THE POINT
of EXISTENCE

OTHER BOOKS BY A. H. ALMAAS:

Essence with The Elixir of Enlightenment
The Diamond Approach to Inner Realization

Facets of Unity
The Enneagram of Holy Ideas

Luminous Night's Journey
An Autobiographical Fragment

Work on Superego

DIAMOND MIND SERIES

Volume I: The Void
Inner Spaciousness and Ego Structure

Volume II: The Pearl Beyond Price
*Integration of Personality into Being:
An Object Relations Approach*

DAIMOND HEART SERIES

Book One: Elements of the Real in Man

Book Two: The Freedom to Be

Book Three: Being and the Meaning of Life

Book Four: Indestructible Innocence

DIAMOND MIND SERIES: III

THE POINT *of* EXISTENCE

Transformations of Narcissism in Self-Realization

A. H. Almaas

SHAMBHALA

Boston & London

2001

Shambhala Publications
Horticultural Hall
300 Massachusetts Avenue
Boston, Ma. 02115
www.shambhala.com

9 8 7 6 5 4 3 2

Printed in the United States of America

⊗ This edition is printed on acid-free paper that meets the American National Standards Institute Z39.48 Standard. Distributed in the United States by Random House, Inc., and in Canada by Random House of Canada Ltd

Library of Congress Cataloging-in-Publication Data
Almaas, A.H.
The point of existence: transformation of narcissism in self-realization / A.H. Almass.—1st shambhala ed.
p. cm.
Originally published: Berkeley, CA: Diamond Books, 1996.
Includes bibliographical references and index.
ISBN 0-936713-09-7 (alk. paper)
1. Narcissism. 2. Self-actualization (Psychology) I. Title.
BF575.N35 A45 2000
158.1—dc21
00–040032

DEDICATION

Dedicated with love, humility, joy and gratitude to
The majestic mystery of Being;
The authentic fulfillment of our lives and hearts,
The essence of liberation,
The truth of divinity,
Our true nature and the true nature of everything,
Our true home,
And ultimate source.

TABLE OF CONTENTS

APPENDICES

NOTES

INTRODUCTION
to the
Diamond Mind Series

The Point of Existence is the third volume in the Diamond Mind Series. This series is a systematic presentation of a particular body of knowledge, which we call Diamond Mind, and its corresponding modus operandi, a way of working with people toward inner realization, which we call the Diamond Approach^{SM}. The presentation is somewhat technical and hence, it will be useful to psychologists, psychotherapists, educators and spiritual teachers, but also accessible to the educated reader. This work is in response to a need being felt in many quarters; a need for a spiritually informed psychology, or conversely, for a psychologically grounded spirituality. This perspective does not separate psychological and spiritual experience and hence, sees no dichotomy between depth psychology and spiritual work. Through a creative critique and investigation, this system incorporates elements of depth psychology—particularly those of ego psychology and object relations theory, and extends them into realms of the human psyche which are usually considered the domain of religion, spirituality and metaphysics.

This body of knowledge is not an integration or synthesis of modern depth psychology and traditional spiritual understanding. The inclination to think in terms of integration of the two is due to the prevailing belief in the dichotomy between the fields of psychology and spirituality, a dichotomy in which the Diamond Mind understanding does not participate.

The Diamond Mind knowledge is a multifaceted understanding of the nature of human beings, our consciousness or psyche, and the potential for expansion of our capacity for experience and inner development. Several points regarding the nature of this understanding will help to place it in context:

1. This knowledge includes an understanding of normal psychological functioning which also sheds light on some prevalent mental disorders. It adopts many of the findings of modern depth psychology, situates them in a more comprehensive view of humankind, and also establishes their relevance for the pursuit of deeper truths about human nature beyond the levels psychology generally penetrates.

2. The psychological understanding is set within a metapsychological perspective that includes a broad outline of the domains of experience and functioning of the human psyche or soul. This metapsychology is not spelled out in any one of the volumes of the series, but is gradually developed throughout its several books.

3. This metapsychology is in turn set within a metaphysical outlook in which psychological experience is situated within a phenomenology of Being.

4. This work demonstrates that what is usually considered psychological investigation can arrive at dimensions of experience which have always been considered to be the product of spiritual practice or discipline. The psychological work is seen here not as an adjunct to spiritual practice, but as a spiritual practice on its own. This is the specific contribution of the Diamond Mind body of knowledge which inspired this series.

5. Not only can psychological investigation lead to realms of experience previously relegated to the spiritual; this work shows that when psychological understanding is refined by an openness to one's spiritual nature, such investigation, if pursued deeply, inevitably will penetrate into the realm of spiritual, religious or mystical understanding. In the course of such exploration, one result is that many currently prevalent psychological dysfunctions, such as some forms of narcissism and schizoid isolation, are revealed as direct

consequences of spiritual alienation, which therefore cannot be truly resolved by traditional psychotherapy. iii

6. This body of work includes a systematic understanding of the domain of spiritual experience, the realm of Being, that can be described in detail in modern psychological language. Thus, it shows that this domain of experience need not be vague, symbolic or incommunicable. This work also includes an exploration of the relationships between this domain of experience and the usual psychological dimension of experience, shedding light on the nature of ego structure and identity. Thus, inquiry into the dimension of Being can be included in some modes of psychological research and investigation.

7. The presentation in the various volumes of the series illustrates methods of investigation, as well as the personal and scientific bases for our conclusions, within a conceptually logical treatment of the various subject matters. However, because of the nature of the field of inquiry, the reader may well be aware of an experiential impact that cannot always be separated from conceptual knowledge. This points to a particular quality of the Diamond knowledge: It is an experiential knowledge that is immediate and intimately human, but which can be elaborated conceptually.

It is my wish that this knowledge will be useful in refining and deepening our understanding of who and what we are as human beings. Perhaps it will make it possible for more of us to actualize our rich potential and to live more complete lives.

A.H. Almaas
Berkeley, California
May 1994

PREFACE

The question of the nature of the self and its relation to Being or the Divine has long been explored by philosophers, mystics, and religious thinkers. Among those who have seriously entertained this question, there has developed a generally accepted set of answers, which of course cannot be conveyed in neat, easily comprehensible statements. In *The Point of Existence*, the exploration of the process of the realization of the self is informed by those traditional answers, and by the methods through which they are achieved. In addition, this book clarifies the relationship between the different approaches of these various traditions and the question of the nature of the self.

The question, "What is the self?" is also being asked by contemporary psychology. In modern theories of psychology, the range of concepts and assumptions about the self is striking. Stephen Mitchell, a psychoanalyst and historian of psychoanalytic thought, writes in his most recent book:

> The most striking thing about the concept of self within current psychoanalytic thought is precisely the startling contrast between the centrality of concern with self and the enormous variability and lack of consensus about what the term even means. The self is referred to variably as: an idea, or set of ideas in the mind; a structure in the mind; something experienced; something that does things; one's unique life history; even an idea in someone else's mind . . . and so on. (Mitchell, 1993, p. 99)

In the course of his writings, Almaas has elucidated many ideas about the self that have arisen in spiritual traditions and in psychology.

vi Is the self ultimately nonexistent? Yes, in the sense Almaas writes about it in *The Void* (A.H. Almaas, *The Void—Inner Spaciousness and Ego Structure*, Berkeley: Diamond Books, 1986), as well as in parts of this book. Is the self a luminous spark of awareness, knowing the Divine, or the real, and revealing the human being as partaking in this divine nature? Yes, this is a central aspect of the self, which is explored in depth in this book.

Is the self an ever-changing flow of awareness, experience, and presence, which can identify with different self-structures, at different times, or become a vehicle for different qualities of Being as they arise? Yes, this is the living organism, the soul, that Almaas defines as the whole self. Is the self a structure in the mind, determined by its biological drives, its history, by conditioning, by language? Yes, this is the nature of ego structure, patterned by imprints, self-images and object relations which shape the flow of experience and determine the ongoing experience of the self. Does the authentic self exist only in the timeless, "transcendent" experience of the mystics, that is in "pure consciousness," or is there an authentic self which is structured, arising in time and space? This question is addressed in *The Pearl Beyond Price* (A.H. Almaas, *The Pearl Beyond Price, Integration of Personality into Being: An Object Relations Approach,* Berkeley: Diamond Books, 1988), where Almaas writes about the self which is a personal integration of qualities of Being, structured by the inherently intelligent manifestation of Being as it arises through, and as, the soul.

In this book, Almaas focuses on the identity of the self, which is related to a particular aspect of the self which he calls the Essential Identity, and describes in detail how issues of narcissism are related to this identity. Understanding and integrating this aspect of the self (which in other work he has called the Essential Self) is a central factor in the capacity of human beings to come to a complete appreciation of their true nature and the nature of Being. In particular, this aspect allows one to recognize oneself as presence or Being, or even as emptiness, in deepening dimensions as the process of realization continues.

Those familiar with Almaas's body of work tend to think of it as a "synthesis of psychological and spiritual work." It is not. This work arises from a level of understanding in which it is clear that, in the

human being, these realms are truly not separate. They can be discriminated, and Almaas's work actually contributes to a clearer discrimination of psychological work from spiritual work. However, his
unique contribution is his understanding of how these realms are
related, how they can be worked with in ways that allow psychological understanding to support spiritual development, and how the discoveries made possible by a comprehensive understanding of the self
can contribute to psychological understanding. Further, like many
philosophical investigations, this work moves from exploration of the
experience of the human subject into the realm of ontology. Almaas's
inquiry powerfully illuminates how the process of freeing the self from
incomplete and false identities leads to a revelation of the nature of the
human self as Being itself.

Beginning with the use of "self" in its ordinary sense, Almaas quickly
moves, in his definition of self as soul, into the realm of self as actual
ontological presence. In elucidating the path through which the self-
awareness of Being unfolds in, through, and as, the human soul, Almaas
describes a process that will be familiar to those who have followed the
quest of those mystics and philosophers whose explorations of the
nature of self and awareness have led to similar discoveries.

However, Almaas utilizes tools that were generally not available to
these thinkers—in particular, the theories of depth psychology, especially self psychology and object relations theory. In the past, Eastern
practitioners, mystics, and the philosophers (particularly phenome-
nologists) who have inquired into the nature of the human subject and
of Being have worked primarily with epistemological questions and
investigative methods in their attempts to see through or render transparent the natural, common-sense view of reality. They have investigated questions like "How do we know what we know?" "What is the
relationship between subjective or internal and objective or external
reality?" and "What is the nature of the knowing subject?" Almaas's
work brings to this inquiry into the nature of self, of consciousness and
of Being, the psychologist's interpretation of the psychic structures that
shape and render opaque the self's experience of itself. With this understanding, questions closer to the concerns of the ordinary human being
can be formulated. For example, the question "What exactly am I longing

viii for, when I desire a love relationship?" will lead a sincere inquirer into an understanding of the self- and object-images which represent certain qualities of the soul that she feels is missing, and eventually to an appreciation of the essential qualities of the self which are often projected onto love objects.

The importance of self psychology and object relations theory is that they allow us to identify and inquire into with great precision the internal structures that shape our identities. "Who am I taking myself to be right now?" "Through what self-image am I responding to this situation?" "How do my self- and object-images determine how I perceive the world?" These questions, whose flavor, import, and resolution resemble those asked in practices of the great Eastern spiritual traditions, become imbued with increased personalness, relevance, and effectiveness when asked in the context of our knowledge of the structures that form the ego.

Spiritual traditions, as well as certain philosophical and psychological bodies of inquiry, have developed substantial bodies of understanding regarding the logical, phenomenological and experiential categories of emptiness and nothingness, as well as of presence and Being. The present work on narcissism begins with the phenomenon of the human being, or soul, as presence, but also passes through a process of de-reification of structures and essences, leading to an appreciation of the primordial emptiness which is a component of Eastern teachings such as Buddhism. Some aspects of the Western philosophical tradition (particularly continental philosophy) have developed an understanding and appreciation of emptiness, but generally without the techniques to actually integrate the awareness of emptiness into our ongoing experience. The understanding of the relationship between narcissism and emptiness in *The Point of Existence* brings new possibilities for embodiment of this aspect of human wisdom.

This particular book emphasizes aspects of the view and method of Almaas's work which move toward deconstruction of ego structures, freeing of the soul from false identities, and spontaneity of experience. At the same time, this work is oriented toward truth and logic. The power and precision of this work arises from a keen appreciation of the importance of understanding the objective structures in which Being

manifests. In fact Almaas's orientation is not at all predisposed toward
freeing the self from structure per se, or breaking down structure. His
orientation, with its working method of openly inquiring into one's
present experience without holding on to prior positions (all the while
noting the inevitable tendencies toward position-taking), investigates
the phenomenon of what is actually present as the experienced self,
with a view to understanding what is determining the experience of
that self. It is true that this method of illuminating the structures which
determine the experience of the self is inherently liberating. However,
the identity of the soul, when it is freed from false (mentally determined) structures, does not simply remain in a homogenous state of
presence or emptiness. Rather, like all the manifest world, it continues
dynamically to unfold, manifesting as various forms arising and passing away. This unfolding has an inherent logic and intelligence, related
to what Greek (and later, Christian) traditions call the Logos. Thus, as
self-realization becomes more established, the experience of the soul is
less and less structured by images in the mind, and more and more
structured by the inherent logic of the dynamic unfoldment of Being.

The longing of the human heart to know its true nature, our passionate desire to know who we are and to know our origin and our
home, is all too easily placated with ready answers. The path described
in this book reflects an approach which is far from a ready answer, but
begins and ends with a sense of humility before the mystery of our
existence. The work of coming to know one's true nature has perhaps
been made easier by the knowledge in this book, but it remains a task
requiring tremendous patience and perseverance.

The understanding of narcissism and its relation to self-realization
which Almaas presents in this book is a product of such patience and
perseverance. Decades of self-exploration, of study, and of work with
hundreds of students, characterized by steadfast love, objectivity,
integrity, and openness, has allowed Almaas to create a new doorway
to knowledge of the structures of our essential human Being, and to
our appreciation of our true nature as the deepest and most universal
nature of Being.

Almaas's work with students takes the form of a method called the
Diamond Approach. This method involves group meetings in which

students systematically explore various qualities and dimensions of the Essence of the self and the nature of Being, and the psychological structures which block our direct experience of our nature as essential Being; various meditation and other practices that support the development of the capacity to sustain open inquiry into one's experience; work with students in smaller groups to support their individual personal inquiry; and for the majority of students, working with a Diamond Approach teacher in regular individual meetings often involving energetic body work.

Since the process of self-realization involves transformation of the self's experience of identity, it exposes and puts pressure on all levels of a student's self-images, and brings up issues that might normally be seen as narcissistic issues. And because narcissism is reflected in all human relationships, issues of transference with teachers at any level of this work, group or individual, are explored as part of the work on understanding one's unconscious object relations structures. The later chapters in this book recount the typical issues that arise in such transference when a student is going through a process of transformation of identity.

Therefore, there may appear, in the text and the case histories, to be an emphasis on working with the transference with the teacher, much like a psychotherapist works with certain phenomena. However, the context of this work is radically different, since the goal of the work is not therapeutic, and since the issues themselves are brought into the student's process by his or her participation in the inquiry method of the Diamond Approach, which actively questions the student's assumptions about identity. Further, the students question systematically not only their object relationships with teachers, but all object relations, with friends, family, colleagues, and the various past and present inhabitants of their inner mental and emotional worlds.

The events reflected in the descriptions of the process of Diamond Approach students in the later chapters of this book reflect many levels of practice and inquiry. These students' experiences are typically the fruition of many years of work. However, these experiences themselves are not exactly the point, nor the fruition. They represent new insights, openings, and transitions in students' work. The real fruition

is our ongoing opening to deeper levels of the self and of Being. This
opening eventually becomes a stable participation in, and appreciation of, the dynamic unfoldment of Being in, as, and through us, as
human beings.

Alia Johnson
Editor
July 1996

BOOK ONE

———————— · ————————

SELF
AND
NARCISSISM

SELF-REALIZATION
AND THE NARCISSISM
OF EVERYDAY LIFE

As human beings we naturally want to be real, authentic, and truly ourselves. We might not all be consciously aware of this drive towards authenticity, but inherently we value being ourselves, especially when it is easy and effortless. Fulfillment comes from knowing what and who we are, and we seek security in this knowledge. We want the sense of who we are to be stable, and we want this stability to be firmly established beyond the need for it to be shored up by external factors. Expressing ourselves is a joy, especially when the expression feels truly reflective of our real selves. It is possible to appreciate ourselves even more when we are spontaneous, rather than self-conscious, as we express ourselves authentically. We can enjoy being creative in our lives, especially when what manifests from within us reveals what lies in our depths, expanding and deepening our experience of ourselves. When our sense of who we are is stable, real, positive, and nonconflictual, we experience a sense of worth.

4   When we know what we want, and see that our desires authentically reflect who and what we are, our self-esteem improves, and we find ourselves enjoying truly human interactions. The more effortlessly secure we are in being ourselves, the more we can afford to open up to others, and the more we can naturally act with generosity and magnanimity. Then we are able to feel more in touch with our humanity, and more willing to be kind and sensitive to others; loving becomes a joy and giving a gift.

However, the moment we feel insecure in our sense of ourselves, the moment we sense that we are not centered in what and who we are, this whole picture reverses. A heavy darkness descends on our experience; we cease to be open or generous, and we find ourselves forgetting our humanity. We begin to feel self-centered and self-conscious, and we become anxiously and egotistically concerned about ourselves. An obsessiveness over how we appear to others develops, and we find ourselves needing an unusual amount of admiration, approval, and recognition. Our self-esteem turns extremely fragile, and we find ourselves unusually vulnerable to feeling hurt and insulted over the slightest lack of understanding or empathy. Our sense of ourselves grows shaky and, rather than coming from within, depends upon feedback from others, making us defensive. Our actions and expressions tend to become false, inauthentic, and reactive, making it difficult to know what authentic action would really be. Without a spontaneous and free sense of who we are, we can only feel empty and unimportant; our lives will lack meaning or significance. Rather than experiencing a sense of value and esteem, we find ourselves feeling worthless and ashamed; rather than enjoying our interactions and activities, we find ourselves beset by anger, rage and envy; instead of being generous and magnanimous, we slide towards exploiting and devaluing others.

The desire to realize and maximize the first condition and to be free from the second is natural, but as we all know this is not so easily done. Even when a great deal of experience and maturity is brought to bear, sooner or later we discover, to our chagrin, that our effort has fallen flat. Out of a recognition for the difficulties of this situation, and out of our love for the truth, we have found it desirable to write this book.

We hope it will be a contribution to the universal human drive to be authentically ourselves.

5

In this book we refer to the first condition—that of freely and spontaneously being ourselves—as self-realization. More specifically, self-realization is a manifestation of a certain human development, a development tantamount to the full maturation of humanness which a human being may attain or arrive at. The state of self-realization has definite experiential characteristics including the ones described above.

The second condition—the condition of not feeling centered in oneself, or authentic and free enough to be oneself—involves many of the characteristics that are usually ascribed to narcissism. These characteristics form a group of traits that define a syndrome, known in psychological literature as narcissistic disturbance, which is seen as a particular disturbance in the development of the self.

Our description of self-realization and narcissism thus far is rather general; it does not reveal the underlying nature of these conditions. Although narcissism is a common element in the make-up of most human beings, its underlying nature, and dynamics, which are not always perceived, are profoundly significant for the understanding of human potential. Narcissism is only beginning to be explored by the prevailing psychological theories of our time. These theories focus more on the pathological manifestations of narcissism than does our work, but they do provide us with an extensive understanding of the development of narcissistic disturbance. All of these theories view narcissistic disturbance as attributable to particular disruptions and malformations in the development of the self. On the other hand, the first condition—self-realization—has been the concern, not primarily of psychological treatises, but of many of the world's spiritual teachings. Even though modern psychological theory addresses the healthy development of the self, which reveals the profound and intricate dynamics in this development, in order to gain a more balanced and complete appreciation of what underlies this condition it is also necessary to turn to the findings of the major spiritual teachings regarding self-realization. In addition, spiritual teachings communicate the subtlety and depth that is possible in human experience and development, levels of experience that can easily be overlooked if we content

6   ourselves only with the psychological theories of the nature and development of the self.

This book, then, is a study in self-realization and its relationship to narcissism. We will explore in increasing depth and detail the nature and underlying dynamics of these two conditions. This necessitates an exploration of the nature of the self and the dynamics of its development. The present exploration is offered as a contribution to the knowledge of self and narcissism in the hope that we can come to understand more completely the process of self-realization, and thus make it more accessible.

chapter 1

Dimensions of Self

W hat makes it so difficult for us as human beings to be deeply authentic and spontaneous, to feel free to be who we naturally are? One aspect of the answer lies in what most spiritual traditions understand to be a case of mistaken identity. Most of us are consciously and unconsciously identified with self-concepts which greatly limit our experience of ourselves and the world. Who we take ourselves to be, as determined by the sets of ideas and images that define us, is very far from the unconditioned reality that deeply realized human beings have come to recognize as our true nature, who we truly are. Numerous approaches, such as psychotherapy, psychoanalysis, and various self-improvement techniques can help us change our self-concepts so that we are more realistic, more satisfied, and more effective in our lives. But only an exploration of the actual nature of the self, beyond the details of its content, can bring us to realms of experience which approach more deeply fulfilling, fundamental levels of philosophical or spiritual truth.

Our experience of ourselves can be transformed from identifying with our mental self-images to having awareness of less contingent, more fundamentally real aspects of the self. It is possible to arrive at a

8   place where we can experience ourselves as the actual phenomenon, the actual ontological presence that we are, rather than as ideas and feelings about ourselves. The more we are able to contact the actual presence that we are, the less we are alienated in a superficial or externally defined identity. The more we know the truth of who we are, the more we can be authentic and spontaneous, rather than merely living through concepts of ourselves.

Among the many methods that shift the quality and depth of experience, those used by religious and spiritual traditions are more effective in contacting deeper dimensions of the self, with a more thoroughly developed understanding of these dimensions and their significance for living life than those used by the newer science of psychology. However, psychology has contributed powerful new knowledge about the human being that allows us to systematically work through the barriers to these deeper levels of self, especially the barriers to integrating these levels into one's identity. In particular, the current understanding of narcissism is very useful for the process of inner realization, the process of learning to contact and appreciate the deeper levels of our nature and allowing these dimensions to actually affect our identity.

The inquiry in this book is part of an exploration which can be found in several lines of tradition in the history of human thought and experience: the exploration of deeper, more objective, or more "real" perceptions of the world and of ourselves than we encounter in ordinary experience. These historical paths include:

1. Western philosophy, particularly the Platonic and neoplatonic traditions, some existentialist and phenomenologist thought, and the mystical/gnostic threads within Western religious (Jewish, Islamic and Christian) traditions

2. Modern psychological research and practice, particularly from the perspective created by Freud and developed within ego psychology, self psychology, and object relations theory (including transpersonal, existentialist and humanistic currents in depth psychology, such as Jung's work)

3. The Eastern traditions such as Buddhism, Vedanta and Kashmir Shaivism, which have developed enormous bodies of understanding

of the nature of self and mind based on powerful techniques of inquiry.

These lines of thought all explore the nature of the human being as self or subject and its relation to existence, to the divine or ultimate reality, or Being. In the West, a particularly potent thread of this exploration began with the Platonic inquiry as developed by Socrates. We will see in the course of our investigation how pursuing deeply Socrates's admonition, "Know thyself," is a powerful path of liberation from the "cave of illusion," and how, in our own times, we have knowledge and techniques available to help us engage in this inquiry with more precision and ease.

The development of depth psychology has enabled us to take Socrates's query to a new level. Freud's discovery of unconscious aspects of the self was a pivotal development in the understanding of human consciousness. The current focus on narcissism in psychoanalytic and psychological research adds further important knowledge about the self.

However, in the current context of psychology this development of our potential for self-understanding has not really penetrated the question of the nature of the self in a way that would satisfy either the philosopher or the mystic's quest. Existential psychology and some aspects of transpersonal psychology have explored this territory, and its explorations have led to a certain degree of integration of philosophical and spiritual understanding with psychology. In general, however, psychological theory is limited by its conceptions of the self, which we will examine in detail in this book. In the philosophic and spiritual realms the pursuit of truth is often limited by ignorance of the unconscious factors that keep our limited conventional view of ourselves and the world trapped in egoic veils, and thus often render spiritual experience as exasperatingly short-lived or unintegratable into our everyday sense of ourselves.

Not only do these limitations affect the theoretical models of the self in the science of psychology and in the traditions of spirituality and religion, but they also affect, in practice, how psychological treatment is conducted, which methods are used by spiritual traditions and psychology to explore the situation of the self, and what defines success in terms of psychological health or spiritual development.

10   Self-realization and narcissism

This book is an exploration of the nature of the self, and the relationship between the knowledge of psychology and that which is the focus of various spiritual disciplines. These realms have much to contribute to one another. Our research has come to an understanding which is not a synthesis of the realms of psychology and spirituality, but rather a fundamental view that encompasses both realms.

This fundamental view has illuminated one clear truth about narcissism: Narcissism is a direct consequence of the lack or disturbance of self-realization. It is the most specific consequence of this lack or disturbance, and can be completely resolved only through realization of all aspects and levels of the self. When one is self-realized, one is consciously identified with the most true, real nature of the self. We cannot present here any simple, common-sense description of that true nature; exploring it has occupied philosophers and mystics for centuries. In the next chapter we will describe in more detail what we mean by self-realization. For now, we will simply say that narcissism involves being identified with relatively superficial aspects of the self, as opposed to being aware of one's identity as Being. This identification with superficial aspects of the self results in a feeling of alienation. The only complete resolution of this alienation, and of narcissism, is the realization of one's truest, deepest nature.

In order to contact the deeper truth of who we are, we must engage in some activity or practice that questions what we assume to be true about ourselves. Psychological methods, as well as spiritual and certain religious ways of inquiring into the nature of the self, all have in common processes of seeing through illusions—inaccurate beliefs about oneself, about other people, and about the world. With a deeper appreciation of the nature of the self, psychology could take these processes much further, expanding both the theoretical understanding of self and its usefulness for the healing and support of human development. Also, the methods and results of spiritual traditions could be made much more effective if they utilized the detailed understanding of the nature and development of the egoic self that has been so effectively explored by self psychology and object relations theory.

Dimensions of experience 11

That there are dimensions to human experience other than those of conventional reality is universally known. Most of us have had profound experiences involving religious insight, deep self-awareness, or some other opening into a realm of Being not generally seen. Visual art, music, and literature aspire to enable us to see or feel aspects of the world or of ourselves without the usual veils. We have been moved by moments of awareness of a larger reality or an unseen force, or by visions or insights, that cannot be explained within the conventional concept of the self. Love and wonder, a sense of light and grace, and peak experiences of oneness in nature are all insights into deeper dimensions of reality.

In addition to appreciating these more commonly experienced deeper dimensions, it is also possible to become aware of the more specifically spiritual dimensions of the human self, what could be called the true human qualities: selfless love, radiant joy, inner strength and will, brilliance and clarity of mind. These qualities are universally acknowledged and valued aspects of ourselves that we can at least participate in occasionally.

Most of the current concepts of depth psychology cannot account for these experiences, and bodies of work which do address these levels of experience, such as Jung's, are generally not informed by the detailed understanding of narcissism which is part of ego psychology. This situation, however, is in the process of changing, and the present work is our contribution to that change.

Even though the existence of the deeper and more expanded dimensions of experience can be easily verified personally by anyone who engages seriously in any of the myriad spiritual practices, and even though there are indeed whole centuries-long bodies of scholarship in which these dimensions are explored in detail by communities of mystics, philosophers, artists and writers, still, the current conventional mind, including the perspective that dominates modern psychology, considers such realms of experience unscientific or unverifiable. (See Appendix A for a discussion of the question of the scientific status of discrimination within these realms of experience.)

12   It is true that the deeper, or spiritual, dimensions of experience are not normally accessible to everyday consciousness. But this is true of many realms of experience. With respect to physical reality, for instance, it took the use of specialized instruments and a body of scientific insight to reveal that the physical world is made up more of space than of solid matter, and that the nature of solid matter is not what it appears to superficial perception. The conventional, "obvious" opaqueness and solidity of the physical world is a limited experience; it is only the way things appear.

By analogy, then, if the psychological researcher insists on validating only the standard levels of the self's experience, concerned merely with disturbances in this conventional experience, we will not end up with a true science of the self, but at best, with something like folklore. A trained psychology professional can see and understand psychological phenomena that are invisible and most unlikely sounding to the rest of us. He might be aware of more objectively real aspects of the self that are invisible to his patients. However, even this greater depth of insight is limited by the prevailing psychological concepts of the self, which do not include or explain what other systems know about the self. In the next chapter we will explore a more complete view of the nature of the self and its relationship to narcissism.

chapter 2

Self and Self-Realization

---•

I n order to pursue our exploration of self-realization, we must elucidate how we are using the word *self*. Our use of the word is unusual in that it refers to an actual ontological presence, not a construct. This emphasis on the actual presence of what is here as the self, rather than on the content of the constructed aspects of the field of awareness, is a crucial aspect of our method of exploration and of our theoretical view.

In our view, the self is a living organism that constitutes a field of perception and action. This is what we call "soul." Fundamentally, it is an organism of consciousness, a field of awareness capable of what we call experience—experience of the world and of self-reflective awareness of itself. In this book we will use the words *soul* and *self* somewhat interchangeably; the meaning of either word is always that defined above. Our understanding of soul is not that it is a split off or special part of the self that is more esoteric or ethereal or spiritual than any other elements. We use the word *soul* to describe the entire organism. This usage reflects the fact that the deepest perception of the self reveals that the entire Being of the self is of the same nature as that which, in conventional reality, is relegated to the spiritual or the divine.

14 As our discussion progresses we will sometimes use *self* and *soul* in slightly different ways. We will predominantly use the word *self*, however, because its connotation can include many aspects of the total self, including its structures. We will use the word *soul* more to connote the dynamic, alive presence of the self as distinguished from the structures of the self which pattern this presence. It is important to allow a slight ambiguity in our use of these words in order for our understanding to be faithful to the deeper perspective. The soul, as an alive conscious presence, is ultimately not separate from the structures which form the ego. It is when they are taken as the self's identity that these structures alienate the soul's experience from awareness of its true nature.

The most striking aspects of this organism which is the self, or soul, are its malleability, sensitivity, intelligence, and dynamism. The soul can take many forms; it is not a rigid structure but a flowing, conscious presence with certain inherent capacities and faculties. The soul learns and the soul acts. The soul is an actual and real ontological presence; it is not simply a product of the body, as much modern thought would define it. However, it is not necessary for the purposes of this book to completely clarify the relationship of the self to the body. Even if the soul were somehow a product of the body, these qualities of consciousness and dynamism of the soul would remain demonstrable, even obvious.

What is conventionally known as the psyche is part of this self. The mind is part of the self, manifesting the capacity to remember, to think, to imagine, to construct and integrate images, to discriminate, analyze, synthesize, and so on. The feelings are part of the self: the capacity to desire, to choose, to value, to love.

In addition to the realms of mental, emotional and physical experience, the self has access to the realm of Being, that is, it can experience directly rather than indirectly, its own presence as existence. The conventional realms are involved in and generally affected by the experience of Being, but when the dimension of Being is experienced there is a profound difference in one's perspective. The reason we have the capacity to experience Being is that the self is an actual ontological presence, a presencing of Being, not simply a construct, and this presence has the capacity to be self-aware. Thus, for the self to become directly

aware of the realm of Being is for it to directly experience its own nature.   15
We will examine this phenomenon in detail in later chapters.

Two capacities of the self are particularly relevant to the development of narcissism as we understand it. The first is *the capacity of the mind to form concepts and structures of concepts in response to experience.* The second is *the capacity of the self to identify with different aspects of experience, particularly with images in the mind and with habitual emotional and physical states.*

Herein lies the mechanism for the "fall" of the self into narcissism. In the beginning of this chapter, narcissism was described as the identification with the more superficial structures of the self. We described the self as a flowing, dynamic presence, an organism with mind, feeling and body (but not identical with any of these), that has an open-ended potential for experience.

The "fall" into narcissism happens as the self forms concepts and structures of concepts, and then identifies with them at the cost of its awareness of Being. These concepts, which the self comes to identify with and to view the world through, are much more opaque and rigid than the open, free, more natural state of the soul. What we describe as the free, spontaneous state of the soul is not a formless or unstructured state. The experience of the soul in a self-realized state is patterned by the intrinsic qualities of its Being, and by the structure of all dimensions of Being, including physical reality. The state of self-realization allows the soul to remain aware of its essential nature, yet at the same time to remain aware of the world of thought and speech, of social life and physical life, and to function in this world.

In Chapter 5 we will elaborate on the mechanism of becoming identified with concepts. For now, we will simply say that this "fall" is not something unnatural, tragic or avoidable. In fact, what we have just described is normal ego development, as described by self psychology and object relations theory.

When, in the course of maturation, or in the context of some identity-shaking life event, or in the pursuit of a spiritual path, we become more open to knowing—or "remembering"—the self in its deeper nature, our narcissism begins to become transparent. If, at these times, we are graced with the opportunity to pursue the truth of our identity rather than

16 compensating for our spiritual dissatisfaction, we can begin to reverse this "fall."

When the soul is caught up in rigid identifications and relations with others and the world, it is not satisfied. In every soul there is an inherent drive toward truth, an inherent desire to feel fulfilled, real and free. Although many people are not able to pursue this desire effectively, the impetus toward the realization of the self is in all of us; it begins with the first stirrings of consciousness and continues throughout life whether or not we are directly aware of it. This impetus spontaneously emerges in consciousness as an important task for the psychologically and spiritually maturing human being. As maturity grows into wisdom in an optimally developing person, this task gains precedence over other tasks in life, progressively becoming the center that orients, supports and gives meaning to one's life, ultimately encompassing all of one's experience.

What is self-realization?

What is the experience of the self when the process of self-realization is complete? What is the actual experience of self-realization? Although self-realization affects many aspects of our experience (including how we relate to others and to the world around us), its central element concerns the nature of our immediate subjective experience. The experience of full self-realization is radically different from the normal ego-bound state; thus, the descriptions in this book may seem alien to the reader. It will help to keep in mind that what we are describing here is the pure state of realization; there are, however, many partial awakenings and openings on the way to the complete experience.

In self-realization our experience of ourselves is a pure act of consciousness. We know ourselves by directly being ourselves. All self-images have been rendered transparent, and we no longer identify with any construct in the mind. There is no reactivity to past, present or future. There is no effort to be ourselves. There is no interference with our experience, no manipulation, no activity—inner or outer—involved with maintaining our identity; we simply are.

We are able to respond, feel, think, act—but from a purely spontaneous and authentic presence. We are not defensive, not judging ourselves, nor trying to live up to any standard. We may also be silent, empty, or spacious. We do not have to *do* anything to be ourselves. We are whole, one, undivided. It is not the wholeness of the harmony of parts, but the wholeness of singlehood. We are one. We are ourselves. We are being. We simply are.

In this experience there is no narcissism. We are at ease, spontaneously real, without psychological artifacts, pretensions, falsehoods. We are not constructed, not even by our own minds. Our experience of ourselves is totally direct and unmediated.

When we experience ourselves like this—directly—we are not inferring anything from past experience or from others' experience of us. Our identity is free from and undetermined by past experience. (Although there is a history of debate in philosophical discourse over whether such unmediated experience is possible, this debate has apparently been conducted in the absence of knowledge of the methods and results of the many practices in the world which result in just such experience.)

In the full experience of self-realization, our experience of who and what we are is not dependent upon nor influenced by any image of ourselves, either from our own minds or from the minds of others. If we do see images of ourselves we clearly perceive that they usually function as distancing and distorting barriers. A student in our work, Lily C., describes such an experience. Lily, in her late twenties, had been working with the author for about three years at the time of this group session, a few months before a summer intensive retreat.

> The problem I spoke up about in the group meeting was that I was afraid to go to the retreat, or rather that I was afraid my life would be so dramatically changed by the retreat that I couldn't cope with it. I felt very small, helpless, and out of control, and these feelings made me feel very frightened, and smaller yet. After I got as small as I could, I suddenly felt so huge that I felt I had no limits at all. I felt like I was the sky, and I felt the sensations of vastness and calm for a brief time, but then I felt nothing at all. I didn't even feel that I was anything, good or bad. I just was. Am.

Lily does not describe here the process of work that transformed her experience from being small and frightened to the sense of purely

18   being. Without getting into too much detail, we can say that the issue that arose for her was the expectation that she would go through overwhelming changes, changes that would conflict with her identity of being small. Exploring this sense of being small revealed that it was simply an image she had of herself. This recognition dissolved her identification with the mental image, which then brought about the experience of space, the vastness she describes. This then culminated in a self-recognition not based on any mental content, image or thought. In this moment, Lily knew who she was, beyond the usual categories of experience, beyond even the concepts of goodness or badness.

The fact that Lily was having a pure experience of self-awareness does not necessarily mean that there was no conscious or unconscious image in the mind, or that there were no memories. Images, memories, and associations can be present or not (they usually are), but they do not determine one's experience of oneself. In that moment Lily was free from her past in terms of her experience of herself. She was free from her mind—from all the memories, images, associations, ideas, emotional reactions, identifications, ego structures, knowledge, and so on—in terms of her experience of herself at the moment.

What is the experiential core of self-realization?

The description of self-realization so far merely elaborates the various characteristics of the experience of being ourselves. It does not communicate the sense of the central element. What are we experiencing ourselves *as*? What kind of positive given are we? This positive given, the actual phenomenon that is present when we are fully experiencing ourselves, is usually a surprise for each individual, and cannot be deduced from our descriptions. It is what characterizes authentic spiritual self-realization and sets it apart from all other psychological experiences.

When we are being ourselves fully and directly, free from all influence of past experience, a quantum leap occurs in the experience of the self. The perception of ourselves departs from the conventional dimension of experience, although most of the elements of that dimension remain available in the experience.

To be ourselves fully, spontaneously, and authentically, means simply   19
to *be*. Not to be a reaction, not to be determined or influenced by image
or experience from the past, not to be according to memory and
mind—is to simply be. This is far more than the colloquial meaning
of the phrase "being oneself." It is the experience of Being. To be—and
in the experience we know this with certainty—is not an action, not
even an inner action. Being ourselves, we find, is being Being.[1]

In self-realization we experience ourselves being present *as* presence. It is not the presence of the body, the emotions, the thoughts. It
is the presence of presence. *To be fully cognizant of oneself as presence
is the central and most positive characteristic of the experience of self-
realization.* (See Appendix B.) The absolute given in perception is presence. Presence is not a characteristic of mind or body. It is a concrete
ontological given, more fundamental than either the mind or the body.
The presence of Being is deeper than our conventional experience of
the existence of our minds or bodies.

Suchness

This way of speaking of our existence is unusual in the modern way
of thought. Presence and Being seem to be philosophers' concepts,
concepts perhaps used in the same way that theistic traditions speak
of God. What is Being? How can we use this concept to describe a very
personal, yet universally available, experience? We do not need to solve
the philosophical conundrums of the ages definitively in order to say
what we mean: In simple terms, to experience ourselves as Being is to
experience our existence *as such,* to experience our own presence, our
own "suchness" directly. It is the simplest, most obvious, most taken-
for-granted perception that we exist. But this existence is usually
inferred, mediated through mind, as in Descartes's "Cogito ergo
sum"—"I think, therefore I am." Existence is background, not foreground, for our ordinary experience. To penetrate into this background, to question our assumptions about reality and ourselves, allows
us to encounter directly the immense mystery of the arising of our
consciousness and of the world.

When viewed from the perspective of the ordinary experience of
the self, the direct awareness of oneself as Being is a very mysterious

20   category of experience. However, for the self-realized individual, it is an ordinary, common experience. In time it becomes the everyday experience of simply being ourselves. Being, here, is not a philosophical notion; it is the concrete experience and recognition of ourselves, before any mediation, conceptualization or labeling.[2] It is the given of perception, the simplicity of being conscious of our existence. Words cannot do justice to this kind of experience; the influence of our thoughts and concepts on our experience of ourselves is so extensive that no description can convey the radical change in nature of experience without that influence.

The experience of Being is not an *idea* we have of our experience of ourselves; neither is it a conclusion we draw from it. It is the concrete, direct and present experience of ourselves as we are being ourselves. What we are is now, a spontaneity of being, an absolute given. We perceive ourselves, then, by being ourselves, by being. We recognize ourselves by being ourselves, by being. We know ourselves by being ourselves, by being.

More concretely, we recognize in the experience of self-realization that to be ourselves is to be aware of ourselves as the presence of Being. It is the direct recognition of the very beingness of our existence, the fact of our "isness." This facticity is not a thought or idea, not a feeling or an intuition, but a very concrete and palpable *thereness*. It is not the thereness of one object or another, like that of one's body, or of a thought. This thereness is a new category of experience. In philosophical and spiritual language it is usually termed "presence." Coming upon the recognition of one's presence as Being is surprising in two ways: first, it is so completely, astonishingly outside the normal identity; second, ironically, it almost always feels familiar, as if one is remembering something, or coming home after being gone for a long time.

We might think that if we are experiencing the absolute given of our perception of ourselves, we will be experiencing our bodies. However, even our experience of our bodies is greatly influenced by the various images, memories, emotional reactions, and associations that are characteristic of the conventional dimension of experience. Ordinarily, we do not really know what the pure experience of the body is; we cannot be aware of how and how much the content of the mind influences our experience of our bodies. The dawning of the experience of self-realization includes the body, but it is not what we usually experience as our body. The body is experienced as part of Being, inseparable from Being, as an embodied expression of Being. But the pure experience of being ourselves is not merely the experience of the body. Being is more than the felt existence of our bodies. In many ways, it includes and transcends the body. Both "common sense" and certain theories of the self consider the body to be the most fundamental reality, but the phenomenon of presence is far more fundamental.

How does the common experience of the self contrast with the experience of self-realization?

Under normal circumstances we experience ourselves only partially. We do not experience ourselves as we are *in* ourselves, in our authentic reality or essence. Instead, we experience ourselves through thick veils of ideas, ideals, beliefs, images, reactions, memories, desires, hopes, prejudices, attitudes, assumptions, positions, identifications, ego structures, labels and accumulated knowledge—in other words, through the influence of all of our past experiences. We literally experience ourselves through the past, through the totality of our personal past, instead of freshly, in the present moment.

Only when we have experienced another way of knowing ourselves is it possible to appreciate the enormous effect all this mental baggage has on our normal experience of ourselves. We see, then, that our awareness of ourselves has become so fragmented, so indirect, so burdened by mental accretions, that even what we take to be authenticity is only a reflection of a reflection of our innate and fundamental authenticity.

The mental images and attitudes that determine how we experience ourselves form the basis of a whole implicit world view. We also experience ourselves only indirectly, as a subject experiencing an object. We are aware of ourselves as an object like other objects, seeing ourselves in the world as one object among others. Even when one is aware of oneself as perceiver or subject, this perception is different from the direct sense of our facticity, from the fact of our existence. We still know ourselves through the veil of memory.

22   As indicated above, ordinarily it is impossible to appreciate the extent of the influence of past experience on our sense of ourselves without having some other form of experience as a referent. What gives us the opportunity to see this omnipresent influence is the direct experience of self-realization, which reveals to us the distance between knowing oneself and being oneself.[3] The self is constrained by the subject-object dichotomy: one is a subject experiencing oneself as an object. In the conventional dimension of experience the most intimate way we can experience ourselves is through such self-reflective consciousness.

In self-realization we experience ourselves as presence, where presence is both Being and knowingness. Here, the cognitive act and being are the same experience. We realize that we are speaking of a level of experience that seems far removed from ordinary experience, and may seem too esoteric to be concerned with. However, thousands of perfectly ordinary people have achieved access to this dimension of understanding, either through religion, spiritual traditions, artistic endeavors, or other kinds of explorations. As we proceed in this book, it will become clear how this level of insight can unfold simply through our maintaining a consistent and open inquiry into our true nature.

The reason we experience knowing and being as a single phenomenon is that presence is the presence of consciousness, pure consciousness more fundamental than the content of mind. Although we usually associate our consciousness with the act of being conscious of some object of perception, experiencing the direct truth and reality of our consciousness requires no object.

When we can finally be ourselves fully, we recognize ourselves as presence, and apprehend that this presence is nothing but the ontological reality of consciousness. We feel our presence as a medium, like a material medium, such as water or clear fluid.

This medium is homogeneous, unified, whole, and undivided, exactly like a body of water. This homogeneous medium is consciousness. The medium is conscious and aware of itself. It is not aware of itself by reflecting on itself, but by being itself. In other words, its very existence is the same as awareness of its existence. To continue the physical metaphor, it is as if the atoms of this medium are self-aware. Presence is aware of itself through self-pervasive consciousness, where

this self-pervasive consciousness is the very substance or medium of 23
the presence itself, not an element added to it.

From the perspective of self-realization, then, the soul is simply our consciousness, free from the occlusive veil of past experience. She can experience herself directly, without any intermediary. She is thus dispensing not only with the veil of past experience, but also with the self-reflective act. She experiences herself by simply being. She knows herself to be a presence, a self-aware medium in which the awareness is simply of presence itself. She is. She is presence, pure and simple. She is aware that she is presence because presence is indistinguishable from awareness.

What does the experience of self-realization feel like?

The experience self-realization, of knowing oneself as self-pervasive consciousness, is felt experientially as an exquisite sense of intimacy. The self-existing consciousness experiences itself so immediately that it is completely intimate with its reality. The intimacy is complete because there is no mediation in the self's experience of itself. We feel an exquisite stillness, a peace beyond all description, and a complete sense of being truly ourselves. We are so totally ourselves that we feel directly intimate with every atom of our consciousness, completely intimate with and mixed with our true identity. The contentment is like settling down peacefully at home after eons of restless and agonized wandering. Clarity and peace combine as the feeling of exquisite, contented intimacy, which is totally independent of the particulars of our situation, beyond the conceptual confines of time and space. The peace and contentment do not come from accomplishing anything, nor are they a result of anything. They are part of the actual feeling of being truly ourselves. We are not only intimate with ourselves, but our very presence is intimacy.

We will describe the experience of self-realization in greater depth as we continue with our study.

chapter 3

Self, Essence and Narcissism

Four concepts are paramount in the understanding of self-realization: self (or soul), presence, Essence, and identity. In precise terms, *self-realization is identity with the essence of the self, which is presence.*

What is self? The soul, as we have discussed, is an organism of consciousness that contains and cognizes all of our experience. Although we have said that self-realization is a matter of being ourselves, this is not a completely accurate description. We have used the phrase "being ourselves" to refer to the sense of being real or authentic. But actually, the soul is always being itself. It cannot be anything other than itself, for it is the very experiencing consciousness.

This consciousness—which is the self—has a fundamental existence, an ontological mode of being. And it can be directly aware of this fundamental existence. This is possible only when we are simply being, not conceptualizing our identity, not reacting, and not manipulating. In other words, we experience our ontological ground when our experience of ourselves is completely unmediated.

Although the self is always being itself, the experience of the self is incomplete until a certain development occurs: self-recognition. In self-realization, the soul recognizes its own nature, the presence of Being. It is this immediate, intrinsic self-recognition that gives the state of self-realization the sense of exquisite intimacy.

What is presence? What is Essence? The self can experience itself either purely and immediately, or through memories and structures created by past experience. When it is seeing itself directly, it is aware of itself in its primordial purity, without veils, without obscurations. It recognizes this pure condition as its ontological nature. This primordial purity or ontological nature is recognized as the self's ultimate truth. So we say the self has an *essence*. The central property of this Essence, or true nature, is that it is an actual ontological presence. Presence is the essence of the self, just as protoplasm is the essence of the body.

What is identity? As we saw in Chapter 2, one of the most significant characteristics of the soul is that it can identify with the content of experience. It can take any impression, for example self-image, and make itself believe that that impression is itself. It can also take a part of the psychological structure and believe it to be the whole of itself. Identifying with an impression or content of experience makes the self feel that it has an identity, and through this identity it then recognizes itself. Our personal history, constituted by our memories, comprises the basic content of our usual identity. This identification with the personal history provides a feeling of self-recognition, a sense of identity, or a sense of self. So in experiencing itself through the veil of memories, the soul not only loses sight of its primordial purity—its essence—but also identifies itself through and with this veil of personal history. The relationship between identity and identification will be discussed further in Chapters 10, 12 and 13.

For now we will simply say that the soul can identify with any dimension of experience—presence, physical body, feelings and emotions, or impressions and images originating from the past. It can identify with its essential nature or with memories, or with specific parts of these memories, or with organized structures of these memories.[4] So the experiential identity of the self can be essential presence—which is known in the present—or it can be another, more superficial, dimension of its experience, which is usually determined by the past.

26   The narcissism of everyday life

In the experience of self-realization, the self recognizes its identity as presence.[5] When a person is identified with something other than the primordial presence, self-realization is absent. He is not then being himself; he is not simply being. He is not one with his essence. The most fundamental and deepest aspect of the soul is absent in his experience of himself. This is the root of narcissism.

In narcissism, the experience of the self is disconnected from its core, from the depths of what it is. It is estranged from its true nature, exiled from its primordial home. The soul's estrangement from its true nature is the basis of narcissism. (Here, we are using the term *narcissism* in the colloquial sense, similar to what is referred to as *narcissistic disturbance* in psychoanalytic terminology. After we present our general account of self-realization and narcissism we will be able to use more precise terminology.)

Narcissism involves identifying with any level of the experience of the self at the expense of its essential presence. In this context, several insights about narcissism arise:

1. Since narcissism is present when the self is identified with anything other than essential presence, whenever we identify with a dimension of experience superficial to our essential presence, we are bound to acquire narcissistic traits. Therefore if we identify with the body, emotions or any mental content, we will experience some narcissistic qualities.

2. As has been amply demonstrated by object relations theory, since all ego structures are based on identifications with impressions from the past, it is clear that the experience of ego cannot be devoid of narcissism. Thus the conventional dimension of experience, which is deeply patterned by these structures (whether healthy or pathological), includes an intrinsic narcissism. Everyone knows that he has some measure of selfishness, self-reference, a need to be seen and appreciated, a deep wish for esteem and admiration from others, and some distortion in his self-concepts. Although we are accustomed to thinking of these traits as normal, they are in fact narcissistic phenomena. They are universal to all nonrealized individuals,

reflecting the fundamental narcissism that is the result of not know-   27
ing oneself on a deep level. This is what we call the "narcissism of
everyday life" or "fundamental narcissism."

3. When a person is working on self-realization, this narcissism is
    increasingly exposed; in fact, it is usually aggravated for some time.
    When we approach the dimension of essential presence we inevitably
    confront the narcissism inherent in our disconnection from that
    presence. The success of the work on self-realization depends, to a
    great degree, upon successfully resolving the arousal and intensifi-
    cation of narcissistic manifestations. The narcissism of everyday life
    is much more ubiquitous, much deeper, and much more significant
    than we usually allow ourselves to see. However, it dissolves steadily
    in the deeper stages of self-realization. Full self-realization completely
    eliminates this narcissism, for it is not natural to the realized self.

4. The identity of the self can be more or less close to the dimension of
    essential presence. The degree of closeness correlates with the extent
    of the person's narcissism, or the level of narcissistic disturbance, but
    involves somewhat different criteria than the general understanding
    of the levels of such disturbance. The more superficial the dimen-
    sion of experience with which the self identifies, the more severe the
    manifestations of narcissism. Even in the dimension of essential pres-
    ence, there are degrees of realization and therefore, different degrees
    of manifestation of, or freedom from, narcissistic issues. In the last
    part of this book we will explore in detail the specific narcissistic
    issues associated with different levels of self-realization.

5. Pathological narcissism, or what is called in self psychology the "nar-
    cissistic personality disorder," is basically a severe form of the narcis-
    sism of everyday life. As a personality structure, it is more deeply and
    strongly crystallized, and thus more rigid, than the character of the
    normal individual. The personality is crystallized around its discon-
    nection from the depths of the soul. The identity of the person with
    a narcissistic personality disorder is superficial, brittle, distorted, and
    feeble because of the extreme disconnection from its own presence.

We will discuss these points extensively as we proceed. Because we
are working with an understanding of the nature of the self that includes

28   dimensions deeper than the conventional, we will be able to pursue these questions regarding narcissism with a precision not yet possible in prevailing psychological theories.

For example, Heinz Kohut, who founded self psychology and remains the most creative contributor to the understanding of narcissism, was reluctant to define the self in any clear or precise fashion. His vague definitions of the self are still considered by many psychoanalysts to be problematic for his theory of the self. Kohut believed that it is not possible to know the self in its reality and essence. To his critics he responds by saying: "The self. . . is, like all reality. . . not knowable in its essence. We cannot, by introspection and empathy, penetrate to the self *per se*; only its introspectively or empathically perceived psychological manifestations are open to us." (Kohut, 1977, p. 311). Kohut's various definitions of the self are discussed in detail in Chapter 7.

In contrast, it is our view that the essence of the self *can* be known, precisely and definitely, and that this knowledge is the central concern of most of the genuine spiritual teachings throughout history, as well as of most philosophical thought. We have observed, further, that the self *per se* can be penetrated by introspection, albeit of a deeper and more refined form than what Kohut describes in his writings. The psychological capacities needed for this penetration are what Kohut terms *introspection* and *empathy*, which can be powerfully developed in the context of spiritual practices.

We consider Kohut's definitions of the self, in both his original and later theories, to be problematic and limited. We will see this in more detail as we study the various narcissistic manifestations. Although we do not completely share his view of the self, Kohut's understanding of narcissistic structures, especially what he called *selfobject* (narcissistic) *transferences*, and the ways of dealing with them, are exceptionally original and useful.

It is central to our view that the self *can* be known in its essence. Further, this insight into the essence of the soul can reveal the deepest roots of narcissism, making it possible to actually resolve narcissistic issues. In fact, in the experience of spiritual realization, we discover that the pure presence of the essence of the soul can be known more directly, more intimately, and more precisely, than can the more external manifestations of the self. This is because the latter are usually experienced through self-reflection and thus indirectly. Self-perception is further obscured by the various contents of the psyche, whereas the essential presence of the self is cognized by *being* it, without the intermediary of extraneous mental content.

Many psychologists, including Kohut, write as if there are many selves, or, more accurately, as if the various manifestations or dimensions of the self can be considered separately without prejudicing one's understanding of the nature of that self. The result is that a psychological researcher comes to believe that he can study the various psychological manifestations of the self and come to an objective understanding of narcissism, without taking into consideration the actual essential nature of that self. Kohut emphasized that the self he was studying was not the self addressed by philosophy and religion. A psychiatrist writing about the self psychology of Kohut makes this clear:

> The term 'self' as used by the followers of Kohut is entirely different than the 'essential self' or, as Kohut (1977) calls it, 'axiomatic self,' of philosophers which is postulated as a center of free will and the basis of responsibility in human behavior. This 'essential self' has a long philosophical history and is related to the metaphysical concept of 'substance' and the theological notion of 'soul.' (R. Chessick, 1985, pp. 86–87)

As Kohut and others have done, defining a certain part or manifestation of the soul as the self in order to study a certain circumscribed phenomenon, can be useful for purposes of analysis, but to take this partial definition of the self as if it applied to all of human experience can lead to endless misunderstandings. When we do delineate certain aspects of the self for study, we must acknowledge and remember that our definition is of a specific, partial manifestation of the self. To do otherwise is actually to duplicate the stance of narcissism, to take a part of the self as the whole.

What is the state of not identifying with content of mind?

When a person is not identified with the content of mind, he will not necessarily experience his identity immediately as essential presence.

30   A more typical development, discussed at length in Chapter 11, and in our book, *The Void* (Almaas, 1986), is that the first thing one is faced with is the experience of emptiness. When one is not identified with the usual content, the experience might be: "There is nothing there!" or even "I am not here!" This emptiness will evoke all kinds of issues and reactions, but eventually it resolves into something more peaceful: spaciousness. The mind feels expanded and open to experience, without identification or attachment to any particular content. This spaciousness in the mind allows for a deep awareness of the fundamental ground of experience, or presence, which may be felt as emptiness. Without the usual identity defining one's experience, one might simply experience, "I am." One can become aware of the central point of one's attention or awareness. Meister Eckhart wrote, "God has left a little point where the soul turns back on itself and finds itself." With the manifestation of spaciousness and the knowledge of the center of one's awareness, one has begun the realization of the Essential Identity, the central identity of the self-aware soul.

What is the status of the conventional elements of experience in self-realization?

When we fully experience and understand essential presence, we are aware of what some traditions term *primordial presence*, and this presence includes other aspects of the self.[6] Awareness of the presence of Being does not exclude awareness of the body and its sensations, feelings and emotions, the mind with its thoughts, images, and ideas, and the totality of the functions of the psyche—such as imagination, thinking, planning, and remembering—and the rest of what ego psychology calls the ego functions. Many spiritual teachings, such as Kabala, Sufism, Kashmir Shaivism, and Taoism, share the understanding of the self as a unity that includes the spiritual dimensions and the usual psychological and physical manifestations.

The complete multidimensional self can be experienced only in the fullest realization of presence. In this condition of primordial presence, thoughts, feelings and images do exist, but in a different way than they do in the conventional dimension of experience. These aspects of the self are felt to be completely inseparable from presence itself, not in

the sense of two things tied together, but in the sense of coemergence.
We do not experience the body as the container of the presence; nor do we experience presence as containing the body. These perceptions might appear in the course of spiritual development, but they are incomplete in that they retain the duality between presence and body. When the experience of oneself as primordial presence is complete, this presence is coemergent with the body.

If we imagine being aware in an immediate way of the general shape and sensations of the body, its various parts and organs, and simultaneously aware of the protoplasm of the body, then we will have some idea of the experience of the body and presence being coemergent. The physical body and its protoplasm form an inseparable unity; they are not two things that are somehow connected. Similarly, primordial presence is the fundamental ground and substance of the body, inseparable from it, although it is itself not physical.[7]

When we experience primordial presence, it is intimately integrated with the various manifestations and dimensions of the self. The body is felt as the same presence as primordial presence, with a specific form. We do not experience the body as a physical object. From the perspective of primordial presence, physicality is simply a form that presence takes. The body is a certain colorful presence within the fundamental clear medium of presence, just as organs are certain patterns that protoplasm take in the human body. In this state, our felt experience is deepened tremendously, and attains a vividness and clarity not possible in even the deepest physical experiences.

In full self-realization we are deeply, vividly aware of all manifestations that arise in the self. Thoughts, feelings, sensations and images are experienced as patterns in the presence, rich with aliveness and energy. The presence changes form, manifesting various contents, but the manifestation is never separate from the presence, and in fact, is nothing but the presence transforming its appearance. Thus, we apprehend the view that Eastern spiritual traditions refer to as *nonduality*. When we are one with primordial presence, its manifestations in the body, thoughts, images, feelings, and sensations, are transparent forms that do not hide the fundamental reality. This perception is beautifully described in the writings of the Dzogchen masters, expressing the

32   teachings of Maha Ati, one of the most elevated teachings of Tibetan Buddhism.

The following passage is from Longchempa:

> Mind and primordial wisdom are like water and its moisture: At all times there is no separation between them, but they are adulterated by the discrimination of mental acceptance and rejection. Mind and its objects, whatever appears, is the essential nature, but by apprehending partiality, openness is restricted. (Tulku Thondup Rinpoche, 1989, p. 324)

A similar view is found in the literature of Kashmir Shaivism, which, in contrast to Buddhism, is theistic. In this nondual philosophy, the ultimate God or Absolute "I," is Shiva, who creates the universe through his creative dynamism, Shakti.

> She . . . who is the goddess embodying Jnana (knowledge), ever knows the totality of categories from the earth up to Siva, which is one in substance with Her Self and is portrayed out of Her own nature on the canvas of Her own, free, clear Self just as a city is reflected in a mirror (from which it is nondistinct). (Jaideva Singh, 1992, p. 2)

This passage extends nonduality to cosmic dimensions; this is one of the implications of complete nonduality.

Perceiving the constant, dynamic creativity of presence displaying the richness and color of all manifestation, we see that everything is unified, making up a harmonious whole. The underlying presence—a nondual medium—unifies its various manifestations in a wholeness that cannot be imagined in an ordinary state of mind. In normal experience we perceive inner forms as objects, separate from each other and existing in some unobservable way in the mind, the body, or the self. Discrete thoughts seem unconnected to the body; feelings are connected only through association; images in the mind seem to pop up from nowhere. This experience is fragmented compared to the awareness of unity.

In full self-realization we not only experience our essential nature—the primordial presence; we also experience the wholeness of the self; nothing is excluded. This integration is not mental, nor is it a product of integrating separate objects. We merely perceive ourselves as we are, in our totality and wholeness.

The term, *Dzogchen,* which refers to this reality, means total completeness. The Tibetan teaching called Dzogchen is oriented toward the realization of primordial presence, which is referred to as *rigpa*—total and complete presence (Longchempa, 1987).

Realization of the whole, nondual but multidimensional self is important for the total resolution of narcissism, because disconnection from any dimension of the self—not only its deepest dimension—creates narcissism. Disconnection from the deepest dimension, that of essential presence, is the fundamental root of narcissism, which gives narcissism its characteristic flavor. Under normal circumstances, the self is more likely to be disconnected from a deeper dimension, and identified with a more superficial one. This is overwhelmingly the most common situation. The reverse can and does occasionally occur, especially for those engaged in a spiritual practice that includes renunciation or abnegation of the surface dimensions of the self (such as the body or the feelings). It is possible to reach deeper dimensions of the soul through some of these methods, but the realization will be incomplete and cannot ordinarily reach the dimension of primordial presence. The dimension of primordial presence alone brings the realization of wholeness. Actually, if the method is powerful enough to penetrate to this dimension and allow a glimpse of it, the practitioner will then have to abandon all suppression and abnegation in order to fully integrate the primordial presence.

How is presence related to change and movement?

Primordial presence brings another kind of completeness. The fact that presence includes the various manifestations of the self in a nondual way, indicates that presence is not a static reality. Seeing that it is always transforming its appearance, we become aware that presence is dynamic. It is not only thereness, but also a flow. Awareness of the transformation of the appearance of presence, or equivalently, the continuous flow of arising manifestations, allows us to experience presence as flowing. In other words, various manifestations and

34   experiences are continuously arising, constituting a continuous flow
of forms of perception. We can experience the coemergence of this
flow *with* presence as the flow *of* presence. The flow of presence is like
the flow of a river, which is always creating ripples, waves, bubbles,
and so on.

This is an advanced perception, in which we understand change,
movement, and transformation in the self-realized dimension. The
mental concept of time becomes inoperative, as we see changes as the
flow of presence, where the flow is not along the dimension of time.
The flow is more the flow of experience, felt as the unfoldment of
Being. We will not delve into the subtle details of the phenomenology
of this perception; we mention it here because the fact that self-
realization involves the experience of flow or unfoldment accounts for
some of the manifestations of narcissism.

As we have noted, it is particularly this experience of the self as a
flow of presence in a dynamic unfoldment that we call the *soul*, the
ancient Western term for the self. The soul is the flow of experience
and the consciousness having the experience; more accurately, it is the
flow of experiencing consciousness. In ordinary experience we do not
experience the soul in its truth or wholeness, but as an individual who
has many parts and various perceptions. In self-realization we experience the soul as the wholeness of the self, in a dynamic unfoldment of
presence coemergent with all content of experience.

Narcissism is an issue of identity, and identity is not the same as
self.[8] Therefore, narcissism is not exactly an issue for the self in general, and we will not explore the nature of the soul in detail.

The problems of identity affect the experience and development of
the self as a whole, which we will address as part of our exploration.
However, the larger questions of the self will be left to another exploration. These questions include the self's properties and characteristics, its various dimensions, elements, and functions, its relation to
the conventional experience of self, the way this conventional experience
develops, the way it is related to ego structures and their development,
the relation of these structures and their development to the essence
of the soul, and the development and refinement of this essence. Of
course, the understanding of the self in its totality is important for

self-realization, but our concern in the present exploration is the study   35
of the central aspect of self-realization, realization of essential presence,
which is the true identity of the soul.

Since our subject is self-realization, which is identity with—and not
merely the experience of—essential presence, we will focus on the
development, characteristics, and problems of identity. In order to
resolve the issue of identity, it is necessary to understand narcissism,
since narcissism is the main psychological issue determining identity.

Our consideration of the totality of the self, including its identity
with Being, makes clear how even healthy ego structures are narcissistic relative to the self-realized state. Without this understanding, the
field of psychology is working with very limited notions of the self,
excluding the most significant dimensions of human experience by
simply defining them away.

chapter 4

The Spectrum of Narcissism

T o begin the next phase of our inquiry, it will be useful to summarize what our discussion has so far established. We have defined the self, or soul, as a living organism of awareness, which can experience itself in, and identify with, many dimensions of experience, from physical reality to the fundamental presence of Being. Self-realization is identifying with the essence of the self, which is presence. This presence can be experienced as the simple, clear existence of fundamental Being, or one might also be aware of the ever-changing forms that presence of Being is taking. Narcissism is the condition that results when the self identifies with any content of experience to the exclusion of awareness of its fundamental Being.

The soul is an organism whose essential identity is presence; it is also a structured, self-organizing dynamic unfoldment of this presence. Being aware of the dynamic unfoldment gives the experience of the self a quality of flow, as we discussed in the previous chapter. Like other manifestations of Being, particularly apparent in biological life, the flow of self unfolds according to an inherent structure of development. In this chapter we will begin to examine the consequences for ego development and narcissism as this unfoldment is affected by the childhood

environment. Many factors in childhood affect the development of the   37
soul, and with the help of the psychology of infant and child development, we can explore very specifically how these factors contribute to
particular forms of narcissism.

In addition to the general phenomenon of narcissism that results
from loss of contact with Being, there are specific phenomena that
result from loss of contact with one's Being as it arises in particular
forms in the course of a child's development. Particular essential qualities of the soul arise at each developmental stage, and problems in
these different stages result in particular narcissistic difficulties. These
difficulties involve not only less than optimal development in the ego
structure, which is addressed in psychological theory; they also involve
limitations in the development of the Being of the self.

Is an infant naturally self-realized?

Even though the self of the early infant must exist in a state of wholeness similar to that of self-realization, we do not assume that the
infant's experience is the same as that of the self-realized adult; in fact,
this is most unlikely because, as we will discuss further, the infant has
not gone through the developmental stages necessary for conceptual
discrimination. However, it is safe to assume that the infant lives initially in a condition that we will term "primary self-realization," since
in the absence of significant disturbances there must be some awareness unmediated by memory, images, or ideas.[9] We can assume that
experience is not yet conceptualized, the self is not yet self-reflective,
and the consciousness is not yet divided by defensiveness. Even if there
is some contraction in the body or nervous system as a result of less
than optimal conditions, or, say, a difficult birth, the infant's experience—at least at times of rest and satisfaction—must be that of simply
being. The actual self, the experiencing consciousness, must be abiding in its true nature, since it is simply and spontaneously being, with
its innocence intact.

We have seen that this wholeness is part of the condition of self-
realization. We have also seen that self-realization is not a matter of
intellectual understanding or even emotional maturity, but rather, a
matter of spontaneously and naturally being—simply being, without

38   conceptualizing oneself. And since the central element of self-realization is presence (which is free, pure, and devoid of mental elaborations), we must accept that at least one component of the infant's experience must be presence. How else can it be? If the self is being itself spontaneously and naturally, there is something there, some actual ontological phenomenon. Remember, too, as discussed in Chapter 2, that the nature of the presence is consciousness. There is no doubt that the infant has an open, intelligent, and sensitive consciousness.

So the infant, in the state of primary self-realization, lives as presence that is undivided, unconceptualized, and whole. If we understand this state of self-realization and accept that the infant has consciousness and experience, this is an inevitable conclusion. This does not mean the infant knows what she is experiencing. She does not know that she is experiencing herself as presence, for she is not capable of this kind of knowledge. If she has any knowledge of this state, it must be nonverbal and nonconceptual. This is exactly what we mean by primordial presence: the direct and immediate sense of one's Being.

Unlike the infant, the adult can discriminate presence from other categories of experience, and we also can conceptualize, so we can call it presence. The most basic difference between the infant's primary self-realization and the adult's self-realization is this capacity to discriminate and conceptualize. It is not clear, however, how different it is from the adult's experience of self-realization. The full state of self-realization, in which there is no self-reflection and absolutely no intermediacy in the experience, has been compared to the infant's original fresh, clear, innocent state. The author, Ken Wilber, has written at length about the confusion among those doing spiritual work who seek a *return* to the state of primary realization experienced in infancy, rather than acquiring this perspective as a development of the maturing self (Wilbur, 1977). So far as we know, the infant's state lacks the depth, expansiveness, power, richness, and the discriminating clarity of the mature state of realization. It lacks the capacity for insight, for intelligent action, for self-knowledge, for appropriate and empathic relating to others, and so on.

We cannot assume that the infant needs the development of its cognitive faculties to experience the wholeness of presence, because the wholeness of presence appears precisely when we let go of our developed cognitive capacities, and abide simply in the spontaneously given condition of who we are. We cannot assume that to experience her presence, the infant needs the development of her physical capacities, because we already know that the infant has perception, and as we have discussed, the conscious presence is more fundamental than the body.

It is not a new or radical observation that the infant is initially in a state of primary self-realization. The fact that a child can simply be is one of the things that adults love in infants and babies. Adults also regret that they themselves have lost this capacity. Since the average baby is spontaneous and natural, is not self-reflective, and has no conceptualized elaboration of its identity, the acute observer can actually learn about Being by observing the infant's presence.

The state of wholeness and beingness characteristic of the infant's primary self-realization is related to the condition that Sigmund Freud termed "primary narcissism." He believed that the experience of the infant is dominated by primary narcissism, in which there is little differentiation between self and other, and between the various parts and impressions of the self. It is a state of primary perfection and bliss. He writes in his groundbreaking paper, "On Narcissism: An Introduction":

> The primary narcissism of children . . . is less easy to grasp by direct observation than to confirm by inference from elsewhere. If we look at the attitude of affectionate parents towards their children, we have to recognize that it is a revival and reproduction of their own narcissism, which they have long since abandoned. . . . Thus they are under a compulsion to ascribe every perfection to the child. . . . The child shall have a better time than his parents; he shall not be subject to the necessities which they have recognized as paramount in life. Illness, death, renunciation of enjoyment, restrictions on his own will, shall not touch him; the laws of nature and of society shall be abrogated in his favor; he shall once more really be the center and core of creation—'His Majesty the Baby,' as we once fancied ourselves. (Morrison, ed., 1986, pp. 34–35)

40   Freud's description highlights the sense of perfection, freedom, pleasure, and power that the baby experiences, which Freud considered
mostly unrealistic and delusional.[10] We postulate, however, that the
parents' responses to the infant reflect an awareness of the actual qualities of perfection and bliss in the infant's state. These qualities actually appear in the experience of self-realization, but in self-realization
we experience them within the realistic, discriminating intelligence of
the mature adult. The concept of primary narcissism was the origin
of Hartmann's concept of the undifferentiated matrix, which describes
the structural characteristics of the infant's experience of self. Initially,
Hartmann coined the term *undifferentiated matrix* to point out that,
at the beginning of life, the ego and the id are undifferentiated from
one another. Other researchers, for instance, Rene Spitz, used other
terms to express this infantile undifferentiation.

> In substantial concurrence with Hartmann about the undif-
> ferentiated matrix, Spitz nevertheless prefers the term nondif-
> ferentiation to extend the concept beyond ego and id. He wishes
> to include nondifferentiation between psyche and soma, inside
> and outside, drive and object, I and non-I, and different regions
> of the body. (G. and R. Blanck, 1974a, p. 51)

Our concept of primary self-realization has elements of both the
concept of primary narcissism and the idea of the undifferentiated
matrix. The infant's initial experience of itself appears to be a state of
equilibrium of consciousness, characterized by a sense of perfection,
wholeness, innocence, bliss, and purity of being. This is all easily acceptable to the ordinary observer, and also to the psychological observer;
it is within the view of prevalent psychoanalytic theory. We add to
these observations our own: The fabric of this consciousness is presence, which presents itself through continuously changing forms. Since
the process of ego development involves construction of and identification with conceptual structures, it is reasonable to assume that the
sense of wholeness and perfection is most complete in earliest infancy,
but diminishes as the infant develops.

      The development of the body, along with the perceptual, cognitive,
emotional, and psychical capacities of the self, engenders and coincides

with a continuous transformation of the essential presence. The soul's presence manifests new forms and qualities appropriate to this development. Although the ongoing substrate of the self continues to be presence, and the baby is a continuity of Being, a flow of presence, the self as a whole is in a constant state of development, maturation, and transformation. The new forms in which the presence manifests along with the effects of interaction with the environment, determine the development of the various dimensions and functions of the self. This continuing transformation also involves an increasing loss of the original wholeness and perfection, because this loss is partly a result of the accumulated memories of experience and their elaboration into images, as well as the development of the ego and its various structures based on these images. But the original and primary condition is that of wholeness, and this wholeness continues to function to some degree in the early development of the child. The dimensions, structures and qualities of the self develop as a holistic, synergistic, and self-organizing process. The forms of the essential presence manifest as part of this development of the total self.

Looking at this transformation from the perspective of the stages of ego development identified by psychologists such as Mahler, we find that the essential presence takes a different form in each of these stages.

Narcissism develops when the soul loses touch with its wholeness, especially as it loses touch with its true nature. The soul loses awareness of its wholeness through the loss of the immediacy of experience, which results from experiencing itself through past impressions. The loss of immediacy is identical with the loss of awareness of presence, and since presence is the "glue" that unifies all aspects of experience, wholeness is gone. The baby loses her primary self-realization (and her primary narcissism) as she begins to experience herself as an object.

An increasing veil composed of memories (and reaction-induced results or consequences) intervenes between the subject—the self—and the object. This duality gradually transforms the infant's experience in such a way that she ultimately loses her identification with the sense of presence. As the infant develops an identity situated in dimensions of experience superficial to her essential presence, she loses her capacity to simply be herself. In a sense, rather than actually losing this capacity, the

42   infant simply forgets it as she gradually finds herself reacting to and manipulating her experience, and becoming increasingly alienated from her true nature. Thus, the loss of contact with her true identity involves the loss of the sense of the perfection and wholeness of the self.

Narcissism develops throughout the early years, not only at one particular stage. The earlier it appears, of course, the greater the disturbance it creates, since disconnection from essential presence in the early stages of development predisposes the child to further disconnection in the later stages. Also, narcissistic disturbances can be more severe in some stages than in others, depending on the changing circumstances of the child's life, such as changes in her relationships with her parents, in her health, and so on. Later we will discuss these factors in detail, but here it is sufficient to note that, although narcissism develops throughout the developmental stages, and although the earlier stages influence the later ones, the nature and severity of narcissistic disturbance fluctuates depending on many factors.

The capacities and properties of all dimensions of the self—mental, emotional, cognitive, physical, maturational, and so on—influence narcissistic disturbances, depending on the stage during which the disturbances occur. As we have discussed, narcissistic manifestations are determined not only by their central causative root, which is the loss of felt contact with the essential presence, but also by the particular qualities of the forms of the soul that emerge in the various stages of development. The fact that specific forms of essential presence characterize each developmental stage is consonant with the phenomenon of specific developmental changes in all dimensions of the self. Our understanding of this phenomenon has developed partly from direct observation of children, but more from the reconstruction of childhood experience during the extensive investigation of adult experience and memory.

Thus, there are different forms of narcissism that originate in different developmental stages. Each form shares the characteristics associated with the fundamental loss of contact with the essential self, but each form also has different characteristics depending upon the developmental qualities and forms of the self in that particular stage from which it originated.

We call this phenomenon the *spectrum of narcissism*, in which each form of narcissism is delineated depending upon the prevailing condition of the soul at a particular stage of development. We have identified four selves ("true selves") related to four stages of development, which are defined primarily by the essential forms in which the soul's presence manifests in these stages. We must remember that there is only one soul, which takes different forms in the different developmental stages, and the four selves are only manifestations of one self. The soul is never actually separate from its fundamental ground, and the same ground is the true nature of each of the four selves.

We also delineate four forms of narcissism corresponding to the four selves, and to each of the four developmental stages. We note here that our description is only an initial delineation that will illuminate our overall view. In Book II, we will focus on the main form of narcissism, central narcissism. The complete working through of the other forms of narcissism becomes relevant on the deeper levels of realization. In Book III we discuss in detail these forms of narcissism and their resolution.

The four forms of narcissism we have identified in our work are:

1. *Oral narcissism,* which results from disturbances in the first few months of life (including the prenatal period), but mostly in the stages that Mahler defines as the autistic and symbiotic stages of ego development.[11] The true self related to this form of narcissism is the unified dynamic soul, the nondual presence. We believe that Otto Kernberg emphasizes this level in his theory of narcissism, which probably reflects the population of individuals he treats. Its manifestations tend to be more primitive than the other types of narcissism, reflecting origins in the oral stage. When this type of narcissism dominates a person's structure, she will tend to manifest severe structural difficulties of the borderline kind. Intense oral rage and envy, as well as insatiable hunger for primitive forms of narcissistic supplies, are the external manifestations of the hidden, empty and powerless self.

2. *Central narcissism,* which results from disturbances in both the differentiation and practicing subphases of the separation-individuation process, spanning the period roughly from seven months to eighteen months, but particularly in the practicing period, and probably extending to the beginning of the rapprochement subphase, up to two years

44   of age. This is the period that most researchers believe to be the specific developmental phase for the narcissistic disorders, which is one reason we call it "central" narcissism. In central narcissism the true self from which the soul is alienated is the Essential Identity. This form is the narcissism that Heinz Kohut emphasizes, again probably reflecting the population of patients he treats. It can be severe and intense, but is not as primitive as oral narcissism. It is characterized by fewer borderline features than in the oral type, greater functional capacity, and an intense need to be special, unique, and constantly mirrored. The idealization of "special" others is a specific trait of central narcissism, as is grandiosity. In contrast, in oral narcissism these characteristics tend to be vague and mixed with various borderline defenses, such as splitting and projective identification.

3. *Individuation narcissism*, which results from disturbances mostly in the rapprochement phase of the separation-individuation process, in the second, third, and sometimes fourth, years of life. The true self is the individuation self, the essential form or true self that we have called the Personal Essence. (See *The Pearl Beyond Price*, Almaas, 1988). This individuated self is the emphasis of the researchers who follow Mahler's theory of ego development with regard to narcissism, as in the case of Marjorie Taggart White, Arnold H. Modell, and Arnold Rothstein (in Morrison, 1986); and G. and R. Blanck (in *Ego Psychology II: Psychoanalytic Developmental Psychology*, 1974b). The narcissistic manifestations are colored by issues of separation-individuation, such as separation anxiety, protection of autonomy, longing for the merged perfection of the symbiotic stage, the rapprochement conflict, and the importance of object relations in the functioning of the self and for self-esteem.

4. *Oedipal narcissism*, which results from disturbances in the oedipal stage of psychosexual development, extending from the beginning of the fourth to the end of the fifth, and possibly extending to the sixth year. The true self is the libidinal self, or the passionate-erotic self, which manifests, and can integrate, the essential aspects of Passionate and Affectionate Love, in which the erotic element is inseparable from the love. This is the emphasis of Alexander Alexander Lowen, the founder of bioenergetic analysis, and partly of Nathan Schwartz-Salant,

a Jungian analyst. (Lowen, 1983; Schwartz-Salant, 1982). Schwartz-Salant distinguishes two levels of narcissism, which seem to coincide loosely with our definitions of central and oral narcissism; in Schwartz-Salant's model, the latter overlaps with oedipal narcissism. Support for, recognition and admiring mirroring of, erotic and affectionate love, emotions in general, body aliveness, and gender identity are all important for individuals suffering from narcissistic disturbances at this level. This level of the self is also sometimes called the "oedipal self." Although Kohut's main focus seems to be on central narcissism, he also understands narcissism to originate in all of the developmental stages. He discusses in some detail the narcissistic disturbances in the oedipal stage, and their resulting characteristics. Our understanding of oedipal narcissism is similar to his, but we see the libidinal self as more erotic and passionate than his corresponding oedipal self. He tends to downplay the sexual component of the healthy oedipal self and to emphasize the affectionate component. The erotic element, as we conceive it, is part of the essential form of Passionate Love, which is love with an ecstatic and passionate affect that is a whole-body experience: a love that seizes both the heart and the genitals without separation.

It is best not to think of the forms of narcissism in terms of strictly delineated categories. All individuals manifest all the forms of narcissism; no one escapes some narcissistic disturbance in all of the developmental stages. The environments in which we grow up are never perfect, and life on earth impinges on our childhood selves in more ways than we can count. There are also unavoidable developmental and maturational causes of narcissism which we will explore, which make it unlikely that anyone can pass through any stage of development without some narcissistic injury.

Although all the forms of narcissism affect each of us, narcissism develops continuously throughout the various developmental stages. The characteristics common to all types go through their vicissitudes throughout our early development, and the specific characteristics develop at each stage. The intensity of the general characteristics will vary from one individual to another, depending on one's overall history. So narcissism might take the form of the normal narcissism of everyday

46   life, or what is called the narcissistic character disorder, or it may develop as a more severe disturbance of the paranoid character, or even some forms of schizophrenia. Also, depending on our personal history, one form or another of narcissism may dominate our character. So a person's narcissism might take mostly the oral form, or the central form, and so on. Of course, more than one form may dominate, or all the forms might be somewhat equally present in our personality.

This model of the spectrum of narcissism provides a possible explanation for the divergent theories of narcissism. It especially illuminates the debate between Kohut's and Kernberg's approaches to narcissism. (The differences between Kohut and Kernberg's views are discussed in later chapters.)

Narcissism is a very general, basic element of ego life. The self of the average individual is deeply and fundamentally narcissistic. The complete resolution of narcissism will elude us until the achievement of self-realization. All that conventional psychotherapy can do is alleviate symptoms resulting from severe disturbances of narcissism, and, when successful, can help the individual to reach the level of the narcissism of everyday life. To proceed further and address this fundamental narcissism, only spiritual development will make a real difference.[12]

We also believe that understanding the spiritual nature of the self can help us to understand even the severe forms of narcissistic disturbance. This perspective can help us to see that we cannot separate our psychology from our spirituality, our psyche from our spirit, for we are fundamentally whole. Our self is one self, and cannot be dichotomized into a spiritual or "higher" self and a psychical or psychophysical self. Perhaps the following multifaceted exploration of self-realization and narcissism will contribute to a healing vision of our fundamental wholeness, and an appreciation of the rich potential for the human soul.

Our approach to self-realization in its relationship to narcissism allows two new possibilities. The first is that it allows us to understand and resolve narcissism at its fundamental roots. This is facilitated enormously by the greater access to essential nature permitted by this view. The mere conception of the existence of essential nature tends to open us up to

perceiving it. The second possibility is that this approach provides us with   47
a new way of working towards self-realization, the method of inquiry
that includes psychological understanding. Traditional spiritual practices
do not include the contemporary Western understanding of self. This
understanding of the self and its narcissism is a central part of our work,
and can also be useful to those engaged in traditional spiritual practices.

PART 2

VIEWS OF SELF

AND

THEORIES OF NARCISSISM

I n the process of self-realization, we undergo a profound transformation of identity. In this process it is invaluable to understand
deeply, precisely and completely the nature of self and identity, as
well as their relationship to each other. In the field of depth psychology there is growing interest in the study of the self; there is, however, no general agreement within the field about the meaning of the
concepts of self and identity. Although these concepts are central to any
discussion of self psychology, they are always being defined and rede-
fined, and frequently used in confusing, unclear, even inconsistent ways
within the same work. Various concepts relating to the self and its manifestations are formulated by different researchers to fit the focus areas
of their study. Confusion ensues when other researchers use these concepts to refer to other areas of study in which they are involved, which
may overlap with areas the concepts were intended to describe, yet differ from them significantly. This is unavoidable at the present stage of
the study of the self, because the subjective experience of the self—which

50   is the data most needed for this research—is much more problematic to describe and define than the data needed for other sciences. This confusion about definitions is part of the reason for the various disagreements in theories of narcissism, the general unclarity in the knowledge of the self, and the plethora of definitions of self and identity.

The confusion becomes even greater, and amounts to outright mischaracterization, when these psychological concepts are applied to spiritual teachings. In addition, different spiritual teachings use profoundly different working definitions of the words self and identity. The only sane alternative remaining for an independent researcher, especially for a newly unfolding teaching about the self, is to create original concepts appropriate to this teaching and then, and if possible, to relate them to the already existing concepts referring to related areas of interest. We have done this to some extent in our work—formulating our own concepts, while at the same time being informed by, both the various developing theories of self and an understanding of the views of self in the major spiritual teachings. The result is that we have developed very precise concepts of self and identity, as well as of other manifestations of the self. In the course of this book it will become clear how our concepts of self and identity relate to the relevant concepts in depth psychology and in the major spiritual teachings.

Our concepts in general are descriptive of the actual phenomenology of lived and felt experience. They are as experiential, or as experience-near (derived from lived experience rather than from theoretical considerations) as we can make them.[13] They arose directly out of the actual experience of the author, his associates and the many students he has worked with.

Some of the concepts originate in levels or areas of experience not available to the normal consciousness, and hence their exact meanings might not be obvious. However, we retain their use because of the perception that they have an evocative power that outweighs the benefits of formulating concepts that are merely theoretically comprehensible. Many parts of this study will yield more readily to openness to the evocative power of some of the words than to conventionally understandable analysis. (See Appendix C for a more detailed discussion of concepts originating from nonconventional dimensions of experience.)

chapter 5

Self and
Self-Representation

———————————————————————————— •

Having given a general account of our concept of the self, we can draw parallels with some prevailing notions of the self and its manifestations. We share with Jung and a few other psychologists, as well as with some spiritual traditions, the concept of the self or soul as the totality of the individual, including one's spiritual nature. Religious, philosophical and spiritual traditions share the belief that the soul encompasses several dimensions of experience and possesses many properties and faculties which conventional psychological views do not include. Our view of the self is closer to that of the Sufi, Indian yogic, and Buddhist views than it is to Jung's, even though Jung's view is original in its illumination of certain aspects of the self.[14] For a discussion of a Christian view of the self, see Chapter 43.

The Sufis view the self as a consciousness that can experience itself within different planes of existence, and that can evolve towards wholeness and spiritual realization. The notion of an evolving self can be seen in the following passage by a Sufi author:

> The Self, called the Nafs, goes through certain stages in Sufi development, first existing as a mixture of physical reactions, conditioned behavior and various subjective aspirations. The

seven stages of the Self constitute the transformation process, ending with the stage of perfection and clarification. Some have called this process the 'refinement of the Ego.' (Shah, 1978, p. 82)

The following passage by the great Sufi philosopher, Ibn Arabi, describes the faculties and capacities of the soul:

> There is nothing but a rational soul, but it is intelligent, reflective, imagining, remembering, form-giving, nutritive, growth-producing, attractive, expulsive, digestive, retentive, hearing, seeing, tasting, smelling, and feeling. (Chittick, 1989, p. 84)

The view of the self as the totality of the person has been familiar in psychoanalytic thinking since the time of Freud, and is reflected in his original usage of the term *ego*. A. Cooper quotes a passage from an unpublished paper by Kernberg, "Contemporary Controversies Regarding the Concept of the Self," in which he states that psychoanalytic theory has always included the concept of the self, that is, the individual's integrated conception of himself as an experiencing, thinking, valuing and acting (or interacting) entity. In fact, Freud's starting point in describing the "I" ("das ich," so fatefully translated as "the ego" in English) was the idea of the conscious person whose intrapsychic life was powerfully influenced by dynamic, unconscious forces (Morrison, 1986, p. 115). This is almost identical to our concept of the self, except that ours includes in this totality other dimensions of experience, for example, essential presence and various dimensions of Being, which are actually among the most powerful forces influencing us. Awareness of these dimensions makes it possible for us to experience the totality of the self directly, but changes the character of experience in ways not anticipated by Freud.

Freud considered the self to actually be the soul, which is the old manner of referring to the self, which he saw as including the "I" (ego).

> He had repeatedly stated that the I is only one aspect of our psyche, or soul, and separated it from the two others, the it and the above-I . . . and that when he was referring to all three institutions, to the mind in its totality, to our conscious and our unconscious life, he spoke of our soul. (Bettleheim, 1982, p. 75)

Even though Freud's appreciation of the totality of the human soul   53
is all but lost in modern psychology, the formulations of psychoanalytic developmental psychology, ego psychology, self psychology, and
object relations theory provide invaluable knowledge about the self,
particularly the development of the ego and its various structures.[15]

For Freud in his later work, and also for most of his followers, the
concept of ego was different from the concept of self. *Ego* referred to
a structure in the psyche, a mental system with a specific organization
and functions, central in the overall experience of the self. Heinz
Hartmann, the founder of ego psychology, made the most precise distinctions between ego and self. This distinction was key to the development of both ego psychology and object relations theory, and most
recently, self psychology. Robert Stolorow writes:

> A crucial bit of groundwork for a functional understanding of
> narcissism was Hartmann's (1950) conceptual distinction
> between the ego (a structural mental system), the self (the
> whole person of an individual, including his body and body
> parts as well as his psychic organization and its parts), and the
> self-representation (the unconscious, preconscious and con-
> scious endopsychic representations of the bodily and mental
> self in the system ego). (Morrison, 1986, p. 198)

The meaning of the word *self* here is that it is the totality of the
individual, so although it is discriminated from the word *ego*, it clearly
includes the ego, for the latter is a structured system within the psyche. Hence, the self includes the self-representation, which is part of
the ego system.

What is the difference between the ego and the self?

According to ego psychology, the ego (and hence the self-representation) is a structure in the psyche, the product of a developmental
process of the first few years of life. At the beginning of life the ego can
be said to exist in potentiality because the self intrinsically possesses
the properties and capacities that make this development possible.
These properties and capacities become integrated in the system ego
as it develops.[16]

54   Object relations theory has become the dominant psychoanalytic theory of ego development. Its main insight is that the ego develops, primarily through the integration of early experiences, into organized mental structures. These mental structures, termed ego structures, are systems of memories that have become organized through the processes of assimilation or introjection, identification, integration, synthesis, and so on, into an overall schema patterning the self.[17]

The processes of assimilation and accommodation go hand in hand during the earliest stages of development, during which the infant organizes its experiences first into patterns and then into patterns of patterns. Eventually meaning is assigned to these patterns, which Piaget designates "schemas":

> A schema, then, is an enduring organization or structure within the mind and is the outcome of the processes of organization—assimilation, accommodation, generalization, differentiation and integration. (A. Horner, 1979, pp. 10–11)

According to object relations theory, the most important experiences involved in the building of ego structures are the child's interactions with its parents. These experiences are retained in the psyche, through memory, as units of object relations. Each of these units is composed of a self-representation (an impression or image of the self), an object-representation (an impression or image of the important other, usually a parent), and an affect coloring the interaction. These units of internalized object relations are elaborated and organized into progressively larger systems by the integration of similar units into overall schema through successive stages of development.[18]

Kernberg calls the organization of internalized object relations the "ego-identity." The overall organization of identifications and introjections (in the form of units of object relations) is accomplished through the synthetic function of the ego, and constitutes the final integration of the ego structure into a sense of self that is continuous in space and time and includes the representational world, which is composed of all the object images.

According to Kernberg, the cohesive self-image on which the sense of self is based is a product of the integration of the very earliest object relations. This ego organization is constantly modified as more object relations are internalized, but later identifications—after the age of approximately three years—add little in terms of the basic structure.

The element of ego structure most central to the issue of narcissism is the self-representation, the overall mental representation of the self, which is called the self-concept or self-image. "It is, in short, an ego function and structure that evolves gradually from the integration of its component self-representations into a supraordinate structure that incorporates other ego functions." (Kernberg, 1982, p. 905) These concepts of self as structures of mental representation clearly contrast with the description we presented in Chapter 2.

What is a representation?

To appreciate the concept of self-representation it is important to understand clearly what is meant by representations. According to Joseph Sandler:

> they are not simply perceptions, which are fleeting and imply no enduring impression. Nor are they simply memories of discrete experiences. Representations are organized compilations of past experiences, relatively enduring impressions, constellations of perceptions and images, which the child culls from his various experiences and which in turn provide for the child a kind of cognitive map, a subjective landscape within which he can locate and evoke the cast of characters and events within the drama of his experience. (Greenberg and Mitchell, 1983, p. 373)

The following passage describes how the self-representation develops:

> From the ever-increasing memory traces of pleasurable and unpleasurable instinctual, emotional, ideational, and functional experiences and of perceptions with which they become

56   associated, images of the love objects as well as those of the
bodily and psychic self emerge. Vague and variable at first,
they gradually expand and develop into consistent and more
or less realistic endopsychic representations of the object world
and of the self. (Jacobson, 1980, p. 19)

It is this concept of the self-representation which plays the greatest role in the various psychological theories of narcissism. Psychoanalytic theory uses the term *narcissism* in a neutral sense. There is
normal (healthy) narcissism, and then there is pathological narcissism.
Hartmann defined narcissism as the libidinal investment (cathexis)
of the self-representation.[19] Healthy narcissism results from a well-
integrated, harmonious, and realistic self-representation being
invested with positive energy or libido. Narcissistic disturbance or
unhealthy narcissism, occurs when there is a problem with the libidinal investment of the self in terms of either the adequacy of the investment or the quality of the energy invested, and/or in the quality of
integration of the self-representation. In simple terms, an individual
is narcissistically healthy when he has developed a stable self-concept
that is realistic, resistant to dissolution or disintegration, with inner
harmony and positive self-regard. Pathological narcissism occurs
when the self-representation is absent, weak, fragmented, disintegrated, or unrealistic, or when it is particularly vulnerable to such
disturbances. Hence, as Stolorow writes, in giving his functional definition of narcissism, "mental activity is narcissistic to the degree that
its function is to maintain the structural cohesiveness, temporal stability and positive affective coloring of the self-representation."
(Morrison, 1986, p. 198)

This is the most commonly accepted basic definition of narcissism
in psychoanalytic theory. Many authors, however, use the term *self* when
they are actually referring to the self-representation. In this case, the definition would be: Narcissism is the cathexis (libidinal investment) of
the self. This is clear in the following statement by Kohut describing the
narcissistic self in terms of the quality of the libido: "Since the self is,
in general, cathected with narcissistic libido, the term 'narcissistic self'
may with some justification be looked upon as a tautology." (Kohut,
1971, p. 26)

Almost all researchers define narcissism as cathexis of the self, rather   57
than the self-representation, but they often differ in what they mean
by *self.* Kohut used the classical definition in his first version of his
psychology of the self, and abandoned it in the second version, basically by changing the definition of the self from the self-representation
to a more general and more experience-near "bipolar self." He did
retain the definition of narcissism as the libidinal investment of the self,
although his considerations did not focus on the libidinal investment.
Different theories use different definitions, but almost all of them
define narcissism as the libidinal investment or cathexis of the self,
and most theorists mean the self-representation when they refer to the
self. We will discuss further certain definitions of self and narcissism
in Chapter 6.

Although the researchers who investigated the development of the
self-representation have done so mainly in order to understand its disturbances, the significance of the concept of the self-representation
for psychological research goes further than dealing with narcissism.
The investigation of the self-representation has also greatly contributed
to the general understanding of the self, especially in the realm of conventional experience. Further, as we will see, the understanding of the
self-representation is a powerful tool for understanding and attaining
self-realization.

Can we differentiate our experience of the self from the self-representation?

It is understandable that most authors use the word *self* to refer to
the self-representation, for it is, in a very deep sense, synonymous with
self. Although the self-representation is a mental construct, we do not
ordinarily experience it as such. Quite the contrary, most of us normally experience the self-representation as the self. This fact is of deep
import, yet it is not easy to grasp its significance. It is not until we
appreciate the significance of this very fundamental phenomenon—
that our experience of ourselves is determined by, and in some sense
identical to, the self-representation—that we can see its deep implications with regard to narcissism. Most psychologists do not see this
connection, partly because they do not clearly discriminate between

58   a mental image and a psychic structure (see note 18). In most circumstances the self-representation is inseparable from the self's experience of itself. Hence, Kernberg's view of the self as a psychic structure is understandable. Only a deeper awareness of the ground of the self, specifically the experience of consciousness as open, contentless space, enables one to consciously discriminate between psychic structures and images.

We have seen that as the self-representation develops it becomes the way we conceive of ourselves. We know ourselves through this self-concept. It determines how we experience ourselves. Ordinarily, we cannot experience ourselves separately from our concept of ourselves. This situation has much more profound implications than most of us appreciate. Yet it does not seem like a startling discovery; rather, it seems obvious. We may naturally think, "Of course, how I experience myself has much to do with how I view myself. How else could it be?" Indeed, how else can it be?

The normal experience of the self includes the belief that its identity is made up of a body, of thoughts, feelings, ambitions, plans, ideals, values, impulses, desires, actions, qualities, and so on. Since the self takes itself to be all these things, integrated and organized in an overall view of itself, it cannot separate from them. This is the experience of the self when it is identified with self-representation. More accurately, it is the self and the self-representation experienced together—as the same reality.

We could say, then, that the self experiences itself from within the self-representation, through the totality of what constitutes this representation. The various images, impressions, and beliefs—the content of the personal history of the individual—which have been integrated into the self-representation, become the lens through which the self not only conceives of itself but, more significantly, experiences itself. The self-representation functions not only as the lens through which the self sees itself, but actually as an inseparable part of the very eye which is the capacity of the self for experiencing itself.

In fact, the self-representation is even more intimately linked to the self's experience of itself than the metaphor of the lens and the eye suggests. The experience of the self is actually *determined* by the self-representation. The phenomenology of the self's experience presents itself through this representation, and hence, what the self perceives and experiences as itself, in its present experience, is greatly determined by it. The self-representation actually sculpts the forms that arise as the phenomenological particulars of the self's experience of itself.

This patterning of the malleable substance of the soul is so inherent in the self's experience that there is no awareness of the distinction between substance and its forms. Under normal circumstances, the self cannot conceive of itself without the particular form it finds itself in. In our opinion, this integration of the self-concept with the self in experience is what the various authors refer to when they speak of the "firm cathexis" of the self-representation.[20]

Given that this cathexis of the self-representation constitutes normal narcissistic health, issues of narcissistic pathology are related to the accuracy or precision of the perception of reality allowed by the developed self-representation, its stability and cohesiveness, how positive its emotional coloring, and how integrated it is in the self's experience of itself.

In infancy, before the construction of the self-representation, there is experience of self, but not recognition of it *as* the self because the infant lacks the capacity to be self-reflective. Thus, the self begins to recognize itself in childhood as the self-representation develops, and not before. This fact holds great significance because, by the time we become aware of ourselves as individuals we are already experiencing ourselves within and through the developing self-representation. So we do not ever perceive the opportunity to recognize ourselves independently from the developing self-representation.[21] Therefore, when there is self-recognition, this recognition occurs via self-concepts, and the child's experience is no longer completely immediate.

To summarize, then, we have identified several factors in the development of the self-concept that lead to such a thorough identification with this self-concept that one cannot differentiate between self and self-concept. These are:

1. the soul's tendency for identification with the content of experience

60   2. the patterning by the self-representation of the forms in which the soul's experience unfolds

3. the lack of capacity for self-recognition in the infant prior to the development of self-representation

4. the loss of immediacy of experience as self-representations form.

An example will concretely illustrate the difficulty in differentiating the self from its self-concept. In dealing with narcissistic issues, or with issues on the level of deep ego structures, one sometimes encounters the experience of fragmentation. As a result of either an already existing weakness in the structure of the self, or deep work that has dissolved ego structures, the individual experiences fragmentation, or disintegration. The sense of fragmentation often feels literal; the person experiences his body in fragments. This terrifies him and brings fears of death. Kohut writes:

> Details of some of the patient's experience of hypercathected disconnected fragments of the body, of the mind, and of physical and mental functions can, for example, be observed during the temporary therapeutic regression from the cohesively cathected grandiose self. (Kohut, 1971, p. 7)

The person's experience of his body being broken into disconnected fragments does not reflect the actual situation. It is an inner experience; the body is still in one piece. How can we explain the graphic and vivid experience of one's self in fragments when in actuality one's body remains in one piece? The usual understanding is that the fragments are not of the body itself, but of its image in the psyche. However, the individual's feeling is that he himself, not an image in his mind, is fragmenting, and thus, he will likely experience physical terror. This is because the image of the body forms a central component in the self-representation. (Mahler, Pine and Bergman, 1975) The individual's sense that he (including his body) is fragmenting makes this experience terrifying.[22] The very least fearful scenario would be that he is *uncertain* whether or not the self (or body) is fragmenting.

This graphically illustrates that in conventional experience we do not discriminate the self from the self-representation. We feel, think, and behave as if we *are* the self-representation.

Probably because he did not discriminate between self and self-concept, Kohut thought of the self-representation as an experience-near concept: "The self, however, emerges in the psychoanalytic situation and is conceptualized, in the mode of a comparatively low-level, i.e., comparatively experience-near, psychoanalytic abstraction, as a content of the mental apparatus." (Kohut, 1971, p. xv) It is an experience-near concept because it springs from our lived experience of the self.

Like almost every other psychoanalytic author, Kohut defines the self as the self-representation by accepting Hartmann's definition of the ego as a "structural mental system," meaning it is merely a concept, even though an experience-near one. Kohut then goes on to use the term to mean the actual self as it is when, for instance, he describes it as empty, depleted, and yearning for mirroring or merger. So for Kohut, the self-representation stands for the person's subjective experience or inner sense of self, even though it is a concept. This usage is understandable but remains unclear and precludes certain discriminations.

The difficulty these authors find in staying clearly within their own definitions of the self is an expression of the same difficulty the average individual has in differentiating the self from the self-representation. This discrimination has a critical significance that is not generally appreciated by either the average individual or by psychological researchers. The discrimination between the self and the self-representation, as introduced by Hartmann and later elaborated by Jacobson, is significant in a way not appreciated by its originators. This discrimination is fundamental if one is to understand normal experience in relation to the condition of self-realization, and hence, to understand some of the main barriers to this realization.

chapter **6**

Self-Representation and Narcissism

•————————————————————————————

I t is critical to understand the significance of the fact that the self-representation is not the actual self; it is the concept of the self. As we saw in the last chapter, this distinction is lost when psychological researchers use the concepts of self and self-representation interchangeably. It might be largely true that this differentiation is not significant for understanding and treating pathological narcissism, since this pathology is due largely to disturbances in the self-representation. Hence, psychoanalytic theory tends not to attach importance to the differentiation between self and self-representation.

Without this differentiation, the common view is that a "realistic" self-image constitutes optimal health and development. However, it was made clear in Chapter 3 that identification with anything other than one's essential presence is inherently narcissistic. Thus, models of psychological health that include identification with self-image will never get to the bottom of the narcissistic phenomenon.

In addition, this incomplete understanding tends to limit the usefulness of depth psychology to the treatment of psychopathology, when it could be so valuable in supporting the realization of the full human potential. For this reason, in this exploration we hope to extend the

present psychological understanding to include the deeper dimensions   63
of experience. Enlarging the view of the self to include these deeper
dimensions is accomplished not through an arbitrary trick of redefin-
ing the self, but in direct response to an extensive knowledge of the
actual lived experience of those whose identities have expanded to
include these dimensions.

The roots of narcissistic disturbance are far deeper than assumed by
prevailing theories of the self. These theories have made possible the
understanding presented in this book, but we will go much deeper
into the phenomena in question, addressing the question of narcissism
at a new depth which takes us past the limitations inherent in the
assumption that the self is the same as the self-representation, and the
assumption that the distinction is not of critical importance.

We noted in the last chapter the main reason that depth psychology
does not sufficiently appreciate the importance of this distinction: The
general view is that the development of the self-representation is inseparable from the development of the self, and is a major component of
it. This is true; the problem, however, is that the self-representation
is usually *equated* with the self. In fact, from the perspective of self-
realization, identification with the self-image is actually the most fundamental cause of the difficulty in being authentically ourselves.

Self-representation is the veil of personal history

We have seen that in order for us to be authentically and fully ourselves,
our identity must include the ontological depth of the soul, essential presence, and that to be presence means simply to be. When we are simply
being, our experience of ourselves is direct, immediate, spontaneous, and
natural, free from the influence of the thick veil of accumulated memories, ideas, ideals, and images. We have also seen that conventional experience does not allow the experience of self-realization because conventional
experience is virtually determined by this thick veil of personal history.
We have noted that ordinarily the self cannot experience itself separately
from the self-representation, and that, in fact, it experiences itself from
within, and through, that representation.

If it has not already been clear to the reader, it now becomes clear
that the veil of personal history is the self-representation. Regardless

64   of how realistic the self-representation is, it cannot contain the true reality of the self.[23]

It follows then that the narcissism of everyday life is an expression of the soul experiencing itself from within, and through, the self-representation.[24] Pathological narcissism is fundamentally the same manifestation, which locates the experience of the self much farther away from the dimension of essential presence, and thus involves a greater alienation from the essential core of the self. Pathological narcissism can include alienation from other, more surface dimensions of the self, that remain accessible to the normal individual, such as the physical and emotional dimensions. The greater distance from the essential core, in addition to the alienation from other dimensions of the soul, manifests not only in the aggravation of traits shared by the normal individual, but also in the development of other more typically narcissistic traits such as a pervasive sense of emptiness, a tendency to fragmentation, hypochondriacal preoccupation, and so on.[25]

How is narcissism related to the real self? Masterson's view

The definition of narcissism as alienation from the authentic depth of the self can be stated as alienation *from the true or real self,* understanding the real self to be the essential core of the self, its ontological truth. The definition of narcissism as alienation from the true self is not unique to us, nor is the notion of the real or true self.

James Masterson, a well-known writer on narcissism, defines a real self and defines narcissism as a disturbance of its development and structure. His use of the term *real,* however, does not correspond to ours. His definition of the real self is, in fact, nothing but the self-representation (or a slight modification of it): "The term 'real self' is used here not as the total self but in the intrapsychic sense of the sum of self and object representations with their related affects." (Masterson, 1981, p. 21)

In our view, this definition refers to a level of false self, since it omits the most important element which makes the self real, its actual presence. We believe, however, that Masterson actually has in mind a self which is not basically a self-representation, although he defines it as such. He attributes to the self capacities—for example, spontaneity,

aliveness of affect, the capacity to experience joy, creativity, self-assertion
and support—which could not possibly characterize a mental construct. So it seems that his actual notion of the self arises from his direct
empathic experience with an actual self whose nature is such that it can
be spontaneous and creative.

The self-representation might develop in a way that does not completely bar access to the essential nature of the self, which is the source
of its spontaneity and creativity, but the self-representation is not what
gives the self reality. A veil that allows some light from the sun to penetrate it can be seen as the normal condition, and a totally opaque veil
as abnormal and problematic, but this does not make the veil the source
of light. To think of the veil as the source is to confuse the self-
representation with the essence of the self. Consideration of the relative transparency or opaqueness of the veil can help to render the
opaque veil more transparent, but it will not allow us to know the sun
directly. Taking the veil to be true reality constitutes a barrier to realizing our full potential. This happens when the psychological helper's
idea of the self excludes its deeper realities. Masterson describes part
of a session with a patient:

> He reported his feeling about the impaired real self as, "I'm
> nobody, an eggshell to be broken. My mother punched a hole
> in the shell and sucked out the inside. There's nothing there. I
> feel no direction, I'm drifting like a spaceship . . ." Outside of
> the grandiose self, "I have layers of self-hate and despise myself.
> There's nothing inside, no essence." (Masterson, 1981, p. 46)

Here, Masterson is describing not merely the self-representation,
but the actual self patterned by the experience of the emptiness inside
the shell of representation. In this experience the soul is identified with
a certain component self-representation, that is, the self experiencing
itself from within and through a certain self-image, which is relating
to a certain image of the object (mother). This description is more
precise than defining the self as a self-representation which is having
a certain experience. The patient's identification with a certain self-
image is causing him to experience himself as an empty shell. Masterson
understands this as the experience of the impaired real self, which

66   means, to be consistent with his formulation, the experience of the impaired self-representation. Our understanding is that the soul is experiencing itself as empty because the individual's identification with the self-representation is making it impossible for him to be himself by disconnecting him from his real core, his essence. In fact, this is exactly what the patient says in his last statement: "There's nothing inside, no essence." The usual psychoanalytic understanding is that the sense of emptiness indicates the absence of some psychic structure. This is true, but more accretion of "healthy" psychic structures does not eliminate this emptiness, except from conscious experience. A narcissistically impaired self-representation is simply a representation that is too weak or too brittle to effectively mask the emptiness of alienation. A narcissistically "healthy" self-representation cannot be the essence of self.

How could a mental representation be the fundamental reality of the self? What self-representation could possibly make this patient feel that he had an essence? Our understanding is that Masterson's patient is expressing, in a direct, simple, and literal manner, a deep truth about his state: He is feeling empty of his essence; the essential core of the self is missing in his experience of himself. We have discussed the experience of emptiness in detail in another book, *The Void* (Almaas, 1986). The interested reader can refer to it, and to our other book, *The Pearl Beyond Price* (Almaas, 1988) for a detailed understanding of the relationships between the experience of emptiness, psychic structures, and Being.

Masterson probably benefitted his patient a great deal, not only because of his understanding of narcissistic development, and not only because of his skill and his human qualities, but also because of his immediate empathic understanding of the true self, which understanding is not encompassed by his theoretical definition of it. This definition does not seem to determine how Masterson works with his patients, since he is clearly responding to elements of the self other than the self-representation. However, his limited definition of the self does make it impossible for his approach to expand directly into the deeper dimensions of the self. Our perspective does not contradict, but simply complements, those of Masterson and others by adding

precision to the already existing understanding of the self, and open-   67
ing that understanding to deeper dimensions of experience.

What is the relation of the real self to the self-representation?

The following report by Pia A. illuminates how an expanded perspective on the self leads to a deeper resolution of narcissistic manifestation and allows access to the underlying spiritual dimensions of
the self. Pia, a woman in one of the helping professions, has been working with the author for several years in a group setting, supported by
private sessions with a teacher trained in our method. Her report concerns a group session in which she worked with the author about a certain issue she had been struggling with:

> *I asked about self-consciousness and concentration. I told you
> I've felt more self-conscious when reading, in other words, rest-
> less, picking on myself, judging or feeling proud of my actions,
> wanting food, sex, etc. It's hard to simply sit and read. That activ-
> ity (reading) seemed to make me more aware of feeling self-
> conscious; however, I notice then that I usually mostly always
> am this way.*
>
> *Part of what I'd been reading was about how it's not pos-
> sible to ever fully concentrate when one is self-conscious. I have
> been, also, reading about having no self. In working with you,
> you pointed out to me at some point that it seems I need my
> parents with me more now, perhaps because of the fear of the
> "no self" state. You explained that the "no self" state I am afraid
> of is not the same as the "no self" state of the Buddhists, that I
> have been reading about. You mentioned that if one is experi-
> encing the Buddhist "no self" state one will not be conscious of
> feeling "no self."*
>
> *You asked how I was feeling. There was emptiness and fear.
> You asked how the emptiness felt. There was more awareness of
> the boundaries around it. You commented that then I was not
> really sensing the emptiness itself, and asked if it was OK to feel
> empty, to which I said "no." You talked of the emptiness that
> accompanies the feeling of being a shell, feeling like an empty shell,
> as an ego state, and not what the Buddhists refer to as emptiness.*

Feeling the emptiness there was a feeling of insignificance. The fear lessened. Then the emptiness became a spaciousness. The boundaries of the shell went away. There was quiet and clarity. Things appeared very bright. It was pleasant to just look at you. It didn't matter whether I had a self or not. There was a feeling of depth in my belly. You acknowledged the state of presence that I was experiencing, which has peace as its most dominant quality.

Pia's experience involves many narcissistic elements, the most obvious ones involving the state of "no self," the fears about it, and the defenses against it. We will return to these later, but here we focus on how the expanded view of the self resolves these narcissistic manifestations by reconnecting with the presence of Being, rather than by building a psychic structure. Pia's report does not describe in detail the interactions between her and the author, but rather delineates the main steps of the process she went through. She started by wondering about the recent intensification of her self-consciousness, inability to concentrate, restlessness, judgment of herself, and desire for food and sex; in other words, there was a general tendency to avoid being with herself, as she sits down to read. It also happened that she was reading about the Buddhist concept of "no self," partly because in her process she was beginning to experience a sense of having no self.

I interpreted her judgment of herself, picking on herself, and increased craving for sex and food, as expressions of her inner need for the psychic presence of her parents (selfobjects, using Kohut's terminology), in either attacking or soothing forms. I also interpreted her need for such inner representations of the parents (or parent) as being related to the fear of "no self" feelings that have been arising in her recent experience. The mental representations of the parents, whether they were attacking or soothing, functioned to cushion her against full awareness of the "no self" state. As she began to recognize this defensive activity, the state of "no self" manifested more intensely. I explained to her then that this state of "no self" is not what she was reading about. This was necessary because her belief that she was experiencing the Buddhist state of "no self" was preventing her from accurately understanding her state. This clarification gave her the opportunity to view her experience freshly, with no preconceptions. At this point the state of "no self" manifested phenomenologically as emptiness, accompanied by fear. She was experiencing herself as an empty shell. Becoming aware of the identification with the empty shell allowed her to experience the emptiness directly, having seen her resistance against full awareness of it.[26]

Fully allowing the sense of emptiness leads to one of the most common manifestations of narcissism, the sense of being insignificant. The affect of insignificance often accompanies narcissistic emptiness, the emptiness that results from the dissolution of the self-concept, as does the feeling of "no self." (We will discuss the various affects which accompany narcissistic emptiness in Chapter 29.) When Pia was able to allow, without resistance, the sense of insignificance and the quality of emptiness, the sense of emptiness transformed to a quality of boundless spaciousness. This ushered her into the dimension of Being, which had the qualities of clarity, peace, and depth.

Pia's process of resolving the narcissistic manifestations of "no self" and insignificance, along with the defenses against them, did not involve establishing any psychic structure or representation. We did not interpret the emptiness as the lack of psychic structure; rather, we saw the manifestations of particular psychic structures (representations of the attacking or soothing actions of the parents) as defenses against the emptiness which was arising in other areas of her experience. The spaciousness which resolved the experience had in fact been veiled by these psychic structures. This clear spaciousness typically accompanies the dissolution of a mental structure, and becomes the space which allows the essential presence to surface into consciousness.

The fact that Pia had been working for some time on narcissistic issues made it possible for her to go through the process she reports here. Our analysis of her report is incomplete, and deeper discussion of it must wait until more material has been presented.

This case demonstrates how dealing with narcissistic manifestations—such as self-consciousness, emptiness, and feelings of insignificance—can lead to a direct awareness of one's essential presence. This is what relieved Pia's fear about the "no self" state, which was at the core of her narcissistic manifestation. She did not resolve the issue

70   with a sense of having a self, but with a state of being that rendered the question of self irrelevant. Since Pia's experience of her presence eliminated the narcissistic manifestations and the defenses against them, it is reasonable to assume that this presence is what was missing when Pia felt she was an empty shell. There are more compelling reasons for this conclusion, which will become apparent in the course of this study.

It is true that the emptiness, and the sense of empty shell that preceded it, resulted from, and is the inner phenomenological reality of, the "no self" state that frightened Pia. It is also true that this state indicates a weakening or dissolution of the self-representation as part of what she was going through at the time. But contrary to what Masterson and most depth psychologists believe, this does not imply that the resolution will involve establishing a psychic structure, which in this case would be the strengthening of her self-representation. However, since her increasing understanding of herself was revealing the self-representation as an empty shell, only tolerating the dissolution of the self-image could bring the issue to resolution. In the process, it was clear that the self-image had actually functioned to veil and contain, and thus to perpetuate, Pia's sense of emptiness.

Pia is not basically a narcissistic person; her narcissistic emptiness does not reflect narcissistic pathology—it does not characterize her daily life. The emptiness was arising mainly because her self-representation was becoming conscious as part of her process of spiritual development. In the typical process of this work, the self-representation is exposed to be the mental structure that functions both to alienate one from one's essential presence, and to veil the resulting emptiness of this alienation, in addition to providing the feeling of self.

When Pia finally experienced the emptiness without the defense of resorting to internalized object relations to shore up her dissolving self-representation, this emptiness transformed into a positive state, a pleasant, clear, and boundless spaciousness. This spaciousness then connected her to the missing essential quality, the peaceful and deep sense of presence, which she felt in her belly.

One final point that can be appreciated through consideration of the above case vignette is that to refer to the self-representation as the "real self," as Masterson does, is not only confusing, but ultimately counterproductive, for it is fundamentally untrue. We will discuss in greater detail the steps of working through narcissistic issues, but this vignette provides an initial glimpse that gives some flesh to our thus far largely theoretical discussion.

What is the relation of the real self to emotions? Alice Miller's view

Another author who defines narcissism as alienation from the true self is Alice Miller, a psychoanalyst known for her popular books on child abuse. She writes in her paper, "Depression and Grandiosity": "Whereas 'healthy narcissism' can be characterized as the full access to the true self, the narcissistic disturbance can be understood as a fixation on a 'false' or incomplete self." (Morrison, 1986, p. 346)

Miller's understanding of the development of narcissistic disturbance, which she bases in part on the work of Winnicott, Mahler, and Kohut, is similar to aspects of our perspective; her view that health is the capacity to be oneself is identical to ours. She describes the self as an experiential reality, as a feeling :

> I regard as a healthy self-feeling, the unquestioned certainty that the feelings and wishes which one experiences are a part of one's self. This certainty is not something based upon reflection, but is there like one's own pulse, which one does not notice as long as it functions normally. (Morrison, 1986, p. 325)

We would mention two points about Miller's definition. First, the spirit of her description indicates a direct feel for the actuality of the self, and an intuition of the experience of self-realization. We see this in her reference to "certainty," and in the observation that the experience is not based on reflection, but is like one's own pulse. Certainty is one of the specific feelings that accompanies the recognition of one's essential nature. One has an immediate and unquestioned certainty that one *is*, and what this isness feels like. One feels present, with the recognition that it is oneself that is present. It seems Miller has a sense of this sense, but she does not discuss it directly. The second point is that although her definition of narcissistic health—full access

72   to the true self—is identical to ours, and even though her formulations indicate some sense of the deeper core of the self, her view of
the true self focuses primarily on the emotional dimension. It is not
clear whether Miller views the true self as characterized primarily by
emotional development and maturity because this is the extent of her
experience and understanding, or because she does not recognize
conceptually the deeper core of the self that she does seem to be aware
of experientially.

In our view, the real self includes the availability, maturity and spontaneity of the emotional dimension of the self, but if we define ourselves at this level our capacity to be ourselves will be limited.[27] In
Miller's words, this is a fixation on an incomplete self.

Without essential realization, emotional maturity and freedom are
limited. The exclusion of deeper dimensions of the self distorts the
more surface dimensions. The self is fundamentally a unity; dissociation from one of its dimensions inevitably affects other dimensions.
The effect of normal narcissism on our emotional life is not resolved
by freeing and integrating the emotions. If treatment of narcissistic
pathology is limited to the emotional level, it can ameliorate the pathology only to the point where the narcissism of everyday life remains.
This amelioration is, of course, very significant to the suffering individual, providing him or her with the capacity to live a satisfying human
life. Also, achieving emotional health makes it possible for some people
to embark on the journey towards the greater maturity of spiritual
realization.

Emotional freedom and maturity are important for self-realization;
disconnection from emotions will cause narcissistic disturbance even
for those with a degree of self-realization. We sometimes encounter this
situation in our work, when a student has done a great deal of spiritual practice but no work on the emotions. Since spiritual work exposes
and intensifies both pathological and fundamental narcissistic issues,
these issues generally distort or limit the person's self-realization unless
they are worked through. Without psychological understanding they
are not easy to deal with.

Emotional freedom and maturity is achieved through the transformation of oedipal narcissism (see Chapter 4). The disturbances related

to this form of narcissism include immaturity or distortion of feelings.   73
However, the self that appears as the resolution of oedipal narcissism
is an essential presence, which forms the core and underlying ground
of the emotional dimension. Thus, we see that defining the real self as
the emotional dimension of experience excludes the deeper element
that can truly resolve narcissistic issues.

Healthy individuals and those who guide them toward self-realization
need to understand the self, not from the perspective of pathology,
but from an understanding which supports the expansion of the soul
toward a more complete humanity. In our opinion, this expansion can
deepen the understanding available to psychotherapy, since it makes
available a more comprehensive and realistic conception of the human
being.

What is the relation of the real self to the body? Lowen's view

Another significant contributor to the understanding of narcissism,
and one who also defines narcissism as alienation from the real self, is
Alexander Lowen, a psychiatrist and former student of Wilhelm Reich.
Lowen pioneered bioenergetics studies, a theory and method of therapy
or growth work based on a synthesis of psychoanalytic theory and
physical-energetic techniques. His view approaches ours when he differentiates between the self and its representation: "There is a difference between the self and its image, just as there is between the person
and his or her reflection in a mirror." (Lowen, 1983, p. 7)

Recognizing the importance of the fact that the self is not an image,
he criticizes psychoanalytic thinking for its emphasis on representation and images.

> Indeed, all this talk of 'images' betrays a weakness in the psy-
> choanalytic position. Underlying the psychoanalytic explana-
> tion of narcissistic disturbances is the belief that what goes on
> in the mind determines the personality. It fails to consider that
> what goes on in the body influences thinking and behavior as
> much as what goes on in the mind. (Lowen, 1983, p. 7)

We agree that psychoanalytic thinking overemphasizes the mind.
Psychoanalytic theory, however, generally does include the body,

74 because the self-representation includes the image of the body; but this is not exactly Lowen's criticism. He is pointing to the fact that present-centered experience includes fresh feelings arising spontaneously in the body, in addition to mental representations. Lowen is oriented toward the phenomena tangibly felt in the body, and his methodology is designed to explore this aspect of experience. It thus tends to orient one toward identifying with sensations and feelings rather than with mental conceptions.

However, Lowen does not seem to fully appreciate the depth of influence of the self-representation. In fact, his understanding of psychological health remains to some degree within the self-image, even when he posits otherwise. This is clear when he defines the self.

> We need to direct our attention to the self, that is, the corporeal self, which is projected onto the mind's eye as an image. Simply put, I equate the self with the living body, which includes the mind. The sense of self depends on the perception of what goes on in the living body. (Lowen, 1983, p. 7)

This definition of the self is problematic in that it does not acknowledge how profoundly the sense of the body is influenced by the representation. The coherent body sense develops simultaneously with, and as part of, the representation. Developmental theory indicates that under ordinary circumstances our experience of the body cannot be separated from the self-representation. Mahler's work on infant development makes this point with great precision.

We have seen how conventional experience is so influenced by the self-representation that it is actually determined by it in large part. Even though the experience of the living body vividly enjoyed in the process of bioenergetics analysis is relatively free from the constricting effect of mental images, it is still significantly determined by subtle components of the self-representation. This influence appears in the fact that one experiences oneself as a body, with shape, size, and other characteristics. Even when one is not identified with the body, one's experience remains centered within a body with shape, very early, unconscious components of size, and other characteristics, the sense of which arises from the body-image. Sandler and Rosenblatt (1962)

paraphrase Freud by stating that: "the self-representations are first
and foremost body representations. In this they suggest that it is
the very processes of differentiation and structuralization that produce the capacity to experience the body image." (G. and R. Blanck,
1974b, p. 54)

How is the body experienced in self-realization?

When our awareness of the body is completely free from any image,
conscious or unconscious, experience moves to a different dimension.
We realize that our experience is no longer centered within the body,
but in a boundless expanse of consciousness, which feels more like
clear spaciousness than anything corporeal. (See *The Void* [Almaas,
1986] for further discussion and case material.)

This is not an experience of the mind that is part of the body, as
Lowen might assume, because this clear spacious awareness is seen to
contain the body and mind. This is not what is commonly called an
out-of-body experience, because the body is more vividly and pleas-
urably sensed than is ordinarily possible. Although this experience of
the body occurs in deeper spiritual dimensions when we experience
ourselves free from any body image, it is not the deepest, and hence
not the most objective, perception of the body. Awareness of the body
completely without mental representation is profoundly surprising. It
moves to dimensions beyond those encountered in bioenergetics analysis, or in any body-centered therapy.

In full self-realization we experience the body as a transparent,
diaphanous form of presence. The form is seen to be more superficial than the ontological reality of presence, which is beyond any form.
This experience of the body is not easy to access; it involves a leap of
consciousness that generally requires a great deal of inner work, such
as decades of intense meditation practice. Many reports from spiritual traditions describe the experience of the body as an open, transparent form of presence. An example is this passage from the Dzogchen
teaching:

> This opening up calls into question the status of what in rep-
> resentational thought is taken to be a determinable entity
> which, as a material thing, is called the body. In this transition

76   from rigidity to fluidity, the body as me-as-embodied is experienced as a process of embodying that which, in the last analysis, turns out to be the spiritual richness that pervades the whole of Being. (H. Guenther, 1984, p. 196)

The experience of the body in the dimension of essential presence indicates that the core of the self is experientially deeper than the living body. This core is the very consciousness that allows us to experience the body as living. Our definition of the self includes the living body, but as we have made clear, also includes more fundamental dimensions. More accurately, it is not that the body is a more superficial reality than presence; it is more that the self is a wholeness that contains all dimensions, including the body, and this wholeness is disturbed when there is dissociation from presence, because it is presence which is responsible for this complete wholeness. Presence is the ultimate ontological ground and reality of all the dimensions. Awareness of essential presence does not negate or devalue the body; rather, it gives it, along with the other aspects and dimensions of the self, a greater sense of integration, wholeness, and lightness.

Lowen might be writing from a position influenced by experiences of presence, but he might not recognize it as such because he is looking at his experience from a conceptual dimension. This conceptual flavor is reflected in his definition, because taking the body to be the ground of experience indicates that one is operating from within the concept of the body. We accept Lowen's thesis that narcissistic disturbance occurs when we identify with an image instead of simply being ourselves, but very deep self-representations determine our experience of the body more profoundly than Lowen seems to appreciate. We can become more deeply aware of the body, and experience it with more freedom, when we let go of images comprising the self-representation. Even then, however, more primitive, deeply unconscious images and structures will determine our identity. Since one naturally conceptualizes new modes of experience within one's assumptions, it will not occur to most people to see certain levels of experience as presence. For example, a person in a spiritual practice might experience a boundless, vast state of awareness; she might even experience her identity as that awareness. But it is likely that even with repeated experiences of boundless dimensions, she will believe that "I am a person, an embodied entity, who is having these experiences." When she has seen through her identity with the body, however, the dominant element in experience is not the living body, but essential presence, which is much more vivid.

It seems likely that Lowen is responding to the actual presence felt as the self, because he emphasizes the direct vitality of feelings so much that it would be difficult to imagine it otherwise. He writes: "And it is this feeling of aliveness that gives rise to the experience of the self." (Lowen, 1983, p. 8) And again: "The self, then, may be defined as the feeling aspect of the body. It can be experienced only as a feeling." (Lowen, 1983, p. 29)

Presence is more like feeling than like thought, which makes it possible to mistake it for the felt aliveness of the body. The unconscious components of the self-representation (like those involved in the primitive body sense), coupled with the assumption that the physical body is the most fundamental level of the self, tend to prevent one from discriminating presence in experience. We believe that these factors have determined the view of the self of many psychological researchers. They certainly determine the self-experience of most individuals, including spiritual aspirants.

Because he includes the living body as an important dimension of the self, Lowen makes a valuable contribution to the understanding of narcissism and its resolution. Although identification with the body is a fixation on an incomplete self, which thus contributes to fundamental narcissism, alienation from the body is one of the causes, and one of the results, of narcissism. Bioenergetics analysis is a powerful method of enlivening the body and opening the feelings. Many of our students work on the body armor and energy. Lowen's appreciation of the living and feeling qualities of the self, his understanding of how its denial is reflected in the body armor, and the relation of this armor to repression and its connection to sexuality and the oedipal stage, make his contribution an original addition to theories about the self and narcissism. We value it especially as an understanding of the libidinal self and its narcissism, the oedipal form of narcissism. We explore oedipal narcissism and its resolution in detail in Chapter 37.

chapter 7

Kohut's Bipolar Self

I n our estimation, Heinz Kohut, a psychoanalyst and the founder of self psychology, has contributed more than any other to the understanding of narcissism and its resolution. We rely on his work throughout this study. Especially valuable to our exploration are his elucidation of various types of narcissistic (selfobject) transference, and his view of narcissism as developmental arrest. In the beginning, Kohut used "self" to refer to the self-representation, but in his later work developed the notion of the "bipolar self." This change reflects Kohut's growing appreciation of the self as more than a self-representation, and marks an important shift to approaching the self as a dynamic phenomenon.

Kohut attributes a core to the self, which he calls the "nuclear self," to which he assigns a specific content. This content is primarily determined by two poles: ambitions and ideals. He views this psychic structure, the "bipolar self," as the essence of the self, as we can see in the following passage about establishing the nuclear self, as "an uninterrupted tension arc from basic ambitions, via basic talents and skills, towards basic ideals. This tension arc is the dynamic essence of the complete, nondefective self." (Kohut, 1984, pp. 4–5)

Even though he defines the core of the self as a psychic structure, 79 Kohut focuses on concepts which reflect felt or observed experience, like ambitions and ideals. His later writings reflect this growing appreciation of the self as an experiential reality, and show the increasing dominance of process thinking in his work.

Kohut views the bipolar self as "a core self . . . the basis of our sense of being an independent center of initiative and perception . . . forms the central sector in the personality, [which is] an energetic continuum in the center of the personality." (Kohut, 1984, p. 7)

This notion deserves further discussion.[28] The center or core of the personality can mean many things; one meaning is that it is the element that is interior to all parts of the personality, in the same way cells are central to the body. In this sense this element forms the core of all its parts.

Here, Kohut seems to be thinking in experiential terms, for we experience ourselves as a continuum of states with a central and permeating aliveness. In fact, Kohut at times writes of the self as if it were a continuum of states; for example, in a case discussion: "to the cohesive experience of the self in time (i.e., to the experience of the self as a continuum of states)." (Kohut, 1971, p. 130) It seems that he is familiar with the experience of the self as an energetic continuum, but continues to see it as mental structure.[29]

Another meaning of something being a center is that it is the central and most important element; for example, free enterprise is central to capitalism. By the centrality of the bipolar self, Kohut seems also to mean that it forms the central part of the personality; it is the most important part, and other parts are subordinate to it. Its development and health would then be paramount in the overall equilibrium and harmony of the total self, according to Kohut. However, he again makes the meaning more literal when he defines the bipolar self as the center of our experience, becoming something like the center of our being "from which all initiative springs and all experiences end." (Kohut, 1978, p. 95). Kohut's formulations suggest a picture of the bipolar self forming a center of a spatial structure, constituting the most central part of it, like the nucleus of a cell or an atom. He actually says that the bipolar self was initially the nuclear self. (See Appendix E.)

80   This concept is important for understanding narcissism. Simply stated, Kohut's notion is that the most significant developmental accomplishment of the healthy self is that it develops, or develops with, a center, which becomes its most important sector. The center is the bipolar self that develops from the original primitive center in early childhood, the nuclear self. Narcissistic health is a result of establishing a cohesive, realistic, and enduring bipolar self, and narcissistic disturbance is due to difficulties in its development and structure.

Although we have no difficulty accepting that the self develops a central sector which becomes its center, we find Kohut's definition of this center to be limited. It makes sense that the center of the self will include structures related to ambitions and ideals, for these are important for the healthy self, but the healthy self must include many other equally important elements. Kohut's definition limits the center of the self to the realm of action and accomplishment, which is central for certain types of personalities, but definitely not for all. It is the narcissistic personality who organizes the self around action and accomplishment, for accomplishment is his primary means of attaining self-esteem. Narcissistic personalities are characterized by problems in the areas of ambitions and ideals because they tend to have grandiose and unrealistic notions of their capacities. One might think that their functioning is disturbed because of distortions in the bipolar self, and it is thus this area that needs attention. This may be true, but it does not make sense to define the self in general based on observations of narcissistic pathology.

Can we use Kohut's definition of self to understand normal experience?

Although Kohut's theory is particularly suited to understanding and treating narcissistic pathology, it becomes problematic when we rely on his theory of the self as a general psychology. His position is supported by many researchers who believe that narcissistic disturbance is particularly characteristic of our times. Even if it is true, however, that narcissism is the psychological malady of our times, the self cannot be defined in relation to this fact.

Although narcissistic disturbance is prevalent in the culture at large, we have no way of knowing whether it is more prevalent now than at other times. It is possible that it is more prevalent, for our times are more materialistic. Excessive concern with the material dimension of life, or exclusive focus on it, tends to alienate the self from its depth. Even though Kohut's definition of the self reflects the contemporary situation, this is not necessarily an advantage in terms of understanding the nature of the self. We think it could actually be a liability, a trap that could keep us in the grips of narcissism rather than freeing us from it. If we confine our consideration of the self to dysfunctional areas, we will exacerbate the situation by excluding elements of the self that could help deal with the disturbance precisely because they are not narcissistic. As we use psychological theory to support our work on self-realization, it is important to avoid the error of defining the human being only from the perspective of pathology.[30]

Also, the fact that a psychic structure is characteristic of the normal individual does not make it healthy in an absolute sense.[31] Although the bipolar self is part of the normal character, its healthy development does not resolve narcissistic disturbance; actually, it lies at its very roots.

Clearly, if our ideals are grandiose and our ambitions unrealistic, we will find it difficult to be authentic and thus to function as a normal, healthy self. The pathologically narcissistic person also tends to delusionally believe that he has attained idealized qualities and accomplishments, thus manifesting what is called the grandiose self. Hence, an amelioration of this condition which enables the self to establish a strong bipolar self (with realistic ambitions and ideals) will expand one's capacity to be truly himself. His condition can move, then, from pathological narcissism to the narcissism of everyday life.

As we have seen, the incapacity to be authentically ourselves is the expression of not being able to simply be. Simply being is not a matter of being anything in particular; it is not a matter of being according to any view of ourselves, realistic or not. Simply being means the absence of any activity, inner or outer, to be ourselves. Simply being is just that: Being.

The extent of the self's alienation is determined by how far the locus of experience is from the true core of the self, which is, in turn, determined

82   by how superficial the self-representation is. We restate this view here
to contrast it with Kohut's view of the self and of narcissism. In turn,
Kohut's ideas allow us to see more precisely the situation of fundamental narcissism.

If, as we posited in Chapter 5, narcissistic disturbance is a result of
investment in the self-representation, then merely correcting the representation only deals with the symptoms and not with the fundamental causes. Thus, defining the healthy self as an inner tension arc
between ambitions and ideals, where ambitions are based on self-
images and ideals are based on ideal-images, is to define narcissistic
health by the very element that disturbs it. Kohut's definition of the
self, then, makes it fundamentally narcissistic, for to live according to
ideals and ambitions means to live according to images, which is the
fundamental narcissistic disturbance.

Kohut's formulation is not mistaken with respect to the experience
of self in the conventional dimension of experience, whether normal
or pathological. His view is an advance in the understanding of the normal self; in particular, his definition of the bipolar self casts new light
on the nature of this self and its disturbances, which is useful for our
present study. Kohut's notion of the tension arc between ambitions
and ideals brings to light an important truth about the dynamic nature
of the self. However, this concept does not do justice to the dynamic
essence of the complete, nondefective self, described in Chapter 3.

This critique of Kohut's model of the bipolar self applies to most
psychoanalytic theories of self and narcissism, particularly to those
which define narcissism as the cathexis of the self-representation. Our
critique actually applies more to the other psychoanalytic theories,
especially those adhering to ego psychology.

chapter 8

The Dynamism
of the Self

———————————————————— •

K ohut's notion of the tension arc as the dynamic essence of the complete, nondefective self brings into the picture of the self the element of dynamism. The tension arc involves a motive for action of any kind: physical, mental, artistic, and so on. In Kohut's words:

> With the term action arc, however, I am referring to the abiding flow of actual psychological activity that establishes itself between the two poles of the self, i.e., a person's basic pursuits toward which he is 'driven' by his ambitions and 'led' by his ideals. (Kohut, 1977, p. 180)

This insight into the nature of the normal self involves two significant ideas. The first is that this nature is characterized not only by the presence of psychic structures, but also by the presence of unceasing psychological activity. The second idea is the delineation of the poles, ambitions and ideals, between which this activity flows.

How does a person act from a state of self-realization?

Just as we contrasted our understanding of the nature of the self with the conventional view in our description of the possibilities of

84 experience in self-realization, so, too, we must contrast the phenomena of change and action from the perspective of psychology (Kohut's
understanding being the most clear and powerful) to the phenomenon
of change and action as experienced when the identity of the self is situated in Being. The abiding flow of experience in self-realization is
neither "driven" nor "led"; it is the natural and spontaneous flow of
presence. The soul unfolds as the manifestation of its essential forms
and qualities. This dynamic property of the self is the basis of all its
action. In the initial stages of self-realization, in which presence is
experienced as the core and inner essence of the soul, this presence
transforms from one quality to another. It manifests sometimes as
love, sometimes as will, other times as intelligence, truth, or individuation, and so on, or as combinations of these qualities. These forms
of presence function as our sense of being, and also as the center of
initiative and action.

The presence is the center of the self, from which all creativity, initiative and action arise. This centeredness gives us the sense of purpose and orientation, and the changing forms provide the specific
motives for action; that is, our action is based spontaneously on love,
compassion, truth, intelligence, and so on. We might have ideals, but
they are not what orient or drive our action. When we act out of love
it is not because of an ideal that loving action is good. We are bound
to act, for good or ill, but when presence manifests in us, in the pure
quality of love for instance, we act spontaneously out of this love. We
act and create naturally out of love, the way a flower blooms in response
to water and sun. We act without self-conscious premeditation, without reflecting on our action to bolster our self-esteem. We cannot help
but act out of the arising quality of our essence, with an innate intelligence. There is an ease and equanimity about the whole affair. Our
actions have a self-existing sense of value and fulfillment, because they
are true to our nature.[32]

In contrast, when the self is not in direct contact with its true center, it develops a center which is a psychic structure. The loss of the
essential center is part of the same process that establishes the psychic
center. This new psychic center of the self, which Kohut calls the nuclear
self (or the bipolar self that develops from it) has a dynamic property,

a certain ongoing psychological activity. This inner activity of the normal self is characteristic of psychic structures in general, but particularly characteristic of the center of the self, as we saw in Kohut's description of the bipolar self which is the center of initiative and action for the self.

Kohut's account of ego activity is general, providing the outlines of its shape: a tension arc which functions to drive and lead the activities of the self. But what is the nature of this psychological activity? What constitutes the drive and the pull? Ambitions and ideals are not, themselves, psychological activities, although they cause the self to act one way or another. Kohut described the poles between which the activity flows, but did not explore the nature of this activity. This inner psychological activity is actually rather subtle, but we can experience it directly and investigate it. The presence of Essence assists greatly in this investigation, because it provides contrast to this activity, making it conscious and rendering it transparent.

What constitutes ego activity?

We need a comprehensive view of the inner workings of the center of the self in order to understand its relationship to narcissism, and hence, to self-realization. This is an involved question; we can only give a sketch of its general outline here. Our books, *The Pearl Beyond Price* (Almaas, 1988), and *Diamond Heart, Book II* (Almaas, 1989), provide a more detailed account of this inner psychological activity, which we term "ego activity" to differentiate it from the dynamism of essential presence. It is based on, and is part of, the self patterned by psychic structures.

The center of the ego-self, the center of its initiative, action and perception, is a psychic structure characterized by a specific pattern and by incessant psychological activity. The pattern, or the particular psychic organization, provides the direction of action, while the activity provides the drive to act. This gives the self a sense of orientation, center, and meaning. The psychological activity includes hope—the self is hoping, consciously or unconsciously, to achieve its aim or ideal. This implies that we project on the future the possibility of accomplishing a certain objective. The content of this objective is dependent

86   upon previous experiences. We can hope only for something we have already had a taste of. The objective does not have to be identical to something we have experienced, but is shaped by many experiences from the past.

For instance, a person might have the objective of becoming a painter. Becoming a painter will involve many things he has never experienced, but the ambition is shaped by the way he believes he will feel, the responses he thinks he will receive, the impressions and influences he expects to make on others, and so on. These are determined or informed by his past experience. His objective and the values he attaches to it become an ideal.[33]

He then experiences hope, which initiates desire for the ideal. This desire is an important element in psychological activity. It is the actual manifestation of the psychological drive. In other words, ambitious striving includes desire, which implies hope. Without hope there would be no desire.

Both hope for a future objective and desire for this objective imply that we experience the condition of the self at the present as not completely satisfactory. This discontent, subtle or gross, conscious or unconscious, constitutes a rejection of the present state of the self.[34] When there is complete acceptance of one's present state, there is no desire and no need for hope. The subtle current of rejecting activity is based on the images which we have of ourselves, and the ideal images that we are trying to actualize. This condition can be conscious, but it is usually an unconscious and implicit undercurrent of the psychological activity of the self.

The psychological activity which is the dynamic center of the ego-self is composed, then, of desire that implies both hope and rejection, and its content is determined by our self-images and ideal images. Thus, the main components of ego activity are hope, desire and rejection.

We are not implying that all human motivation arises out of the flow of hope, desire and rejection, for we recognize that the self is fundamentally a dynamic wholeness. The dynamism of the self is an evolutionary force which has the *a priori* property of functioning as an "optimizing force." This force is recognized by many of the spiritual teachings of humankind. See Appendix F for a discussion of his force.

Ego activity and the dynamics of Being

One way of envisioning the situation of the ego-self is that its dynamic core, ego activity, is an incomplete and distorted manifestation of the dynamism of Being. From this perspective, we can appreciate the fundamental truth that it is the dynamism of Being which underlies all activity and creativity. However, this dynamism can be functioning naturally according to its own intrinsic design, recognizable as an optimizing force, or it can function in an errant, distorted, or incomplete manner, recognizable as ego activity.

Ego activity is not always led by ideals or driven by ambitions; it is a more general, ongoing motion of defending against pain or seeking pleasure. Also, the ego is always acting directly or indirectly to preserve the self-representation. It preserves ego structures, including the "nuclear" structures of the center of the self. When this activity becomes organized and channeled according to ideals and ambitions through the establishment of higher level psychic structures (as Kohut conceptualized them), it becomes the tension arc of the bipolar self. Thus, the tension arc of the bipolar self is a particular manifestation of ego activity, one central to the narcissistic sector of the self. As will be discussed in later chapters, our observation is that the cessation of ego activity actually results in the dissolution of some psychic structures.

Kohut's definition of the self in terms of ambitions and ideals restricts his understanding of the inner activity of the self, which has a broader and more basic function. As we have seen, because the nature of the self is fundamentally Being, it is part of the general flow of all Being and shares the quality of dynamic, spontaneous, ever-changing manifestation.

The dynamism of Being, as experienced in the deeper stages of self-realization, is a spontaneous and natural flow of presence. In the human soul the presence functions as the inspiring and motivating center of initiative, action, and creativity, and its intrinsic patterning functions as the guidance that directs the activity. This activity is totally spontaneous, and free from the constricting influence of psychic structures. The self is intrinsically intelligent, and this intelligence is part of the inherent intelligent structure of Being. This intelligence manifests as appropriate responsiveness to the needs of whatever situation one finds

88   oneself in. When love is needed, the dynamism manifests presence in the aspect of Love, which guides us to act in loving ways; when strength is needed, it manifests Essence in the quality of Strength, guiding us to act with strength and vitality. Past experience is available to the intelligence without defining the truth of the self. The dynamic essence of the self, here, is not an ambitious activity trying to actualize a certain objective that fits its ideals; rather, it is a completely nonselfish, dynamic flow of the essential nature of the self as it unfolds naturally and authentically. Authenticity means that the inner flow and the external action are the matter-of-fact reality of the self being itself, just as the heart beats because it is its intrinsic nature to do so.

Action based on ambitions and ideals disconnects the self from its innate dynamism. The activity is bound to be somewhat unauthentic, for regardless of how near the ideals and ambitions are to the actual condition of the self, they cannot be identical to its condition in the moment because they are based on structures most likely laid down in early childhood. In fact, activity based on ambitions and ideals is a kind of substitute activity, reflecting our inability to contact the real dynamism at the center of the self. This is the sense in which the tension arc of ideals and ambitions is a false dynamism, an impostor that takes the place of the real thing. The unrealistic ideals and grandiose ambitions of narcissistic individuals are exaggerated manifestations of the fundamental narcissistic condition. So we can see that in narcissistic pathology, just as the unrealistic self-images and ideal images are distorted and exaggerated manifestations of fundamental narcissism, which is disconnection from the core of the self, the tension arc of the unrealistic ambitions and ideals is the distorted and exaggerated manifestation of the disconnection from the dynamism of Being. Our discussion indicates, also, that the normal tension arc of ambitions and ideals is the normal manifestation of the disconnection from the dynamism of Being.

From this perspective, to live according to ambitions and ideals is the very essence of the narcissistic condition; this is a manifestation of the self that is not being itself. Self-centered individuals are typically ambitious, and extreme ambition is usually considered narcissistic. Ambition has never been considered a true spiritual quality; it is acceptable in modern society primarily because of the increasing materialism of the time. The prevalence of personal ambition is possibly a manifestation of the narcissism typical of contemporary society. Also, we commonly understand that when a person is strongly focused on living up to ideals, he is not contented to be himself. Such idealism is considered societally abnormal only when it reaches extreme proportions.

Our argument that identification with ambitions and ideals constitutes and perpetuates narcissistic disturbance may be easy to see in the case of ambitions, but harder in the case of ideals; in most societies high ideals are a sign of maturity, even of spiritual refinement. However, having high ideals is not the same as having ideals based on ideal images of self and objects. We might have high ideals in the state of self-realization, but they do not originate from psychic structures that define who and what we are. These high ideals are the influence of the qualities of Essence on the self.

It is difficult not to develop ideals into psychic structures that define the self. In fact, it is difficult even to engage in spiritual practice if we are not inspired by ideals. The inevitable presence of ideals based on psychic structures, however, simply reflects the limitation of our self-realization. As long as we are not fully self-realized, some psychic structures define the self, and ego activity is based somewhat on ideals. The more we are self-realized, the less we rely on ideals because we experience a growing trust that the dynamism of Being will manifest what is needed. Ultimately, we do not need high ideals because we have integrated into our being their very source. Our actions might appear from the outside as if they are inspired by high ideals, but in fact, we are merely manifesting our true nature.

Another, more fundamental reason why the definition of the self as the bipolar self imprisons the notion of self within the narcissistic disturbance, is that basing our sense of self on an inner activity oriented towards an objective in the future automatically disconnects us from our essential nature. Presence cannot be found in the future. If we are oriented to the future, we are not being in the present. This does not mean that in a self-realized state we cannot plan or think of the future. We can plan and think without rejecting our present state.

The future orientation of ego activity in general, and the tension arc of the bipolar self in particular, disturb the present-centered property

90 of presence. To simply be means to be now, and not to try to be something that matches an ideal. Trying means not being. This is the reason we do not try to live according to ideals in the state of self-realization. We can measure our state from the perspective of an ideal, but this is not the same as defining our identity by this measurement. So we see that the tension arc between ambitions and ideals is not only an expression of the loss of contact with the dynamism of Being, but by its very nature serves to disconnect the self from Being.

Since presence is the condition of the self when it is simply being, it can arise only when we are accepting our present condition. Thus, the rejection implicit in the activity of the bipolar self makes it impossible for the self to be completely present in the now.

To summarize, then, three of Kohut's contributions to the understanding of the self are particularly important for our study:

1. The self develops a center, the bipolar self. This center becomes the central sector of the self.

2. The center has two poles, ambitions and ideals.

3. The center of the self is characterized by the flow of psychological activity, termed a tension arc.

Kohut relates narcissism to this central part of the self. The firm establishment of a cohesive and realistic center characterizes narcissistic health and narcissistic disturbance is due to disturbances in this development.

Our discussion and critique of the views of the self and narcissism in the theories of Kohut and other psychologists has established the following:

1. Viewing the depth of the self as primarily emotional fixates the self on a partial manifestation of its nature, and hence, perpetuates narcissism.

2. Identifying the self with the body also fixates the self on a partial manifestation of it, which both causes and is the outcome of fundamental narcissism.

3. Ego activity, which is the dynamic property of the center of the ego-self, perpetuates the disconnection of the self from the deeper

truth of its Being, and hence, both causes and is caused by funda- 91
mental narcissism.

4. Identification with mental representations, or a psychic structure patterned by such representations, is the most fundamental cause of narcissistic disturbance.

5. Fundamental narcissism, the specific and most central manifestation of the disconnection from the essential core of the self, the presence of Being, underlies all other forms of narcissism.

6. Pathological narcissism is a distortion or an exaggeration of fundamental narcissism.

7. Fundamental narcissism is an intrinsic property of the ego-self, which is the self as experienced in the dimension of conventional experience.

———————————————————— · PART **3**

IDENTITY:
EGO STRUCTURE
AND ESSENCE

We have discussed how the self develops with, and partially through, the establishment of the self-representation, and how this development influences the self to the extent of determining its ongoing experience. The self develops not knowing itself separately from its representation, experiencing itself from within and through this representation, to the extent that the self identifies with it. Thus, the representation is the means by which the self knows and recognizes itself. This has deeper implications than we have so far discussed, which we will now explore in order to illuminate the representation's relation to narcissism, and hence, to self-realization.

What are the major manifestations of the self patterned by the self-representation?

What are the main psychological patterns, the primary structures? We can look at this question from the perspective of our lived experience

94   as well as from the perspective of developmental psychology. In normal personal experience the ego-self is what we experience as ourselves. We experience the self as an entity among other entities. We do not experience ourselves as part of something else, but as an entity in our own right. We experience our existence as our own, fundamentally separate and autonomous from other entities or phenomena.

It is possible for us to experience ourselves not as an entity, but this is unusual. There are basically three situations in which this is possible. The first is in early infancy before the development of a separate sense of self. Most developmental theories hold that the neonate is not aware of itself as a separate self, that at the beginning experience is not referred to a self differentiated from the rest of the perceptual field.[35] The second situation is severe psychopathology in which the normal sense of self did not develop or developed inadequately.[36] In some unusual circumstances this condition can arise transiently in the normal self. The third situation is the state of self-realization, when we experience presence as boundless. In this case, the experience of the self is the oneness of the universe, or awareness of the soul as part of the fabric of this oneness. In general, however, normal experience definitely includes a sense of being an entity. In fact, "entitihood" constitutes the barest minimum of the sense of self for a human being.

We normally experience our sense of self as more than the sense of being an entity, and more than the sense of being a living psychophysical organism. The basic sense of being an entity appears more specifically as being an individual, a person. The experience is of ourselves as individuals, persons with human bodies, with human characteristics and qualities. We are individuals who can interact with other individuals, and who have significant relationships with significant other individuals. The sense of self is differentiated here as a feeling of individuality, of personhood with unique personality traits and characteristics. Each of us experience ourself as an individual with an inner psychological life, that finds itself, and expresses itself, in a personal life. Being an entity, however, is not identical to being an individual; individuality presumes entitihood, but entitihood does not entail individuality. The relevance of this apparently subtle discrimination will become clear as we proceed. It is particularly important for understanding the later stages of self-realization.

chapter 9

Identity

O ur discussion thus far has involved how we develop as individuals, each basically an entity with individuality. However,
the soul has another characteristic that also characterizes
individuality, which differentiates each self from other selves. Every
normal self is an individual, but each individual has something about
him that makes it possible for him, and for others, not only to recognize that he is a person, but also to identify who he is. This is not just
the sense of individuality, for all people are individuals, but another
manifestation by which we distinguish one individual from another.
This manifestation is a combination of many characteristics of the particular individual—physical, mental, emotional, behavioral, moral,
spiritual, and others that are undefinable. The combination of these
personal characteristics makes up an integrated whole, a gestalt, which
allows us to know that someone is this particular individual, and not
someone else.

Recognizing this overall gestalt makes us feel that we really know a
particular person. The more we know a person, and the more intimately
we know him or her, the more we know his or her particular gestalt.
Greater familiarity allows us to sense this gestalt even more deeply,

96   more completely, and the deeper and more complete our knowing-feeling-sensing of this identifying gestalt, the more particular and specific it becomes. We can come to know not only the various characteristics that make up this gestalt, but also the psychological quality that is its essence or distilled flavor. Yet, even when we know intimately the gestalt of a particular person, it remains difficult to define.

Most of us are aware that our bodies have certain characteristic smells which, although they are easy for us to identify, are at the same time difficult to define or to describe. We can also know the psychological "scent" in an individual familiar to us, a sense of the quality that identifies this person, the essence of his identifying gestalt. Knowing the person in this way is like knowing him from inside, knowing the feel of him, the dominant quality that characterizes his inner atmosphere.

This identifying gestalt is of course also experienced from the inside, by the person himself. We not only experience ourselves as entities and as individuals, but we also feel another sort of self-recognition. This self-recognition is not inferred from the various characteristics that constitute our identifying gestalt, but is felt directly, as a certain familiar sense by which we intimately recognize ourselves. We recognize ourselves without noting the various properties of our body and mind but simply by this inner sense, through the familiar overall quality of our inner atmosphere.

This inner sense that characterizes each one of us is usually so familiar that we do not know it is there unless we experience its absence, or a threat to its presence. We become aware of it more easily when it is absent or disturbed, than by directly feeling it. But it is possible to identify it in our lived experience. This feeling of identity is related to, and might be composed of, and at least partially generated by, the identifying gestalt. However, it is a unique category of experience. This inner recognition of oneself, as a feeling, an affective tone, a psychological quality, can only be called identity.

Just as the sense of being an individual is not exactly the same as that of being an entity, so, too, the sense of identity is not the same as these. We can recognize ourselves as entities. We can recognize ourselves as individuals. And we can simply recognize ourselves. This pure self-

recognition is the direct experience of our identity; it is possible because
the self has an identity. If not for this identity, we would not be able
to recognize ourselves by merely feeling ourselves; we would have to
infer our identity by observing our characteristics.

Self, entity, individuality, identity

We have now differentiated four categories of self-experience: self
(or soul), entity, individuality, and identity. Soul is the totality of the
human being, primordially a wholeness. In self-realization we recognize it as the experiencing consciousness. In the dimension of conventional experience the soul experiences itself as an entity. This sense
of entity is the basis of the self experiencing itself as an individuality.
The self, as an individuality, can recognize itself directly because it possesses an identity, which it experiences as the feeling of identity. These
concepts are the basic and most general patterns of the experience of
the self in the dimension of conventional experience. They are the primary experiences, or psychic structures, of the normal self. We have
delineated them so precisely because such precision is necessary for
completely understanding narcissism and self-realization.

The self-representation influences the self by patterning its experience such that it knows itself as an entity with a separate individuality, which has an identity. This is the result of the development of the
self as the self-representation is established in early childhood. Developmental psychology explores this process extensively, as we will discuss
shortly. However, this exploration has been subject to a great deal of
unclarity, confusion and disagreement regarding the above four concepts. Frequently they are used interchangeably; such usage is a result
of this confusion, and also produces more confusion. For our purposes it is important to define these concepts clearly, first with respect
to lived experience, and then in relation to the various developmental theories.

It is difficult to become aware of the actual soul directly. We usually
experience it through its manifestations; the self is always present in
the manifestation because the manifestation is simply a particular form
of it. So it is difficult to know the self itself because we are usually
focused on the form of its manifestation.

98   To become directly conscious of the manifestation of self as an entity is unusual. The sense of being an entity is so basic that we naturally believe it to be intrinsic to what we are, and not an acquired perception. Indeed, although developmental psychology has demonstrated that this sense is a developmental achievement, it is assumed to be not a pattern that is formed, but a reality that is recognized in the course of development. The view is that the sense of being an entity is an intrinsic quality of the self, although to experience it and identify with it is a developmental achievement. In the deeper dimensions of spiritual awareness, however, the sense of being an entity is seen quite clearly to be not intrinsic to the self. One sees clearly that it is an acquired pattern.

The sense of being an entity is the most general aspect of the self-representation. It can arise clearly in awareness and be questioned experientially only at deep levels of understanding the nature of the self; we need not discuss it in detail in our present study.

Of the four primary categories of self-experience we are discussing, individuality is the most familiar in direct experience. However, we normally do not experience even this property very consciously or precisely. We simply have a general sense of being an individual, or a person, or an individuality. Personal individuality and its essential counterpart are the subject of our previous book in this series, *The Pearl Beyond Price* (Almaas, 1988).

Identity is also familiar in normal experience, but it is even less clearly recognized. Identity is the most important element of the self for our exploration because it is directly related to narcissism and self-realization. As we have remarked, the concepts of self, entity, individuality, and identity are frequently used interchangeably in psychological literature. We always use them in the precise ways we have defined them. This precision is possible because they are very clearly experienced and discriminated in our work with students. These basic patterns of the self are interconnected in ways that we will explore. Although it is not always important or relevant to differentiate between them, precise differentiation is important for some aspects of our work of self-realization.

Edith Jacobson has been criticized by many of her colleagues for "splitting hairs" in her discrimination of different psychological phenomena. Indeed, from many perspectives it is difficult to see the 99 relevance of such fine discriminations. She not only differentiates between the self and the self-representation, as does Hartmann, but also between the sense of entity and the sense of self or feeling of identity. This last distinction is clear in the following quotation:

> I would prefer to understand by identity formation a process that builds up the ability to preserve the whole psychic organization—despite its growing structuralization, differentiation, and complexity—as a highly individualized but coherent entity which has direction and continuity at any stage of human development. The objective process of normal identity formation finds reflection at any stage of development in the normal subjective feeling of identity. (Jacobson, 1980, p. 27)

The differentiation between entity, individuality and identity, and especially between individual entity and identity, is clearer in the work of Margaret Mahler and her colleagues, who built on Jacobson's discriminations. Mahler's description of the separation-individuation process elaborates the development of the structure of the self as the individuality with the two structures—entity and identity—as major parts of the self-representation. Her theory addresses the development of the self as an individuality; she sees the experience of the self as an individual as the final achievement of the separation-individuation process. This individuation involves developing object constancy and self constancy. The achievement of object constancy is seen as an indication of the full psychic separation of object-representations and self-representations, and the arrival at a mature level of object relations, as, for example, in the ability to relate to others as individuals in their own right. "Self constancy" refers to the establishment of individuality. Mahler writes:

> The task to be achieved by development in the course of the normal separation-individuation process is the establishment of both a measure of object constancy and a measure of self constancy, an enduring individuality as it were. The latter achievement consists of the attainment of the two levels of the

sense of identity: (1) the awareness of being a separate and individual entity, and (2) a beginning awareness of a gender-defined self-identity. (Mahler, 1975, pp. 223–224)

Mahler's understanding of the two levels of the development of individuality—the first involving the sense of being an individual entity, and the second involving self-identity—is almost identical to the picture of normal experience presented above. The difference in our view is that we see that the self's sense of individuality and identity are both based on the sense of being an entity. The important point here, however, is that the individuality of self has two main levels: a sense of being an individual (separate) entity and a sense of identity.

We find it interesting that, although Mahler's differentiation of self-entity and self-identity is very specific and clear, it is not, as far as we can ascertain, utilized much in prevalent psychoanalytic thought. As we have noted, most theories use interchangeably the concepts of identity, entity, self and individuality.

According to Mahler, the sense of separateness or entitihood develops from core self-representations that include the representations of the external experiences of the body and its surface, while the sense of identity develops from component self-representations that include, and are crystallized around, the inner experiences of the body. She writes:

> The infant's inner sensations form the core of the self. They seem to remain the central crystallization point of the 'feeling of self,' around which a 'sense of identity' will become established (Greenacre, 1958; Mahler, 1958b; Rose, 1964, 1966). The sensoriperceptive organ—the 'peripheral rind of the ego,' as Freud called it—contributes mainly to self's demarcation from the object world. The two kinds of intrapsychic structures together form the framework for self-orientation (Spiegel, 1959). (Mahler, 1975, p. 47)

The idea is that the self-representation falls into two major groups, one crystallized around the boundaries of the body and the other around the inner sensations of the body. The first group becomes integrated into a structure that gives us our sense of separating boundaries, the sense of being an individual entity ultimately based on the representation of the contours of the physical body. The second becomes integrated into a structure that provides us with a sense of identity, ultimately based on the inner experiences of the body.

The normal, healthy self is thus characterized by the sense of being a well-rounded individual who is basically an autonomous individual entity with a cohesive and stable sense of identity. The experience of being an individual, especially in relation to self-boundaries, is explored in detail in *The Pearl Beyond Price* (Almaas, 1988). In that book we investigate the sense of being a person both in the normal experience of the self, and in spiritual development, and the relationship between the two. Here we are focused on the self's experience in relationship to identity as opposed to individuality.

It is important to be clear that the identity is not the self itself, but a specific attribute or function of the self. Identity is a major element of the self, which develops as part of its development. The normal identity is the expression of one major structure of the self which develops through the establishment of the self-representation, as seen in the above quotations from Jacobson and Mahler. However, there is little information in the writings of depth psychological about the features and functions of this structure, and even less about the immediate experience of the "sense of self" or the "feeling of identity."

Identity is an important part of being a human being. In normal circumstances, it is inseparable from the sense of being an individual. It is not ordinarily differentiated in immediate experience, but each individual knows that he or she has a feeling of identity that is part of the sense of being an individual.

chapter 10

Functions of Identity

• ————————————————————————————————

T he primary function of the self-identity is self-recognition. Every normal individual has the capacity to recognize himself, to feel directly the unique and familiar sense of "I." The word *I* usually refers to the total self, but there is also the feeling of "I-ness" which accompanies the self, and which is part of distinguishing the self from others. Generally speaking, except under certain circumstances, this "feeling of identity" is difficult to discriminate. As we have mentioned, it is most easily delineated as a specific feeling when it is temporarily lost or threatened.[37] In such circumstances we can recognize it as a psychic structure, and perceive that although it is usually an inseparable part of the self, this feeling of identity is only a particular structure of (and in) the self.

The work of spiritual development can bring to awareness this quality of identity, since such work tends to penetrate and reveal the various structures of the self. We see an example of this in the following report from a long-time student, James E., describing some work he did with the author in a group setting. He works in one of the helping professions, but has lately been interested in a career in business. He has been bringing his conflicts about inadequacy and satisfaction regarding work to the group. A narcissistic flavor is evident in the way he regards these difficulties, how they affect his self-esteem, and the sense of meaningfulness of his life and work.

James begins this segment of work by wanting to understand his chronic feeling of deficiency, the sense that he lacks capacity. He realizes that this sense is not realistic because he has been functioning adequately in the world, as if he does have capacities. Realizing that the deficient feeling is not accurate exposes a certain image of deficiency that he identifies with, which is no longer true about him. The work then focuses on why he identifies with this deficient image since he knows from experience that it is not accurate. It becomes clear that he feels he needs this structure, the deficient image, for something, which we then try to discover. He writes about his discovery, and the resulting transformation of his experience in the group session:

> It became clear that identifying with my personality and my self-image as lacking capacities was a way of having identity. Seeing myself with capacities, I felt without identity, not able to recognize myself as I have always known myself. I felt like nothing. My experience of being nothing was at first frightening, without identity. As we worked I began experiencing contact with you. I began to feel in my belly a strong, warm sense of being substantial, with substance of my own. I felt as if capacity came from this state, this place inside me, and without effort, and when needed. I felt love along with these feelings. While working, I had a strong clarity that what I need comes from inside me. From nothing comes the source that makes all the sense in the world to me. I felt a definite separation from my personality, and experienced Being. While working with you, I understood the nature of this work much more deeply than ever before. I felt like there was a bubbling stream inside me, a source of everything. I felt a major transformation, or rather a shift to something much more real.

This report raises many important questions, but we will deal with only a few and leave the rest for later discussion. The most important element of this experience is the loss of the feeling of identity, which James felt as the loss of his familiar sense of self-recognition. He lost

104   this feeling by separating, or disidentifying, from a self-image, in particular his deficient image of himself. This illustrates that the sense of
identity is determined by a self-image, a component self-representation,
exactly as Jacobson and Mahler believed. This self-image had developed as part of his early object relations, and had become a part of his
sense of himself. He had worked through initial levels of the sense of
deficiency and was functioning in the world adequately. However, the
deficient self-image remained in spite of his actual situation, and our
exploration revealed the function of this image, which James had not
recognized before this work. He saw that the deficient self-image functioned to provide him with a feeling of identity, that it was part of the
structure of his self-identity. Of course, the overall self-identity develops through the integration of myriad self-representations; in this session he has seen through one of them.

   Another important observation in this report is that seeing through
the self-image exposes a certain emptiness, the feeling of being nothing, which always occurs when a self-image dissolves. This emptiness
then allows the realm of essential presence to arise, in this case, as the
particular qualities related to contact and functioning. The presence
of these qualities resolved not only the issue of identity but also that
of deficiency. The resolution of the sense of deficiency indicates that
the question of identity here is related not only to narcissism in general, but specifically to individuation narcissism, which is related to the
Personal Essence, with its qualities of contact and capacity to function. See *The Pearl Beyond Price* (Almaas, 1988) for more details. We
will elaborate on these points in the discussion of individuation narcissism in Chapter 36.

   Another function of identity indicated in James's report is that of
identification with something in particular. The self has the capacity
to identify with any of its manifestations, such as impressions or images.
So not only was the deficient self-image present in James's mind, but
also he was identified with it. If he were not identifying with the image,
he would have only become aware of an image in his mind that he did
not take to describe him. He would have felt some other identity not
patterned by this particular image. Thus, he not only had a mental
image of deficiency, he both felt and believed that he was actually

deficient. He could not dissociate himself from this felt conviction   105
until he saw, by reflecting on his functioning in his life, that this image
of deficiency was not objective.

The tendency of the self to identify with images caused James to
take the deficient image to be himself. The identity provided him with
both a feeling of identity and a descriptive content of who and what
he is. Note here that the feeling of identity is not the same as a self-
image—the sense of identity is not the particular representation, but
a feeling or tone based on the representation. In fact, the feeling of
identity is based on the totality of all the representations in the structure of self-identity. We can now see the significance of distinguishing
between the feeling of identity and its content, and better understand
Jacobson's seeming "splitting of hairs" discussed above. James maintained the unrealistically deficient self-image not only because it was
part of his unconscious identity, but also in order to identify with
something.

This case also demonstrates the soul's capacity for identification,
which it possesses in lieu of a given structure of self-identity.[38] We all
know that we sometimes take ourselves to be a certain way that turns
out not to be a true description of ourselves, as James did with the
deficient self-image. We call this process "identification," in the sense
that the self takes the particular content to be not only descriptive of
itself, but to *be* itself. James really believed that he lacked capacity, and
emotionally felt the accompanying sense of deficiency. He was convinced that deficiency was part of his very identity.

Identification is a process that can possess the self so completely that
we believe, for all practical purposes, that we are the content we are
identifying with. Not only do we believe we are the content, we also live
as if we are this content. For example, if a woman identifies with an
image of being ugly, she will feel ugly, believe she is ugly, and behave as
if she is ugly. She will have this complex of experiences even if she is
actually beautiful according to others' perceptions of her. When we are
identified with a certain content, such as an image, state, or function,
we are not capable of perceiving ourselves apart from this content.

Thus, James actually felt deficient, and the woman in our example
will actually perceive herself as ugly when she looks in a mirror. So

106   these self-images are not only mental beliefs or opinions. The effect of identification is much deeper. Most self-images are implicit; that is, we are not usually aware that we are identifying with an image. When we see an identification clearly, the identification tends to break down, as we saw in James's report.

The fact that the process of identification is largely unconscious is what makes self-images so persistent even when they are unrealistic. The process of spiritual development expands our awareness of the self such that we become conscious of various identifications one after the other, at deeper and deeper levels. We increasingly realize the extent of our identifications until we see that even the way we experience our bodies is dependent on identifications, particularly with the body-image.

As we have noted, depth psychology, including ego psychology and object relations theory, posits that the self develops through the integration of myriad self-representations; thus, the sense of self is based on identifications. For example, Kernberg describes the process of the development of psychic structures as that of establishing identification systems (Kernberg, 1979). The theories of depth psychology, however, implicitly take the position that these identifications with the content of the self are truly descriptive of the individual, and hence, would survive even with full awareness of the identifications.

We question two things about this position. The first has to do with the nature of the process of identification. This process is basically a complex psychic action of the self, which includes remembering, imaging and cathexis, among other things. This psychic process can cease, and does cease under certain conditions. One of these conditions is awareness of it, which can manifest as the recognition that one is taking oneself to be one thing or another. The process of identification is essentially a mental activity. If the mind ceases this activity, the identification dissolves, even if its content is accurate. Many meditation practices are based on disidentification, which is a practice of becoming aware of the content of identification and also of the process of identifying. This awareness dissolves the identification, and generally brings one to a state of inner spaciousness devoid of any image of self.

Dissolution of self-images   107

The phenomenon of the dissolution of self-images upon their becoming clearly conscious is actually involved in the uncovering techniques used in depth psychological work. This dissolution makes it possible for distorted images of oneself to change when they emerge in consciousness. Another step in this process, however, reveals that these uncovering techniques can also dissolve realistic images of the self. In general, psychologists and psychiatrists do not take these techniques that far. As one self-image dissolves for a patient, another arises, so the analyst or therapist does not have the opportunity to observe what happens when there is no self-image in the mind. Even when a self-image does dissolve without being immediately replaced, the practitioner is not likely to give the arising spaciousness enough attention to enable him to recognize its significance in relation to the self-image, since his model of the possibilities of experience probably does not include the state of inner boundless space.

In our work one of the main methods is simply to take these uncovering techniques further than is done in analysis or psychotherapy. Various identifications are revealed, and begin to dissolve as we become aware of the mental process of identifying with them. This is what happened in James's process when he began to feel inner spaciousness, which then ushered him into the domain of Essence. Thus, we question the notion implicit in most psychological theories: that identification with self-images will remain even when they are conscious.

The second problem with the position of depth psychology regarding identification is that it posits that the component self-representations forming the sense of the normal self are faithful renderings of the reality of the self. This is not the case, even with images which are ordinarily considered realistic. These images quite naturally seem to be realistic and faithful renderings of the reality of the self because it is those representations which pattern and define the experience of this self. However, given the premise (widely acknowledged by spiritual traditions) that the self is ultimately presence, the normal self-representations are ultimately unfaithful renderings of the reality of the self. The fact that the self-representations are intrinsically unrealistic becomes apparent as deeper experience arises; in fact, even relatively accurate self-images are

108   seen ultimately as false. This perception is part of a development which involves the dissolving of self-images as they fully emerge into conscious awareness. Self-realization involves the transcendence of the so-called "normal" self-representations, as happened in James's experience. His last statement, *I felt a major transformation or rather a shift of awareness from personality to something much more real,* shows how the dissolution of an unrealistic identification does not necessarily lead to another identification, but can precipitate the experience of a spiritual reality that transcends the self-representation, which James calls "personality."

James's experience is an example of the premise stated in Chapter 1: It is possible to experience the self independent of the content of identifications. The awareness of a fundamental presence, with no activity in the mind (which may be felt as emptiness or spaciousness), results when self-images are dissolved by explicit awareness of them.

Another function of identity is to locate the experience of the self. James's familiar identity involved self-recognition and identification with a certain content, and also situated his experience in the dimension of conventional experience. This again has to do with the function of identifying. The self not only recognizes itself through the identity, but also perceives itself and reacts emotionally to its perceived situation, from within the self-representation one happens to be identifying with at the moment. In effect, the identity locates the experiencing awareness of the self in whatever representation we are identified with.

To summarize, the following structure defines the conventional experience of the self:

1. We are identified with a particular self-representation.

2. We experience ourselves within and through this self-representation.

3. This self-representation is related to an object or objects.

4. The set of object relations, that is, self-representations in relation to object representations, constitutes the object world of the self, and determines the entire world view.[39]

Objectified self in objectified world

In addition to identifying with a particular self-representation, we also experience ourselves within the overall self-representation because we are always identified with it, partly consciously, but mostly unconsciously. This locates individual consciousness within a general background patterned by the overall self-representation and its world.[40] The overall self-representation is the background of any particular moment-to-moment experience, the foreground of which is determined by shifting component self-representations. So the identity locates the individual consciousness both in the particular component self-representation the individual happens to be identifying with in the moment, and within the overall self-concept with its representational world.

Thus, the identity determines the self's domain of experience, by locating the awareness within the self-representation. Under normal circumstances, this domain is the conventional realm of experience. In James's last statement above, we see that when his identity dissolved and he did not resort to identifying with other self-representations, the location of his experience moved from the conventional dimension to the dimension of essential presence.

This perspective illuminates both ordinary experience and the experience of self-realization. The functions of self-recognition (feeling of identity), recognition of the self-pattern (identification), and of locating the experience of the self all combine to locate the sense of self in whatever dimension of experience the self-representations involve. It is not only experience that is located by the identity, but the self itself, so far as a person is aware of himself. In any identification, the "I" is experienced as being located within the particular realm associated with the representation the self is identified with.[41]

For example, a person's experience of herself will be largely mental if she is alienated from her emotions or is not in touch with her body. If a person is more identified with her feelings, she will feel most "herself" when concerned with them, and may not be identified with or even interested in what is happening on intellectual or physical levels. Thus, the sense of "I" of a given character may have a typical or habitual location, so to speak. Of course, one may at different times locate the sense of "I" in different realms of experience, including dimensions of essential presence.

Our identity is our most intimate sense of ourselves. It is like the center of ourselves, the intimate, unique flavor of ourselves, the experiential

110   essence of the "I" and its locus. Our identity is so intimately associated with the self that we locate ourselves at the site of its identification.[42]

The fact that identity locates the experience of the self points to other functions of identity. Identity determines the locus of consciousness, awareness, perception, and observation. The feeling of identity is inseparably connected with the center of perception, what is usually referred to as "the observer." This is the ordinary experience of all normal individuals; everyone experiences the sense of "I" as the center of perception. The reader can confirm this by spending a few minutes paying attention to his or her inner experience.

Anyone who pays attention to the sense of the "I" as the center of perception is likely to find the observer located somewhere in the body. Some people experience the observer centered in the head, in the back of the head or neck, or in the back of the body in general. Our perception of ourselves is almost always clearly oriented in space. For example, a person observing her inner experience might find that she is looking from the head downward, or from the back forward, or from the surface inward. Her perception will inevitably have a locus or center, and thus a direction.

If, in such processes as self-observation or awareness meditation, we observe the observer itself, only one of two outcomes seems possible. The first is that a new center of observation is created by this maneuver. So the observer merely shifts location.[43] The other outcome, which is the goal of awareness meditations, occurs when no new center of observation manifests. It is not only the observer that dissolves in this condition, but also the feeling of identity. The disappearance of the familiar sense of identity is something that parts of the self will quite naturally resist; this is why such experiences are not easy to achieve, and generally occur only in the context of a lengthy, dedicated practice.

In advanced stages of meditation, practitioners experience the absence of the center or locus of observation, called the *diffusion* of the observer. This indicates that one is experiencing awareness as boundless presence (or space), centerless and omnipresent.[44] This phenomenon is described in accounts of the meditation practices of the Buddhist Mahamudra or Dzogchen, as in the following verses by Padmasambhava:

And when you look into yourself in this way nakedly (without any discursive thoughts), since there is only this pure observing, there will be found a lucid clarity without anyone being there who is the observer. (Reynolds, trans., 1989, p. 12)

This description illuminates the dramatic contrast between the experience of self in the context of nonidentified awareness and the conventional experience of identity, in which everyone experiences herself or himself as the center of observation, and perceives this center as located in space (usually within the physical body).

In addition to functioning as a center of observation, perception, and awareness, the structure of self-identity has other functions which are difficult to distinguish until we have the experience of the identity dissolving. In the experience of "no self," as in Pia's report in Chapter 6, when one experiences the identity as absent, one may also feel that one doesn't recognize oneself, as in James's report at the beginning of this chapter. In initial experiences one is also likely to feel uncentered, lost, disoriented, not knowing which way to go or what to do, or even the sense of not being able to do anything. Clearly, this phenomenon is different from loss of memory, although that might also result in loss of the feeling of identity. It is more a sense of loss of a psychological self-reference. Losing the sense of self-recognition disturbs the element we depend on to know what to do and what direction to take in life; hence, we may feel disoriented and lost. How can we discern a meaningful direction or action if we do not know ourselves? Actions, plans and goals are meaningful only in relation to one's identity. So loss of identity is bound to manifest, at least sometimes, as disorientation and lack of direction. There is a common expression for this state—we say we are "not feeling centered."

This returns us to Kohut's definition of the bipolar self: "This structure is the basis for our sense of being an independent center of initiative and perception." (Kohut, 1977, p. 177)

The nuclear self, the core of the bipolar self as defined by Kohut, is related to what we have been describing as the self-identity. Our discussion of identity has shown that in addition to ambitions and ideals, the identity itself is a source of initiative and action. The self-identity structure includes self-representations which underlie ambitions and

112   ideals, but it also includes other categories of representations which are important sources of action and initiative. We do not need to go into detail here, for it is a common understanding that people have other motivations, like compassion, love, self-expression, or aggression, that impel them to act. The existence of these other motivations does not necessarily contradict Kohut's formulation, because they can function as the ground for ambitions and ideals.

Ambitions and ideals are expressions of major substructures of the self-identity, organizing the various components of identity—specifically those related to motivation for action—in higher level organizations structured around the categories of ambitions and ideals. This is how Kohut views the development of the bipolar self, seeing the two poles as the two primary substructures of the self, with the ambitions pole developing through the integration of childhood grandiosity, and the ideals pole through the integration of the idealization of the parents (Kohut, 1977, pp. 179–186).

We have established, then, that identity in general, and not only its substructures, functions as the center of initiative and action. This is an important point; in some sense the maintenance of a given identity is part of the motivation of most psychological activity. In fact, it is sometimes the main motivation, as we saw above in the case of James. Furthermore, in some situations this activity has the purpose of maintaining identity per se, rather than maintaining a particular identity.

What is the relation between identity and the bipolar self?

In his notion of the bipolar self, Kohut is trying to capture the actual felt sense of identity. In this passage he speculates about the feeling of the abiding sameness over time:

> I came to hold the view that the sense of abiding sameness along the time axis—a distinguishing attribute of the healthy self—is laid down early as the result of the abiding action-promoting tension gradient between the two major constituents of the nuclear self. (Kohut, 1977, p. 183)

It is difficult, however, to imagine how the tension gradient could provide one with the sense of abiding sameness along the axis of time.

What do ambitions and ideals have to do with this attribute of the self?   113
Perhaps the fact that they do not change much contributes to this attribute, but then there are many other characteristics of the self that do not change appreciably over time; in fact, some change much more slowly than ambitions and ideals. But then Kohut is not referring to particular ambitions and ideals, but to their action-promoting tension arc. Nevertheless, why would this particular manifestation of the self be the one responsible for sameness in time?

Kohut is cognizant of the fact that the sense of abiding sameness along the time axis is fundamentally related to identity, as seen in the following statement from his discussion of time continuity: "In the last analysis, only the experience of a firmly cohesive nuclear self will give us the conviction that we will be able to maintain the sense of our enduring identity, however much we might change." (Kohut, 1977, p. 182) Kohut views the attribute of abiding sameness along the time axis as a manifestation of an "enduring identity," but believes that it is the nuclear self that gives us the capacity to maintain this identity.[45]

We concur with Kohut that it is the feeling of identity that provides the self with the sense of abiding sameness in time regardless of the changes that the self goes through. This is actually a simple observation; everyone feels the sense of sameness by having an enduring feeling of identity. Identity is not only a feeling that is intimately associated with the self, but it is also an enduring feeling, familiar to the self since the inception of its awareness of itself. According to depth psychology (for example, in the formulations of Jacobson and Mahler), the feeling of identity is a manifestation of the structure of self-identity, which develops in early childhood as part of the overall self-representation, becomes established by the third year of life, and undergoes very little change from then onward. According to that view, the self begins to have the sense of self-recognition (feeling of identity) simultaneously with the development of its patterning, so it really never knows itself before the development of this attribute.

Although it is difficult to see how the tension arc of the nuclear self could be what maintains the identity, we have pointed out that ego activity in general, of which the tension arc is one manifestation, contributes to the maintenance of identity. However, the identity is

114   maintained by other processes, such as identification, internalization, synthesis, integration, organization, and so on.

In our opinion, Kohut was actually looking at the identity itself, but
for various reasons, one of which was his focus on narcissistic disturbances, he was able to see only some of its attributes.[46] We agree with
Kohut, however, that one function of identity is to give the self the
feeling of abiding sameness along the time axis.

Kohut includes in his definition of the self attributes that are not
actually part of the self-identity, but part of the self-entity. He writes:
"This structure is the basis of our sense of being an independent center integrated with our experience that our body and mind form a unit
in space and a continuum in time." (Kohut, 1977, p. 177)

One could say that Kohut is defining the bipolar self by combining
segments from both structures of individuality, entity and identity. In
our opinion, this is not the case. First self-identity is already integrated
with the self-entity; the two are substructures of the overall structure
of the self-representation. The other, more important reason is that it
does not make sense to think of the sense of entity as being the center
of perception and initiative, because there are conditions where one
can experience oneself as an entity without the sense of identity, as is
implied in the reports of both Pia and James, and in the case from
Masterson. In this condition one feels that one is an entity, but with
no identity and no center of action.

Our conclusion from this discussion is that Kohut is referring to the
structure of identity in his definition of the bipolar self, but that this
definition lacks the precision necessary for understanding identity and
its various functions, and specifically, its relation to narcissism.[47]

chapter 11

Disturbances of Identity

---·

The self-identity functions not only as one's sense of identity, but also as the center of the self, especially, as we have seen, in relation to perception, initiative, action, creativity, orientation, and centeredness in oneself in general. The sense of centeredness is also closely related to the feeling of identity.

In our view, then, the individuated self is defined by boundaries and center, corresponding to the two structures conceptualized by Mahler, entity and identity, respectively. In terms of personal experience, we experience ourselves as having both boundaries and a center. The boundaries differentiate and separate us from the rest of the environment, and provide us with the sense of being an entity. The center is a locus or source of action, which we feel as a sense of enduring identity; it gives us the sense of inner balance and orientation.

According to Mahler, self-boundaries develop in relation to the external body image, and self-identity develops in relation to the inner sensations of the body. We can imagine these structures of the self in spatial terms, where boundaries form a shape with external contours, and the identity is a center inside this form. The image that comes to mind is a sphere (or any solid) with boundaries and a center. The sense

116 of entity corresponds to the external form of the sphere, its surface, and the sense of identity corresponds to the center of the sphere.[48] A helpful image is that of a cell, or even an amoeba, which has a boundary (the membrane) that makes it an entity, and a center (the nucleus) that contains its inner program for functioning. It is possible, as we have noted, that Kohut had this image in mind when he named the center of the self the "nuclear self." The nucleus has qualities some of which are unique to each particular cell, and which identify it. The cell structure is analogous to the primary structure of the self-representation, the total body-image, whose skin provides boundaries, and whose inner felt atmosphere provides the feeling of identity.

Weakness of identity

Disturbances in the development of the self can occur either in the sector of either entity or identity, or, of course, in both. When the development of identity is incomplete or distorted, the identity is brittle, feeble, shaky, superficial, incomplete, distorted, and/or unrealistic. It is thus vulnerable to injury, disintegration, and loss. When the self's vital center, the center of her psychological balance and harmony, the place in her that allows her to know herself in an immediate way, is not firmly established or stable, she will experience her feeling of identity not only as uncertain and vague, but sometimes as threatened, or even as destroyed or lost. This weakness or loss of identity may manifest as the feeling that she has no self, or as a sense of deficient emptiness. These feelings indicate the absence of a sense of center. One feels like an entity without a center, a body without insides, as seen in Masterson's patient in Chapter 6.

A person with an unstable or absent center of the self is likely to feel lost or disoriented, and may have a sense of not knowing what to do. She may feel depressed, for she not only does not deeply know herself, she has no clear or firm sense of who and what she is, and thus does not know what to do. Without a clear sense of her self, her actions will lack a sense of significance.

Even if she is able to cover up the lack of orientation by adopting external goals and aims, her accomplishments will feel empty and meaningless since they are not serving her own sense of value, and do not originate from her own initiative. Her life is likely to be pervaded by a sense of meaninglessness, pointlessness, aimlessness, and superficiality. She is vulnerable to a sense of fakeness because her life and actions do not express who and what she is, but support a facade that hides, to various degrees of effectiveness, inner impoverishment, lack of significance, and the absence of an inner center. In some sense, she is not in her life, because she does not know herself in any depth.[49]

This precarious situation places her in the position of having always to protect and defend her identity, to try constantly to strengthen and maintain the cohesiveness, stability and positive affective coloring of her sense of herself, and to seek external supports to shore up her identity. These maneuvers usually manifest as exaggerated self-reference, a sense of self-importance, and preoccupation with her self-esteem and value, as she attempts to counteract the fragility of her identity and the associated sense of insignificance. She might have a strong need to be seen, appreciated, and admired, because a shaky identity needs an inordinate amount of attention to support and stabilize it. She may feel a sense of uniqueness, and entitlement to special attention. Her conception of herself might thus become grandiose. Such grandiosity is both an expression of the unreality of her identity and a way to cover up the underlying sense of deficiency and worthlessness. Another way her narcissistic disturbance might manifest is in her seeking relationships with people whom she can idealize, as she attempts to meet her need for external support from a "perfect" object which reflects her grandiose self-image.

She might have a shallow emotional life, with limited capacity for empathy. Her capacity to know and feel herself, and therefore others, is limited by the shallowness and incompleteness of her identity. She lacks compassion and real love, not only towards others, but also towards herself.

She is unusually sensitive to insult and extremely vulnerable to hurt. She is predisposed to feelings of intense rage and anger as a reaction to perceived hurt and insult, and also to defend against the feebleness of her identity. Her inner impoverishment may manifest as intense envy and jealousy of others who seem to be enjoying a fulfilled life, while hers feels empty and meaningless. She tends to be emotionally

118   isolated, going through life mechanically and without real joy, except on occasions of external acclaim, admiration, and acknowledgment.

We observe that disturbances of identity are reflected primarily in narcissistic manifestations. Many researchers have seen that narcissistic disturbances are actually disturbances of the identity. Mahler's statement makes this clear:

> Their basic conflict is to be sought and found, we believe, in the primitive narcissistic struggle that was acted out in the rapprochement crisis, but that may have become a central internal conflict pertaining mainly to their uncertain sense of identity (Erickson). (Mahler, 1975, p. 230)

However, as we have pointed out, in accounting for narcissism most depth psychology does not differentiate between the self and its identity sufficiently to avoid referring to both structures interchangeably. For instance, R. Stolorow, in his paper, "Toward a Functional Definition of Narcissism," appears to appreciate the question of identity with respect to narcissism:

> Elkisch (1957) observed that certain of her patients would gaze at their images in the mirror in order to restore a lost sense of self-identity. Referring to the myth of Narcissus, Lichtenstein (1964) formulated that narcissism refers not to the love of oneself but to the love of one's mirror image, and argued that the 'mirror and the act of mirroring introduce problems of the emergence of a primary identity, of identity confusion, of loss of identity, and of identity maintenance as well.' Narcissistic object relationships are to be understood as regressive efforts at identity maintenance through mirroring in the object. (Morrison, 1986, pp. 199–200)

Yet, Stolorow does not seem to differentiate between the identity and the self-representation, as we see in the following passage (a continuation of the above quotation):

> Eisnitz (1969) formulated that narcissistic object choices serve to stabilize and supplement a weakened self-representation. Arlow & Brenner (1964), Murray (1964), Kernberg (1970), and Oremland & Windholz (1971) all noted that grandiose fantasies

of magic omnipotence and unlimited entitlement may be attempts to repair various injuries to and degradation of the self-representation and to ward off the threat of its dissolution. (Morrison, 1986, p. 200)

Some of this latter group of authors might actually mean identity when they refer to the self-representation, but the differentiation between the two is clearly considered irrelevant in their views of narcissism. It is true that narcissism is related to the firm cathexis of the self-representation, as discussed in Chapter 6, but it is important to discriminate the two precisely. The resulting precision of our model is crucial to the understanding of the issues of self-realization.[50]

How is narcissism different from borderline conditions?

Although it is true that narcissism affects the overall self-representation, our observations point to identity as the specific central psychic structure responsible for narcissism and its disturbances. Narcissism relates to our experience of ourselves in general, but specifically, as it affects our sense of identity. The overall self-concept determines our identity, because the totality of ego identifications (and all object relations connected to them) influence its development. But this does not mean that narcissism is specifically related to the totality of the self-concept. To think of narcissistic disturbance as disturbance to the self-representation in general posits it as a form of the borderline condition, which it is not. The borderline individual is usually less functional than the narcissistic character, more outwardly dependent and clinging, more prone to regressive disorganization and disintegration, more aware of ego weakness and deficiency, with more predominance of splitting and projective identification, and with a more vague and amorphous structure. In contrast, "the surface functioning of the narcissistic personality is much better than that of the average borderline patient." (Kernberg, 1975, p. 230) The narcissist might exhibit borderline features, but his reality testing is usually intact and his tendency towards disintegration is less severe. When there is disintegration, it is generally temporary and reversible. (Kohut, 1971)

Kernberg tends to see narcissism as a form of the borderline condition, while Kohut, especially in his later theory, views the borderline

120 disturbance as a more severe form of narcissism. It is possible that Kohut's shift of focus from the self-representation to the bipolar self is a reflection of his appreciation of identity itself—in contrast to the overall self-representation—in relation to narcissism.

Our view is that narcissistic disturbance is a disturbance of the identity, while the borderline condition is a disturbance of the totality of the self-representation. This means that the borderline condition is a disturbance not only of the self-identity but also of the self-boundaries, particularly of the sense of being an individual entity demarcated from others. It is thus a more severe disturbance than narcissism.

The difference of view between Kernberg and Kohut regarding the two conditions can be resolved easily if we recognize that Kernberg bases his thinking on the notion of the total self-representation, while Kohut bases his on the concept of identity, which is part of the self-representation. If one's central concept of the self is the total self-representation, then narcissistic disorders will be seen as a subset of the borderline condition, because, according to our understanding, it is a disturbance of a subset of the self-representation, that is, the self-identity. If one's central concept of the self is the identity, then the borderline condition will be seen as a more severe form of narcissistic disorder, with some different features, because it is a more comprehensive disturbance of the self.

From this perspective, the borderline individual usually has narcissistic disturbances, but the reverse is not necessarily true.[51] Issues of entity, reflecting borderline disturbance, manifest as lack of integration, cohesion, and wholeness; ego inadequacy, dependency, and infantile tendencies; issues of separation and separation anxiety, and a preponderance of splitting mechanisms. Some researchers view the difference between the narcissistic and borderline personalities in terms similar to ours, as in the case of W.W. Meissner. He writes, in his paper, "Narcissistic Personalities and Borderline Conditions: Differential Diagnosis," after discussing different ways of differentiating between the two disturbances: "Another way of putting it is that the borderline issues are concerned with self cohesion more than self esteem; the narcissistic issues are concerned with self esteem more than self cohesion." (Morrison, 1986, p. 427).

In our view, cohesion can involve the identity or the entity, and this 121 determines in a more exact way whether we are dealing with a borderline or narcissistic issue. It does seem that Meissner is referring to the total self-representation when he discusses cohesion.

Another author, Settlage, comes much closer to our perspective. After presenting two possibilities that might account for the difference between the two kinds of disturbances, viewing the borderline condition to be the more severe disturbance than the narcissistic, the first related to time of inception, and the second to intensity of defensive response, he writes:

> And thirdly, the difference may come to be understood in terms of the area of personality involved in developmental arrest and pathologic formation, for example, involvement of the sense of self and identity as these can be distinguished from ego capacities and functions per se. (Settlage, 1977, pp. 810–811)

In our opinion, all three considerations are important to the distinction, but the third one, which is the view presented in this chapter, is the most significant for explicating the difference between narcissism and borderline conditions as manifest in symptoms and in characterological features.

Structure, identity and action

The structure of the self-entity is responsible not only for the self's demarcation from others and from the external world, but also for functioning. We have observed a certain relationship between the structures of entity and identity, in relation to action. Just as identity is the center of initiative and the source of motivation for action, individual entity is the executor of action. More accurately, it is the total self which acts, but action requires two necessary elements: The first is the motivating center out of which arises a direction for action, and the second is the structure of functional capacities needed for carrying out the action.

This model is analogous to the functioning of the body, in which it is the musculoskeletal system (corresponding to entity) which acts—

122   such as in eating, but the motivation for the action originates in the inner sensations of the body (corresponding to identity), like hunger. It is also similar to the situation of the amoeba, in which the protoplasmic mass with its membrane is what acts, but the instructions and patterns for action originate from the nucleus.

The acting self is a totality, but it has, so to speak, a legislative branch and an executive one: The legislative branch is basically the self-identity and the executive branch the self-entity. Both branches are needed for meaningful action, for the complete action of the integrated self. Disturbances of either branch interfere with action. When the legislative branch is defective, there are no clear indications or motivations for action; this is narcissistic disturbance. The narcissistic individual can act, since the functional capacity is generally intact. In other words, the narcissistic individual does not feel, "I cannot do," but rather, "I do not know what to do." The borderline individual, on the other hand, experiences his main difficulty as ego inadequacy, in which he feels, "I cannot do."

The narcissistic individual can act, and even excel, when he adopts external guidelines, such as performing well in a job situation. We believe that this is because the execution of action is related to the self-entity, rather than to identity. Even extremely narcissistic individuals who have little sense of identity are capable of adequate, and sometimes superior, execution of action. They can be very successful in careers and can hold positions of responsibility. This is usually not the case with borderline individuals.[52] This difference between narcissistic and borderline individuals in terms of functional capacity is not absolute; it is simply a general pattern.

As we have pointed out with regard to other lines of argument which emphasize precise discrimination regarding self-structures, this precision is useful for understanding pathology and character, and is crucial for working through issues confronted in the process of self-realization.

chapter 12

Identity and
Essence

—— •

Thus far, our consideration of narcissism in relation to identity has dealt more with narcissistic disturbance than with issues of self-realization. In order to complete this consideration we must spell out the relationship of narcissism to difficulties in the sense of identity.

What causes the identity to develop as weak, shaky, and distorted? What is the structural phenomenology of a disturbed identity? We begin to answer this question by remembering Alice Miller's definition of narcissism: "Whereas 'healthy narcissism' can be characterized as the full access to the true self, the narcissistic disturbance can be understood as a fixation on a 'false' or incomplete self." (Morrison, 1986, p. 346)

Miller associates the vulnerabilities of identity with an individual's identification with a false or incomplete self-representation. To put it precisely, the identity is vulnerable because it is based on a false or incomplete self-representation. Also, since identity is a part of the self-representation, its disturbances involve both how faithful the representation is to the actual self, and the extent to which the self identifies with the representation.

124 The self-representation can be false in some respects, or incomplete, or both. If we identify with a self-concept that does not reflect the true self, then the identity is false; in other words, we are mistaken about who and what we are. This alienates us from ourselves and exposes us to continual challenges from our environment which threaten our identity. False aspects of the self-image cannot be completely supported by either our internal or external environment.

When the self-representation excludes aspects of the self, this incompleteness will cause the sense of self to be weak, distorted, or both. This is partially due to the pressure of the actual self on the identity. Any real part of ourselves that is excluded by what we take ourselves to be will create conflicts in the sense of identity, since its mere existence threatens the identity. For example, if our identity does not include our anger, or our love, then our identity will be threatened when anger or love arise forcefully in consciousness. Hence, the incompleteness of our self-representation leaves our identity vulnerable to the truth of our actual self, just as the falsehood of the representation leaves our identity in an untenable position in relationship to all of reality.

How does alienation from parts of the self affect identity?

Incompleteness of the self-representation also weakens our identity by disconnecting it from the possible support of excluded aspects of ourselves. In our example above, a person who believes herself incapable of anger, whether that belief comes from a sense of weakness, incapacity, or a false sense of virtue, will lose the support of her healthy aggressive and discriminating strength. A person who has excluded the experience of love from the self-representation will, of course, suffer great impoverishment of experience. The more the deeper aspects of the self are excluded from the identity, the more superficial and weak it is. As in Miller's formulation, we have seen how excluding our emotions and feelings, or our vital connection to our bodies, as in Lowen's account, can contribute to narcissism. Considering narcissism in terms of identity clarifies how these forms of alienation from the actual self produce various narcissistic characteristics, particularly vulnerability. Alienation from important dimensions of the self weakens identity.

The most deeply impoverishing alienation in ego experience is alien- ation from the essential core of the self. There are subtle but fundamental differences between this and alienation from other dimensions of the self. We discussed in detail in Chapter 6 how experiencing the self from within and through the self-representation automatically alienates the self from its Essence and core, the true presence of Being.

This alienation causes the identity to feel deeply weak and vulnerable. Since the self-concept excludes the dimension of Being, the very ground of the self is absent from experience, which naturally makes one feel weak and unsupported. Identity mediated through this incomplete self-representation is also bound to be superficial because it excludes the depth of the self.

Since the presence of Being is not only the inner core of the soul, but also its true nature, a self-representation which excludes Being is not only incomplete but also distorted. Recalling our discussion of the perception of the body in the experience of self-realization, we will remember that the body is not experienced as a solid object in time and space, but as the embodiment of presence, as a particular form that Being assumes. We perceive directly that the body is not the solid object that the self-image portrays it to be. It is interesting to note here that if we are able to transcend, even slightly, our ingrained idea that we are what ends at our skin, we see that the experience of the body and the senses is much more flowing and sensitive to our environment.

The conclusion we are compelled to adopt, supported by direct experience and the knowledge of the deepest spiritual teachings of humanity, is that the self-representation is inevitably incomplete, false, and distorted, when it excludes the essence of the self, which is Being as presence. This incomplete identity also gives one a sense of weakness, vulnerability and superficiality.

If we integrate this observation with previous segments of our exploration, we are led to a shocking conclusion. We have seen that since presence cannot be captured in a representation, the self-representation cannot include essential presence. Thus, since the normal ego identity is part of, and an expression of, the self-representation, the self-identity is inherently incomplete and distorted. Thus, normal identity is inevitably weak, superficial, and vulnerable.

126   Recalling Mahler's notion that the structure of self-identity is based on representations reflecting the inner core of the self—for Mahler, it is the body—we can see that the incompleteness of the self-representation specifically affects the substructure of self-identity. It is thus this substructure that is weakened by the absence of Being in the self-representation. This account clarifies our view of the fundamental narcissism of everyday life. It shows that the conventional experience of the self as determined and patterned by the self-representation, is bound to involve a fundamental weakness of identity.[53] Also, the relation between narcissism and self-realization can now be understood in relation to a specific psychic structure, the self-identity, and a particular affect, the feeling of identity.

There are further implications: The fact that the self-representation inherently excludes Essence means that we cannot maintain the familiar sense of ego identity and at the same time feel Essence as our nature.[54] Armed with this insight, we have a precise way of understanding the extreme difficulty of attaining self-realization, since most individuals find it almost impossible to experience themselves, with equanimity, without their familiar sense of identity.

Although complete realization of the self as Being is a very advanced attainment, we can experience Being in other, less radical, ways. As we have seen, our experience of ourselves can move nearer to or farther away from the dimension of Being. Since one of the functions of identity is that of identifying, that is, the capacity to locate the observing consciousness in whatever manifestation of the self the representation happens to be patterning, the identity can locate the experience of the self more or less near the essential dimension. The nearness to Being will depend partly on the depth of the dimension of the self captured in the self-representation.

It is not, however, this particular feature which actually brings about the experience of Being. Rather, it is a feature of the process of identifying itself, namely, the possibility of disidentification, that allows us to experience Being. The identity can be more or less rigidly identified with a particular content of the self. Some aspects of the identity, typically the more false ones, are felt as shaky and easily challenged. This leads to a certain grasping or tightness of identification, creating rigidity rather than flexibility in the sense of who one is. Psychodynamic theory and practice have explored extensively the defense mechanisms employed to maintain our rigidly fixed identities. When a person's sense of identity is particularly weak, he can become desperate to identify with any content that will give his identity structure. In this situation, the function of identifying becomes extremely rigid, and we cannot easily allow any distance from a particular notion of ourselves. We might feel fear, or even terror, that any crack in our sense of ourselves will threaten the structure, cohesion, and stability of our self-identity.

What we would normally call a stronger identity is somewhat secure, cohesive and stable. This stability allows the identity more freedom to be flexible, so that the self is more relaxed with respect to particular contents or patterns of experience. A person who insists to himself, "I am never angry," is less free and flexible than one who is sensitive to the bodily and emotional affect of anger, and can say, "I am sometimes angry and sometimes not." An even greater freedom, clearly, belongs to those who can say, "I'm angry; I wonder why this situation is making me angry." Here, the self does not feel threatened by some distance from the particular content of identification. This capacity is termed "disidentification." When we are disidentified from a particular content and do not move to another identification, we disidentify to some extent from the self-representation itself, and we are then much more likely to directly experience our essential Being.

In such an experience, we are likely to retain some background identification with the overall self-representation; however, the flexibility of the identity allows us to not resist the awareness of the presence of Being when it arises. The self-representation remains present in the consciousness, but because this identity is relatively secure, we do not feel so threatened by the presence.

This does not mean that the more we experience essential presence, the more we will include Essence in our identity. The actual presence of Essence cannot be part of a self-image. When we have consistent experiences of Being, our identity in general becomes increasingly flexible, and we find ourselves more easily and more frequently experiencing some disidentification. The capacity for disidentification

128   becomes an enduring aspect of our experience as our identity becomes stronger, more realistic, and more flexible, due to the integration of more aspects of ourselves.[55]

The capacity for disidentification can develop in two ways. The first is by increasing the capacity to tolerate greater distance from certain self-representations, which allows us to experience Being more easily. This occurs in the inner development of some spiritual aspirants, as a result of certain practices.[56] But this capacity for disidentification is seldom complete. When other self-representations manifest in response to life situations, we may remain completely identified.

This understanding addresses the phenomenon of spiritual teachers who are supposed to be spiritually developed, but then behave in strange or destructive ways in certain situations. There have been many cases in which a highly acclaimed teacher or guru behaves in a disturbed manner which does not accord with what is known about spiritual development. Some people take these situations to mean that the particular teacher (or guru) is not really spiritually developed. However, the truth of the situation might be that the teacher can experience and manifest very deep spiritual states and insights, but his development is incomplete because his realization is obscured when certain unresolved self-representations (and their object relations) arise in his consciousness under certain circumstances, and he cannot disidentify from them.[57]

The second way the capacity for disidentification develops is that our overall self-representation becomes so much more complete that our identity becomes very flexible. This ultimately leads to a strong general capacity for disidentification such that we can actually be disidentified from the overall self-representation while still maintaining our identity. This capacity requires thorough clarification, that is, objective understanding and seeing through delusions regarding the various segments of our self-representation. It also requires a measure of balance in our spiritual development: balance in relation to mind, heart and body for example; balance in relation to stillness and movement, knowledge and expression, and so on. Imbalance in these areas might involve disidentification weighed on the side of some segments of the self at the expense of others. One might have worked through some segments of the self-representation but not others.

The capacity for global disidentification allows us to be permanently in touch with our essential presence, although the identity and the self-representation remains in experience. This condition allows the experience of self-realization to arise, at least occasionally, when the identity relaxes to the extent of total absorption by (or into) essential presence.[58] The more this capacity for global disidentification develops, the more frequent, and the deeper, are the experiences of self-realization. This development continues, in principle, until permanent, full self-realization, where total global disidentification coincides with complete absorption of the self-representation, and complete openness and flexibility of identity.[59]

Complete flexibility of identity raises the phenomenon of disidentification to a new level, beyond the normal egoic experience. This flexibility involves the dissolution of self-identity, or more accurately, the cessation of the activity of identifying. This condition, which occurs in isolated experiences of self-realization but is the permanent condition of full self-realization (enlightenment), is what is referred to by some traditions as "ego death" or "the death of the self."[60]

In this state of complete annihilation of identity, one does not have identity in the usual sense;[61] our identity is now with the presence of Being. In other words, our identity has shifted from the self-representation to Being. To understand this condition we need to answer two questions: What does it mean not to identify? What is identity in the essential dimension?

Before we embark on this exploration, we need to address the significance of the above discussion with respect to narcissism. Our observation that the deepest root of narcissism is the absence of self-realization and the additional observation that in full self-realization the normal sense of identity dissolves, combine to give us a deep insight about narcissism: The presence of the normal identity is the root of narcissism. This implies two further insights, at different levels of the self. The first is that not only is normal identity fundamentally weak and vulnerable, but its very existence is responsible for this weakness, and thus it cannot become completely stable. In other words, the normal self (or more accurately, the ego-self) is inherently narcissistic because its identity is inherently weak and vulnerable. This weakness is due to the inevitable

130   incompleteness of the self-representation, and therefore cannot be eliminated as long as the self-representation forms our sense of identity.

Second, since the fundamental narcissism of everyday life is an
expression of normal identity, complete resolution of narcissism
requires that we cease to use self-representations for self-recognition.[62]

What does it mean not to identify?

Identification is not merely the presence of the content of experience; the self cathects it to define and support the identity. Since the
identity is the center of perception, one experiences oneself from within
and through this content. Not to identify, then, is to not engage in this
psychic act. Here we are saying "not identifying" rather than "disidentifying," because what is involved is not an action, but the cessation of
an action.

But what is this nonaction? For one thing, we are not locating our
identity within any particular content. Not to locate our identity within
any content means not to engage in any psychic activity for the purpose of self-recognition. We are not doing anything in order to know
ourselves. Since the normal identity depends on the ego activity of recognizing oneself through self-representations, this identity will dissolve when the activity ceases.

Furthermore, not to identify means not doing anything to form an
identity. This means we are not looking self-reflexively at ourselves or
conceptualizing ourselves. If we are not experiencing ourselves self-
reflexively and conceptually (whether with old or new concepts), then
we are experiencing ourselves immediately, directly, and nonconceptually. We are then aware of ourselves by merely being. In other words,
not to identify is simply to be. This is the experience of self-realization.

When the self is not engaged in the act of identifying, it is merely perceiving itself. It is the pure awareness of what is present in consciousness. This pure awareness is totally direct and unmediated. The self is
not experiencing itself through a representation, so there is no identification. So awareness and being coincide in complete nonidentifi-
cation. This is the experience of presence in self-realization. But since
all our normal notions of self-recognition involve awareness of ideas
about and images of ourselves, how can there be self-recognition in the

situation of no identification? This brings us back to our second question: What is identity in the essential dimension? Our next chapter will
address this issue.

chapter 13

Essential Identity

—————————————————————

To understand how identity, or self-recognition, is possible in the essential dimension, we need first to investigate the feeling of identity itself, and not the structure of self-identity, because in self-realization there is no psychic structure based on representation.[63]

Depth psychology does not explicitly explain how the affect of identity develops from the integration of self-representations. Although accepted unanimously in object relations theory, the assertion that ego development leads to the feeling of self and identity has never been truly explained. The theory is that early in childhood we construct self-representations, and through the integration of these representations we attain, among other things, a sense of self, a sense of being an individual with a feeling of identity. Actually, object relations theory establishes only that representations are formed, and that through the function of integration, a unified self-concept results, which patterns the self and its experience. The question of why and how representations get attached to a concept or feeling of self, or what creates the actual sense of identity, is never really answered.

Why and how does a feeling of identity develop? 133

If there were no sense of identity in the beginning, how could representations be referred to a self that cannot be separated from the identifying feeling of the same self?

The usual notion in object relations theory is that the psychic structure formed by the unified representation gives one a feeling of identity. But this structure is only an image, along with sensations, feelings, and perceptions, as, for example, Jacobson says:

> the image of our self issues from two sources: first, from a direct awareness of our inner experiences, of sensations, of emotional and thought processes, of functional activity; and, second, from indirect self perception and introspection, i.e., from the perception of our bodily and mental self as an object. (Jacobson, 1980, p. 20)

This does not explain the development of the sense of identity. Besides the structure of self-images, the impressions that go into a psychic structure involve mostly pleasure and pain, and include things like temperature, tension, relaxation, sadness, anger, love, fear, movement, thinking, and so on. How can these categories of experience lead to the category of self, and especially to the category of identity? The feeling of identity does include all these categories of experience, plus images, inner and outer. But this does not explain the nature and source of the feeling of identity itself.

Mahler deals with this difficult question to some extent, by talking about the "core identity." She is aware, however, that it is not known how this identity comes about. Discussing the differentiation subphase, she writes,

> In our observational research we could clearly see the infant-mother interaction patternings, but we could as yet only guess and extrapolate the internal patterning that contributed to the 'coreness' of the primitive body image at its inception (*cf.* also Kafka, 1971). (Mahler, 1975, p. 53)

Mahler devotes a chapter of this book to the issue of the development of identity, entitled "Reflections on Core Identity and Self-boundary Formation." She begins by describing the difficulty in understanding

134   how the overall self-representation comes about. "The steps of building the self-representation from the self-object representations of the symbiotic phase are rather elusive." (Mahler, 1975, p. 220) She attributes part of the difficulty to the fact that it is not possible to tell exactly what the infant feels inside his body. "What the infant feels subjectively, inside his own body, especially in the beginning of extrauterine life, eludes the observing eye. That is to say, behavioral referents are barely existent." (Mahler, 1975, p. 220)

Mahler then discusses some of the possible processes related to identity formation, reflected in the child's joyous reaction to being mirrored, like wiggling, moving his body and so on: "This obvious tactile kinesthetic stimulation of his body-self, we believe, may promote differentiation and integration of his body image." (Mahler, 1975, p. 221) Tactile kinesthetic stimulation gives the infant familiarity with his sensations and body environment and contributes to body image differentiation, but it says nothing about how the feeling of identity comes about. Mahler ends the chapter by stating that neither observational methods nor psychoanalytic reconstruction of past experience can trace the development of the sense of self:

> We must emphasize again that the development of the sense of self is the prototype of an eminently personal, internal experience that is difficult, if not impossible, to trace in observational studies, as well as in the reconstructive psychoanalytic situation. (Mahler, 1975, p. 224)

There must be a factor, or a combination of factors, that makes it possible for the self-representation to develop in such a way that one ends up with a feeling of identity. It appears that this factor cannot be discriminated and clearly recognized except through essential perception. From this perspective, it is not true that "behavioral referents are barely existent." The referents do exist, but to recognize them for what they are requires some essential experience. Mahler and others do see these referents in children's behavior and attitudes, but generally misinterpret them, as we shall discuss shortly.

To recognize the factor responsible for the sense of identity, one must recognize a certain essential quality, the essential aspect of Identity. The

Essential Identity is one of the pure forms in which presence manifests   135
in the soul. (In previous books we have referred to this quality as the
Essential Self.) When we know the Essential Identity, the Self of Essence,
it becomes possible to see and understand the behavior and attitudes
that express it.

Our understanding, based on both direct observation of infants and
reconstruction of adult experience, is that this manifestation is present in the infant from the beginning of life. It can be observed even in
intrauterine existence. In most infants, however, the Essential Identity
is present only occasionally, becoming more predominant in the differentiation subphase, and then becoming the dominant essential
aspect in the practicing subphase of the separation-individuation process. The Essential Identity can be seen from the time when we notice
a certain look of alertness and directedness suddenly appearing in the
infant. This look can appear even right after birth, but rarely, and for
only short periods of time. Some infants seem to have it more than
others. The presence we see in the infant at these times is the Essential
Identity. It is related to this specific look of alertness. This look, which
gives the feeling that the infant is present in the look, is one of the
behavioral manifestations of the Essential Identity which Mahler
observed. She writes:

> Observing the infants in our set-up, we come to recognize at
> some point during the differentiation subphase a certain new
> look of alertness, persistence and goal-directedness. We have
> taken this look to be a behavioral manifestation of 'hatching'
> and have loosely said that an infant with this look 'has hatched.'
> (Mahler, 1975, p. 54)

Mahler's interpretation of this look as "hatching" is an excellent
reflection of what is happening on the essential level: When the
Essential Identity is present, then, in a sense, the child is truly born.
He is not only simply being, but he is being his true identity, the
Essential Identity. He is self-realized. He is also unique and distinct
from all others. The essential presence of the soul is no longer the global
nondifferentiated primal self, but a definite manifestation that allows
the infant to experience herself as differentiated from the rest of reality.[64] Mahler discusses the difficulty in defining this manifestation, a

136   difficulty characteristic of defining any state of Being: "The new gestalt
was unmistakable to the members of our staff, but it is difficult to define
with specific criteria. It is probably best described in terms of state *(cf.
Wolff, 1959).*" (Mahler, 1975, p. 54)

It is interesting that Mahler and her colleagues observe the manifestation of the Essential Identity and understand it as "hatching,"
which is a kind of birth, but do not directly relate it to the sense of self
or the feeling of identity. When a person who does not think in terms
of Being or essential reality clearly observes a manifestation of essential presence, it is inevitable that the phenomenon will be interpreted
according to the observer's conceptual framework.

The Essential Identity is a simple, pure sense of presence which feels
like self, like "I." It is so simple that it is a subtle matter to differentiate it from other feelings. It is what gives the self the capacity for self-
recognition in the essential dimension. It is not the typical sense of
identity that most of us know. The typical feeling of identity is only a
reflection of the essential identity.[65]

When we say that the Essential Identity gives the self the feeling of
identity, we do not mean that it is the usual kind of feeling, like an
emotion or sensation. The feeling of an essential presence is part of its
very substance; it is a quality of consciousness, a felt knowingness, a
state with a recognizable quality. The closest we can come to describing the present quality is to call it a feeling of identity.

We believe that this quality is the prototype of the feeling of identity.
This pure feeling of identity is a basic self-existing category of experience. It is not a combination of feelings or images, or the result of such
a combination. It is elemental; thus, we call it a Platonic form. The self's
feeling of identity in the presence of the Essential Identity is simple and
immediate, unlike the normal sense of identity which is an affect based
on past experience. Although this affect does differentiate each person's sense of self from others, it is not as clear and definite as the sense
of identity in the Essential Identity. The normal sense of identity is usually somewhat vague, and we do not generally become aware of it unless
we experience its absence. The following report from a woman about
her experience of absence of identity while working in a group session
illustrates some of the issues that arise in experience:

I began to talk about the tensions I was noticing in my head. It
seemed that the fatigue and spaciness were from being in my
head all the time. I started to feel hot and confused about what
point I was trying to make, what I was trying to work on here. I
relaxed my eyes at some point and started to feel sad and angry.
I noticed a hurt feeling in my heart. I had a feeling like some-
thing was missing in my body. I felt it was a sense of who I am.
Then all feelings went away and I felt empty. It felt light and
pleasant. I noticed that when I took my glasses off the emptiness
expanded. My body was there but it was not a boundary. The
emptiness was inside and out. It was a still, pleasant feeling.

At first this student did not recognize her sense that her normal identity was absent. She first felt a hurt and the sense of something missing, with a lot of confusion; most individuals experience this confusion when the sense of identity is absent. An investigation into her feelings was needed before she recognized that it was her feeling of identity, her sense of who she is, that she missed. At the beginning she felt something unspecified was missing because she was used to experiencing her sense of identity without consciously discriminating it. We also see in this report what happens when one understands this experience without rejecting it or reacting to it: The deficient emptiness which typically accompanies the absence of identity transforms to a spacious emptiness characterized by the feeling of peace.

We have noted that the usual feeling of identity is a vague sense of self-recognition with which we are always identified. But we rarely isolate or directly contemplate it. Doing so actually tends to precipitate the experience of the Essential Identity, as is demonstrated by the results of the traditional spiritual practice of constantly asking oneself the question, "Who am I?" This practice can lead to increasing disidentification with the more superficial aspects of the self, particularly the self-images, until one's experience of self shifts to the dimension of Essence, with the true identity as the center of the self. One feels simply, "I am present, this is me." This sense cannot be completely described, but it can be recognized.

The Essential Identity is the purest, most specific, and most differentiated form of essential experience. This complete definiteness and

138   delineation of perception is not possible in the conventional dimension of experience; it is specific to the intrinsic discriminating property of the domain of Essence.

The Essential Identity is supremely singular and amazingly unique. We readily recognize this unique singularity as our true Self. The Essential Identity, then, provides the self with the capacity for self-recognition in the essential dimension. We recognize ourselves in a very direct and simple manner, with a feeling that we have always known our true Self, even though we have always identified with the vague sense of identity belonging to the ego-self. Thus, the Essential Identity is the capacity of the self to recognize itself without reference to any experience of the past, or any self-image, or even any memory. We recognize ourselves because we are present as ourselves, as the presence which is authentically ourselves. This pure, unmediated self-recognition is innate, inherent in the self, but it is available only when the self ceases to identify with the content of experience, and thus allows the Essential Identity to arise.

In the following passage, a student describes her experience of the Essential Identity while listening to a group discussion. She had been working on issues related to her sense of self for some time, and this experience is the result of an intensive period of investigation. We especially notice her excitement and happiness about recognizing her true self; this is a common response to this experience.

> *I especially wanted to thank you for your talk today. As I said, it seemed a perfect culmination for the aim I have had the last four weeks. While you spoke today I felt a fire inside my chest, and I felt that I am special. It was as if for that time I was something real—me. I felt a kindness for myself I have never felt and saw even more how I try to prop myself up or tear myself down. I feel so grateful for this experience and so excited about what I feel and have seen. I am looking forward to my work in this group, but what is happening now is so alive and real.*

As the Essential Identity, we realize that the vague sense of identity we have always been aware of indirectly is only a reflection, a distant reminder, of this singular and unique sense of self.

It is interesting that in ego psychology the sense of self—specifically
the feeling of identity—is the most difficult to understand, while in
essential experience, it is the most definite and singular. In no other
area is it so clear that the absence of the concept of Being in most depth
psychology gives rise to ambiguity and incompleteness.

In essential experience the identity is definite and singular, with a
sense of freedom, lightness, joy, and delight, as we saw in the report
above. There is a sense of excitement, playfulness, and adventure. We
feel interested in ourselves, excited about our life, wanting to live and
enjoy it. We feel our preciousness and specialness and the preciousness and delight of living. Life feels like an adventure with unlimited
potential and exciting possibilities. The following report is from James
E., whom we have seen dealing with individuation narcissism. He is
now working with central narcissism and has been experiencing feelings of hurt and a sense of having no value or importance. At some
point in this work he focused on feeling not recognized for who he
really is. He reports a segment of work he did in a group session.

> *Before I started talking, I felt scared, burned out, and hurt—the
> things I had been feeling for the last month. I also felt at some
> point a sense of clear spaciousness, and a crystal kind of clarity.
> Then I started feeling something sparkling, like flashes of light.
> I became aware of a presence like a point of concentration in my
> head. It felt just like a point, no dimension to it, but seemed inde-
> structible; there was no question of it being destroyed or altered
> by anything outside. When I felt this concentrated presence in my
> chest, it made me want to laugh and smile. I stopped myself, still
> holding on to the hurt. Then I felt it warm my whole chest. It felt
> wonderful! The hurt left, it felt like I was healing. There was an
> itch in the center of my chest where the hurt had been. I felt espe-
> cially close to myself. Somehow I felt very different, like a child
> and not knowing how to relate to other people, a little embar-
> rassed, I think. After group I felt a lot of peace and happiness. Later
> when my wife and I made love I felt the pointed presence in a
> very wonderful way.*
>
> *My mind questions this (of course!), Is it real? Could I have
> such a thing? But the experience is still there and my questions*

140 *just disappear when I sense this presence. When I sense this pres-*
ence, that feels like a point of consciousness and joy, as I move
around, it seems the whole rest of me, body and mind, is there to
move it around.

We can compare this experience of the Essential Identity with
Mahler's description of the practicing subphase of the separation-
individuation process.

> During these precious 6 to 8 months (from the age of 10 or
> 12 months to 16 or 18 months), the world is the junior tod-
> dler's oyster. Libidinal cathexis shifts substantially into the ser-
> vice of the rapidly growing autonomous ego and its functions,
> and the child seems intoxicated with his own faculties and
> with the greatness of his own world.
>
> The chief characteristic of this practicing period is the child's
> great narcissistic investment in his own functions, his own
> body, as well as in the objects and objectives of his expanding
> 'reality.'
>
> The child concentrates on practicing and mastering his
> own skill and autonomous (independent of other or mother)
> capacities. He is exhilarated by his own abilities, continually
> delighted with the discoveries he makes in his expanding world,
> and quasi-enamored with the world and his own grandeur
> and omnipotence. (Mahler, 1975, p. 71)

We could not have described the experience of the Essential Identity
more eloquently. Here Mahler shows her exquisite perception of the
manifestations of the true Self. She had said that there are no referents
to the inner experiences of the child, but what she describes here are
the exact behaviors and attitudes that express the presence of the
Essential Identity. It is clear from her descriptions that the Essential
Identity becomes dominant in the practicing period.[66] Mahler further
writes: "We may assume, however, that the earliest perceptions are of
the order of bodily sensations. . ." (Mahler, 1975, p. 220) The fact is
that sensation is the closest description of the feeling of Being. Its feeling is very much like a sensation of something, but much more clear
and precise than a physical sensation.

How is the Essential Identity experienced?

The Essential Identity is not an image or representation, nor is it dependent on an image or representation. One directly experiences presence by being presence. The Essential Identity is a definite presence with no boundaries. This is inconceivable under ordinary circumstances, in which we assume that we are a bounded entity. But imagine a radiant point of light, definite, precise and clearly differentiated. A point is nondimensional, without separating boundaries. It is the source of light, and it is the light itself.[67] The radiant light goes on forever; it is not bounded by spatial distance. If we now imagine the light to be consciousness or awareness, then we have a very good impression of a definite conscious presence which is boundless. One experiences oneself as a brilliant point of light, conscious and aware. Since one is a dimensionless point, one feels singularly definite, but with no sense of boundaries. The Essential Identity feels like a concentrated presence, a precious and pure presence of consciousness, with the characteristic sense of self and identity. The sense of definiteness, singularity, uniqueness, and preciousness are so lucid and complete that it is not possible to appreciate without having the direct experience. Visually, one might see some beautiful image like the image of a brilliant star. But this hardly conveys the profound feeling of significance of the experience. It is an experience of pure consciousness, of lucid awareness and alive presence, in its most singularly definite form.

Our understanding is that object relations theory has erred in conceptualizing the development of identity as beginning with self-representations and ending with the sense of self and identity. The implication is that identity does not exist at the beginning, but does exist at the end of ego development. Our understanding, based mainly on direct perception but also on observation and analytic reconstruction, is quite the contrary: Identity exists at the beginning of ego development. The Essential Identity is present before the development of representations, and is what makes it possible for the self to have the sense of self-recognition.

The fact that the Essential Identity is a differentiated and unique quality allows the self to recognize itself but to recognize itself as a differentiated and unique existence, with a definite sense of identity. Even

142   the earliest self-representations already include the feeling of identity. As the development of the self proceeds, the various self-representations coalesce into the overall self-representation, structuring the self in such a way that it retains the sense of identity. However, this final sense of identity is now based on the *structure* of self-identity. One believes by then that this structure is who one is, and is thus cut off from the Essential Identity. (See *The Pearl Beyond Price* [Almaas, 1988] for more details of this process.) Let us describe in some detail how we conceive of this process.

1. During the symbiotic phase the self is in a nondifferentiated state in which the dominant form of essential presence is what we call the Merging Essence. One product of this phase is the internalized merged representations, primitive representations of the self that are not separate from representations of the mother. The Essential Identity rarely manifests at this time, because the infant's perceptual capacities are not developed enough to feel it very definitely and thus, cannot sustain it.

2. During the differentiation subphase, another essential quality, which we call essential Strength, becomes dominant. This quality contributes to increasing the capacity for perceptual discrimination, which affects development in two ways. It enables the infant to differentiate his image and manifestations from those of the object. Also, the capacity for differentiated consciousness makes it possible to manifest as the Essential Identity. This period involves maturation of the capacities of perception and cognition as the presence of essential strength affects the developing self.

3. In the practicing period the Essential Identity becomes dominant, partly due to the increased capacity of perception and cognition in terms of differentiation and discrimination and partly due to the development of locomotion. This is because, at the beginning of its manifestation, this form of presence has a dynamic quality, an excitement and activity similar to the sense of the toddler running around full of excitement and joy.

4. During the differentiation subphase some representations have some sense of identity because the presence of the Essential Identity

during the experiences generates the representations. Let's imagine an   143
interaction with the mother during this time, when the Essential
Identity is present. The child is this self; he experiences himself as a
differentiated, unique existence with a sense of identity. The feeling of
identity is inseparable from the differentiated sense of existence. The
child feels definite, distinct, singular, and unique. However, he is not
conceptually aware of the Essential Identity. He does not look at it and
say, "That is me." He is indistinguishable from it. He is experiencing
identity, but he has no image of something called Essential Identity.
He is completely identified with the Essential Identity, and has no distance from it. The experience of the Essential Identity is through identity and not through reflection.

So the child feels unique and singular without conceptual awareness
of the Essential Identity. This is a characteristic of the experience of
self-realization. One is, but one is not reflecting on the isness. This is
the state of "no mind," or of empty mind, in which the mind is not
filled with representations.

However, the child is aware of his physical sensations, emotions,
expressions, body image, and so on. The Essential Identity is such a
deep source of consciousness that when we are realized on this level,
the center of awareness is located at the essential depth of the self;
hence, other levels of experience are felt to be somewhat external to
that depth. So the child is aware of the usual categories of experience,
but with some distance from them. In other words, his awareness of
the Essential Identity is a nondualistic perception, and his awareness
of all other categories of experience is dualistic, involving the dichotomy
of subject and object. Thus, he cannot represent his sense of identity,
but he can represent the rest of his experience. So he feels a definite
sense of identity, but at the same time he is aware of a delineated impression connected to himself. By "impression," here, we do not mean just
a picture; we are referring to an overall "gestalt" of physical sensations,
emotions, ideas, and so on.

Consequently, the child's experience includes a preverbal impression of the Essential Identity and at the same time an objectifiable
experience of body and mind. This objectifiable experience of
body-mind is what becomes represented in the self-representation,

144   which is then present in his consciousness with the wordless, implicit experience of Self. Since he is not objectively aware of the Essential Identity, the child inevitably connects the feeling of identity to the representation. This explains how the infant comes to associate the representation with the category of self. The Essential Identity is present, and its sense of uniqueness and singularity helps his maturing perceptual faculties to differentiate his representations of himself from those of the object. And because the representation is related not only to the body, but also to a clearly felt sense of self identified with a specific feeling, it becomes a *self*-representation.

The final result is that the child internalizes a self-representation, an image or an impression, that is associated with a sense of self. The representation includes the feeling of identity, which characterizes or colors it. The infant experiences the sense of identity as coexistent with, and in fact as an important part of, the representation or image connected to his body. So self-representations are always connected with, or imbued with, a sense of a differentiated and unique self, colored by a feeling of identity which gives it self-recognition.

It is important to note that the self-representations in psychic structures are memories. The Essential Identity is not present in these structures; what is there is the memory of the feeling of self connected with the Essential Identity. This explains how the self-representations become imbued with the feeling of identity.

5. These self-representations are the building blocks of psychic structures which are organized into a unified self-representation. Since each representation has a sense of self which is actually a memory of the sense of the Essential Identity, the unified self-representation that develops is imbued with a feeling of identity. The final feeling of identity is a composite of all the myriad memories which include the original sense of identity. This sense is colored by all the experiences in the child's history and is also influenced by the intrapsychic processes involved in the structuralization of the self. So clearly, one's feeling of identity is colored by the significant emotions, sensations, images and perceptions that constitute one's experience. It is not a pure sense of identity; its characteristic qualities are determined by the personal history.

We see, then, why the normal feeling of identity is a pale reflection   145
of the original feeling of essential identity. It is not only a memory of
the original feeling; it is a memory contaminated by all of one's history. This normal feeling of identity becomes the center of the self
responsible for its usual capacity of self-recognition.

6. The final outcome of development is a unified self-representation
which is experienced as a sense of being an individual with personal
boundaries and a feeling of identity. The feeling of identity is, then,
an expression of the substructure of self-identity, which develops primarily through the integration of the inner impressions of the body,
which include the impression of the Essential Identity. Thus, the original clear and precise feeling of identity, which is characteristic of the
Essential Identity, is replaced by the normal sense of identity felt in the
conventional dimension of experience.

At the end of this development, then, the self is no longer experienced as an ontological presence. One is cut off from the true self by
identification with representations. One's sense of self is now determined by a representation constructed from past object relations, and
structured by the development of internalized object relations, just as
object relations theory contends. However, our analysis demonstrates
that this theory is not the whole story. The feeling of identity in the
self-representation is a vague memory of the true feeling of identity,
which existed at the beginning as a characteristic of the Essential
Identity. The normal sense of identity is a reflection of something real,
but this vague feeling is only a pale reflection of the original, precious
self-awareness of one's true nature.

chapter 14

Essential Identity, Essence, and Narcissism

•————————————————————————————————

B ecause the Essential Identity is the true identity on the essential level, when the self loses contact with it, it loses the capacity to be identified with Being; thus, it loses the capacity for self-realization. In order to understand this point more exactly, we need to investigate the relationship between the Essential Identity and Being in general.

As we have seen, the presence of Being, which is the essence of the self, manifests as a structured dynamism in which presence arises in various forms. We call these manifestations aspects of Essence. Each of these pure forms of Being possesses phenomenological qualities along with specific functions in relation to the self. The Essential Identity is one of these forms. In the last chapter we discussed two of its qualities—the sense of being a unique, differentiated locus of existence, and a feeling of identity.

Each aspect of Being is an expression of the same reality. Each of them is part of the essence of the self, constituting its ontological core. The Essential Identity additionally provides the self with the capacity to identify with Being, to be Being.

What are the ways of experiencing Being?

There are basically three ways to experience Being, two of which are related to the functions of the Essential Identity. Let us take, for example, the experience of essential Truth, one of the pure forms of presence.[68] The first way the self can experience essential Truth is easily accessible; the self experiences truth as presence, without experiencing itself as presence. In this condition we retain the normal feeling of identity. We experience ourselves as an individual, with a sense of identity, who is experiencing the presence of Truth. In this situation the subject is the conventional self and the object of perception is the presence of Truth. We might feel this presence to be our truth, but it remains an object. This level of essential experience retains the perspective of the conventional self. We might relate to the presence of Truth as if it is something we possess. But for the self to believe it "possesses" Being is like the body believing it possesses protoplasm. Since this belief is untrue it will tend to disconnect the self from its essential nature, because Truth is an aspect of this essential nature.[69]

The second and third ways of experiencing Being arise from the functions of the Essential Identity. We have said that the Essential Identity provides the capacity to situate one's awareness in any form or dimension of Being. For instance, we may experience Being in the aspect of Truth, not in a subject-object relationship, but by experiencing ourselves from within and through essential Truth.

In this direct experience of Truth we do not perceive ourselves experiencing Truth, but we are present *as* Truth. We recognize ourselves as the presence of Truth. We do not feel like an individual self experiencing Truth, but more like the presence of consciousness intimately aware of itself as Truth. There is no question of self experiencing Truth. The presence of Truth is the same, here, as the awareness of Truth. The awareness is identical to the presence, which is identical to the Truth. It is like solid gold aware of itself in each atom. This awareness of itself has the specific cognition of Truth. This is the pure experience of Being in the aspect of Truth.

The third way of experiencing Being is similar to the second, with an added quality. The Essential Identity provides the self not only with the capacity to situate awareness within Essence, but also provides the

148   feeling of identity. In the experience of oneself as Truth, the identity is not experienced as separate from the essential presence, Truth, but as indistinguishable from it. So rather than experiencing ourselves as Truth experiencing itself as Truth, we experience the Truth as self. In other words, the sense of identity makes our identity the essential quality of Truth.[70]

In this mode, we experience Truth as identity. In the second mode there is only the aspect of Truth in the experience. In the third mode, Truth and identity are completely coemergent, absolutely nondual. If we express the second mode of experiencing Truth we will say: "There is only Truth," while if we express the third way, we will say: "I am the Truth." Both modes of experience are nondual, but we see here two kinds of nonduality. The first mode of experience of the nonduality is absolute identity, while the second is absolute coemergence.[71] We may experience self-realization in either of these modes. Self-realization is the direct, nondual experience of one's Being.

What is the relationship between the Essential Identity and narcissism?

These last two modes of experiencing Being indicate the importance of the Essential Identity for self-realization. The Essential Identity makes it possible to experience Being as self. This fact is the origin of the term *self-realization* being used to refer to the complete realization of the potential of the self, the completion of the inner developmental task, the complete fulfillment of the optimizing thrust of Being. Although the full realization of the potential of the soul includes the resolution of many issues and the integration of the totality of Being, the central issue for transformation of the identity itself is narcissism.

In that light we can now give a more precise definition of narcissism: Narcissism is not simply alienation from Being, but more specifically it is the loss of the Essential Identity. Given our discussion of the function of the Essential Identity to allow identification with one's true nature, it is clear that this loss is the central factor in our incapacity to know ourselves as Being, and thus, in our narcissism.

Although self-realization involves the full and nondual integration of Essence in all its forms and dimensions, the Essential Identity is the

element responsible for the central part of this integration because it 149
makes possible the nondual experience of Being. Otherwise, one can
integrate Being only in a dualistic way, continuing to believe that one
"has" a quality of being rather than recognizing it as oneself.

In the process of spiritual development, and specifically in the
Diamond Approach, we first integrate the various forms of Being. So
we integrate presence in the qualities of Peace, Kindness, Love, Truth,
Strength, Clarity, Space, Knowingness, Intelligence, Existence, and
so on, until we are permanently in contact with the dynamic flow of
essential presence. This development requires the resolution of many
issues: a specific constellation related to each of the pure forms of
Being, the psychic structures underlying them, and the object relations constituting such structures. This accomplishment, although
rare and difficult, is still not a complete integration of presence because
we still identify with a self-image based on representations. At this
stage we are developed only to the extent of the first of the three modes
of essential experience.

The next step in the integration is to shift the identity from the
domain of psychic structures to that of the essential presence itself.
This is the transition to self-realization, that is, to the second and third
categories of essential experience. See Appendix H for further discussion of this process.

What is the relationship of the Essential Identity to the spectrum of narcissism?

We saw in Chapter 4 that narcissism manifests in different forms that
reflect the different forms of essential presence from which the soul is
alienated. In addition, all forms of narcissism involve general characteristics related to the alienation from the true self, which leaves the
self with a psychic structure which is fundamentally empty. Since the
general characteristics of narcissism are due to the loss or absence of
essential realization, they reflect specifically the alienation from the
Essential Identity itself.

It also happens that the Essential Identity is dominant in the practicing phase of Mahler's separation-individuation process. Thus, the
characteristics of central narcissism, which are specific to this stage,

150   are also the general characteristics of narcissism. This is why we call this form of narcissism "*central* narcissism."

Since realization of the Essential Identity is the resolution of central narcissism, the most fundamental form of narcissism, we will now focus on the exploration of central narcissism, discussing the other forms of narcissism only briefly. We can thereby clarify our understanding of the roots of narcissism and understand more completely how this primary psychological barrier to self-realization can be resolved.

Our discussion up to this point has laid the groundwork for exploring the realization of the Essential Identity, the transformation of central narcissism, and the relationship between the two. Moving on from our general discussion of self-realization and narcissism, we will begin the specific study of the central elements of each. The realization of the Essential Identity represents the primary accomplishment in self-realization and the resolution of central narcissism amounts to the resolution of the most fundamental disturbance of narcissism.

BOOK TWO

———————— • ————————

SELF-REALIZATION
AND
CENTRAL
NARCISSISM

PART 1

CHARACTERISTICS AND DEVELOPMENT OF CENTRAL NARCISSISM

The central and most common characteristics of narcissism result from the alienation from the Essential Identity.[1] These characteristics are common to all forms of narcissism and to all individuals whose identity resides mainly in the dimension of conventional experience. From this point on, we will use the term *narcissism* to refer to central narcissism.

In the Diamond Approach[SM], understanding and resolving central narcissism is part of our work on spiritual development.[2] Individuals with marked narcissistic disturbances will face this segment of the work from the very beginning of their involvement in the spiritual process, and narcissistic issues are likely to continue to dominate their process. In this case, the narcissistic issues pervade all other issues, giving the whole process a narcissistic cast. For most people, however, the manifestations of central narcissism remain for some time in the background, intensifying occasionally due to the particulars of their overall process of development. Issues of central narcissism arise mostly as

154   reactions to life circumstances that challenge one's narcissism. The working-through process is similar to that of students who are markedly narcissistic.

In spiritual work, we can progress for some time without fully confronting our narcissism. This is because, for at least a few years, our development deals with issues that do not challenge the deeper structures of the self, such as those of self-identity or self-entity. Pursuing the open inquiry involved in our work brings up issues and conflicts related to the superego, neurotic or character conflicts, the pain and defenses related to early abuses of different kinds, and character distortions. The work challenges our inaccurate beliefs and assumptions about ourselves and reality, and exposes issues of separation and individuation, dependence and independence, and so on. Understanding these issues and clarifying the ego structures underlying them connects us to Essence. (See Appendix G) This process goes on for some time, with varying degrees of accomplishment, depending on our endowment and history, until the connection to Essence becomes more or less established. Then, at some point in our process, we are bound to arrive at the understanding that our development is incomplete because we are still identified with the surface of the self, rather than with its core.

The beauty, depth and fulfillment attendant to the repeated or continuous experience of the presence of Essence activates our desire for a more fundamental integration of Essence, reflecting the guiding pressure of the optimizing force of Being. We become increasingly aware that our continual suffering, the limitations on our freedom and fulfillment, and our still incomplete access to the realm of Essence, result from continuing to identify with the self-representation. We become increasingly uncomfortable with our identification with the usual self in the conventional dimension of experience; it becomes ego-alien.[3]

chapter 15

Manifestations of Central Narcissism

From this point on, our discussion will focus on the actual process of self-realization and the narcissistic issues that arise as part of that exploration. We will follow the typical process of practitioners of the Diamond Approach^{SM} the methods of which are described in the Introduction. The issues and insights we describe are likely to be relevant not only to practitioners of the Diamond Approach^{SM}, but also to those pursuing other spiritual paths. Also, since our method makes possible the illumination of deep ego structures by bringing them to consciousness without identification, our exploration will continue to shed light on the nature of narcissism by revealing an increasingly precise understanding of the deep structures of the self.

Our central method of working—engaging in consistent inquiry into our essential nature—quite naturally begins to put pressure on the structure of our self-identity, exposing its narcissistic characteristics. As this happens we become more aware of the narcissism in our character. Ironically, we begin to feel more narcissistic! For example, we become more acutely aware of our self-centeredness, or of our sensitivity to others' opinions. These characteristics may have always been there, but at this stage we begin to notice and to question them. This

156   focus spontaneously arises from our investigation of our essential nature and begins a new and much deeper phase of our spiritual work. We begin to be curious about aspects of our experience we have up to now taken for granted.

An important aspect of this development is that it arises as a result of our continuing process of inquiry. It happens without premeditation and without being set up by spiritual beliefs about one's identity. This development does not need to be initiated from the outside, nor worked on through some specific practice. In Buddhism and Hinduism, for example, focus on the nature of the self is part of many practices from the very beginning, whether or not the question is naturally arising in the student's process. We believe that the method of open inquiry that we practice in the Diamond Approach^{SM} makes such directed questioning unnecessary because sincere exploration of the truth of one's experience will inevitably lead to the question of identity. In this way the student is guided by his desire to know the truth of who he is, not by an idea taken from a teaching.

The narcissistic constellation proves to be the most central, deepest, most sensitive, and frequently most difficult, part of the personality to work with. The student increasingly discovers that the issues he confronts now, in these deeper dimensions of realization, are the most painful ones. These issues are more emotionally sensitive involving feelings of vulnerability, hurt, and reactivity. Other issues arise at this level of spiritual work, but narcissistic concerns usually dominate the student's process.

Narcissistic issues are extremely difficult to go through by ourself, because it is very hard to see one's own narcissistic issues. Clearly, these issues are the closest to our sense of who we are, for our very identity is in question. At this level a teacher can be helpful, even indispensable. The student needs the teacher at these times more than he did for other issues, because the narcissistic issues make him feel lost and disoriented. The states and issues that arise at this point are similar to those of pathological narcissism, but at this phase of development they do not generally reflect pathology. Rather, they reflect the increasing awareness of the fundamental weakness and emptiness of the normal identity.

In pathological narcissism, on the other hand, this weakness is chronic, indicating the lack of integration of the sense of self and identity, in which the underlying emptiness and unreality are chronically exposed. Theories of depth psychology posit that the emptiness and unreality are due only to the lack of integration of the self, as reflected in the following passage from Kernberg:

> A lack of an integrated self is also characterized by chronic feelings of unreality, puzzlement, emptiness, or general disturbances in the 'self feeling'(7) as well as in a marked incapacity to perceive oneself realistically as a total human being. (Kernberg, 1975, p. 316)

As we have seen, these feelings are much more fundamental, for they are products of the alienation from Being. Therefore, regardless of how narcissistically healthy a student is, these feelings and states arise as he increasingly experiences Being and comes to see the unreality of his usual sense of identity.

What are the specific manifestations of central narcissism?

When the narcissistic constellation approaches consciousness, the way it manifests depends on how resolved our narcissistic issues are. Here, we will discuss general characteristics that indicate the presence of these issues.

Self-esteem and essential value: A major concern is the question of value, which manifests as preoccupation with self-esteem, and various maneuvers meant to gain more of it or avoid losing it. The student becomes sensitive about his sense of worth, obsessively evaluating himself and his actions, and is unusually sensitive to the evaluations of others. He becomes more interested in making a good impression on others, insecure about whether he is, and generally unable to be objective about how others perceive and value him. He cannot help but try to gain value from others through his actions, expressions, utterances, appearance, accomplishments, and so on. He may tend to compulsively praise and congratulate himself.

These developments express the student's growing awareness of a deep sense of low self-esteem. When he explores and understands these

158   manifestations, he sees that the state underlying them is a sense of being deficient and worthless. Often this sense of worthlessness simply alternates with the inflated state. Some individuals tend to identify with the defenses against this painful sense of deficiency, attempting to shore up their self-esteem. Others ("closet narcissists") tend to feel these affects more directly and identify with them. The underlying difficulty is the same; both types of individuals share the preoccupation with the question of value.

The issue of self-esteem reflects the loss of contact with our intrinsic value. This sense of value is lost when we are alienated from the true self. Self-esteem is a certain affect that relates to investing the self-identity with positive energy, libido, or value. Kernberg writes:

> Jacobson (7) has pointed out that the normal 'self feeling' derives from the individual's awareness of an integrated self, while 'self esteem' or 'self regard' depend upon the libidinal investment of such an integrated self. The level or intensity of self-esteem or self-regard indicates the extent to which there is a narcissistic investment of the self. (Kernberg, 1975, p. 317)

This description applies to the normal self which is generally invested with positive instinctual or affective energy. However, when a person has come to a point at which this very identity is in question, he will inevitably face a crisis of self-esteem, since the structures that have been cathected and valued are now being revealed as disconnected from his true nature. The issue arises regardless of the degree of positive regard of the self one might usually have. The decrease in self-esteem experienced at this point highlights a deeper underlying absence of value, which is exposed as the narcissistic features of the normal self become more transparent. In fact, the affect of self-esteem is a reflection of a true feeling that characterizes an essential quality of the soul which we call "value."

Experiencing the aspect of Value has a positive and pleasurable feeling, with a sense of deep satisfaction and sweetness about the fact of our existence. This pleasurable and fulfilling feeling is quite tangible and clearly discriminated as "value." It is the innermost value of the self. It clearly reveals that the self possesses an intrinsic value that is inseparable from the fact of its existence. Value is not only an affect, 159 but a manifestation of our ontological truth, an inherent quality of our core presence.[4]

When we are alienated from our essential presence—that is, when we are narcissistic—we are inevitably alienated also from the quality of Value. We are disconnected from our sense of innate value by the mere fact that our identity is situated in the conventional dimension of experience. This alienation from Value becomes apparent when the manifestations of central narcissism begin to approach our consciousness. We become aware of the lack of Value inherent in our normal sense of identity as this identity becomes transparent and is revealed as empty.

This understanding of the issue of self-esteem or value is satisfactory if one accepts our view of narcissism. In contrast, the theories in depth psychology that explain self-esteem are diverse and unclear. Our view does not contradict these theories, which are basically accurate when applied to the dimension of common experience. The diversity of views simply points to the deeper ground of the issue of self-esteem. It also shows that the question of self-esteem is always problematic for the normal individual, for the "normal" self is always alienated from the intrinsic Value of the true self, regardless of how narcissistically healthy it is. So in spiritual work, the issues of self-esteem that manifest as the narcissistic constellation arises, are simply the intensification of a condition that has heretofore been in the background.

Narcissistic vulnerability: Another issue that arises when the narcissistic constellation begins to be dealt with is sensitivity to narcissistic hurt. This is what we call narcissistic vulnerability. It manifests as the tendency to feel hurt, slighted or humiliated at the slightest indication of lack of empathy, understanding, approval, value, admiration or recognition.

Some defend strongly against this vulnerability, but even if we defend against it we feel disturbed about the absence of narcissistic supplies. The student might act as if he does not care, but how he feels inside is a different story. The vulnerability is always there because of the fundamental weakness of the normal identity. Vulnerability is usually not in the foreground and is defended against in many ways, but becomes

160   more conscious as the narcissistic constellation approaches consciousness. This sensitivity might readily present itself in the student's experience, or the defenses against it might come to the fore first, and will need to be worked through before he can feel the sensitivity directly and fully.

Need for mirroring: The normal need for mirroring becomes exaggerated at this point. This need is one element of the overall functioning of the normal self, but at this point it takes center stage, revealing its importance for our sense of identity. We become more aware of our fundamental need to be seen, recognized, admired, appreciated, and so on. This need has two elements: The first is the need for someone outside us to see us accurately, understand what we are about, how we feel, what we think, and so on. It is a matter of another person functioning like a mirror for us, thus shoring up our sense of identity. The second need is that the mirroring feedback has to be not only accurate, but extremely positive. We need to be seen with admiring and appreciative, even idolizing, eyes.

The need for mirroring reflects the insecurity and instability of the sense of identity. The individual expects the positive empathic feedback to shore up this self-structure. However, because this insecurity reflects the fundamental weakness of the ego identity, which is due to the alienation from the Essential Identity, it is an expression of a deeper need. This deeper need is for our true self to be seen and appreciated, simply because it is not seen, by anyone—ourselves or others.

We agree with Kohut that the need for mirroring is a natural developmental need, but we view it somewhat differently. We will go into this in much greater detail when we discuss the mirroring transferences in Chapter 28. Here, we will give only a general impression.

The need for mirroring is connected with the quality of awareness in self-realization. Self-realization involves direct awareness and perception of our true identity, in which our presence is consciousness. The absence of this direct perception of ourselves manifests as a need for it. In other words, the need to be seen, and seen in a positive light, directly expresses the absence of self-realization, for the latter is a positive awareness of our inner core. This need becomes directed toward external objects because in early childhood the child does not have the capacity for self-reflection.

In the discussion in Chapter 13 about the arising of the Essential Identity 161 in the practicing period, the child is the self without awareness of what he is being. At this time he needs the external mirror to reflect this state, to be able to know himself, for his beingness to be confirmed and supported, and to feel that who he truly is is loved, cherished, and wanted. Otherwise, he will feel unsupported, isolated, and alone.

Typically, this need for one's true self to be seen and confirmed is not adequately met; instead, more superficial aspects of the child are seen and responded to. These aspects end up composing the self-representation, and thus the normal identity. This explains why a person in the process of self-realization, with a normal self (which, according to Kohut, must have received adequate mirroring), begins at this point to experience such a pressing need for mirroring. It is not merely the need of the normal identity to be shored up by mirroring due to its lack of cohesiveness—as Kohut believes—but more important, it is the fundamental need for the Essential Identity to be seen. Because this aspect of the soul was not seen and was thus alienated, its development is incomplete in this respect. In the course of approaching or integrating the Essential Identity, the student feels urgently the need to complete this development. He feels that he wants to be seen, and to be seen with admiring eyes, and to be seen for who and what he truly is. It is a specific dimension of himself that needs mirroring.

The more pathologically narcissistic an individual is, the more he needs his usual feeling of identity to be seen and supported. So it is more accurate to say that a person needs mirroring for whichever dimension of the self did not receive adequate mirroring in the past. This puts us in agreement with Kohut, with the added observation that even for the normally healthy self, the essential presence, and specifically the Essential Identity, rarely receives adequate mirroring. Thus, the need for mirroring is chronic and pervasive; it is the "normal" need for mirroring that is socially accepted. But for a student undergoing a spiritual process, it intensifies as the normal identity reveals its fundamental emptiness, and the deeper need of the true self to be seen and realized becomes conscious. The more narcissistic the individual happens to be, the more intensely and desperately he will experience his need to be seen.

162   *Specialness and uniqueness:* The need for external mirroring feedback typically becomes focused on the need to be recognized as special and unique. This need reflects an exaggerated belief in one's specialness, which in turn reflects an underlying feeling of being insignificant. So the student feels either an exaggerated sense of specialness, importance, and uniqueness, or painful feelings of insignificance and unworthiness; or the two sets of feelings might alternate, depending on the adequacy or absence of narcissistic supplies. These inner states may or may not manifest in overt attempts to appear special and important. Appearing special, more than being special, is what matters, because this is a specific manifestation of the need for mirroring.

Grandiosity: The needs for specialness and importance are qualities of central narcissism. These needs manifest at some point as unrealistic and grandiose beliefs about who one is, what he can do, and what he has accomplished. He may believe he is the best, the most powerful, the most irresistible, the most intelligent, and so on. He may feel he has capacities or qualities or accomplishments far superior to his actual abilities. Of course, this grandiosity complicates his need for mirroring, because he believes these imaginary qualities should be mirrored. This, in turn, intensifies his vulnerability and sensitivity, because reality is always a threat to this unrealistic assessment of himself.

Central narcissism always involves some grandiosity, but only when it is pathological is the central identity with the grandiose self. In the normal self, the grandiosity is part of the self-representation, and the greater this part the greater the narcissistic disturbance. Grandiosity is usually an unconscious component self-representation, but constitutes the central segment of identity in pathological narcissism. (See Chapter 20 for more discussion of grandiosity and its relation to the Essential Identity.)

Idealization: Grandiosity may alternate with, or be hidden by, an inordinate need to find persons to idealize. The need to idealize someone specific is normal, but it is a more desperate need for the narcissist, and is needed for the normal individual when the narcissistic constellation approaches conscious experience in the work of spiritual development. The idealization becomes more extreme, and one tends to believe that one's idealized figure possesses unusual perfection

and power. He uses the relationship to the idealized figure as a sup- 163
port for his sense of identity, to gain a sense of power and perfection
from the association with the idealized figure.

Deficient emptiness: One of the most characteristic manifestations
of narcissism is the painful state of emptiness, in which one feels a
deficient inner nothingness—a vacuity, as if one has nothing inside,
no substance. This poverty of inner life, experienced as an actual phenomenological nothingness, is usually accompanied by feelings of
unreality, meaninglessness, pointlessness, and insignificance. He feels
his life has no meaning or sense, his existence has no significance, and
his action no point or real aim. These feelings reflect his alienation
from essential presence, which is, in the deepest sense possible, the
true significance and meaning of his existence, for the presence is his
true existence.

There might also emerge other painful affects, accompanying the
emptiness or separately, such as feeling lost, aimless, purposeless, disoriented, not knowing what to do, and the inability to initiate any
meaningful action. These affects are specific manifestations of the loss
or absence of the feeling of identity, which may be experienced directly
as a sense of no self, as a feeling of not being able to feel one's familiar
identity. The lack of identity may also manifest as the specific feeling
of having no center and no orientation, because identity functions as
the center of the self.

Narcissistic rage and envy: The narcissistic individual, or the normal individual at this phase of development, is prone to intense anger,
an irrational rage, which may take the form of acute explosions or be
chronic and vengeful. This narcissistic rage is provoked by the slightest—real or imagined—narcissistic insult, such as not being seen,
understood, or appreciated, in the way one feels he deserves. Narcissistic
envy may arise; one hates anyone who has (or seems to have), a rich
inner life or external acclaim and feels pain about not having what the
other has.

Fakeness: A singularly defining manifestation of narcissism is the
feeling of being fake, unreal, lacking authenticity. This may appear first
as the fear of being found out, without knowing what is going to be
found out. When the person goes deeper into this fear he may discover

164   that he is afraid to be found out to be phony, that it will be seen that he is not for real. This sense of phoniness is a reflection of the fact that the normal identity is devoid of the real self, the essential presence. He might even feel himself to be an empty shell, devoid of substance or reality. The sense of phoniness, or the feeling of being an empty shell, appears in this phase of development as a result of approaching the truth of the emptiness of his normal identity.

Depression: For some individuals the emptiness and meaningless-ness may manifest as a certain kind of depression: heavy, hopeless, and helpless. One feels meaningless emptiness, a heavy and sluggish lack of enthusiasm about life, an absence of joy and excitement about one-self, one's work, and one's prospects. It is not a matter of feeling guilty and sad, but of feeling a heavy emptiness, a dry and arid inner life.

Lack of support: The person increasingly feels a sense of lack of sup-port, as if he is unable to stand on his own feet, psychologically. He might feel a lack of balance, even physically. This lack of support appears ini-tially as a strong need for external support, which may manifest as var-ious maneuvers to gain it. All these manifestations reflect his growing awareness of the weakness of his identity. Kohut believes this need for support is a natural developmental need for selfobjects, from which the individual can never be free. We share with him the conviction that it is a natural developmental need, but we do take the position that one can be free from such need, specifically in the condition of self-realization. The growing awareness of this need indicates not only the inadequacy of external support in his past or present, but also, and more signifi-cantly, the absence of his own inner support for his sense of his true identity. The sense of lack of support increasingly manifests as the actual truth of his identity becomes more transparent. The normal sense of identity does need external supports, from a real selfobject or an inter-nalized one, and the pressure of the awareness of the unreality of this identity reveals also the unreality of what has been used to support it.

We will discuss most of these manifestations in much greater detail and depth when we investigate the details of the psychogenesis of nar-cissism and the various steps of working through it. The account of narcissistic manifestations we have given does not significantly differ from the accounts of various depth psychologists, except that our

account describes the normal manifestations of any individual as he
or she approaches the state and issues of self-realization, while in depth psychology, these manifestations are considered to be pathological.[5]

As we continue our exploration of self-realization and narcissism, it is important to distinguish between these manifestations as symptoms of psychopathology (as when they are chronically central in one's experience), or as temporary, normal phenomena in the phase of the transition of identity from the common dimension of experience to that of Being. All these narcissistic traits are present in the normal experience of the self, but they are only part of this normal experience, usually in the background. Nevertheless, they are narcissistic manifestations, related to alienation from Essence, and hence, tend to intensify when one finally confronts this alienation. One realizes, then, that one's life has been empty and insignificant in a way that most people are unaware of. The direct experience of Essence, and the new appreciation of a different order of depth and meaning, exposes the dimension of conventional experience as empty, shallow, and meaningless, just as the normal individual views the experience of the pathologically narcissistic individual. (Kernberg and Kohut list other manifestations that are specifically pathological, and which do not necessarily intensify as part of confronting the alienation from Essence.)[6]

The intensity, depth, and extent of narcissistic issues and manifestations one confronts in this process differ according to the degree of narcissistic disturbance. Some students understand these manifestations when they experience them, and go through them with relative ease. Some become somewhat overwhelmed and find it difficult to experience clearly or understand these conditions. Some become stuck within such states almost all the time. It is difficult for this latter group to disidentify from such manifestations, and they tend to act them out, indicating a more severe underlying narcissistic disturbance. For some individuals, these manifestations are compounded with neurotic, schizoid, or borderline features and defenses, which complicate the situation and make working through the narcissism more difficult. For example, obsessiveness, hysteria, defensive isolation, splitting, and ego inadequacy make it more difficult to clearly comprehend the specifically narcissistic manifestations.

166   However, the narcissistic manifestations tend to predominate as we progress to deeper states of self-realization, and tend to intensify each time a person approaches another level of self-realization. This may mean that narcissistic manifestations will continue to be present, not necessarily intensely, but as reminders of the barriers to self-realization.

chapter 16

The Development
of Narcissism

O ne's view of the way narcissism develops not only provides
a perspective from which to understand it, but also largely
determines the methodology one adopts to deal with it. At
least in part, resolving narcissism involves the correction of distorted
development, as well as the completion of failed or arrested aspects of
development. In particular, our understanding of the development of
narcissism determines how we understand its resolution, and thus
affects not only our general theoretical position, but also the particulars of technique in dealing with narcissistic issues.

The main currents of the understanding of the development of narcissism in depth psychology are exemplified by Kohut and Kernberg.
Our findings correspond somewhat to their positions, but a discussion of how our understanding differs from them will be useful.

Kohut's view

Kohut believes that the self develops in early childhood by building
structures through its interaction with early careholders. In his first
theory of the self he used Freud's concept of primary narcissism as the
beginning of the infant's experience of the self. The perfection and

168   bliss of the nondifferentiated condition of primary narcissism is the infant's initial natural state. This perfection is disturbed due mostly to the inadequacies of the environment. The child tries to hold on to the original perfection in the next state of development, in which the self and object become gradually differentiated.

> The equilibrium of primary narcissism is disturbed by the unavoidable shortcomings of maternal care, but the child replaces the previous perfection (a) by establishing a grandiose and exhibitionistic image of the self: the grandiose self: and (b) by giving over the previous perfection to an admired, omnipotent (transitional) self-object: the idealized parent imago. (Kohut, 1971, p. 25)

The child imagines that the perfection still exists, but now qualifying herself or the object. Seeing the perfection as qualifying the self creates a grandiose self, which becomes exhibitionistic in order to display this self and gain confirmation of it. Believing the perfection to be in the object, she sees the object as omnipotent and perfect, in other words, an idealized object. Both the grandiose self and the idealized parental imago are imaginary and unrealistic, for neither she nor the parent possess such perfection or power. Kohut believes that this creation of unrealistic images is part of the normal development of the self, dealing with the loss of primary narcissism. The child employs the central mechanisms of "I am perfect," and/or "you are perfect, and I am part of you" to preserve a part of the original experience of narcissistic perfection. However, this is only one stage of the development of the self, and these structures undergo a specific modification as development continues.

> Under optimal developmental conditions, the exhibitionism and grandiosity of the archaic grandiose self are gradually tamed, and the whole structure ultimately becomes integrated into the adult personality and supplies the instinctual fuel for our ego-syntonic ambitions and purposes, for the enjoyment of our activities, and for important aspects of self-esteem. And, under similarly favorable circumstances, the idealized parent imago, too, becomes integrated into the adult personality. Introjected as our idealized superego, it becomes an important

component of our psychic organization by holding up to us   169
the guiding leadership of its ideals. (Kohut, 1971, pp. 27–28)

We see here the beginning of Kohut's view of the bipolar self, although at this point he is not defining the self as bipolar. According to Kohut, this process of integrating the grandiose self and the idealized parent imago enables the self to establish the central structures needed for narcissistic health. In other words, the normal self develops through the establishment of psychic structures that provide the self with realistic ambitions and ideals, rather than developing as a grandiose self with the need to idealize others.

> If the child, however, suffers severe narcissistic traumas, then the grandiose self does not merge into the relevant ego content but is retained in its unaltered form and strives for the fulfillment of its archaic aims. And if the child experiences traumatic disappointments in the admired adult, then the idealized parent imago, too, is retained in its unaltered form, is not transformed into tension-regulating psychic structure, does not attain the status of an accessible introject, but remains an archaic, transitional self-object that is required for the maintenance of narcissistic homeostasis. (Kohut, 1971, p. 28)

Disturbances of the process of integrating the grandiose self and the idealized parent image interfere with structure-building, and one's sense of self becomes arrested at this stage of development, rather than developing with the structures that provide ambitions and ideals. This is how narcissistic pathology develops, according to Kohut's early theories. Thus, we see that narcissism is basically a fixation on an earlier stage of development, in other words, some elements of the self cannot develop further because of this fixation on the grandiose self and the idealized object.

In his later theory, Kohut abandons ego-psychological terminology, and defines the development of the self as the development of the bipolar self that begins as the nuclear self. In this theory he departs from the concept of primary narcissism. He develops the concept of self-objects, which are objects the child experiences as part of herself, and thus are not seen as objects in their own right, or with their own needs,

170   but are there to satisfy the narcissistic needs of the self. The child expects to have control over such objects, like she controls her body movements. Kohut differentiates two primary kinds of selfobjects, basically the selfobjects related to the grandiose self, and the selfobjects that are the idealized objects. He defines their functions in terms of these two configurations, thus identifying the nature of the environmental response needed for the integration of the two configurations. In one of his latest papers, "The Disorders of the Self and Their Treatment: An Outline," which he co-wrote with Ernest S. Wolf, Kohut says:

> There are two kinds of selfobjects: those who respond to and confirm the child's innate sense of vigor, greatness and perfection; and those to whom the child can look up to and with whom he can merge as an image of calmness, infallibility and omnipotence. The first type is referred to as the mirroring selfobject, the second as the idealized parent imago. (Morrison, 1986, p. 177)[7]

It is natural for the child to need both mirroring and idealization. She needs her grandiosity and sense of perfection to be mirrored and admired so that they can be integrated into the self; she also needs to idealize a figure in her environment in order to share in his perfection and power. She needs the mirroring in order to retain some of the original sense of perfection, until she is able to be more realistic about herself. At this stage of development, she can tolerate only incremental inattunements to her grandiosity, and when this inattunement happens gradually and empathically, she will—to the extent of her developmental capacity—internalize these corrections of her self-image in a gradual process of taming her grandiosity. In this way, psychic structures are organized into a realistic image of the self, with a sense of vitality and ambition. Gross and/or chronic lack or inadequacy of the mirroring response leaves the child with her grandiose self unintegrated, for at this stage she is unable to tolerate such inattunement, whether the inattunement is due to faulty perception of her, or even correct but faulty according to her image of herself.[8] Similarly, the idealized object needs to respond to the child by allowing her to idealize him, and allowing this idealization to break down gradually, in due developmental time, as a consequence of the child's increasing cognitive capacities for perception and her increased

ability to tolerate narcissistic deprivation. Otherwise, her need for the   171
idealized selfobject will persist and the psychic structure responsible for
ideals will not develop.

Kohut calls the specific process through which the primitive narcissistic configurations become integrated into the self as psychic structures "transmuting internalization." It is a process of internalizing the
primitive selfobjects in a way that transmutes the self, developing it
from its original amorphous condition with primitive selfobjects to a
structured self that has its own ambitions and ideals.[9]

Failures of selfobjects are unavoidable; when they are minor and
nontraumatic they lead to the healthy development of the bipolar self;
when gross and traumatic, they lead to narcissistic pathology.

Kernberg's view

Kernberg follows Hartmann in his definition of narcissism as the
libidinal investment of the self. He also views the normal self similarly
to most depth psychologists, as an intrapsychic structure consisting of
multiple self-representations and their related affect dispositions.
(Kernberg, 1975, p. 315) We have already described Kernberg's perspective on the development of the self (see Chapter 5), which is basically its increasing structuralization through the development of the
self-representation, as the main outcome of the separation-individuation
process. He associates the development of narcissistic disorders with
the difficulties in the overall development of ego structures based primarily on the internalization and integration of object relations. This
is mainly a matter of emphasis; Kernberg emphasizes both the self and
the object in the development of psychic structures, while Kohut
emphasizes the self, viewing the object as a selfobject. However,
Kernberg disagrees that narcissistic problems are due to a fixation on
normal developmental steps in childhood.

> The structural characteristics of narcissistic personalities can-
> not be understood simply in terms of fixation at an early level
> of development, or lack of development of certain intrapsy-
> chic structures. They are a consequence of the development
> of pathological (in contrast to normal) differentiation and
> integration of ego and superego structures, deriving from

172   pathological (in contrast to normal) object relationships. (Morrison, 1986, p. 271)

Kernberg sees idealization as the defensive projection of the grandiose self, and the grandiose self as a pathological structure developed for defensive purposes. The idea is that when the child encounters severe difficulties, especially in her relationships with her primary caretakers, she defends against the intolerable reality in these interactions in many ways, one of which is building specifically defensive psychic structures. This interferes with the normal process of development by setting up pathological structures rather than normal ones. Kernberg believes that this process occurs soon after differentiation between self and object images through a defensive refusion of these images.

Kernberg's view includes the development of many kinds of images of self and other, primarily actual and ideal ones; the latter images reflect what the child wishes herself and her parents to be. Under normal circumstances, the actual images go into the formation of the ego psychic structures, constituted by the overall self and object images, while the ideal self and object images go into the formation of the superego. In narcissistic disorders, however, the actual self-images, ideal self-images, and ideal-object images coalesce into one structure—the grandiose self.[10]

Thus, in Kernberg's view narcissism results when the self develops into a pathological structure that interferes not only with the differentiation between self and object images, but with the differentiation between the ego and superego. This development interferes not only with one's relationships with others, but with the tension between ego and superego, which normally provides the normal self with guidance, self-esteem regulation, and conscience. The point most relevant to our discussion is Kernberg's notion that the grandiose self is not a fixation on a normal developmental image of the self, but rather, is a defensive pathological development of an abnormal structure. The grandiose self, and the narcissistic structures in general, are basically defensive structures, which primarily defend against dependency, especially oral dependency.[11]

In this model, the lack or inadequacy of oral satisfaction leads to a kind of disintegration, inner poverty and weakness, and hence to a need to defend against this state. The defense is constructed through the integration of idealized object images, idealized self-images, and 173 realistic aspects of oneself. So to defend against that original state of helplessness and need, the person develops a grandiose self which is a feeling of, "I'm not like that, really. I don't have those needs. I'm not so weak. I'm not so deficient. I am powerful and perfect." The disturbance that this structure is defending against is similar to what Kohut refers to, especially in his first theory, as a disturbance to the primary narcissism, but which is more specific and extreme: It is a state of extreme helplessness, emptiness, and deficiency, even a state of disintegration, which is similar to the disintegrated borderline state.

This is the reason Kernberg considers the narcissistic personality a variation of the borderline structure. He posits that the child develops a grandiose self to defend against a borderline disintegrated state. Thus, the main difference between his model and Kohut's is the origin of the grandiose self. Kernberg says the origin of the grandiose self is not a fixation but a pathological development, while Kohut believes the grandiose self is a fixation at an early stage.[12]

Our view

Our account of the views of Kohut and Kernberg regarding the development of narcissism prepares the ground for us to present and compare our views. The comparison will clarify some of our ideas and observations, especially since our view developed in the context of the knowledge of Kohut and Kernberg's understandings, and utilizes some of their formulations.

The formulations of depth psychology, as reflected in these two major viewpoints, posit that the development of narcissism is due to specific disturbances of the development of the self as a psychic structure. The differences are mainly around the nature of this disturbance and how it is handled. Our view does not contradict this perspective, but views it from a larger frame of reference. We regard the disturbances of structural development as only part of the development of narcissism, and not the most fundamental one. Narcissism is fundamentally the central expression of the alienation from one's true self, where this true self is not only the vitality of the experience of the body and the emotions, but also, and most significantly, the inner core of

174   the self, its essential presence. In this context, disturbances of the development of the psychic structure of the self are manifestations of relatively severe alienation manifesting as pathological forms of narcissism. Again, we note that theories of depth psychology account for the development of narcissism only partially.

The main difference between our view and the prevailing models of depth psychology is our view of the self. In our view, a human being is born a living presence, a soul, with various essential qualities inherent in that presence.[13] This living presence possesses all the potential of humanity, all its properties and capacities.[14] The self of the neonate, with its perceptions, sensations, feelings, images, impulses, processes, and movements, has its ground in primordial presence, the source of all of these psychic manifestations. The essential presence itself constitutes the identity of the infant, more than any particular manifestation. This understanding of the nature of the self represents our main contribution to the understanding of the self, and constitutes our main divergence from the major theories in depth psychology.[15]

It is of paramount significance for understanding the self, its development, and its disturbances, to include the self's ontological ground (its essential presence) in our view of the self. The human self is fundamentally a presence of Being whose potential includes not only the commonly known capacities and functions, but also (and most significantly for our study), all the various aspects and dimensions of Essence. The fullness and richness of the essential core constitutes the true source and substance of most of the self's qualities: its Love, Pleasure, Satisfaction, Value, Intelligence, Strength, Will, and Nourishment. The development of the self is an expression of the optimizing force of its Being, in which its essential potential unfolds and expresses itself, in part, in unique and real individuality of the self. Thus, the psychic being, the self or soul, actualizes its potential as beingness while functioning in the world of humanity. The process of development of the true individuality, as discussed in detail in our book, *The Pearl Beyond Price* (Almaas, 1988), includes the process of ego development. This process involves the properties and capacities of the self, both essential capacities and what ego psychology calls ego functions, in developing the self into a sense of being a real person.

This personal self develops not only through the maturation of its cog
nitive, physical, and emotional capacities, but also through the manifestation of the essential forms appropriate for each stage of development.

So in our understanding of the development of the self, we adopt
the general outlines of object relations theory regarding the development of the self as a psychic structure, and add the arising of the essential qualities of the soul as part of this development. In the following
chapters, we will examine the development of narcissism in more detail.

chapter 17

Factors in the Development of Narcissism

•————————————————————————————

The factors leading to the development of narcissism can be divided into five major categories: (1) epistemological-phenomenological; (2) maturational; (3) representational; (4) environmental; and (5) constitutional. We return to our understanding that the structure of the self develops through establishing representations, which form structures by patterning the consciousness field of the self. Certain properties of this process make it inherently problematic, as well as vulnerable to interferences and disturbances. The inherent problems in the structuring of the self through representations are reflected in the epistemological-phenomenological, maturational, and representational factors of the development of narcissism. The vulnerability is reflected in the environmental and constitutional factors. The inherent factors are significantly interrelated, but we can discriminate between them. Traditional spiritual teachings tend to consider only these inherent factors, while depth psychology tends to include only the environmental and constitutional factors.

Epistemological-phenomenological factors

The representations which constitute the structure of the identity of the normal self are impressions integrated from the past, which by their very nature are unable to contain essential presence, and thus, alienate the self from its essential core. Essential presence cannot be captured in any kind of memory. Awareness of oneself as presence is the immediate experience of beingness, while retained impressions are many steps removed from this immediacy.

Therefore, to recognize ourselves with and through this memory, or any impression from past experience, is bound to exclude essential presence from our sense of self. Hence, the nature of essential presence and the epistemological stance involved in identification with psychic structures combine to make the developed self—a psychic structure— fundamentally narcissistic.

This development creates epistemological barriers to self-realization by rendering the content of experience opaque: The self cannot see through or beyond its concepts of itself or the world.

A person who engages in spiritual inquiry does not at the beginning expect to have her perception of herself and the world entirely and radically changed. However, in the transformation from one's normal identity, which might involve some experiences of essential realities, to recognizing oneself *as* the essential nature, many assumptions inherent in the conventional world view must be seen through.

One such assumption, for instance, is that a human being is an entity fundamentally separate from other entities, which are also fundamentally separate from each other. Another, related, assumption is that the dimension of solid physical reality is the most—or even the only—fundamentally real existence. Another assumption is that one's concepts about the world, about other people, and about oneself are actually objective, accurate representations.

This category of assumptions constitutes what we are calling phenomenological barriers to self-realization. It is these barriers which are addressed in most traditional spiritual practices, which use methods that are specifically designed to confront them.

From the point of view of seeing narcissism as a failure of self-realization, one could say that the mistaken assumption is the very stubborn belief that the concept of the self *is* who one is.

Besides the body of exploration in spiritual tradition, a central thread in the field of Western philosophical thought concerns epistemological

178   questions regarding the experience of the self. This body of thought has penetrated the naive assumptions of conventional thought regarding the nature of self and world, and brought profound appreciation of the difference between mental constructs and more fundamental reality. However, this tradition does not focus on actual methods of transforming the experience of the self. Existentialist psychology is the field that most clearly addresses these epistemological questions in the context of a philosophical understanding integrated with psychological knowledge.

Maturational factors

Another factor in the development of psychic structures working against retaining contact with essential presence is the limitation in the infant's cognitive capacity. The capacity for discriminating perception does not exist at the beginning of life in the mature form we know in adult experience. It develops gradually in the earliest months of life. This limitation means that the infant does not recognize himself as a discriminated phenomenon; the infant is being himself without knowing himself.[16]

The knowledge that develops gradually is focused on the external, and includes parts of the self that are in contact with people and with the environment. Thus, the infant's initial conceptual knowledge involves the more superficial aspects of his experience. At the beginning, the mind is able to discriminate only the grossest and hence, most superficial, aspects of the experience of the self. The capacity for subtle discrimination does not develop until much later. The infant mind cannot conceptually discriminate essential presence, the subtlest dimension of the self. Thus, the self-representations that develop contain the superficial layers of the self, but exclude the deepest core, because representation depends on conceptualizations, or at least on discriminations.[17] Thus, since the Essential Identity is not a discriminated aspect of the infant's experience, it tends not to survive as part of the self-representation.

However, the main reason for the infant's limited self-knowledge is that the capacity for self-reflection does not exist at the beginning. It develops as part of the maturation of the cognitive functions. Thus, the infant's perception is always directed outward, so to speak. He does not have the capacity to turn back and look at his "inner" experience, let alone to turn back and reflect on himself. In some sense, he is aware only of the "front" of his experience.

At the beginning, the capacity of the infant to simply *be* is intact. He is, without knowing it. His being himself is completely natural and nonconceptual. He does not know that he is being himself, for he does not even have the concept of self. He is being presence when he is being himself. Our discovery in the experience of self-realization reveals that in simply being, one is identified with presence; and when observing young infants we see that there is no self-reflection and no alienation from immediate experience.

Thus, the infant is totally identified with presence without knowing that he is, for his experience is nonconceptual. He has no idea about presence, but it is his very substance, consciousness and identity. This state is due not only to the presence of Essence, but specifically to the fact of childhood self-realization: He is not simply experiencing Essence; he is *being* Essence. To refer to our classifications in Chapter 14, he is experiencing Essence nondualistically, in the second or third kind of essential experience.

At the same time, however, the infant experiences other parts of himself objectively, the way he perceives "external" phenomena. He can see and touch parts of his body; he can hear his voice and can gradually discriminate various sounds and noises; he can feel sensations and inner movements. However, he is not aware of his body in the way an adult is. He sees its shapes and colors, but isn't necessarily aware of its contour. We cannot say that he is aware of his chest or head, for instance. He does not have a coherent awareness of his body. He is aware of various kinds of sensations and impressions, but they are not sorted into categories of "chest" or "arm." He might not actually be aware of the parts of his body where there is no specific sensation or movement. He has sensations when and where there are physiological processes going on, like hunger, full bladder, pain, and so on, and when he moves. Also there are sensations and impressions due to contact with external objects, animate and inanimate. These impressions and sensations, plus the sights and sounds of his body, accumulate and are retained in the psyche as impressions. These impressions

180   become organized gradually into an overall impression of his body, a body-image. It is this integrated image of his body that makes it possible for him to experience his body as a whole body, rather than as a sea of impressions. This integrated image also makes it possible for the infant to then experience his head or arm as a coherent entity.

Thus, the experience of the body as a coherent manifestation is a development in the mind. The body image is basically a concept. Although we normally think that the experience of the body is a direct perception, it is actually filtered and organized by the concept of the body-image. It is actually a mental pattern, not perception *per se*. This is an example of the notion in object relations theory that experience of the self develops through the construction of representations that pattern experience. The development of the body-image described above is an important component of the overall self-representation.

The significant point here is that the child can represent his body because from very early on he perceives it objectively. Thus, this level of his experience forms a fundamental pattern of his identity. He can also perceive his affects, movements, interactions with others, and the various manifestations of these others from the beginning, at first vaguely and then with increasing discrimination. It is because he can experience them objectively, as content of experience, that he retains them in memory and hence conceptualizes them.[18]

In the original condition of primary self-realization, which coincides with that of primary narcissism, the child does not possess enough discrimination to differentiate between his essential presence and the various contents of the self. In the next stage, where the Essential Identity is his dominant presence, the child's capacity for discrimination has matured some. But he is identified so totally with the presence of the Essential Identity, at least when it is manifesting, that he is not able to perceive it. He is being it; he actually feels what it is like to be it, but is not able to objectify it because he is not self-reflective.

This lack of self-recognition in the infant has several consequences for the development of the self. First, it means that the infant does not recognize essential presence, and the Essential Identity in particular, as his true self and identity. His mind does not know that it is him. So he does not conceive in his mind the notion that he is being himself.

Having not recognized his early self-realization, he never appreciates   181
its significance. We note again that this is because his cognitive and perceptual capacities are not mature enough for this recognition.[19]

Another consequence is that the Essential Identity is not retained in
the usual memory, for one cannot retain something in memory that
was never discriminated in experience. Since this experience is not represented, it does not become part of what patterns the developing self.

Even though there is no conceptual memory of the state of realization of the Essential Identity, we have seen many times the interesting
phenomenon of students remembering infant experiences of being
this identity. It seems that the adult capacity to discriminate makes it
possible to recognize the nature of the state, even though the state
itself—as it is remembered—is nonconceptual.

Although Essence itself cannot be represented, some facets of the
experience of childhood self-realization may be retained in memory.
We have in mind the pleasurable feelings, the sense of freedom and,
most important, the feeling of identity. These feelings survive only in
diluted and distorted form because the child never recognizes what
they are actually about, and thus attributes them to other contents of
experience. For example, the feeling of identity, which survives in the
normal feeling of identity as a pale reflection of the original feeling,
becomes associated with the surface content of the self. So what remains
of the original experience of essential presence becomes attributed to
the surface layers of the self that are represented.

Because the self loses contact with essential presence as it develops the
capacity for self-reflection and discrimination, this development goes
hand in hand with the gradual loss of childhood self-realization. By the
time the child is able to reflect on himself he is no longer identified with
essential presence, and certainly not with the Essential Identity.[20]

We conclude from this discussion that the immaturity of the perceptual and cognitive capacities in early childhood is one of the factors leading to narcissism.

Representational factors

We explicated these factors exhaustively in Chapters 5 and 6, in our
discussion of the relationship of self-representations to narcissism, so

182   here we need only summarize our previous discussion. The self develops its structure, or structures, by establishing self-representations. The self as structure is the soul patterned by the integrated impressions of its past experiences. The self experiences itself, then, from within and through this representation, that is, indirectly. The self-representation functions as a layer between the consciousness that is the experiencer and the self that is experienced. So the development of the representation involves the loss of both the nonduality and the immediacy of the original experience of the self.

The loss of immediacy involves the loss of essential experience, and the loss of nondual experience involves the loss of the condition of self-realization, the nondual experience of Essence. So representing oneself leads to alienation from the essential core of the self. Therefore, the development of representations which form the structures of the self is one of the factors in the development of narcissism.

Representations alienate the self from its essential nature in another fundamental way, also discussed in previous chapters. The capacity for representation is a natural property of the mind. The mind discriminates things according to concepts in the memory. Our normal self-recognition through self-representations thus depends on conceptual memory. The mind tells us who we are. This happens to everyone, since the mind believes it is its job to tell us who we are. But our sense of who we are as defined by the mind can only involve knowing ourselves through memories, and thus, through concepts.

No matter what we experience, even nonconceptual reality, the mind will try to define our identity according to that experience. The moment this definition occurs we are identified with a concept, and this concept can only be a memory. This is the usual knowledge of self.

We are not saying that this pattern of development is not necessary, or shouldn't happen. We are simply describing what happens. This is how the mind functions; we end up taking ourselves to be something according to the mind, and thus become identified with concepts of ourselves. This is the simple meaning of the idea that our identity is an expression of self-representations.

When we are self-realized, we are aware of ourselves as completely pure, completely virginal, and completely new. We may say, "It feels like such and such." We may conceptualize our experience. But if we take that description to define us, if we hold on to a memory to define who we are, then we will have lost our self-realization.

So, even though the development of self-representations is a natural property of our mental functioning, it alienates us from our essential Being. Narcissism, then, is a natural and unavoidable result of identification with self-representations.

We believe that spiritual development must be seen not only as a correction to normal experience, but more importantly, as further development of the self. Much spiritual work functions to correct the delusions of the self regarding its true nature and the nature of the world by encouraging disidentification with self-concepts. However, we understand the natural unfoldment of the soul to lead to one becoming discontent with, and seeing through, one's identifications. This unfoldment need not involve a rejection of the capacity for conceptualizing; it can simply allow an increasing transparency of mental concepts as the appreciation of our nature as essential presence reduces our identification with self-representations.

Environmental factors

The environmental factors contributing to the development of narcissism are the effects of the child's interactions with his early environment, represented primarily by his parents and immediate family. Most spiritual teaching methods do not address these factors and do not envision a psychological understanding that can free the individual from the influences of early childhood. In fact, the common position in traditional teachings is that dealing with the epistemological-phenomenological and representational factors is sufficient to dissolve blockages caused by the environmental factors. This is because the former factors are more fundamental and actually function as the ground of the psychological issues and conflicts related to the latter. Most traditional methods of self-realization are based on moving beyond representations and the associated psychic structures. They focus on establishing nonconceptual consciousness or awareness, either by transcending the content and activity of the mind in general, or by activating spiritual phenomena—like presence—which are already

184   nonconceptual. For example, a Zen Buddhist might be attempting to "go beyond the mind," the Christian mystic to "surrender to God," the Sufi to achieve "annihilation in the Divine."

This is the reason so many spiritual teachings seem to distrust or devalue intellect. Their attitude toward the mind does not actually reflect a devaluation of the mind per se, but reflects a recognition that conceptualization can support the alienation from the true nature of the self, the nonconceptual essential presence. This is why these traditions emphasize "no-mind," nonconceptual reality, surrender of one's beliefs and identity, and so on.

The relatively new understanding of depth psychology gives us an opportunity to work directly with the consequences of the environmental factors, which manifest as structural difficulties and psychodynamic issues. We believe that these issues are more significant barriers to self-realization than most spiritual teachings appreciate. In our work with many students, we have found that the barriers against self-realization are complex and intertwined reflections of all the factors in the development of narcissism. The work is less effective when we deal only with fundamental factors. Individuals involved in spiritual practices that deal exclusively with the fundamental factors run into great difficulties when issues and structures related to the environmental factors affect their practice. In fact, spiritual practices, especially the effective ones, tend to activate the narcissistic issues related to the environmental factors.

For example, consider a method that works on activating presence directly and thus transcends mental content and activity. Suppose a person is successful in his practice, and experiences essential presence. What usually happens (under normal circumstances and for most individuals) is that the experience does not last. Furthermore, it is likely that the person will begin to experience many kinds of difficulties—psychological, physical, or functional. These difficulties are usually considered a natural part of the spiritual journey, which will pass in time if one perseveres in his practice. If we observe closely, however, we will see that these difficulties are actually produced by his spiritual experience. They are usually connected with psychodynamic issues or structural conflicts and disharmonies that result from the fact that experiencing essential presence has taken his experience beyond some of his psychic structure and its object relations. For instance, he might experience separation anxiety, because the experience of essential presence means to his unconscious that he is more distant from his internalized image of his mother. Or he might experience a deep hurt about not being seen, because experiencing essential presence involves experiencing a part of himself that is actually not seen yet by anyone. This situation tends to activate the old hurt about not having been seen in the past. In this example the spiritual practice—which focuses on the fundamental factors—activates issues arising from environmental influences, which the practice is not designed to deal with. It is true that if the individual in this case were completely successful in applying the spiritual practice, he would be able to transcend the arising difficulties. If he were no longer identified with any childhood self-representation, he would not have an issue about separation from the mother. So if his practice is deep enough, he will be able to experience the essential presence without this issue arising. However, how many people can apply a spiritual practice with complete success from the beginning? In our opinion, it is just this sort of scenario that makes people unable to pursue many traditional spiritual paths. In this example the separation anxiety will almost certainly not be felt consciously or understood, but might be acted out, say, in the person deciding that it's really more important to pursue a relationship with a lover than to do this practice, which really doesn't have enough emphasis on love anyway.

Although the fundamental factors are subtle and deeply embedded, the consequences of the environmental factors are frequently much more difficult to handle, let alone resolve and free oneself from. Many people in this situation have a great deal of difficulty dealing with the consequences of their childhood experience, and are not able to benefit from practices that deal only with the fundamental factors. Because of these issues, many individuals cannot manage to perform spiritual practices in any real or committed manner.

We therefore take the view that dealing with all the factors causing narcissistic issues is the most efficient approach in the work of self-realization. In the Diamond Approach^{SM} we deal with whatever level

186   of self the student happens to be experiencing, and work towards understanding it without taking a rigid position about what element of experience to focus on. We allow the student's exploration to guide us to the factors most relevant for his or her present experience. The work may focus on one factor for some time, or several, or may move from one to the other.

Since the identity structure develops through the integration of internalized object relations, the child's experiences in his actual relationships are the primary determinants of the development of his sense of self. This is a basic tenet of depth psychology. The child needs these interactions for this development, which not only affect it, but actually form it. The influences of these interactions can be divided into two groups: (1) those that affect the development of the self in general; and (2) those that specifically cause narcissism.

The general factors which interfere with the development of the self contribute to the self's alienation from its essential core and thus to narcissism. This group consists of all the consequences of inadequate satisfaction of the child's needs during the various stages of development. The child's needs change according to what phase of development he is passing through, and the parents (at the beginning specifically the mother) must satisfy these needs adequately, and also must respond flexibly to the changing needs.[21]

Inadequate care creates distortions in the developing structures of the self, resulting in many kinds of psychological difficulties, among these, narcissism. These inadequacies—for example, insufficient positive merging in the symbiotic phase—affect the child by making it necessary for him to react to his situation in order to get what he needs. This reactivity tends to disconnect him from his essential presence. For example, the infant's need to react when the environment is not responding, which becomes more intense and chronic the greater the inadequacy, takes away his basic condition of relaxation; thus, he loses his capacity to simply be.[22]

In addition to specific subphase inadequacies, general difficulties of the self contribute indirectly to the development of narcissism, because any intolerable condition will lead the child to erect psychological defenses against experiencing it. This again results in increased alienation from his essential presence, since a psychological defense involves avoiding the present condition of the self. The child cannot try to defend against his experience in the present moment and at the same time remain in touch with his present essential nature. Thus, all ego defenses, necessary though they are for the psychological balance of the inadequately cared-for child, contribute to his disconnection from his essential core, and thus to his narcissism.

Not only defenses, but many kinds of structures develop in defensive ways. Some ego structures actually develop specifically for defense, for example, those which constitute the schizoid character. In attempting to avoid dealing with very painful object relations, the child defends by isolating himself from his felt experience in general. This defensive detachment isolates him not only from his emotions, but also from his essential presence, characterized by vivid affects and qualities of aliveness. If he were in touch with the essential presence, he would lose his capacity to isolate himself from his emotions, because the presence would open him to his present experience, whatever its content. This disconnection from the essential core makes the schizoid character narcissistic on some level.

Another example of how defensive structures can contribute to narcissism is the person who was abused physically, sexually, or emotionally. He must develop measures to deal with his trauma, any of which will disconnect him from Essence. He cannot afford to stay in touch with his essential presence because this would put him deeply in touch with himself, confronting him with the full impact of the abuse. For example, he may develop structures such as obsessive thinking or defensive hostility to keep his experience shallow enough to deny his pain and helplessness.

The interested reader can find detailed explorations of these general factors and their related manifestations of self in our previous publications, such as *The Pearl Beyond Price* (Almaas, 1988) and *The Void* (Almaas, 1986).

In the next chapter we will explore the environmental factors specifically connected with the development of narcissism in the infant and child.

chapter 18

Specific
Environmental Factors

The environmental factors contributing to narcissism relate to
the development of identity, that is, to the child's assumption
of his unique characteristics, capacities and qualities.
Problematic interactions with his environment lead to difficulties in
being truly himself. Depth psychology has explored these factors and
their relation to narcissism, as we see in the following passage by Kohut
and Wolfe, from their paper, "The Disorders of the Self and Their
Treatment: An Outline":

> The self arises thus as the result of the interplay between the
> newborn's innate equipment and the selective responses of the
> selfobjects through which certain potentialities are encour-
> aged in their development while others remain unencouraged
> or are even actively discouraged. (Morrison, 1986, p. 182)

Each child is born with a certain potential that includes many qualities, capacities, properties, functions, forms, and levels of experience
and behavior. For these qualities to be established and developed, they
need to be related to in specific ways. The child needs for the important
persons in his life to relate to him in specific ways that encourage the
emergence, establishment, and development of the various components

of his potential. Such encouragement and support enable the child to   189
grow in a way that integrates the full range of his potential as a human
being. Inadequacy of the specific kinds of relating needed by the child
limits the unfoldment of his potential and his capacity to be himself as
his potential unfolds. The main specific factors that contribute to the
development of narcissism are:

1. *The child is not seen for who he is.* Being seen is probably the deepest narcissistic need; the child needs this external mirroring not only
to confirm and solidify his arising sense of self, but even to know this
sense in any definite way. His sense of self does exist on the essential
level but, as we have seen, he still does not see himself; he is not conscious of his state of childhood self-realization.

When the important people in his life do not see him he may feel
alone and isolated, as if he is from a different species. He may feel unwel-
come, or not "at home." He may feel unimportant and insignificant,
wondering, "Why won't they see me?" But most of all, his arising sense
of identity remains unrecognized and unconfirmed, and as a result he
will most likely doubt it himself. Even if he manages to know and see
himself in some way, he will feel totally alone because his identity—who
and what he truly is—is not seen. This state of aloneness is too intolerable for a child, so he has to find a way to avoid it. Most of the time,
the way to do this is to be something that the parents can see and will
respond to.

The child's need to be seen includes his external manifestations: his
actions, feelings, expressions, preferences, capacities, accomplishments,
motives, and their observable qualities. When any of these elements is
not recognized or appreciated by the important people in a child's life,
he is likely to become alienated from these elements. This factor in
narcissistic disturbance is recognized by depth psychology.

What about his essential core, the true place of his feeling of identity? The same thing happens as happens to unseen external qualities;
the child grows up alienated from his essential core if it is not seen by
the important others in his early life. Thus, almost everyone grows up
alienated from his essential presence, for who has parents who can see
Essence? Most parents do not see their child's essence because they are
not aware of their own essential presence. This is probably the most

190   significant environmental factor in the development of narcissism. In other words, the child becomes narcissistic because his parents are subject to the narcissism of everyday life.

The child is bound to feel unrecognized on the essential level even when his other, more external manifestations, are seen. The external manifestations are just that, external, while essential presence is his inner nature, his very beingness, who he really is. He is also bound to feel not seen without exactly knowing what is the him that is not seen. Thus, the child's sense of identity includes the manifestations that have been seen, but that identity also includes a vague sense of emptiness. This emptiness reflects the alienation from his true self and identity.

2. *Although being seen is a fundamental need, it is not by itself enough.* The child also needs his arising self to be related to. It is possible to be seen and not related to. Sometimes an important aspect of the child is seen but not responded to. Being seen and not related to is not as bad as not being seen at all, but it is bad enough to cause narcissistic alienation. The arising potential of the child needs to be related to for the child to be able to relate to it himself.

A parent may see a certain quality in the child and for various reasons not relate to it. She may ignore it because she does not know how to respond to it, since she cannot relate to that quality in herself. She might see it, but misunderstand what it is, attributing it to other manifestations which she can relate to. This last scenario is common, especially when the Essential Identity is present. A parent might see the preciousness and brightness of this essential presence but not understand that is actually who her baby is. (We noted this in discussing how Mahler and her colleagues interpreted this manifestation in children they were studying.) She may attribute the brightness to intelligence, for instance, and then relate to this intelligence while ignoring the real thing, the Essential Identity.

The fact that the failure of relating to any level of the child's self contributes to narcissism is appreciated in psychological theory. Here, we are emphasizing the deeper levels that are ignored not only by normal parents, but also by most theorists of child development.

The child cannot tolerate not being related to. It makes him feel alone and isolated, ignored and unrecognized, and probably rejected and unwanted. He feels unimportant, insignificant, ignoble, and unlovable. He is likely to end up believing that there is something fundamentally wrong with him. Most children blame themselves for not being related to and end up hating the most precious element in themselves. They strive to develop those aspects of the self that are seen and appreciated. Thus, the child's self develops empty of its center and essence, identifying only with his external manifestations. This is his fake identity.

3. *Even though the child might be seen and related to, he might be misunderstood and thus alienated.*

When a child's manifestations, actions, motives or expressions are interpreted incorrectly, this misunderstanding has a deep wounding effect on the child because he is not related to as who and what he is. The child will not only feel hurt and betrayed, but is likely to become confused and uncertain about his sense of himself. The child's self not only needs to be seen and related to, but seen accurately and responded to accordingly, for his sense of self to develop accurately. Otherwise, some qualities will be incorporated into his sense of self in a distorted way because they will be integrated into his sense of self compounded with the misunderstanding. Clearly, this particular disturbance affects most children's relation to essential presence, because even if the parent is open enough to see her child's essence in a vague way (for instance, because of intense love), she is likely to misunderstand it. She may understand his expressions or motivations, but misunderstand who he is. This is a fundamental failure of the environment; it is not possible to estimate the extent of devastation to the growing self of the child as he becomes alienated from who and what he is, his inner preciousness and truth.

We cannot blame the parent in this instance; she might be a normal and healthy mother who loves her child and does her best to provide him with what he needs. Her limitation is part of a societal norm, and she will not know otherwise unless she is fortunate enough to see what Essence and self-realization are. The degree and kind of the parent's misunderstanding affects the degree of the child's alienation. She might interpret the wonderful qualities of her child, which are actually the visible qualities of his essence, to be a specialness

192   unique to her particular child. It is true that these qualities are unique and special; Essence, and the Essential Identity in particular, are the special and precious elements in the self. However, they are common to all children. The parent believes that her child is special because she senses something about him that is different from other children. The fundamental narcissism of the parent is what gives her this perspective.

Parents almost always attribute unusual qualities or capacities to their children, as if they are unusually fortunate compared to other children. The fact may be that their children are unusually fortunate, but this does not make them different, better or more fortunate than other children. They are unusually fortunate because they are born with, or more accurately as, Essence, which is the most special and fortunate thing in all the universe. In other words, their children are special and fortunate because they are born human, with a human soul whose inner nature is the preciousness and wonder of Essence.

Many parents feel convinced that their own child is "unusually bright," or "the most beautiful I've ever seen." They feel, "I don't want his purity to be seen, for he might be envied"; "He is going to be the best"; "I can't help but see that he is the most precious thing that ever lived," and so on. Because awareness of these intrinsic qualities of Essence is rare in adult experience, the parents cannot help but believe that their child is born with unusual and rare qualities.

The parent does not see that these wonderful qualities are those of Essence in general, true about any human being who is being his essence. If she were seeing him as Essence, she would know that these wonderful qualities are not unusual, and are not particular to her child. This misunderstanding can manifest in having unusual expectations for her child, becoming disappointed when these qualities fade, feeling inflated and special herself, and so on. If the parent happens to be narcissistic and grandiose, she may attribute manifestations of her baby's essence to some kind of divine or extraordinary gift.

This lack of understanding again contributes to the child's alienation from his essential nature, and hence contributes to his narcissism. This point is important because everyone, including depth psychologists, believe that this admiring attitude is appropriate and

necessary for the child's narcissistic health. They do not see that   193
although the child does need this admiration, he needs it for his true
nature, not for a comparative "specialness." The parents' failure to see
that the source of these qualities is his actual true self wounds the child
deeply, and makes him feel that their love is not really for him.

4. *The feeling quality of relating to the child is also important.* The child
needs not only to be seen, recognized and related to, but also to be
appreciated, admired, and loved for who he is. He needs to be seen in
a positive light, to feel welcomed, wanted, cherished, prized. He needs
to be valued as precious, special, and unique. He needs this positive
and admiring mirroring to recognize and establish his arising sense of
who he is.

Kohut appreciates the child's need for this admiring mirroring.
However, there is no theory in depth psychology that explains this
need. Why does the child need such positive feedback? Why does the
feedback need to include not only acceptance and love, but also glow-
ing admiration, and an attitude that the child is special and precious?
The closest thing to an explanation from Kohut is his view that the child
needs this adoration to protect his narcissistic vulnerability, which is
due to his imaginary grandiose view of himself. In other words, the
child needs this kind of adoration because he has a grandiose sense of
himself which needs to be supported by such adoration until he is able
to see himself more realistically. In describing how the mature self of
the parent will respond to the changing needs of the child, Kohut and
Wolfe write:

> It can, with a glow of shared joy, mirror the child's grandiose
> display one minute, yet, perhaps a minute later, should the
> child become anxious and over-stimulated by its exhibition-
> ism, it will curb the display by adopting a realistic attitude vis-
> a-vis the child's limitations. (Morrison, 1986, p. 183)

We believe that the situation is not as simple as it appears, and that
the child is not as delusional as Kohut and Wolfe believe. The child's
grandiosity is not a groundless delusion. There is a deeper reality to
the need for admiration and adoration than the need to have a false
grandiose self supported. What needs to be seen and loved is not only

194   the external, physical, emotional, and mental manifestations of the child, but more important, his very presence, his true self and identity. This true self, the Essential Identity, is actually what is precious and special in the child. It is the spark of Being in him, the most beautiful, wonderful, magnificent preciousness in his self. It is important and significant because it is the fundamental true nature of his self and the source of his true potential, the source of everything beautiful and majestic in a human being.

Given that this is the nature of his being, how can the child feel seen and appreciated if he is not seen as special and precious and amazingly wonderful? The child needs such admiration to make him feel seen and appreciated, because adoration is the appropriate response to the presence of Essence. Anyone who has a clear experience of essential presence will understand this need immediately, because when he beholds this presence he is filled with adoration and exquisite appreciation. This admiring response accurately mirrors the true self, not the grandiose self.

We believe that this interpretation gives a much better explanation for this narcissistic need than the one held by depth psychologists. Parents express this adoring attitude towards their children not only because of their grandiose projections, but also because the children are truly and actually adorable and special in their essential nature, and the parents are responding to these essential qualities. Essence is precious, beautiful, wonderful, and the most lovable quality in the whole of existence; so the parents are not being unrealistic when they feel this way about their children, even though they might mistakenly believe that these qualities are unique to their own child.[23]

This discussion clarifies why the absence or inadequacy of loving, valuing, and admiring mirroring from parents contributes to narcissism. The greater the inadequacy of this admiring mirroring, the deeper and more profound is the child's alienation from his essential core, and the more pathological is the resulting narcissism.

Sometimes a child is loved and admired, not for who he truly is but as an extension of the mother, or as something she has projected. She might love him, for instance, because he happens to be her child and not because she really sees him and loves what she sees. She admires an extension of herself, not him. Or she might admire something she projects on him, for instance, the expectation that he will be like her 195 idealized father, rather than seeing what he actually is. For the child's need for mirroring to feel satisfied, the admiring attitude must actually be a mirroring; in other words, the child needs to feel that it is directed to his true self, not to an external part of him or to the parent's projection. Without this true mirroring, the child will grow up feeling deeply unloved, even though he might be seemingly surrounded by love. This lack will contribute to his loss of contact with his true self.

5. *Lack or inadequacy of support.* The developing self needs to be supported in order to retain and develop its capacity to be. The quality of support may not become explicit if it is adequate. If the child is actually supported he doesn't necessarily feel supported; he simply doesn't feel unsupported. When support is not available, the child feels unsupported and the issue of support arises. The child does not even know what it is like to be supported, when he is. Because the awareness of support arises only when it is lost, the child who does not have it experiences its absence but is not aware of when it has been there. Many people grow up feeling, "My father was never there for me," when this is not completely true.

Support is related to the qualities of the parents' presence and behavior that make the child feel that there is strength, solidity, calm, certainty, and confidence that she can depend on. The soul of the young child is vulnerable; it cannot yet depend on its own resources to feel supported and upheld in regard to her sense of being herself. She needs to be bolstered by an external solid presence of confidence, certainty, strength, and reliability.

When the child can just relax and trust that the parent will be there—will know what she needs, be available to take care of her, to protect her and provide her with whatever she needs—her own sense of identity will be solid and stable. The reliable, solid, external presence helps to solidify her sense of being herself.

Kohut understands this need for external support as the need for the idealized selfobject; support then comes from merging with its power and bliss. "Since all bliss and power now reside in the idealized object, the child feels empty and powerless when he is separated from

196   it and he attempts, therefore, to maintain a continuous union with it."
(Kohut, 1971, p. 37) This view is consistent with our observations. We
understand the genesis of idealization differently, but we agree that
the child tries to gain support by idealizing the parents, imbuing them
with magical omnipotence and bliss. We also believe that the need for
support is more general than the need for idealization, the latter being
its most obvious component.

It is more what the parent is than what she does that functions as
support. The child needs to perceive her as a solid and calm presence,
sure of herself and her capacities, for him to feel the security and support to simply be, instead of anxiously having to try to maintain himself. Kohut seems to understand this point, but he views it in terms of
grandiosity and idealization.

> In other words, it is not so much what the parents do that
> will influence the character of the child's self, but what the par-
> ents are. If the parents are at peace with their own needs to
> shine and to succeed insofar as these needs can be realisti-
> cally gratified, if, in other words, the parents' self-confidence
> is secure, then the proud exhibitionism of the budding self of
> their child will be responded to acceptingly. (Morrison, 1986,
> p. 182)

To interpret this situation in terms of Being, we can say that the parents' calm and solid presence, their confidence in being themselves, the
harmony in their beingness, and the expression of this beingness, support the child's identity with his essential presence. The confident sense
of being acts as a support for the child, not only to feel secure enough
to simply be himself, but to feel confident that his parents will be there
for him. Support for his exhibitionism is only a part of this general support, and is actually a distortion of the real situation.

As Kohut emphasizes, it is not only the parents' confidence in themselves which supports the child, but also their mere presence. This
presence can be physical, emotional, or essential presence, supporting
the physical, emotional or Essential Identity of the child, respectively.
We will explore in detail the question of support and its essential counterpart when we deal with idealizing transference in Chapter 23. Here,

it suffices to say that absence, insufficiency, incompleteness, or unreliability of support leaves the developing self abandoned and prematurely on its own. The child's sense of himself will develop as somewhat shaky and tentative, since he has not had the support to sustain the capacity to be himself.

6. *Children often experience expectations and demands to be something they are not.* Most parents receive their child with some notions about what they want and expect him to be. The expectations are mostly unconscious, but some levels are conscious and forcefully stated. The parents perceive and respond to the qualities of the child that they expect, and hence only these are supported, leaving the rest of his potential undeveloped. The more external the elements that the parents expect and perceive, and the more their expectations diverge from the child's true qualities and capacities, the more he feels that who he is, is not valued and loved. As a result, he tries to become what his parents want and expect him to be. Alice Miller writes about this situation, understanding it as reflecting the parent's narcissistic needs:

> This does not rule out strong affection. On the contrary, the mother often loves her child as her self-object passionately, but not in the way he needs to be loved. . . . Instead, he develops something which the mother needs, and which certainly saves his life [the mother's love] at the time, but nevertheless may prevent him, throughout his life, from being himself. (Morrison, 1986, p. 326)

Sometimes the parents might fail to see the child's true self, but might not expect him to be anything in particular. When they not only do not see him, but also want him to be a certain way, this is an even bigger rejection for the child; not only is he not seen, but he must mold himself in their image of him. So his identity is based on pleasing his parents.

Even the particulars of his potential that arise are affected by the responses of his mother. Mahler believes it is the specific unconscious need of the mother which, out of the infant's infinite potentialities, draws out those in particular that create for each mother "the child" who mirrors her own unique and individual needs. (Mahler, 1968)

198   Mahler's view illuminates the great significance and extent of the parents' influence on the child's self.

The totality of the parents' selves and their life situations exert a selective influence on the child's development. Depth psychology has investigated the manner in which the imbalanced condition of the parent's self, manifesting in part as expectations, results in the imbalanced development of the child's self. Expectations result in narcissism, focusing on the external manifestations of the self also result in narcissism, and admiring capacities and qualities instead of the child himself results in narcissism, ". . . for he senses that so long as it is his qualities which are being admired, he is not loved for the person he really is at any given time." (Alice Miller, in Mahler, 1968, p. 329)

Miller's statement illuminates the observation that the condition of the parent's self greatly determines the content of the child's self. Since the parents cannot mirror or encourage in the child the dimensions of the self they do not know or have not integrated, as is most often the case, they cannot mirror the child's essential presence. Thus, the fundamental narcissism of even healthy parents forms a general background of expectation for the child, who, in a sense, inherits this fundamental narcissism and perceives it as part of how a human being is expected to be in normal society.

Because the child experiences the parents' expectations as different from who he actually is, he feels betrayed by the parents. Even the general narcissistic condition of the parents is perceived as a betrayal. Because the child is completely dependent on the parents, this situation leads to his betraying himself to avoid aloneness and the loss of love of the parents. This, the greatest of all betrayals, is an important part of the development of narcissism, and constitutes an emotional issue central to the resolution of narcissism. In general, this sense of betrayal is completely unconscious until later developments take place, for instance when a person is in the process of individuation and separation from the parents' expectations, he may feel then the cost of his accommodation to the parents' defining of him. Another level of development is the process of spiritual realization, in which glimpses of essential nature tend to reveal the emotional pain involved with the parents' failure to support and mirror this true nature. Seeing one's essential nature gives one a painful awareness of what was betrayed by the parents and by the self's accommodation of the parents' world.

7. *The child may experience a lack of attunement to his state, his needs and his expressions, which can result from any of the above factors.* This is caused by the parent responding inappropriately to the needs and expressions of the child. The child needs to be seen and responded to not only positively, but also accurately and empathically. The response needs to be attuned in terms of timing, in terms of kind, in terms of frequency and intensity, and so on. For instance, if the child is crying because he is wet, and the mother carries him and comforts him and nurses him, she may be loving, but she is not really responding to the child's need. If response is not exact, the child will be influenced negatively. He will not have his immediate need met, with whatever consequences this might entail. In terms of narcissism, it means he is not seen as he is at the moment. When the present condition of the child's self is not attuned to, the child feels a lack of support for being himself.

Perhaps the parent cannot recognize or understand the child's needs, or perhaps she has other reasons for not responding accurately. She might be reactive or hostile toward the child. She might know the child is hungry, but not respond because she happens to be angry. "Good. Cry more." This is lack of attunement. Or the child might be feeling vulnerable for some reason, but the parent's response lacks sensitivity to the vulnerability, teasing him or humoring him when he is feeling hurt. Inattunement can be gross or subtle, superficial or deep, chronic or occasional, but it will always affect the child by wounding his sense of himself.

Lack of attunement involves a lack of empathy, which is an expression of the parent's own narcissism. So again, the narcissism of the parent leads to the narcissism of the child. The severity of the narcissism of the parent determines to a great extent the degree of the child's narcissistic alienation. If the lack of empathy is gross and chronic, the child might become depressed, or even psychotic. In less drastic circumstances, a child will become moderately narcissistic, or basically normal, with a narcissistic lack of sensitivity to his essential nature.

200   8. *A certain class of inattunements involves destructive actions and attitudes on the part of the parents toward the child.* Hating the child, abus-
ing him, misusing him, exploiting him, neglecting him, depriving him,
or abandoning him inflict so much pain and suffering that the child
cannot stay in touch with himself. This category of factors affects many
aspects of development, but here we will discuss only the particular
feature that leads to narcissistic disturbance. These destructive acts
and attitudes are intrusions on the precarious self of the child at the
beginning of its development. In addition, there is a class of actions
that are specifically intrusive, like not respecting the child's privacy, be
it physical, emotional or mental. The parents might intrude on the
child's physical space, by entering his room unannounced or even
unwanted, arranging it the way they prefer and not giving him any say
in the matter. Or they might always choose his clothes for him, not
respecting his wishes, or interfere unreasonably with his choice of
friends, activities, and interests. In some cases this intrusive treatment
affects the child to the extent of determining completely what the child
says, does, wears and expresses, so that the child ends up having no
preferences, feelings, or opinions of his own. How then can he possibly be himself?

Constitutional factors

The last category of factors in the development of narcissism is not
an external environmental factor, but has to do with the state of the
body and its effect on the development of the self. The infant might
be born with a body or nervous system damaged or imbalanced in
some way. For instance, in the last decade research has revealed that
some emotional difficulties are due to chemical imbalance.

The following passage discusses some of these findings in relation
to aggression:

> The events of 'fetal androgenization' of the mammalian
> brain—and indeed, also the mammalian body . . . fall in the
> subcategory of embryogenesis; they show that the tendency
> to aggression in adulthood is influenced by the amount of
> testosterone circulating in early life (before birth in monkeys,
> just after birth in rats), and, furthermore, that this effect is

almost certainly the result of long-lasting changes in the brain.
(Konner, 1982, p. 195)

This well-researched book discusses the biological underpinnings of other emotions: fear, joy, lust, love, grief, and gluttony.

Biological factors have been documented in relation to the propensity toward anxiety and depression. Chronic difficult emotional states may contribute to the development of narcissism because such painful affects, some of which the parents may not be able to remedy at all, might make it difficult for the child to stay deeply in touch with himself. We cannot discuss this factor in any detail because we do not have much experience of it.

Some depth psychologists believe that congenital predispositions to some affects, such as rage, may predispose an individual towards narcissistic manifestations. Kernberg writes:

> These patients present a pathologically augmented development of oral aggression and it is hard to evaluate to what extent this development represents a constitutionally determined strong aggressive drive, a constitutionally determined lack of anxiety tolerance in regard to aggressive impulses, or severe frustration in their first years of life. (Kernberg, 1975, p. 234)

This is an interesting proposition, but we have no evidence for or against it; Kernberg is pointing here to severe cases of narcissistic disturbance, a class of individuals with whom we have no experience. We include this category of factors in the development of narcissism for completeness.

Another situation, which is not necessarily a constitutional factor but which may have similar effects, is the occurrence of sickness or disability in early childhood, especially at the time when the sense of self is developing. This can be seen as an environmental factor if we take the body to be the specific environment. The child is bound to experience the chronic or transient loss or disability of a body part as a narcissistic insult. The body, with its organs and functions, is the prototypical selfobject. Any significant physical disturbance is bound to create a sense of loss of support. Even though the support lost is physical—for instance with the loss of an eye, or the functioning of

202   limbs, since the young child does not differentiate self into physical and mental, the sense of being oneself may become undermined. Of course, how the parents handle the situation is paramount here. The loss or limitation of mental functions may also affect the child's sense of identity, again depending on how the situation is treated by the parents.

chapter 19

The Process of
the Development
of Narcissism

————————————————————————————————•

We can now summarize our view of the way in which narcissism develops. The general thrust of our understanding is similar to the perspective of the Jungian analyst, Schwartz-Salant: "In terms of Jung's approach to the psyche... it would be the rejection of the Self, the failure to live one's true pattern, that leads to what we now call the narcissistic character disorder." (Schwartz-Salant, 1982, p. 23) In this view, narcissism is the result of not becoming what we are meant to be. The Jungian view of one's "true pattern" is not the same as the Kohutian view of the "nuclear program." The "true pattern" of the self refers to the intrinsic possibilities one is born with. It is considered a reflection of an archetypal reality. This concept corresponds to our view that the soul has a "blueprint," analogous to the DNA in the cell nucleus, which shapes the pattern of development. Kohut's "nuclear program" is a pattern that is set in early childhood, constituting one's earliest and most archaic ambitions and ideals.

Kohut writes:

> It seems very likely, for example, that, while traces of both
> ambitions and idealized goals are beginning to be acquired
> side by side in early infancy, the bulk of nuclear grandiosity

consolidates into nuclear ambitions in early childhood (perhaps mainly in the second, third and fourth year), and the
bulk of nuclear idealized goal structures are acquired in later
childhood (perhaps mainly in the fourth, fifth and sixth years
of life). (Kohut, 1977, p. 179)

From the point of view of the development of the soul as the unfolding of a true pattern or blueprint, narcissism results from disturbances
of the unfoldment of a person's intrinsic pattern, as well as the dissociation of this unfoldment from the essential ground and nature of
the self.

This inner core of the self transforms constantly, manifesting in the
qualities, and their functions, needed for the self in its moment-to-
moment experience, and for its overall development. The unfolding
of the inherent qualities of the self is intimately linked with the maturation of the various psychic and physical capacities of the self. These
processes form a unified process of transformation and development,
which bifurcates as the self becomes alienated from Essence.

Essential presence unfolds in forms that largely coincide with the
phases of ego development discussed in Chapter 3. How much the
child manifests a particular quality in each of the developmental phases,
and how much she integrates it into her experience of self, depends
on the factors affecting the development of narcissism presented in
the last few chapters. Some children are fortunate enough to manifest
these essential qualities throughout the crucial early stages of development. Some are less fortunate; their situation allows them to stay in
touch with their essential nature only in the earliest phases of their
development. The child who grows up with a "normal" self usually
falls between these two extremes, where the developing structuralization of the self is accompanied by a gradual alienation from the essential core. The healthier her development, the more contact with her
essential nature she retains.

To summarize the process which we have described: For the normal self, the final result of development is the formation of the sense
of self with two major components, those of entity and identity. This
development of structures is concurrent with gradual alienation from
essential presence. This alienation is reflected in the identity structure

in its feeling of identity. Narcissism is, then, the result of the development of this identity. The identity depends for its cohesion, stability, and strength, on the completeness and realism of its underlying structure, which is a major substructure of the self. This, in turn, depends on the distance of this identity from the essential core, which is determined by the overall effect of all the factors causing narcissism. The various environmental factors influence the child not only by alienating her from the depths of her self, but also through becoming integrated into the developing structure of the self, thus determining her identity. A normal person's identity is weak, distorted and incomplete because it excludes much of her potential.

The severity of narcissism depends not only on the extent of alienation from the essential presence in general, but also, and more specifically, on the extent of alienation from the Essential Identity. It is easy to see this in a very simple way. The Essential Identity is the factor responsible for the initial feeling of identity, that makes it possible for the child to develop and integrate the normal sense of identity. More specifically, the normal feeling of identity is based on memories of the original pure feeling of identity characterizing the experience of the Essential Identity. This means that the child's final integration of this sense of identity will depend in part on the degree to which she experienced the Essential Identity in terms of frequency, duration, and depth.

The alienation from Essence begins at least from the time of inception of psychic structures for, as we have discussed, these structures become established by the development of self-representations that pattern the experience of the self. Experiencing the self through representations is antithetical to direct experience of essential presence. The specific loss of identity with Essence—which is the fundamental root of narcissism—is the alienation from the Essential Identity. This particular alienation is the cause of central narcissism in particular.

The capacity that is lost when identity with the Essential Identity is lost is the ability to experience oneself as the forms of essential presence. It is in the nature of the soul to become identified with any content, and it is natural that the soul's experience is open to experiencing identity with essential presence. But identification with mental structures precludes this experience.

206   Indeed, even though the Essential Identity is the identity of Essence, it is actually what makes it possible for the child to establish self-representations, for it provides her with the capacity to experience herself as a differentiated existence with its own sense of identity. As we discussed in Chapter 14, these self-representations are associated with an original sense of self, which the Essential Identity provides.[24]

The Essential Identity is the specific essential form that functions as the true self in the period roughly analogous to that of the practicing phase of Mahler's separation-individuation process. Thus, this period in the child's early life stands out as the specific developmental phase for the genetic development of central narcissism, and because this form of narcissism is the one underlying the basic well-known features of narcissism, their genetic phase is also the practicing period.

There is almost universal agreement in depth psychology that the practicing period is the most central developmental phase for the development of narcissistic disturbance. Kohut writes:

> The narcissistic transferences are therapeutic activations of developmental phases which probably correspond predominantly to the transitional period between a late part of the stage of symbiosis and an early part of the stages of individuation in Mahler's sense. (Kohut, 1971, p. 220)

Mahler recognizes the central importance of the practicing period for narcissism, although she sees that the other stages contribute:

> The autonomous achievements of the practicing subphase are the main source of narcissistic enhancement from within. Most infant-toddlers of the practicing stage show three contributories to narcissism at their peak. These are (in an exaggerated way and in individually different proportions): self-love, primitive valuation of their accomplishments, and omnipotence. (Hartocollis, 1977, p. 73)

As the above quotations clearly demonstrate, however, there is no clear explanation of the association of narcissism with the practicing period. Our view is that it is because the Essential Identity dominates as the true self in the practicing period.

chapter 20

The Truth of the Grandiose Self

———————————————————— •

M any psychologists consider the grandiose self the most characteristic element of narcissistic disturbance.[25] Our view offers an explanation of the genesis and the significance of this characteristic.

Mahler's observational studies demonstrated that during the practicing period, the child behaves as if she is all-powerful, all-knowing, and completely wonderful. She has much less fear of separation, a greater sense of autonomy and adventure, and a kind of blindness about her limitations, both physical and mental. Mahler describes the child's inflated sense of ability and fearless adventure as the attitude of relating to the world as if it is "the junior toddler's oyster." (Mahler, 1975, p. 271) She falls and stumbles, but she picks herself up, full of enthusiasm and confidence. She makes great strides in maturation and development. Adults can see that her sense of confidence and ability is unrealistic, for she is still quite limited physically and mentally, and is still very much in need of the parent's care and protection. For this reason, Mahler concludes that children are delusional and grandiose about their abilities in this phase.

We can, however, understand this sense of grandeur and omnipotence differently when we realize what it feels like to be the Essential

Identity. The Essential Identity fills the consciousness with a special kind of preciousness and with a sense of omnipotence and omniscience. We feel that we are completely wonderful, completely able, and totally indestructible. We feel all-loving, all-knowing, and all-powerful. There is a sense of completeness and totality. When students come upon the experience of the Essential Identity, these qualities are always present, as we saw in James's report in Chapter 13, when he says:

> *I became aware of a presence like a point of concentration in my head. It felt just like a point, no dimension to it, but seemed inde-structible; there was no question of it being destroyed or altered by anything outside.*

These characteristics are actually true of the Essential Identity. We presented in previous chapters only those qualities relevant for our discussion, but this aspect has many other qualities. It is an indestructible source of pure love and awareness. It cannot be touched, cannot be hurt, and cannot be marred. The late Indian teacher of self-realization, Sri Nisargadatta Maharaj, describes the Essential Identity like this:

> When you realize yourself as less than a point in space and time, something too small to be cut and too short-lived to be killed, then, and then only, all fear goes. When you are smaller than the point of the needle, then the needle cannot pierce you—you pierce the needle! (Nisargadatta, 1982, p. 464)

When we are self-realized we have these characteristics on the Being level. They are well known within various spiritual traditions. When the Essential Identity arises in the practicing period, the child feels these grand qualities. However, as we have discussed, she is not consciously aware that she is being the Essential Identity, so her realization is different from the mature self-realization of an adult. She *is* the Essential Identity completely and nondualistically, but at the same time she is dualistically aware of her body-mind. So she believes that these characteristics of her true self are the properties of her mind and body.

On the Being level, the Essential Identity has no limitations, since the identity is directly in touch with the timeless, vast, ontological ground of being; but because she is experiencing these qualities intuitively while aware of the body-mind objectively, the child comes to believe that her body and mind have no limitations, which is obviously a delusion.[26] *The* *delusion is not the feelings and attitudes of grandeur and omnipotence, for these are the actual feelings of the Self of Being. The delusion is in attributing them to the body-mind.* The limitless qualities become grandiose when attributed to the body and the mind. The child's imperviousness to hurt is an expression of her identity with the Essential Identity of Being. It takes her a long time to become aware that these feelings of grandeur and omnipotence are false, in the sense that they are not true about her body and mind. When this happens, she is thoroughly disappointed and deflated. This usually occurs at the beginning of rapprochement, the third subphase of the separation-individuation process. This is the big fall, the realization of limitation and dependency. Mahler writes about the child, in the beginning of this subphase, at the middle of the second year of life.

> However, side by side with the growth of his cognitive faculties and the increasing differentiation of his emotional life, there is also a noticeable waning of his previous imperviousness to frustration, as well as a diminution of what has been a relative obliviousness to his mother's presence. (Mahler, 1975, p. 76)

The child also becomes aware that her wishes are not always identical to those of her mother, which juncture marks the beginning of the loss of the omnipotence of the dual unity.

> This realization greatly challenged the feeling of grandeur and omnipotence of the practicing period, when the little girl had felt 'on top of the world' (Mahler, 1966b). What a blow to the hitherto fully believed omnipotence; what a disturbance to the bliss of the dual unity! (Mahler, 1975, p. 90)

Here, at the end of the practicing period and at the beginning of rapprochement, both the dual unity and the sense of grandeur and omnipotence are lost, as a result of the maturation of the child's cognitive and perceptive faculties in conjunction with increasing identification with the body-mind. Dealing with this colossal disappointment becomes the task of the rapprochement subphase and an important fulcrum in the development of the child's self.

210   Since the child lacks discriminated awareness of her Essential Identity, she does not understand that it is this identity that is truly grand and in a sense all-powerful, but her physical-emotional-mental self is not. She never learns that she is more than the psychosomatic organism. This situation has far-reaching consequences. One of these is that the perception of vulnerability, limitation, and dependency, without the ability to discriminate these from the experience of the Essential Identity, leads to the abandonment of identity with the latter. The child loses her nonconscious self-realization. She pushes away the sense of grandeur and omnipotence because she feels it is not true, and in the process, she pushes away her Essential Identity.

The significance of this step cannot be appreciated until we are deeply involved in the process of self-realization. We know the extent of the loss in childhood only when we consciously regain the Essential Identity.

The practical consequence of the shift from the Essential Identity to identification with the body-mind is that the child becomes more realistic about her physical and mental capacities, which is necessary for both survival and normal life. She is now especially aware of her body, its feelings and sensations, its abilities and its image. By the end of the practicing period and during the rapprochement subphase, we begin to see "the baby's taking possession of his own body and protecting it against being handled as a passive object by the mother." (Mahler, 1975, p. 222)

The important point for our present discussion is that the feelings of omnipotence and lack of limitation are not delusional in the way psychologists like Mahler and Kohut believe. Also, contrary to what Kernberg believes, these feelings are part of the normal development of the self, and hence, are not originally defensive. However, this does not mean that we agree with Kohut's view of the grandiose self and disagree with that of Kernberg. The situation is not so simple. First, we do not believe that the original feelings of omnipotence are delusional; they are a normal part of the experience of the self in the practicing period. In fact, the child's feelings of omnipotence reflect a truth more fundamental than what the ordinary individual feels to be real. They reflect the child's contact with her essential nature, which the normal

adult self has forgotten. The self develops from a base of truth, and not   211
delusion, although this truth is so deep that the normal adult self cannot conceive of it.

What is the relationship of the grandiose self to the Essential Identity?

What Kohut and others call the grandiose self is actually the Essential
Identity, or more accurately, the condition of the soul as it is patterned
by the Essential Identity in the practicing period. We hasten to clarify
that this normal grandiose self of the practicing period is not the same
as the grandiose self of the narcissistic adult. The latter is a psychic
structure, not an essential presence. So where does the narcissistic
grandiose self come from? It is an imitation of the Essential Identity,
a fake "shell" which develops around the end of the practicing period
and the beginning of the rapprochement subphase.

In the development of narcissism, the child does not let go of the
sense of omnipotence at the end of the practicing subphase and the
beginning of the rapprochement phase, but holds on to it as her primary identification. More accurately, her self-representations include
the sense of omnipotence and specialness of the Essential Identity. For
the normal person, the self-representations regarding the capacity of
the body-mind become more realistic as the child's increasing awareness of limitation and identification with the body and mind develop.
However, when the sense of vulnerability that arises from the perception of separateness and limitation is too difficult to tolerate, the child
resorts to various defensive maneuvers such as retaining the sense of
omnipotence as part of the central self-representation. She denies its
falsehood with respect to her mind and body and ends up believing
that the omnipotence is truly characteristic of her bodily-mental self.
(See *The Pearl Beyond Price* [Almaas, 1988], Chapter 30, for other
defensive maneuvers at this juncture of development.) So the magical
omnipotence, which was not only developmentally normal at the practicing subphase, but also an authentic characteristic of her true self at
this stage, becomes a grandiose belief. The more severe is the denied
vulnerability, the greater is the dominance of the grandiose self in the
developing sense of self, and the more narcissistic is the individual.

212   This understanding clarifies several points. First, the grandiose self is not the Essential Identity, but a self-representation based on it. Second, it is based on a normal developmental experience of the self; in other words, it can be seen as a fixation on, or a regression to, a normal developmental stage. This view is similar to Kohut's. Third, it is a psychic structure that functions, especially in the narcissistic personality, mostly as a defense against intolerable affect. This view is similar to Kernberg's.

Thus, we see that the grandiose self of the narcissistic individual is both a fixation on an early stage of development and a defense against deep narcissistic vulnerability. Hence, our understanding of the grandiose self implies that both Kohut and Kernberg are correct in their views of the grandiose self and that there is no contradiction between these two views. Both fixation and defense are important fulcrums for the development of narcissism. This is not the whole story, however.

The developed self is holding on to feelings and qualities that once were part of a normal developmental phase. The psychic structure captures what it can of the experience of the true self at that developmental phase. This is how any psychic structure develops. Our description so far differs from Kohut's view of the grandiose self in two respects. First, in his later version of the psychology of the self, the grandiose self of childhood is not based on real feelings. In his first version of the psychology of the self, he considers it a remnant of primary narcissism; the child tries to retain the bliss and power of primary narcissism by imagining that she is omnipotent. This is similar to our view of the narcissistic adult grandiose self, except that Kohut takes the origin to be the stage of primary narcissism. Actually, the Essential Identity is an element of the primal self in the stage of primary narcissism, but in the experience of the primal self (the unstructured soul), it is not differentiated. The primal self does not distinguish between surface and core, between self and identity, or between self and object. This discrimination has to wait until the differentiation subphase of the separation-individuation process makes it possible for the self to tolerate the presence of the Essential Identity in a sustained manner. The Essential Identity has characteristics similar to those of the primal self, but it is a much more differentiated and definite sense of identity. So it is possible for us to accept Kohut's first version of the origins of the 213 grandiose self of childhood if we remember that it is a real presence and not an image in the child's imagination.

Kohut does not explain the grandiose self in his second version of the psychology of the self, except to say that it is a normal element of the self at a particular developmental stage. In his later theory he regards the grandiose self as a fixation on an early, but developmentally normal, unrealistic sense of self. In this view, the child's sense of omnipotence is delusional. However, our understanding of the truth of the grandiose self makes sense of the fact that this particular phenomenon arises in the first place. For an infant to produce an experience of omnipotence and specialness as a defense against vulnerability or helplessness seems less likely than, for instance, producing a schizoid defense of shutting down one's openness in response to the fear of lack of support or rejection. Where could this sense of omnipotence come from in a completely helpless human infant? We have described how knowing oneself as the Essential Identity brings about the sense that one has qualities of vast potential, uniqueness and grandeur normally attributed to the grandiose self, but without the delusions about one's human limitations.

The second respect in which our view of the grandiose self differs from that of Kohut has to do with his view that the adult grandiose self is an arrested development of the childhood grandiose self. First, we need to see that it is not the Essential Identity which is fixated, but some of its qualities. The Essential Identity itself cannot be fixated because it is not a discriminated representation. So the grandiose psychic structure is a fixation not on the presence itself, but on some of the affects characterizing this presence. Kohut's view implies that one continues to experience the same grandiose self from childhood through the adult years, although frequently unconsciously. However, if we accept the premise that the source of the omnipotent and special feelings is the reality of the Essential Identity, then we see that the grandiose self is not exactly a case of arrested development, but of a shift in identity from the Essential Identity to a structure that remembers and tries to imitate some aspects of that Self. More accurately, the grandiose self is a fixation on this shift.

214   We can also contrast our perspective on the grandiose self with that of Kernberg. Although we agree that the narcissistic grandiose self is a psychic structure that defends against intolerable narcissistic vulnerabilities, we question his understanding that the grandiose self is constructed by integrating disparate images, namely those of actual and ideal self-images, and actual and ideal object-images. This would mean it is not a representation of something that the child actually experienced, nor a reflection of an actual state of the self at any stage of development, but a completely fabricated image of something imaginary that never existed. This is in marked contrast to our view that although the narcissistic grandiose self is a structure, and although it is defensive, it nevertheless reflects an actual early experience of the self.

Kernberg's view that the grandiose self is constructed through a refusion of already differentiated representations is not easy to contrast with our view. It takes us to subtle levels of observing different developmental stages. The grandiose self integrates the sense of limitlessness and power of the presence of Being from several developmental stages, specifically, from the essential qualities of self in primary narcissism and central narcissism. This structure tries to capture some of the qualities not only of the Essential Identity, but also, and significantly for Kernberg's formulation, qualities of the primal self. This means that the narcissistic individual's grandiose self includes nondifferentiated components, because the primal self is in a nondifferentiated state of existence. We are then dealing not only with central narcissism but also, and perhaps more predominantly, with disturbances to primary narcissism, namely, oral narcissism. We have noted (see Chapter 4) that this form of narcissism seems to be the focus of Kernberg's formulations. In any case, our understanding is that the grandiose self that is a defense against the vulnerabilities of oral narcissism is most likely based on the primal self, and hence, a representation of some of the qualities of an actual felt state of the self in its earliest stages of development. So it is a fixation at, or a regression to, an actual developmental stage, although it is a defensive structure.

With regard to the defensive function of the grandiose self, Kernberg's formulation is more relevant to the borderline structures, for there is

more deficiency, a greater tendency towards disintegration, and hence   215
more need to defend against such vulnerabilities.

We have observed the pattern of a defensive grandiose structure based on the primal (undifferentiated) self in individuals with more borderline structures. For example, when such persons approach spiritual work they tend to idealize, and may experience easily, states which involve merging with an idealized object, loss of the normal sense of ego boundaries, experiences of unity, and so on. However, our work with normal individuals confirms our perspective that the Essential Identity is the primary origin of the grandiose self.

These similarities and differences between our view of the grandiose self and those of Kohut and Kernberg have important implications for our approach to the process of working through narcissism. We must address the defensiveness of the grandiose self, while taking into consideration that it is a fixation on nondefensive feelings the individual actually felt as a young child. The defensiveness of the grandiose self needs to be allowed to unfold in the working relationship with the teacher, as Kohut recommends, while interpreting and understanding its defensive nature. The student needs empathic understanding of the truth within the grandiose self, not rejection of it as completely groundless. In fact, she needs to arrive at the understanding, or even the memory, of the grandiose stance as reflecting authentic feelings, which she came to use for defensive purposes. Not interpreting the feelings of omnipotence as delusional, although they are by now defensive, may give her the opportunity to see that these feelings represent an authentic childhood state. When she can see their delusional element, she might then appreciate their real source, the Essential Identity. This latter insight often precipitates the experience of the Essential Identity.

chapter 21

The Phases of
the Development of
Narcissism

•———————————————————————————

The process of alienation from the essential presence and identity goes through several phases before culminating in the formation of the self-structure and its identity. We can relate these phases to the various levels of narcissistic disturbance, or to various emotional disruptions due to alienation from Being. They are not necessarily phases in terms of time sequence; rather they are the vicissitudes of the narcissistic alienation that one finds in different experiential levels. The relationship between the various phases is basically psychodynamic, and only sometimes genetic. We call them phases because we encounter them in a sequence as we move from the normal sense of identity to that of the Essential Identity. In our work of self-realization, one moves through several states and manifestations of the self as one penetrates the sense of identity and moves deeper into the experience of the self, until one arrives at essential presence.

The narcissistic constellation

We will present this group of states and experiences in the reverse order from the sequence one encounters in the process of working through narcissism, assuming that this reverse order is the order in which these states arise in the process of alienation. We call this group of states, conditions, and structures of the self, "the narcissistic constellation."

1. The disconnection of the self from its essential presence manifests as a profound and deep wound to the self. It is as if the very core of the self is yanked out from within it. This is the specific narcissistic wound, the hurt that expresses the pain of this fundamental loss, and reflects the actual state of loss. All of the factors which contribute to narcissism, compounded by the self turning away from its connection with essential presence, lead to this narcissistic wound. Centrally, the narcissistic wound is caused by the decathexis of the Essential Identity.

2. Alienation from the Essential Identity leads to the loss of the profound sense of value and preciousness intrinsic to the sense of one's identity with Being. Value is a quality of Being which, when lost, leads to a loss of self-esteem. When we are in touch with Being, self-esteem is experienced as an intrinsic feature of the self, as part of one's inalienable human inheritance. The wound of the loss of value is intimately associated with the narcissistic wound.

3. The alienation from the Essential Identity results in narcissistic emptiness. This feels like a deficient emptiness, the specific deficiency being the feeling of absence of the sense of self. It is the loss of identity. Instead of clear and definite self-recognition, the person feels an emptiness, a phenomenological nothingness, with an accompanying sense of no identity. She feels that her self is missing. This deficient emptiness makes her feel lost, with no center, no orientation, no purpose, no meaning.

   A typical reaction to this deficient emptiness comes in the form of superego attacks. One feels one is worthless, not important, not good enough, or perhaps fake. The deficient emptiness is the feeling of having no self, which can feel like a lack of center or orientation. When this emptiness is arising, superego reactions—self-attacks, such as feeling one is worthless, not important, or not good enough— might arise as resistances to directly experiencing the deficiency. These reactions are partly due to disconnection from the value of Being. A healthy reaction at this point might be the sense of remorse of conscience, for failing to be authentic.

218   4. The emptiness and the wound make up one structure, the emptiness-wound. The emptiness and the wound are intertwined elements of narcissistic alienation. The emptiness-wound is where the hurt and vulnerability are felt. In experiencing the lack of all other aspects of Essence, one generally experiences both the emptiness and the hurt about its lack or loss, but emptiness and hurt are experienced separately. Only in the loss of contact with the Essential Identity does one experience the hurt and emptiness inseparable from each other, as two elements of the same felt state.

5. Reactions to this injury include narcissistic rage, envy, and depression. The rage has specific narcissistic features, such as lack of empathy and a sense of entitlement. These affects have a function in the overall narcissistic development, which we will discuss later.

6. The narcissistic injury, that is, the emptiness-wound and its various associated affects and reactions, is covered over by the self-identity, through the identification with self-images and their associated affects. The overall structure of self-identity is sometimes experienced as a shell around the deficient emptiness. This shows very clearly that the experience of being an empty shell—which is reported frequently by individuals suffering from narcissism—refers to the psychic structure of self-identity, and that the emptiness inside this shell is the direct consequence of the alienation from the Essential Identity.

7. One does not usually experience the shell directly as a shell; if she did, she would be aware of the deficient emptiness. The more she becomes aware of the truth of her identity, the more likely she will become aware that she is a shell, and the more aware she will become of the emptiness. The usual experience of what we are calling the shell is the sense of self characterized by a specific feeling of identity. Because of the normal feeling of identity, the ordinary individual is not directly aware of her fundamental narcissism. As she becomes aware of her fundamental narcissism, she will recognize that her feeling of identity is based on a structure which she can perceive directly as an empty shell. This will usually make her feel phony or fake.

8. The more narcissistic the person, in other words, the greater the distance from the Essential Identity—indicating greater narcissistic injury in childhood—the more her identity is based on the grandiose self.

We call the totality of the self-images the shell, because the sense of being a shell-like structure surrounding an empty space is a very common way that people experience the normal identity as it becomes conscious. Normally, of course, this structure is unconscious; one doesn't experience the shell as a shell, one simply experiences a sense of identity. For most people, this shell is not a grandiose self; it's just a sense of identity. For the narcissistic personality, the sense of identity is a grandiose self because the grandiose component self-representations dominate the sense of identity.

However, we must not forget that the shell is nothing but the soul itself, the actual self identifying itself through representations and hence patterning itself according to past experiences. It is the self structuring itself largely according to the parts of itself recognized and related to by the parents, and the environment in general. The empty shell results when the consciousness disavows the core of the self and identifies with the surface of who it is.

We present now a report from a student, Natalie R., of some work she did with the author in a group setting, as part of her work of dealing with the narcissistic sector of her personality, in which she was intensely engaged for some time. The report is general, but elucidates in a personal way the main points we have been discussing. She writes:

Saturday night I worked with you on the conflicts around my narcissistic needs. The more I communicate to others about myself, and the work I do here, feelings of deep hurt, anger and hatred arise. I feel misunderstood and unappreciated by others. Insecurity comes when I sense that my presence brings up issues and emptiness for them. There is a feeling of unsupportedness in my identity, so I compensate with grandiose thoughts and internalized surges of rage and righteous indignation. I resist the feeling of insignificance. I want my point to shine in the sky in a special way. I don't want to have to be fake in order to get recognition. I'm deeply hurt by others' insensitivity to my feelings, as

I perceive it. I felt deeply saddened that my parents didn't recognize what was real in me. All my life it was as though I've been trying to prove my value to them. I felt sad that at times I've used the work and all its knowledge to gain value.

By the end of our interaction I felt peaceful, with the ordinariness characteristic of the perspective of our work. The hurt lingers as I sense how desperately I wanted and continue to want appreciation for just being. The compassion for myself begins to heal this wound.

Natalie's work is typical of many students working through these narcissistic issues. Understanding one's patterns and becoming aware of the painful affects associated with them typically brings compassion for oneself, which gives one the capacity to tolerate the feelings around the wound, rather than avoiding them by acting out defensive feelings and strategies.

PART 2

ESSENCE AND NARCISSISTIC TRANSFERENCES

At this point we begin to describe the work on self-realization: the actual steps of the process of working through the narcissistic constellations and the full realization of essential presence. The method is what we described in the introduction as the Diamond Approach^SM. Although most of our understanding comes from the experience of those who have pursued this particular spiritual path, it does appear that those on other paths face many of the same issues and barriers that we explore in this segment of our book. However, in the absence of sustained exploration of psychological issues, practitioners in various spiritual traditions may not face these barriers with conscious understanding. They may attribute them to other factors in their lives or act them out unconsciously. Barriers to deeper experience may be penetrated by spiritual practice, but for most practitioners there remains a gap between the deeper experience and the day-to-day identity. For some few, this gap may be closed when certain very deep realizations are achieved. The material

222   we present here is a contribution to understanding the barriers to self-realization encountered by all practitioners and students of spiritual development.

The Diamond Approach[SM] is a process of experiential inquiry into the self, inviting the self to reveal its truth as a direct living understanding. At some point the inquiry begins to focus naturally on the self-identity structure of the self. For the majority of students, the truth that reveals itself at the beginning is the psychological truth of this ego structure, the psychodynamic processes that express and sustain it, and the personal history that went into its development. This confronts the student with awareness of the environmental factors that caused her narcissism, leading to the challenge and dissolution of the many levels of defense and rigidity in this structure. The inquiry proceeds further into the fundamental factors causing her narcissism. For a long time, she finds the environmental and fundamental factors linked together in a complex, but ultimately comprehensible, manner.

We can see the psychodynamic aspect of the work that leads to the realization of the Essential Identity as a regression, or as the retracing of the process of the loss of this self and the development of the shell, as we discussed in the last chapter. The process generally follows the previously mentioned phases in the reverse order. Frequently, this entails psychological regression, but not always. Therefore, our discussion will follow this reverse order, exploring at the outset the first narcissistic manifestations students generally encounter, and going deeper as we traverse the above steps backward. From this point, the movement of our exploration will be a direct penetration of the narcissistic constellation, moving from the surface to the depth.

Sometimes it is possible for a person to penetrate to the emptiness, or to the Essential Identity itself, without working through the surface layers, like the shell. Such a person has not generally dealt with the narcissistic issues, but has managed to penetrate the surface layers. In most circumstances, the surface layers will reassert themselves, and she will have to deal with them in order to stabilize and integrate the condition of self-realization. Often, individuals who engage deeply in a spiritual practice end up experiencing the emptiness without knowing how to deal with it, or they might experience the Essential Identity

without understanding its relation to their psychological experience.   223
In these cases, the narcissism will generally remain untouched.

To truly deal with the narcissistic issues one must go through the shell in a very specific way. It is not enough to experience only the narcissistic emptiness; understanding the shell is an important part of the process of understanding and working through the narcissistic constellation. The most important part of this work, the part where a school and a teacher are almost indispensable, is that of exposing to consciousness the narcissistic situation. Most people are not aware of the narcissistic nature of many of their expressions; in fact, they resist such awareness. The student needs to experience directly that her sense of identity is not real, that what she takes to be her identity is really nothing but an empty shell. Most people do not have this awareness; they walk around taking their normal sense of self to be real, that it is who they truly are. They do not question their normal sense of self in the conventional dimension of experience. So a major body of work, which in some sense begins the whole process, involves inquiries and practices which lead to the realization that what one is taking oneself to be is not the real thing, but an empty thing. When a person arrives at this understanding the process begins.

chapter 22

Meaninglessness and the Flame

I n the work of self-realization, the first and most important part of working on the narcissistic constellation involves exposing the shell. This means realizing directly that what we take ourselves to be is not real, that it is an empty shell, a facade constructed from images and identifications. For most students in our work, this happens completely naturally, in the course of self-exploration. It is not necessary for the teacher to introduce or create these perceptions. Simply by exploring our continuing experience of ourselves and inquiring into its meaning and truth, we come to see that what we take to be our identity is actually an empty mental construct.

One of the main ways a person arrives at this understanding is through maturation of the well-integrated self. Maturing through a life lived with a competent ego integrating one's experience, we are likely to experience some relaxation of the defensive ego structures. With the relaxation of these structures, we may then become aware of a sense of emptiness and meaninglessness, a sense that our life is pointless. This may happen, for example, when we live our lives according to our ambitions and ideals and actually complete our inner program. We can then relax and we can afford to be flexible in our positions and

attitudes. This entails letting go of some of our defensive positions.   225
Also, accomplishing our goals may give us a sense of inner value and
felt wisdom, but the deepening of this wisdom will eventually require
a transformation of identity. Frequently, an individual who has arrived
at this awareness through maturity becomes interested in the deeper
aspects of existence and seeks answers in philosophy, religion, or spiritual practice. This natural process is frequently what begins the inner
search, especially in a well-integrated ego. It is the proverbial midlife
crisis, although often, of course, the quest leads one to seek meaning
in external life or activities.

Meaninglessness

It is important to understand this significant juncture in the maturation of the normal self for what it is: a spiritual juncture. The sense
of meaninglessness, pointlessness, and emptiness in one's life is not due
to being in the wrong life situation, like the wrong job or marriage.
The soul is becoming aware of its inner existential emptiness. Changing
external life situations will genuinely relieve our inner emptiness only
if this change is part of a larger and deeper change. Recognizing that
this meaninglessness and emptiness are actually expressions of the lack
of self-realization makes it possible to begin looking in the right direction, so to speak: to begin one's inner search for deeper truth.

Various religious or spiritual ideas, therapeutic approaches which
"explain" one's emptiness as a lack of gratification in one's history or
relationships—or even more external factors such as new work projects, new relationships, even new possessions—are all too available to
fill the hole of meaning in a person's life. But if this emptiness is filled,
even with notions of spirituality, it is not possible to penetrate the emptiness and become available to the arising of one's true nature. In our
work, we approach this—as all questions—with open-ended inquiry,
in which the student is invited to investigate his feelings to discover
their truth within his personal experience. The teacher guides him only
to inquire sincerely and points out his assumptions and defenses regarding his self-awareness. A certain understanding informs this approach:
We observe that with an inquiring, empathic but noninterfering support, the individual will move naturally and spontaneously towards the

226   truth of his experience. This allows the meaninglessness, and its underlying emptiness, to become more conscious, revealing that the emptiness is in his self, and not in those external situations.

At this stage, the student experiences the emptiness not directly and phenomenologically, but more metaphorically and existentially, as a general, sometimes vague, sense that life lacks meaning. Many existentialist writings about meaninglessness and emptiness are based on this general sense of pointlessness. This feeling is a vague recognition of the emptiness underlying our sense of self and identity. Our narcissistic emptiness is partly revealed by the gradual relaxation of the shell, but is still veiled by some identification with that shell. The sense of meaninglessness characterizing the mid-life crisis, then, is an expression of one's underlying narcissistic emptiness, which is manifesting gradually as our external sources of meaning, and our plans and ambitions, are wearing out their usefulness.

This sense that one's life is meaningless is related to the boredom and loss of excitement and value that the individual with a narcissistic personality constantly experiences in his various relationships and activities. Writers on narcissism have noted that the experience of meaninglessness is common in very narcissistic people. Narcissistic emptiness underlies the identity of both the normal and the pathologically narcissistic individual, but for the latter the shell has developed inadequately, and hence is vulnerable and brittle. In both cases, this emptiness reveals itself when one's life situations are not sustaining the narcissistic shell. Although the very brittle narcissistic shell crumbles easily and thus frequently, the normal individual's more firm, cohesive, and realistic shell can sustain much more narcissistic loss. Thus he can live his life believing in the reality of his identity until his sources of narcissistic supplies finally wear out. The wisdom accumulated in the course of living his life also contributes to making the shell more transparent, revealing its emptiness and ushering in a sense of meaninglessness.

Why does the narcissistic emptiness manifest as meaninglessness? Meaninglessness is absence of meaning, but in this case meaning is not a matter of something we tell ourselves; it is not a conceptual meaning, or a story about our lives. Our story about our lives, and our iden-

tification with our history, will actually feel meaningless when this   227
issue is arising. The meaning that is missing is a sense of experiential
significance, a sense of profundity and substance in our experience, a
sense of the value of our existence and activities. The experience of the
Essential Identity clearly involves such a sense of meaning.

The point of existence

Self-realization fulfills the meaning of our lives. The true significance of all experience is the essential presence. The point of existence
is the Essential Identity. It is profoundly significant that the Essential
Identity is experienced directly as a brilliant point of presence, a point
of Being, which is true existence. We can say, then, that meaninglessness is pointlessness, and the feeling of pointlessness is an indirect
awareness of the absence of the essential point, the Essential Identity.

When we feel that there is an essential point missing in our experience, without which our existence and life are pointless and meaningless, we might interpret this absence metaphorically. But it is actually
a literal experience of our existential condition. The sense of meaningfulness does not define self-realization, nor does such realization
give us a conceptual picture that we can then identify as the meaning
of life. Self-realization effaces the feeling of meaninglessness by eliminating the alienation from our spiritual core.

In ordinary perception, one might experience the absence of presence, but interpret it as meaninglessness because he does not know
what presence is, or even that there is such a thing. He interprets the
absence from within his known world, in this case as meaninglessness.[27]

The flame

Experiencing meaninglessness without attributing it to our external
life situation confronts us with the fact that we do not know what it is
really about. We feel it, without completely knowing the truth of it. If
we have the support to not resort to incomplete and indirect explanations and avoidances, and the curiosity to inquire into our experience,
we will be able to stay with the sense of meaninglessness, especially if
we feel a deep aspiration to uncover its truth. Our curiosity about, and
interest in, finding out firsthand about the truth of our experience can

228   become a burning, even a passionate question. This is the inner spiritual inspiration, the true motive behind the spiritual quest, the search for meaning, which is actually the search for the essence of the self.

To pursue this search, we need to be interested in the truth of our experience, unhampered by biases about what this truth might be, or even in which direction to look for it. When we sincerely desire to know the truth, we feel that our soul is on fire. We become an aspiring flame, a burning question mark. We aspire towards the truth without mentally knowing what we are searching for. This flame of the search is the soul that has *awakened* to its existential condition and discovered the emptiness of that condition. We know that something is amiss, and we passionately want to uncover the truth of it. In the very substance of our soul we want to find out for ourselves.

The flame of the search is ignited only when we accept our unknowing, and still aspire to discover the truth of our situation. It will be dimmed, even extinguished, if we anaesthetize ourselves with the belief that we know the truth, or if we accept someone else's explanation or teaching without discovering the truth in the intimacy of our personal experience. When we sincerely acknowledge our ignorance, because we genuinely love the truth, the flame can become a passionate and consuming fire.

As a soul matures, this inner flame can be sparked through normal life experience. Another way this process can come about is through exposure to spiritual work. The student's intentional work on understanding himself will gradually expose the superficial defensive structures of the ego, while the discovery of Essence in its various aspects—the true nature of the soul—will exert a pressure on the ego identity.

The initial discovery of Essence begins a journey of discovery, a period of wonderful experiences of Essence. It feels like a honeymoon. Little by little, however, it dawns on the student, to his dismay, that there is a big problem. He becomes aware that although he experiences his essence, in some deep and disturbing sense it is still not him. He does not recognize directly and nonconflictually that it is truly him. His experiences of Essence seem to be only experiences that sometimes happen to him, the same "him" he always was.

Simply experiencing Essence does not necessarily lead to confronting the shell. Many devotional practices, for example, produce essential experiences without bringing up the question of identity. The experience can be attributed to the guru, or the divine, without shaking up the normal sense of identity. Only one's consideration of the possibility that the self is Essence will ultimately lead to the understanding of the shell. The student will recognize that it is because of the shell that he does not take himself to be the Essence.

To use our terminology from Chapter 14, we can say that the student realizes that he has been experiencing Essence within the first type of essential experience, in other words, in a dual manner. He, as the self, experiences Essence, instead of experiencing himself *as* Essence. The more he contemplates this situation, the more he perceives that he is identifying with an empty shell. As this happens, the feelings of emptiness and meaninglessness arise quite poignantly.

Narcissistic transferences

For most students, then, the pressure of maturation and the work of understanding reduce the identification with the shell and soften the ego defenses, gradually resulting in some transparency of the self-identity. This brings up feelings of meaninglessness, and at this point the deeper narcissistic defenses become more active. As awareness of the familiar identity approaches consciousness, it becomes apparent that the strongest defenses against perceiving its emptiness are the "narcissistic transferences," that is, the narcissistic elements of the student's object relations. As the emptiness of the shell approaches conscious awareness, one's relationships to others become more markedly narcissistic. Kohut called the narcissistic object relations *narcissistic transferences* (he later named them *selfobject transferences*), referring especially to those seen in the clinical situation with the analyst. The narcissistic transferences generally function to shore up the sense of identity, to make that sense of identity feel supported. In our work these transferences arise in the student's relationship to her teacher.

The narcissistic transferences are present for everyone all the time, but are usually in the background. In our work they come into the foreground, and become the focus of the work when the emptiness of the normal self-identity becomes increasingly obvious. Working with the narcissistic transferences is the primary psychodynamic work on

230   the narcissistic sector of the self. Working with these transferences is a way of exposing the emptiness of one's sense of self, especially for students with significant narcissistic personality components. Awareness of narcissistic transference *as* transference again will bring out the sense of meaninglessness.

Three factors elicit narcissistic emptiness and meaninglessness: first, the normal process of maturation in which one outgrows defensive aspects of the identity; second, the pressure of doing spiritual work and experiencing essential presence, which tends to expose the relative unreality of the level of personality identifications; and third, working with the narcissistic transferences, that is, bringing to consciousness the object relations that have been supporting the more superficial sense of self and helping one to avoid the sense of emptiness.

These narcissistic transferences are very powerful; they are not easy to work through. However, it is necessary to work through them in order to expose the support for the superficial identity, as well as to deal with the defenses against emptiness, helplessness, and aloneness. These defenses prevent our openness to the realization of our true essential nature. We will discuss these issues in detail in later chapters.

According to Kohut, there are two main groups of narcissistic transference, reflecting the two primary narcissistic structures that constitute the bipolar self, and relating to the two kinds of selfobjects:

> those who respond to and confirm the child's innate sense of vigor, greatness and perfection; and those to whom the child can look up and with whom he can merge as an image of calmness, infallibility and omnipotence. The first type is referred to as the mirroring selfobject, and second as the idealized parent imago. (Kohut and Wolfe, in Morrison, 1986, p. 177)

Activation of the object relationships to these early kinds of selfobjects are termed mirror and idealizing transference, respectively. To understand Kohut's idea that the formation of narcissistic transferences will involve the regression to, or activation of, those early stages of normal development, we must recall his view of the origin of narcissism as a fixation on the early structures that constitute the two

poles of the self. According to Kohut, when a person begins to form 231
those narcissistic transferences with an analyst or a teacher, or any
individual, he is regressing to those early modes of relating.

For the narcissistic individual, working through narcissistic transference involves not only a regression, but also involves confronting a
strong fixation on these archaic structures. The more narcissistic the
person, the more narcissistic transferences characterize her object relations. In a less narcissistic person, it is when the shell approaches conscious awareness that the transferences will begin to dominate.

chapter 23

Idealizing Transference

In our work, a critical aspect of the transformation of narcissism is working through transference with a teacher, as well as the more general transference in one's life. We will briefly explore the narcissistic transferences, elucidating their relevance to our work on self-realization and their relation to essential presence. The work of Kohut and his followers contains more detailed discussion of the various modes of narcissistic transference. (See References.)

While both mirroring and idealizing transference intensify when a student begins working on identification with the ego self-identity—the shell, for normal personality structures the idealizing transference usually predominates at the beginning. Students with narcissistic structures tend to manifest the mirroring transference early in the process.

The student who is dealing with narcissism tends to relate to his teacher and to significant others in his life like a child does when it is developmentally normal to need an idealized selfobject: "Since all bliss and power now reside in the idealized object, the child feels empty and powerless when he is separated from it and he attempts, therefore, to maintain a continuous union with it." (Kohut, 1971, p. 37) The student believes, at least unconsciously but often consciously, that his teacher possesses perfection and greatness. This perception is based not on reality but on his own narcissistic needs. He does not question this image of his teacher, believing it to be true, and feels blessed and fortunate to have such an extraordinary teacher. He cannot help but adore his teacher, believing him to be the best thing that has ever appeared on the earth. His mind might be somewhat incredulous of the intensity of his love and admiration, but his feelings are completely convincing.

Kohut believes that the reactivation of the relationship to the idealized selfobject is necessary to enable the individual to resume the development that was arrested at the stage when it was actually needed. According to Kohut, successful development occurs when the child is able to internalize the functions of the idealized object.

> Under optimal circumstances the child experiences gradual disappointment in the idealized object—or, expressed differently: the child's evaluation of the idealized object becomes increasingly realistic—which leads to a withdrawal of the narcissistic cathexis from the imago of the idealized self-object and to their gradual (or, in the oedipal period, massive but phase-appropriate) internalization, i.e., to the acquisition of permanent psychological structures, which continue endopsychically, the functions which the idealized self-object had previously fulfilled. (Kohut, 1971, p. 45)

This describes the development of the structure of the self related to guiding ideals, one of the main poles of the bipolar self. So, according to Kohut, the development of narcissistic normality involves not only an idealized selfobject, but the integration of the functions of this object through an incremental disappointment, as a result of gradual realization of its limitations. Absence, loss, sudden or severe disappointment in the idealized selfobject is too difficult for the child to deal with, and precludes optimal internalization. If the idealization breaks down too quickly, then the gradual process of integration and internalization does not happen. "The child does not acquire the needed internal structure, his psyche remains fixated on an archaic self-object, and the personality will throughout life be dependent on certain objects in what seems to be an intense form of object hunger."

234 (Kohut, 1971, p. 45). Without the capacity to maintain the home-ostasis of the self, his sense of self is insecure and he needs to idealize an external object in order to feel some calm, cohesion, and self-esteem.

As a student's narcissistic issues begin to be addressed, this need intensifies. It is as if the person is making a new attempt at integrating the functions of the idealized object. However, this integration will occur only if the transference is handled appropriately. Life situations offer many opportunities for idealization, but we rarely manage to use them for internalization and building of psychic structure because situations do not normally allow us to optimally deal with our disappointments. According to Kohut, the understanding and skills of the analyst make the relationship to the analyst a good place to deal with idealization, its breakdown and the resulting disappointments.

In psychoanalytic circles this view of idealization is widely accepted, but not universally. Kernberg's view of the idealizing transference is similar to his view of grandiosity. He sees it as a pathological development that defends against painful and threatening object relations, and not a fixation or regression to a normal stage of development. Specifically, he believes that the idealizing transference is a projection of the pathological grandiose self onto the analyst.[28] This difference in view is significant in that it affects how the teacher or analyst deals with idealization. If it is a defensive structure, it needs to be confronted and analyzed as such from the beginning; if it is an attempt to resume development that was arrested at the normal stage of idealization, then it needs to be responded to with empathy and understanding, and not confronted at the beginning.

Our view parallels that of the Jungian analyst, Schwartz-Salant, who thinks that idealization can have a primarily defensive purpose, blocking painful or threatening feelings, ". . . or else it can represent the healthy mobilization of the positive Self in the form of projection: one's own better or potential qualities are 'transferred' to another and experienced as characteristic of that person." (Schwartz-Salant, 1982, p. 43) His idea is that the self integrates aspects of its spiritual potential by first projecting them onto external figures, then internalizing them as psychic structure, and that this process—which is natural in childhood—is what is operative in some idealizing transferences.[29]

This is different from Kohut's view, although we share with Kohut 235 the notion that idealization is a normal developmental stage. It is similar to Kernberg's idea that it is a projection; however, it is not a projection of a pathological defensive grandiose self, but rather, of the person's true qualities. It is in the more severe, mostly borderline, narcissistic individuals that Kernberg worked with, that idealization involves mainly the projection of the pathological grandiose self. However, in the normal-to-neurotic range of ego structures typical of the individuals we work with, the idealization is mostly a regression to, or activation of, an earlier normal stage of development.

Idealization and the need for support

In working with and resolving the idealizing transference, the student goes through somewhat predictable stages. The first is establishing the transference. Some will resist this phase. Kohut discusses some of these resistances, and contends that it is possible to discover through the dreams or associations of the student, some indication of a person's fears about this kind of transference. He writes:

> Is the mobilization of idealizing cathexes, for instance, feared and resisted because the narcissistically invested objects which the child tried to idealize were cold and unresponsive. . . . In the prestages of an idealizing transference there may also appear indications . . . that the patient is afraid of the extinction of his individuality by the deep wish to merge with and into the idealized object. (Kohut, 1971, pp. 87–88)

This latter reason for resisting the idealizing transference may manifest as the fear of disappearing, losing oneself, becoming overwhelmed by the power of the object, or being too dependent.

An instructive example of resistance to the idealizing transference is the case of Daniel N., a long-time psychotherapist, who had been working with the author in both group and private settings. His resistance manifested first in the group, where every once in a while he would get upset and angry at me, questioning the way I was working with another student, and wanting to approach his feelings as realistic professional criticism of my performance. This conflicted with his

236   imagined fear of my reprisal, his need for my help and with his general friendliness. It gradually became clear in his work that his distrust of me, and his continuing need to test me, functioned in part as defenses against focusing on how he actually felt about himself and me. I worked with him with gentleness, acknowledging his insights into my work when they had some truth, but still confronting his fear, distrust and aggression, which were clearly not warranted under the circumstances. This revealed a need to defend against seeing my caring for him, which he could not tolerate. This exposed difficult feelings of vulnerability and sadness. His defensive suspiciousness of me became the focus of our exploration, revealing a paranoid defensiveness against a projected image of a punitive authority. This led to exploring facets of his early relationships with both parents, in which he felt his mother to be critical, aggressive, and intrusive, and his father weak and unavailable. He felt that neither of them listened to him, and the fact that I listened with caring helped him to trust me more, after seeing through his defensiveness.

In time, Daniel realized that he had not been able to idealize his parents; in addition to his mother's aggressiveness and his father's weakness, both were poor and uneducated, and he felt ashamed of that. He finally realized his fear that I might not be able to deal with his issue, or be present for him in the way he needed. This recognition gradually allowed him to recognize and express warm and loving feelings towards me, and to feel held and understood in his work with me. This developed into a positive transference, with the idealization slowly escalating, but it remained difficult for him to acknowledge it. He started to like the group a great deal more than before, felt steadily better about himself and his work with me, and his needs for mirroring and support became increasingly apparent and acceptable.

From the beginning, I had sensed in Daniel a deep need to idealize me unquestioningly, but he had a strong fear of dependence and vulnerability, which he believed would expose him to a cruel object (mother) or an unavailable and unreliable object (father). Only after understanding all these conflicts and developing his trust in my holding capacity and commitment, was he able to let go, relax and feel his love towards both his father and myself. This became the ground from which his need to idealize could emerge and be acted out. I could see his enjoyment and happiness in having the chance to idealize, to finally find an idealizable selfobject. However, it was also clear to me that he was not ready to see his idealization of me, or more accurately, to feel its extent and depth. I did not try to analyze it away because for some time I did not see it as defensive, but rather, as helping him to explore very deep and vulnerable parts of himself and his history.

Kohut's position is that the idealizing transference will establish itself spontaneously if we work through the resistances against it. This corresponds with our findings. Also, we allow the transference to emerge without either interpreting it away or encouraging it, as in the case of Daniel, above. We share with Kohut the understanding that it is important not to interpret the idealizing transference as it is emerging at the beginning. Since it is an expression of a deep need, interpreting it before it is in full bloom would risk causing the student to feel that we are saying that we don't like it, we cannot take it, we are disapproving, that he cannot have his need met, or that he cannot have the parent that he still wants. This is a very tricky point. Usually, this transference develops gradually. One reason we allow it to emerge little by little, instead of interpreting it right from the beginning and eliminating it, is because we cannot work through it if we do not allow it to happen. It has to come to full bloom for the individual to know what it is, and to appreciate the extent of his need for it.

The next stage arises when this idealization of the teacher is disrupted by something that the teacher does or fails to do. It is usually disrupted simply by the fact that the teacher is not perfect and the idealization is not realistic. Regardless of how perfect the teacher might be, she will never fit the idealized image of the student, and the student will at some point notice the discrepancy. When the student sees something in the idealized figure that doesn't fit with the imagined perfection, there is a disappointment and a loss of the idealized image. The student will experience even slight failings of the teacher as lack of empathy, attunement, appreciation, understanding, sensitivity—but most importantly, as the loss of the teacher's support.

This loss often brings up the defensive reaction of anger, rage, and hatred. The student hates the teacher for not living up to his image of

238   her and feels that she has failed him, or even betrayed him. Psychodynamically, every time the idealizing transference is disrupted, the student experiences unconsciously, if not consciously, the loss of part of his structure, a part that provides him particularly with the sense of support for who he is. This is a loss of the support for the narcissistic equilibrium—the sense of self-esteem and stable self-existence. However, the student does not initially recognize the loss of support implicit in the loss of the idealized object. He first goes on the defensive, experiencing rage toward the teacher, blaming and devaluing her. This rage may manifest as cold withdrawal from the teacher, or even vindictive devaluation. This might seem counterproductive or disruptive to the teacher-student relationship, but it's actually a blessing in disguise. If the teacher understands the situation and is skillful in her interactions with her student, and if the student is sincere and mature enough, there is the unique opportunity here of the student seeing his teacher as she is. More significantly, there is the possibility of a quantum jump in his inner transformation.

The next stage emerges when the student manages to be sincere enough about his feelings, and the teacher is aware of the situation and is compassionate and skillful enough to help him tolerate it. This stage begins as the student recognizes that he is angry because he feels disappointed and betrayed. Feeling and recognizing the disappointment allows the student to begin to move through the initial defensiveness. He does not appreciate how dependent on the teacher he has been until he acknowledges the painful—sometimes devastating— disappointment that lies underneath the rage and cold withdrawal. The rage is both a reaction to the disappointment and a defense against it. It is as if the student feels towards the teacher: "How can you be that way! I have trusted you all these years, I put my life in your hands, I depended on you, and now you have failed me. I hate you, for you have betrayed me and disappointed me."

We find Donna D., coming to her private teaching sessions with the author, feeling frustrated and angry at me and the work we do together. She feels angry and disappointed because I do not see her as special and value her in a special way. This intensifies into deep hurt and intense rage, and she starts seeing its connection to her father, whose imminent death is one of the circumstances causing the emergence of these feelings. She begins to doubt and reject the kind of work I do with her. The anger and rage are not only toward myself and her father, but also towards God and Being, the states of Being that she has been experiencing. This gradually reveals a deep disappointment in me which, when we explore it, we find is connected to the loss of a certain idealized image of me. The idealization broke down when she perceived that I failed to see her specialness and treat her in the way she felt she deserved. This indicated the presence of the grandiose self, which we were not able to confront until much later, after the idealized transference had been sufficiently worked through.

Investigating the idealized image she had of me—as strong, loving, and caring in an unusual way—led us to explore the way she viewed her father. It was difficult to acknowledge her feelings towards her father as idealization, partly because he was dying, and partly—most importantly, we discovered—because she needed this idealized image of him to cover up an early state of helplessness. Confronting Donna's belief in his unusually devout love and strength, and her belief that she received these supports from him, by pointing to her intense need for mirroring and support—a need which contradicted her belief in what she received from him—exposed her idealization of him. She saw then that she had actually given up her own capacities of will and love by believing that she received them from him. Her disappointment in me became now the acknowledgment of her disappointment in her father, who did not give her enough mirroring and admiration, as much as she now knows she needed. This confronted her with painful states of humiliation and vulnerability, which were relatively easy for her to tolerate and understand, not only because of my empathic understanding of her, but also because of her capacity to experience essential presence. Her repeated experiences of her real inner resources, like essential love and strength, gave her the confidence and trust to tolerate the painful affects.

It is important that the student directly and fully experience the deep hurt associated with this disappointment if his process is to go deeper in such an investigation. This emotional hurt is very significant; it is actually a stage of self-experience that can surface only after the

240   disappointment is acknowledged. It is experienced as a deep and painful psychic wound. This experience of wounding directly expresses the loss of psychic structure. The wound may feel like something was ripped out of one, leaving a sense of devastation and enfeeblement.

Kohut says that the initial reaction of rage and despondency is usually followed by various regressions in an attempt to deal with the loss; the regression can be to any earlier stage or structure.

> In the idealizing transference the working-through process thus concerns the following typical sequence of events: (1) the patient's loss of the narcissistic union with the idealized self-object; (2) the ensuing disturbance of the narcissistic balance; (3) the subsequent hypercathexis of archaic forms of either (a) the idealized parent imago or (b) the grandiose self; and, fleetingly, (4) the hypercathexis of the (autoerotic) fragmented body-mind-self. (Kohut, 1971, pp. 97–98)

We observe these regressions in some students occurring more often in more narcissistic structures. The regression to the merging experience sometimes appears as a recourse to some forms of spiritual experience. The person, in some sense, seeks a kind of merging with God or with the cosmos, and thus feels supported, which helps him to reestablish the narcissistic equilibrium. Although these same spiritual states are actually deep attainments when they arise in their true, nondefensive place in the student's process of transformation, resorting to them in this situation amounts to avoiding the narcissistic vulnerability.

Dealing with these defensive regressions by understanding their function confronts the student with the nature and significance of his idealization of his teacher. At this point our work diverges from Kohut's. He writes about how he works with the disruption of the idealizing transference, or any kind of narcissistic transference.

> In a properly conducted analysis, the analyst takes note of the analysand's retreat, searches for any mistakes he might have made, nondefensively acknowledges them after he has recognized them (often with the help of the analysand), and then gives the analysand a noncensorious interpretation of the dynamics of his retreat. In this way the flow of empathy

between analyst and analysand is remobilized. The patient's self
is then sustained once more by a selfobject matrix that is
empathically in tune with him. (Kohut, 1984, p. 67)

Kohut conceives of the flow of empathy as significant for the resolution and cure, a view we share with him, but we do not give it the
same degree of significance. We see this flow of empathy as necessary
for the student to go deeper, but it is the resolution of the deeper parts
of this issue that is responsible for "cure"—or in our work, transformation. The student will feel supported and sustained, as Kohut says,
but this is not a true resolution of the issue of idealization.[30] Kohut
believes that in childhood the person did not have the chance to go
optimally through the breakdown of idealization, and now the analyst may use the situation to complete this developmental task, utilizing his empathy and support to compensate for what was missing in
the early childhood situations.

We concur with Kohut in this, but our interest is in how this process can support a deeper process of transformation. Kohut does
acknowledge that another level of work is necessary at this point, but
it is not what we have in mind. He sees that when the student understands the disruption of the supportive relationship, and reestablishes
the relationship, and this happens several times, a new kind of material
begins to surface:

> There will gradually emerge a host of meaningful memories
> which concern the dynamic prototypes of the present experi-
> ences . . . and memories that have always been conscious will
> become intelligible in the light of the present transference
> experiences. (Kohut, 1971, p. 98)

This is what typically happens when a transference is seen clearly as
a transference, as we saw in the cases of Daniel and Donna, above. It
is the reason for working on transference manifestations. Memories
of childhood situations in relation to idealization, and to the idealized
objects, arise at this point, and the student has the opportunity—with
the teacher's support—to understand and work through those early
painful experiences. Kohut does not consider this part of the working-
through process to be the critical factor needed for the transformation,

242 and again we concur. Where we differ is in what we see as the critical factor. Kohut considers the empathic bond to be the specific factor needed for the transformation of narcissism. He considers the process of transformation, or cure:

> as a three-step movement, the first two steps of which may be described as defense analysis and the unfolding of the trans-ferences, while the third step—the essential one because it defines the aim and the result of the cure—is the opening of a path of empathy between self and selfobject, specifically, the establishment of empathic in-tuneness between self and self-object on mature adult levels. (Kohut, 1984, pp. 65–66)

The main idea is that, through the process we have been discussing, the student will relinquish his archaic forms of dependence on self-objects, and replace them with more mature forms. It is Kohut's con-tention that the person never transcends the need for selfobjects to support his narcissistic equilibrium, and that the most one can hope for, in terms of the transformation of narcissism, is the ability to sat-isfy his narcissistic need in more mature and realistic ways.

> True, psychological structure is acquired through psycho-analysis and the self becomes more firm. But this increased firmness does not make the self independent of selfobjects. Instead, it increases the self's ability to use selfobjects for its own sustenance, including an increased freedom in choosing selfobjects. (Kohut, 1984, p. 77)

This is a very significant assertion; on this point he takes issue with the depth psychologists who emphasize independence and autonomy, like Mahler and others. There are three important points in this claim that we will explore in detail, to illuminate our divergence from Kohut, and thus to clarify our own perspective. The first point is the under-standing of how the transformation of narcissism occurs. The second is the question of what the most important factor for this transforma-tion is. The third point is the understanding of what this transforma-tion amounts to. According to Kohut, the transformation occurs within the empathic milieu, where the gradual disappointment and the restora-tion of the narcissistic relationship lead to a gradual building-up of

psychic structures, through the process he refers to as "transmuting   243
internalization." Functions that are assigned to the idealized figure, and
necessary for the maintenance of the equilibrium and strength of the
sense of self, are gradually internalized, due to the frustration that arises
when the student realizes that he cannot always count on the teacher
to perform such functions for him.

In Kohut's words:

> Replicas of the experiences of. . . optimal frustration (identi-
> fications) are established in the mind via the mechanism of
> introjection. . . . The child's drives are opposed originally by
> the prohibitions of the parents. If these prohibitions are of
> nontraumatic intensity, the child incorporates the parents'
> drive-restraining attitudes in the form of innumerable benign
> memory traces. . . . As a result of having introjected many
> experiences of optimal frustration in which his infantile drives
> were handled by a calming, soothing, loving attitude rather
> than by counteraggression on the part of his parents, the child
> himself later acts in the same way toward the drive demands
> that arise in him. (Kohut, 1984, p. 109)

If we read "narcissistic needs" for "drives," we get the picture of how
narcissistic structures are built by the working-through process. The
structure of the self is transmuted by the incorporation of new, more
realistic elements, through the gradual integration of the qualities and
functions of the idealized object.

The second point at issue with depth psychology is that the factor
necessary for this transformation is that the student feels empathically
understood by the teacher. Kohut goes so far as to suggest that it is this
experience of being understood, and not that of insights into one's psychological functioning, which is the significant factor: "While expansion of consciousness and of verbalizable insight are often encountered
in the late stages of successful analyses, some unqualified analytic successes include in the main neither of these gains." (Kohut, 1984, p. 76)

The third point is the one we noted above, that narcissistic transformation ("cure") involves relinquishing primitive forms of relationship to selfobjects, and replacing them with more mature ones, where
one's sense of self still needs external support, but now with ". . . newly

244   acquired ability to identify and seek out appropriate selfobjects—both mirroring and idealizable—as they present themselves in his realistic surroundings and to be sustained by them." (Kohut, 1984, p. 77).

In this instance, we can compare Kohut's understanding to our view of how transformation happens, by resuming our discussion of the stages of working through the idealizing transference as we observe them in our work. When the idealization is recognized as a transference of early object relations, the empathic bond is reestablished, and the genetic psychodynamic material starts emerging, as the student begins to remember his early relationships with his parents in terms of idealizing needs. However, there is one important difference: The emerging memories are viewed not only from the perspective of idealization, but also, and most significantly, from the perspective of what the idealized parent was to provide the child—namely, support for his developing sense of self and identity. The student can understand and acknowledge his need for narcissistic support when he comprehends that the disruption of the idealizing transference means the loss of the teacher's support for his narcissistic equilibrium. When he recognizes the need for narcissistic support that underlies his tendency to idealize, he often begins to recall his childhood situation in terms of the availability and quality of support.

Another case history will illustrate this process. As Sam L. arrives at one of his private teaching sessions with the author, he is feeling despondent and angry. Inquiry into what is happening reveals that he is feeling disappointed in some of his business associates for not being as responsible as he thought they were. This exposed his thus far unacknowledged idealization of the business community as responsible and competent. Sam then recognized that this idealization was his way of feeling supported by these businessmen. Spontaneously, then, he remembered how much he needed his father to support him. Feeling this deep need for the support he never got from his father opened up a big wound, a deep sadness and hurt that he had never felt.

This session was part of a larger process of Sam seeing his need for support, his issues about it, and the various conflicts it caused in his life—in his relationship with his wife, whom he felt did not support him in his business, with the members of the group, whom he felt did

not behave in a way that supported the activities of his work, and so 245
on. It is important to note here that the issues of idealization and the
need for support arise not only in relation to the teacher, but usually
in all of one's life situations. Frequently, idealization of the teacher is
confronted only after it is seen in other life situations.

As we see in Sam's case, the actual need turns out to be the need for
narcissistic support, for the strength, calm, and certainty in the parent that will function to support the child's developing—and still fragile, feeling of identity. It is this need for support that drives the child
to idealize the parent, for this idealization is needed for the child to
feel adequately supported. We will explore shortly why this need turns
particularly to idealization, but for now we want to stress that the need
for narcissistic support is more fundamental than for idealization. This
position is actually simply a clarification of an understanding common
in depth psychological theories regarding the relation of idealization
to the need for support, as we see in the following quote from Kohut:

> Unconsciously fixated on an idealized self-object for which
> they continue to yearn, and deprived of a sufficiently idealized
> superego, such persons are forever searching for external
> omnipotent powers from whose support and approval they
> attempt to derive strength. (Kohut, 1971, p. 84)

At this point, it is clear that the central function the idealized object
provides for the student, which the student needs to "internalize," is
a kind of support. At this juncture of the process of working-through,
the relevant childhood situations are remembered or recognized in
their appropriate light, as issues around support.

The next stage becomes the exploration of, and working through,
the need for support, the lack of support, and the various ways that
the student tries to access it. We explore this stage in three segments:
the various strategies that the individual utilizes to support his feeling
of identity; the state of absence of support; and the actual quality of
support. At this point, the student finds that many of his manifestations function to support his sense of identity, but that the central
object relation—whose primary function is to support his identity—
is the one with idealized selfobjects. He finds that all his internalized

246   object relations function, at least partly, to support his identity, because, as we saw in Chapters 6 and 10, these object relations constitute the very building blocks of the psychic structure of self-identity. Since the feeling of identity is based on the integration of all self-representations, and since each self-representation is intimately linked to an object-representation, this identity is dependent on all these internalized object relations, and on their activation in various transference situations in the individual's life.

The student also finds that he uses, both consciously and unconsciously, his body and his image of it as a support for his feeling of identity. He also uses his environment—both animate and inanimate, his interests and activities, his roles and involvements, his capacities and skills, his possessions, his ideals and philosophies, his accomplishments and successes, even his failures and problems, almost everything in any way related to him, for the same end. Exploring one's sources of narcissistic support is necessary for a more complete transformation of narcissism, but at this point it is working through the idealizing transference that provides the student with the most concrete opportunity to integrate the support he needs for his self-realization.

chapter 24

Narcissistic Helplessness

K ohut's approach suggests that the student's recognition of his need for support, and his working-through of his childhood situations regarding support, when done within the empathic bond with the teacher, will be enough for him to internalize the teacher's supportive functions. However, this involves internalizing an object relation which will create or support a certain psychic structure. This approach will not work for the purpose of completely working through narcissism. Although it's valid for the purpose of healing pathological ego structures, this understanding holds a view of support—basically as supportive actions and attitudes—that supports development in the direction of ego structures, and not toward self-realization.

This argument will become more clear as we explore the issue of absence or loss of support. In our work there is a consistent focus on the felt sense of the student, including body sensations. This focus reveals that it is not only on the level of the object relation that the lack of support is felt. When the student feels that the teacher is not acting supportive, in his present felt sense of his bodily state he feels a lack of support, which may manifest as a feeling of weakness. When the student

248   actually feels the sense of lack of support, this experience activates another sense, the feeling of weakness of self, or vagueness of identity.

Thus, there are two aspects of the experience of narcissistic vulnerability: The first involves a sense of lack or loss of support; the other, loss, weakness, or lack of identity.[31] The student experiences the loss of external support as a weakness of a certain kind. He may feel as if his bones are getting soft and losing their strength and solidity, and hence cannot support him. He may feel spineless, or that his backbone is soft or brittle. He may feel that his legs are weak and unable to support his weight, or they feel small and skinny, or soft and mushy. He may feel small, helpless and unable to support himself, or structureless and amorphous like a jellyfish.

An example of this phenomenon is the case of Penny W., whose narcissistic issues focused mainly on her difficult relationship with her husband, by whom she felt emotionally abused. She could not stand up to him because she needed him for psychological support for her identity. She could not let go of her idealization of him regardless of how much pain he caused her, and regardless of how much aggression and narcissism she saw in him. Recognizing her intense need for his support, she felt a big hole open up in her belly. Penny tried many strategies of deflection in the session, to avoid feeling the affect in this emptiness. Finally, as I pointed out her attempts to distract herself from the difficult state that was arising, she began to feel the hole as a sense of no support, as having no foundation to stand on, as if there is no ground under her. This was combined with painful feelings of worthlessness and undeservingness. Staying with the sense of lack of support, she started feeling a gradual loss of definition in her structure, until she felt like a pile of mush. She referred to herself in this state as a "blob."

In subsequent sessions Penny dealt with the narcissistic hurt about her mother and father not seeing what is real and loving in her, but seeing only the negative and deficient, as her husband tended to do. A great deal of hurt and anger arose, along with a sense of betrayal and abandonment. At some point she experienced the essential aspect of Strength, which made it possible for her to feel some separation from her mother. During this phase of her process, she arrived one day at her private teaching session feeling angry at me, disappointed in something

I had done in the previous session. Investigating the flaw in my work
that disappointed her, it turned out that she felt I had not been clear.
This exposed her idealized image of me as one who is always clear and
knows what is going on. Seeing through the idealization, she began to
feel unseen and abandoned. This brought about a deep wound in her
chest, and feelings of being a small, helpless, and alone child. This
evoked and clarified some aspects of her relationship with her father,
whom she felt abandoned her when he divorced her mother. Penny
realized that she had always had an idealized image of him in fantasy,
an image that became the basis of her dream about the kind of man she
might someday find. Feeling the abandonment by her father caused
her to feel a deep longing for her mother to hold her—indicating a
movement of regression to an earlier, merging kind of idealization. By
this time she was feeling very weak and unsupported. This state manifested in many ways in the course of the ensuing months and took her
a long time to work through.

When a student is fighting the awareness of these states of weakness
and lack of support, she often experiences physical tensions in the legs
and back, and aches and pains in the lower joints: the hips, knees, and
ankles. The resistance against these somatic manifestations of lack of
support may lead to physical injuries to these joints, because of the awkwardness caused by physical tension and imbalance. These manifestations indicate that a person is somaticizing the sense of lack of support.

As the student becomes more directly aware that he is feeling a lack
of support, the felt sense becomes more definite and concrete. His legs
may feel light and empty, insubstantial, even ghostly. This can progress
to feeling the emptiness in the legs and the lower body as a definite sense
of vacuity, as in the case of the hole in the belly that Penny felt. Only
when the student accepts the feeling that he has no inner support does
he finally recognize this lack as a specific emptiness, a state of deficient
nothingness, which feels like a lack of support.

Loss of idealization and deficient emptiness

We find, then, that the state of lack of support is the psychological
recognition of an existential emptiness, a deficient state experienced
phenomenologically as nothingness, or vacuity. Retracing our steps,

250   we can see that the breakdown of the idealizing transference produces a state of deficient emptiness, with a sense of lack of support. It is our experience that fully experiencing this emptiness is necessary to resolve the need for idealized selfobjects.

Self psychology and object relations theory explain this emptiness as the absence or loss of a psychic structure, or as a consequence of the loss of a certain object relation. We find this explanation only partly accurate. It is true that when a certain object relation (in this case the idealizing transference) or a psychic structure (in this case the structure related to ideals or to the superego) is lost, this emptiness usually arises. However, this does not mean that the emptiness is necessarily the absence of this object relation or of the psychic structure. An alternative explanation would be that the loss of the object relation and/or psychic structure merely reveals an underlying emptiness. Our perception is that the idealizing transference functions to support the sense of self, but does so by veiling this underlying emptiness. Thus, the idealizing transference is a defense against this underlying emptiness.

We saw in Chapter 11 that the normal sense of identity is inherently weak and brittle since it lacks recognition of a more fundamental identity, the Essential Identity. It naturally follows that the normal sense of identity, and the structure of self-identity it is based on, is not only inherently weak and insecure, but also cannot be supported in any true way. Truth cannot support something false. The normal identity is ultimately an empty shell, which is not supported internally by anything authentic. When this shell is deeply investigated, then, it will inevitably be found to lack true support. Underlying the identification with the shell, we always find an emptiness characterized by the affect of no support. The ego sense of identity is supported by psychic structures based on internalized object relations, and by transference situations, that are enactments of those object relations. The idealizing transference is the primary object relation specifically utilized for the purpose of supporting this identity.

This understanding clarifies narcissistic idealization, which supports a feeble and shaky sense of self and also demonstrates that all kinds of idealization, whether we call them primitive or mature, function to shore up one's identity. Because of its intrinsic incompleteness and unreality, the normal identity always needs this support, regardless of how strong this identity might be felt to be. In fact, it is our understanding that all idealizations are simply variations, on and reflections of, the narcissistic idealization. We see then that any identity based on ego structures (which is true of both the normal identity and the grandiose self of the pathologically narcissistic individual) inevitably needs external support, such as the idealization of others. This also explains why the normal individual develops deep idealizing transferences similar to those exhibited by narcissistic personalities, when dealing with the aspect of his spiritual transformation relating to the sense of identity. In our work, we understand this development of the narcissistic idealization as intensification of normal idealizations, due to the greater narcissistic need for support which arises when the normal identity is challenged by expanding spiritual transformation.

This returns us to a point in our discussion of Kohut's view of the transformation of idealizing transference. He asserts that one never transcends the need for external selfobjects, that transformation—cure, in his terminology—is a matter of relinquishing the need for archaic and primitive forms of self-selfobject relationships, and replacing them with more mature and realistic ones. We agree that the normal self cannot transcend the need for external sources of narcissistic support, regardless of how strong or firm one's sense of self becomes. Only realization of the Essential Identity, that has no inherent weakness or insecurity, liberates the self from the need for external support.

If we limit our conception of the human potential to the conventional dimension of experience, as Kohut and most depth psychologists seem to do, then we are bound to come to the conclusion that human beings can never be totally autonomous narcissistically, that we will always need external sources of narcissistic support and supplies. This conception leaves out the truth that most genuine spiritual teachings of humankind have expressed: that there *is* such a thing as true and ultimate liberation. This liberation includes fundamental independence from external sources for one's inner equilibrium. Reduction of the human potential to identification with mature, realistic object relations negates the phenomenon of the full realization of individuals like Buddha or Lao Tzu, who proclaimed full and absolute

252   independence from others with respect to their sense of self, well-being, and inner equilibrium. More fundamentally, this model, like many others in depth psychology, excludes the most fundamental truth about the human spirit: that it is Being itself, completely independent from mind, psychic structure, or object relations.

The further development that a student undergoes in the course of working through the idealizing transference demonstrates that it is possible to directly experience this ground of being or real identity. Fully experiencing the deficient emptiness of support is the transition to true resolution and transformation. Kohut's view that in the process of working-through, this emptiness is eliminated by the development of new psychic structures, or by the firming-up of insufficiently developed ones, is definitely true. This development is unavoidable when the teacher handles the transference appropriately.

However, if we hold to the understanding of deficient emptiness presented above, another, deeper, process can commence when we recognize the idealizing transference, and our strategies for gaining narcissistic supports as defenses against this deficient emptiness. This recognition will naturally arise if we do not take the stance that this emptiness needs to be eliminated. In fact, we do not need to take any position about this emptiness, but only inquire into it, to discover what it is truly about.[32]

The recognition of the need for support, specifically, the need to support our sense of self, will naturally precipitate the feeling of no support, as we saw in the cases above. If this feeling is not defended against, it will reveal an underlying emptiness characterized by a sense of deficiency of support. The emptiness may provoke many associated feelings and self-images, as we have seen, like feelings of helplessness and weakness, and images of smallness and lack of structure. This usually brings up from the unconscious deeply repressed, painful object relations and their associated emotional states of abandonment, betrayal, depression, terror, even fear of death and disintegration. These are reactions to and associations with the deficient emptiness. We must then clarify these reactions and associations in order to understand the genesis of the emptiness. This process requires awareness of, and disengagement from, judgments and superego attitudes about the deficiency.

This process finally reveals what the specific feeling of deficiency is, 253
what lack of support makes us feel. We begin to realize that what we
feel is that we do not have our own support. This is possibly the first
clear indication that there could be such a thing as one's own inner support, for the sense of self—based on ego structures—cannot conceive
of this possibility, just as Kohut could not. This lack of our own inner
support feels like a particular kind of helplessness. It is not general ego
deficiency, the ego weakness having to do with functioning and one's
sense of being an immature individual.[33] It is helplessness about supporting our sense of who we are. When a student finally recognizes it
precisely, she usually feels, "I don't know what to do," or "I can't do
anything." To illustrate this important development, we will present
another student's experience.

Julia begins work in a small group setting by telling me that she has
been feeling terrified. She informs me that this feeling has been increasing for a few weeks, and that she has been working on narcissistic
issues. In previous group meetings she has worked with various aspects
of her transference, including her idealization of me. I ask her what she
is terrified about. She mentions that she has been feeling ungrounded,
that it has been difficult for her to feel present, that her competence
in her work has suffered, and that she feels she is about to fall apart.
She also felt disappointed in the work we have been doing together,
judging herself to be slipping back, that she has lost all the realization
and transformation she has been sincerely working on.

Knowing that Julia had a relatively normal structure, I was not
alarmed about her fear of fragmentation, but I was curious about what
was causing it to arise. As she spoke, it turned out that she felt she was
going to fall apart because she felt ungrounded, as if she had no moor-
ing or anchor. By then she was shaking in her lower body, feeling terrified and not present, as if spaced-out. This revealed a feeling of
weakness in her legs that, in turn, exposed an emptiness in her lower
body. The feeling of not being grounded, as having no anchor, turned
out to be the psychological expression of this emptiness. Here, she
realized she was feeling the absence of inner support, a realization that
was helped along by her awareness of my support for her, in seeing me
calm, confident, and empathically in contact with her. This is not

254   idealization, for it is a real trust, based on direct intuition, which she needed in order to go deeper. At this point idealizing transference would not be sufficient to support her continuing unfoldment.

When we investigated the terror, Julia saw that she felt hopeless and helpless. When I asked why, she informed me that it was because she didn't know what to do. She felt the emptiness expanding, dissolving her boundaries, and extending into her head. She felt unknowing and helpless, and that she did not know what to do, even that she was unable to do anything. She judged herself for this helplessness and felt hopeless and terrified about it. When I asked her what made her feel she needed to do something, this intensified the shaking in her body. She felt she had to do something and that she was supposed to be able to do something—hence the judgment. Inquiring about what it was in relation to her feeling that she did not know what to do, it dawned on her that she did not know what to do to be herself. Here, it became clear that she had gone through many of her strategies for getting support to enable her to be herself and was not able to use any of them at this time.

Inquiring about what it means to be herself, she found that she does not know what to do to merely be. This clarified what the judgment and rejection were about, namely, that she believed this unknowingness and inability to be a deficiency, a personal failing. When I asked her whether she ever knew what to do to be herself, she realized that she thought so; she believed that the various things she does in her interactions, plus the various spiritual practices and processes that she has been involved with, are ways for her to be herself. But she realized now that, in truth, she had never known what to do in the immediate moment, or directly, to be herself.

This state of helplessness, which feels like we do not know what to do to be ourselves, is precisely the feeling of missing our own inner support. The greatest barrier against understanding and resolving this situation is the judgment of ourselves as inadequate based on the conviction that we can, and ought to, know. That is why I suggested to Julia to be completely open to her experience, to see whether she could remain with her experience without the judgment, and without any idea or position regarding whether she can or ought to know what to

do. Basically, I supported her to inquire into this state of helplessness   255
with an open, nonjudgmental mind.

It took Julia some time, and some working through issues about trusting me and herself, before she was able to stay with her experience of helplessness with an unbiased attitude. As she managed to let go of her bias and judgment, she realized that the terror subsided, that her state became more neutral, even pleasant. She was quite surprised to find out that she was feeling more and more present. She felt simple and free, and quite clear. I asked her about her state, and she said she felt she was being herself. She experienced her state as simple presence, free and unencumbered. She kept saying, "It is not that I am present, but I am presence." This was the first time she experienced presence in this nondual way. She became clear about the difference between experiencing presence, as she had been for few years, and experiencing herself *as* the presence.

When I asked Julia about the question of support, she had a second major insight: "I *am* support." Support was simply the way she experienced her presence. This resolution was not a matter of having support, but of discovering support as inseparable from her very presence. When I asked her about the feeling that she did not know what to do to be herself, it was clear to her that it is not a matter of doing anything, for being is not an activity; it is pure presence.

chapter 25

Support and Being

The most important insight needed for a student to move from the deficient lack of support to the actual state of support is the recognition that the feeling of helplessness, of not knowing what to do to be oneself, is not an actual deficiency, nor a personal failing. It is rather, the recognition of a fundamental truth about the self, which is that we cannot do anything in order to be, for to be is not an activity. We can come to this understanding only through the cessation of intentional inner activity. At this point, not to know what to do is a matter of recognizing the natural state of affairs, for since there is nothing that we can do to be, then it is natural that we cannot know what to do. There is nothing to know because such knowledge is impossible. Nobody knows what to do to be, and the sooner we recognize this, the easier is our work on self-realization. In fact, feeling that we don't know what to do to be ourselves is the beginning of the insight that we don't need to do anything.

This fundamental insight underlies many advanced spiritual practices, such as those of surrender and "nondoing" meditation. We can arrive at this insight by exploring the question of support for identity, but it is another matter to remember and practice it. When we truly learn this fundamental truth, then we have become wise; for self-realization is now an effortless relaxation into the nature of who we are, and this is the presence of Being. Nothing more need be done; the transformation is a matter now of spontaneous unfoldment.

This understanding informs the highest teachings of many ancient traditions, although Taoism is the main tradition associated with emphasis on the wisdom of nonaction. Another is Kashmir Shaivism, which teaches through three principle upayas, or means, but also offers the wisdom of nondoing as an ultimate means.

> Beyond these three upayas, sambha voupaya, saktopaya and anavopaya, there is another upayas, although it is not actually an upaya, yet it is mentioned in Kashmir Shaivism. This upaya is called anupaya. The word 'anupaya' means 'no upaya' . . . in anupaya the aspirant has only to observe that nothing is to be done. Be as you are. If you are talking, go on talking. If you are sitting, go on sitting. Do not do anything, only reside in your being. This is the nature of anupaya. (Laksman Jee, 1988, p. 40)

As we begin to understand this perspective, we may learn that one's helplessness is based on a delusion: the belief that there is something we need to do in order to be ourselves and the resulting conviction that we can know what it is. This is one of the basic delusions of the ego life of the self. It is inherent in narcissism that we will attempt to do things to support our sense of identity. So the self is always engaged in inner activities of remembering, imaging, identifying, repressing, projecting, idealizing, and various self-manipulations to shore up our insecure sense of identity. We observe this in the inner psychological activity of the bipolar self, the tension arc of Kohut, and its underlying ego activity, which is actually needed to support the normal identity. The issue of real support emerges clearly only after we have penetrated the various external manifestations of this ego activity, and have experienced essential presence directly and immediately. The experience of essential presence functions naturally to expose these psychological activities. And since the idealizing transference is the primary object relation that the self utilizes for support, it becomes the most important area to explore

258   in order to uncover the true state of support and the accompanying wisdom of nondoing.

The nondoing we learn at this stage of transformation is not the absence of activity in general—physical or psychological. It is the cessation of the particular activity whose specific purpose is the formulation and support of a sense of self and identity. Clearly, there is nothing wrong with activity; we need it for living. We cannot live without physical activity, and we need thinking for many purposes. But when we use our thinking, and our psychological activity in general, to construct and support an identity (i.e., to try to be ourselves), then we are using the mind inappropriately. It is not the job of the mind to tell us who we are. The recognition of who we are is the function of the Essential Identity, whose mere presence is sufficient for self-recognition. This is being ourselves, and knowing ourselves, directly and immediately, without even self-reflection.

There are many routes by which we might arrive at the state of existential helplessness, and most of them involve a lot of activity. Many spiritual practices and exercises are designed for the very purpose of ceasing this activity. In the path of spiritual transformation, a great deal of uncovering and understanding are necessary for us to be able to experience this helplessness objectively, impartially, and without defensiveness. So we cannot take the attitude that doing nothing is the real practice, and stop all practices. If we do that, it is more than likely that we will merely continue with our ego activity unconsciously, and will develop only laziness. Many spiritual disciplines use the ego activity intentionally, with a great deal of energy and effort, to gain as much as possible from it; but at the same time, they use it in a way that tends to expose its nature. For such disciplines to be successful, the activity must be such that in time its nature and function are revealed.

Since we do not need any inner activity to support true identity, if we *were* able to simply cease all this activity, then we would need no practices for self-realization. However, this is impossible for almost everyone; thus the necessity for the various disciplines and practices. These disciplines will always bring the student to the realization of nonaction when the complete transformation of self-realization is attained.[34]

As we saw in Julia's case in the last chapter, support is not an activity, but a manifestation of Being. When we finally accept our narcissistic helplessness and experience it in a totally open and impartial manner, the deficient emptiness loses its deficiency and reveals itself as a vast spaciousness. The transformation of deficient emptiness into space is made possible when we accept the deficient emptiness. This process involves the transformation of self-image, namely, the relinquishing of the conviction that we could know what to do and that we are inadequate because we cannot. (See *The Void* [Almaas, 1986] for a detailed discussion of the transformation of the self-image and its relationship to the experience of inner spaciousness.) The emptiness feels deficient because it is pervaded by the deficient concept of ourselves, which is based on a delusion. Letting go of the delusion dissolves the self-image and liberates the emptiness from the pervasive feeling of deficiency. Emptiness reveals its true nature as a deep and peaceful inner spaciousness.

Diamond Will

Inner spaciousness is the necessary step for the emergence of Being in the essential manifestation of support for nondoing. It usually manifests as an experience of presence in a new form which has the characteristics of solidity, immensity, immovability, strength, groundedness, definiteness, precision, and clarity. We feel solid, as immense as a mountain, as immovable and grounded as a column, but as clear and definite as a cut diamond. We have the innate certainty that we can be, for we are, simply and easily. There is an implicit confidence in our capacity to be ourselves, and a determination about and commitment to it. The psychological feeling is that of a singular and clear recognition of support—of our own inner support. But it is not our own in terms of ownership; we perceive that it is inseparable from the Being that we now recognize as ourself. We may feel supported, we may feel the presence of support, or we may feel that we *are* support.

We now recognize that support is a way of experiencing Being, our Essence. This is what Julia was experiencing at the end of her work above, and what every student realizes when they finally experience support directly. It is what arose for Donna, above, after she dealt with

260   her idealizing transference with me and after she acknowledged her life-long idealization of her father. For several weeks she experienced the sense of support and immensity. She felt herself as firm, hard like a crystal, but pleasant and loving. This allowed her to experience her power, and to recognize her love of Essence and truth even more deeply. The state of essential support felt sometimes like a solid density in her belly, or an incredible solidity and substantiality in her legs.

The characteristics of solidity, groundedness, immovability, and confidence are the characteristics of Will on the Being level. In fact, we find that support of any kind is always connected in essential experience to Will. (See note 34.) Will is one of the pure forms in which Being manifests, and it is always a sense of groundedness, definiteness, and certainty that provides the self with the confidence and the capacity for commitment and perseverance along the path of transformation. It usually has a sense of purity and sacredness, although it is not a quality commonly considered to be spiritual.

The aspect of Will manifests at the beginning stages of the spiritual journey, making possible the student's true commitment, patience and perseverance. It is one of the several aspects that are central for transformation, like those of Loving Kindness, Strength, Peace, and Joy.

Will emerges again in deeper stages of transformation, not only as a specific aspect, but as a whole dimension of Essence, a plane of Being where all aspects manifest as Will. This dimension, which has to do with the question of supporting spiritual transformation, manifests Essence in all its pure qualities—Love, Kindness, Clarity, Strength, Joy, Truth, Peace, Fulfillment, Contentment, and so on—but always as Will. In other words, in this dimension, we experience Love, for instance, with its sweetness and appreciativeness, but also with the characteristics of solidity, definiteness, confidence, and commitment. Love is then experienced as supportive. This kind of experience is not known in the conventional dimension of the self, and it might not make sense from that perspective, but it makes a great deal of sense from the perspective of many spiritual traditions.

The support that emerges when we go through the narcissistic helplessness is a manifestation of Being which is this whole dimension of Will. We refer to this as Diamond Will for reasons we will discuss shortly.

Understanding this quality will clarify many issues regarding idealization and its transferences.

Recognizing that the support that resolves the idealizing transference is an essential manifestation of Being, makes it clear that there is
no way to gain true support from external sources. It is an aspect of
our very Being, and the most that an external source may provide is
guidance towards recognizing it within ourselves.

This brings us back to our consideration of Kohut's view of the transformation of narcissism. We have noted his emphasis on the empathic
bond between teacher and student, and discussed our view that the
importance of this bond is not only to provide what was missing in
the student's early childhood, but to provide sufficient holding for the
student to venture into the narcissistic helplessness and terrifying
emptiness. Also, this empathy gives the teacher the information and
skill necessary for guiding the student deeper, to contact his own real
support. It is clear from the cases above that the empathic bond would
not by itself reconnect the student with his own true support. The
insight into the helplessness, the understanding that the deficiency is
not a real one, and the recognition of the delusion behind both, are
pivotal in the transformation of this narcissistic manifestation. It is
these insights that are primarily responsible for this transformation.
In fact, the transformation is bound to occur if we achieve these
insights, even in the absence of the empathic bond. We see, then, that
although the empathic bond is helpful, it is not the central factor in
the transformation, and insight into the functioning of the psyche
retains its traditional place of central significance.

What is the truth of internalization?

Another aspect of Kohut's view is that the transformation occurs
through internalization of the functions of the idealized object and
the consequent development of needed psychic structure. This is the
established view among depth psychologists. It is of utmost importance
to understand this conception, which is a prevalent model of the way
human beings develop and mature. Basically, the view is that a human
being develops by internalizing the soothing, calming, and regulating
functions of the objects—the parents in childhood, and the teacher

262   (analyst) in adulthood. We question two elements of this model. The first is that what is internalized, and hence established within the self, are mechanisms and functions. The second is that inner development occurs by internalizing something that is not intrinsic to the self.

Clarifying the precise difference between Kohut's view and ours on this question of internalization will help us to see more clearly the dividing line between the psychological level of understanding the self, and the understanding of the self in relation to Being, which we are developing here. We saw in the cases above that what was established was not a psychic mechanism, but a connection with an inherent part of ourselves, the aspect of essential support. It is true that we do not realize it until it is established, but this does not mean that it is internalized from an external source. The external source can at best invoke essential support in us, and teach us how to relate to it, but we discover it within ourselves as an inherent element of our humanness. In fact, all the spiritual qualities in the path of self-realization are integrated not through a process of internalization, but a process more like the lighting of one flame by another. The teacher guides the attention of the student to his own already-existing resources, because the teacher knows how these resources appear in experience and can see the identifications that are blocking the student's experience of them.

When we understand deeper levels of the human potential, we see that the internalization of psychic structures is only one of the mechanisms in the development of support for the self. When the self is in touch with its essential nature, support comes increasingly from Being itself. As the soul recognizes and integrates this presence, it develops a wisdom whose source is the essential presence itself. This wisdom can expand the horizons of our understanding of human development.

The concept of internalization can also help us understand another question important for self-realization: What exactly is psychic structure?[35]

Even in the work of self-realization of normal individuals, the healing of segments of the self that approach narcissistic pathology might require a stage of internalization. Furthermore, internalization is usually part of the overall process of the integration of essential presence. But this internalization is not primarily responsible for the

transformation. Since the primary transformation of narcissism is the   263
discovery and the permanent establishment of essential presence, as
the student's realization goes to very deep levels, even those structures
that have been built in relation to the teacher and the work will be
exposed. When this occurs, what sort of structure could remain?

Is there essential structure?

Is Diamond Will a psychic structure? Students sometimes describe
it as a structure, as did Daniel above. As he learned to deal with his
relationship to me and to "let go" in my presence, he began to experience the sense of solidity of the Diamond Will. He also felt warmth,
peace, confidence, and joy, as qualities of this solidity. The qualities
became bright colors in his inner vision: brilliant green, luminous
black, shiny silver, and bright yellow. He saw and felt them to compose
a structure that reminded him of a medieval cathedral. He felt the
solidity of the cathedral structure, the spaciousness of the great expanse
inside it, and the colored faceted crystal lattices all around it gave him
feelings of warmth, happiness and peace. He felt supported, present,
and authentic.

"The cathedral" is one of the names for the Diamond Will because
it frequently appears in consciousness as an inner form resembling a
cathedral. We may call this a psychic structure, but not in the usual
meaning of the term. It is not an organization of remembered impressions. In this experience, the consciousness is actually structured by
the spontaneous arising of an essential form, a beautiful and magnificent form of presence. This presence actually exposes the usual psychic structures, especially composing the structure of self-identity and
its supports. It exposes the self-identification as a fake structure with
fake supports, as we see in the following case.

Martin has been working with the author for some time; at this
juncture we find him expanding in his life in many ways. He has mar-
ried a woman he loves and is expanding his work and becoming more
autonomous in it. Although he has experienced the Diamond Will and
worked through some of its issues, issues of support are emerging
again. He feels that he is not supporting himself in a way he needs, in
his work or in his marriage. As he explores the issue, he sees that he

264   has been denying some of his wife's limitations because of the need to idealize her. This exposes his denial of his mother's insufficiency, made necessary by his dependence on her. Martin starts feeling some tension in his back, along the spine. He realizes that this tense spine is a kind of support, composed of identifications with both parents. Awareness of this psychic structure began to reveal an underlying emptiness, until it became an empty husk, which felt to him like a false support for his familiar, old identity, which was standing in the way of his expansion. The emptiness expanded, dissolving the false support-structure, and the Diamond Will emerged anew. At this point, it emerged in the aspect of Truth, as a substantial presence with the feeling of truth, which makes him realize that only truth is a real support. This, in turn, made it possible for Martin to feel his sense of presence as his true identity.

The psychic structures established to support the familiar sense of identity, such as those which internalize the functions of the idealized object, are fundamentally false because they support a false identity. All psychic structures based on past impressions are found to be false when the emptiness underneath them reveals their unreality.

Our exploration reveals, then, that the idealized object functions as a support for the familiar, but inherently weak, identity, and also as a defense against acknowledging the absence of true inner support, which we call the Diamond Will. The relationship with the idealized object supports the familiar identity, and thus masks narcissistic helplessness. Since this helplessness is an expression of the deficient emptiness—which signifies the absence of inner support, the idealized transference is specifically a defense against acknowledging this absence and the painful emotional states connected with it.[36]

chapter 26

Essential Origins
of Idealization

———————————————————————————— •

H aving explored idealizing transference and the dimension of Diamond Will, we can see more clearly the connection between the idealized object that is needed to support one's narcissistic identity, and the essential quality that is the support for the true identity. The idealized object is usually seen as big, strong, powerful, perfect, intelligent, and loving. These characteristics are like the experience of the Diamond Will: immense, powerful, loving, spacious, and solid. We saw in Chapter 20 that the grandiose self is a distorted image of the Essential Identity. In relation to the Diamond Will, which is the true support for the Essential Identity, the image is not only distorted, but projected on an external object, usually a parent or teacher. *This is the source of idealization: The perfect qualities of the idealized selfobject are not merely created from the needs of the child, but reflect the qualities of something real.*[37] These qualities, which are considered by depth psychologists to be delusional idealizations, are the real characteristics of the only thing that can support the child's real identity: the Diamond Will of Essence. The child needs the idealization, which is simply the projection of the Diamond Will on the parent, because he knows—albeit unconsciously and indirectly—what he needs to sustain his sense of true identity.

266   The question of what makes the child develop in such a way as to project something of his own on external figures remains unanswered. We do observe that the adult self projects the Diamond Will on the idealized figure, and we can only conclude that this originates in childhood development. We also have more direct evidence from our exploration of students' childhood situations that the child does project the Diamond Will on the idealized parent. However, there is a difference. The adult idealization not only indicates the need for support, it also functions to mask the lack of support (the sense of deficient emptiness) which is uncovered when this idealization is disrupted. On the other hand, the child's idealization does not seem to mask a state of deficiency in the child; it simply expresses his need for support. The child's attribution of the perfect qualities of the Diamond Will to the idealized parent appears to be a natural part of development. This is why we question whether it is a projection.

A report from a student, Anna, illustrates an experience of Diamond Will which does indicate the possibility that the infant experiences Diamond Will in some contexts of support from the parent. It also indicates that, in some situations, the answer to the question of whether it is projected becomes moot because it is experienced at a time when the self-identity is not entirely separate from the parent, and the experience of the child is patterned by merged representations. Thus, you could say the child is not separate enough to project; she experiences the quality simply as part of the situation and does not discriminate exactly whether it is hers or the parent's. This situation is similar to Kohut's idea that holding on to the idealized object is part of the tendency to hold on to elements of primary narcissism, just as the grandiose self is.

> *In the context of my personal life I was working through deep barriers to sustaining the work in the face of the narcissistic catastrophe of losing my intimate relationship. At the same time in my relationship to you and the group I was feeling strongly that I did not want to depend on you or the work for guidance and support for my process, although I was clearly aware that this dependence did exist. I needed you and my friends to see and support where I was. But this need was hard to tolerate.*

In this meeting, you were talking about mirroring. I had been *passionately exploring the question of what is mirroring really. What's it for? In the course of sitting there listening to you I became very heavy, depressed, leaden. I felt alone, abandoned. I might as well be dead. No life, no love. I just completely surrendered to that state. Profound depression and heaviness. A big lump of dead rock. But in the back of my mind I am listening to you and really wondering about mirroring. Then in a moment I saw it. I saw what is really happening when a mother sees a baby. The insight was, what is seeing and what is being seen are the same thing. No boundary; the intense golden love and the seeing together. The room was transformed into this beautiful golden structure. It is the essential reality seeing itself. Even if the mother doesn't know it, even if it will be forgotten and lost, at this moment the mother's seeing and love makes possible this powerful structure of light and love.*

Then to my amazement, for a long time afterward the dominant state was the felt sense of the Diamond Will, immovable, unaffectable, immense, but at the same time direct and simple. In intimate situations with a friend I could feel I was in a much deeper place than my friend, but it didn't matter. I didn't need my friend to be where I was, and didn't feel the usual narcissistic hurt that I wasn't seen. I felt completely free to be myself whether there was support and mirroring or not.

One conclusion we might draw from this experience is that, since the child is the Essential Identity and the mother's love and support and mirroring are there, the child experiences the support as Diamond Will since that is what is actually there on the essential level as support for the true identity. In fact, we can see another aspect of the situation which would make the child associate the Diamond Will with the parent: The child who is unsupported, who is uncomfortable or frightened or abandoned in the absence or nonattunement of the parent, is not completely, freely abiding in her essential presence, but is reacting in order to try to get what she needs. At that point she is experiencing the absence of support. When support comes, it generally comes in the form of the parent. It is possible, then, that as the child relaxes back into the open flow of presence (with the implicit identification with

268   the Essential Identity), the quality of Diamond Will will also be present. Such a scenario would depend somewhat on the state of the parent. Loving support would be much more likely to allow the child to rest in essential presence than resentful or cursory caretaking.

In sum, the child could experience that when the parent is there, this dimension of support is experienced, and when the parent is gone, it sometimes disappears. Then, as the representations of self and parent develop, the quality of the Diamond Will might remain associated with the parent, rather than literally projected.

A self psychologist may think that the adult idealization is merely a resumption of the early one, and it is not a projection but a needed delusion. However, this does not explain why helplessness and lack of support arise when the idealizing transference is disrupted. These manifestations indicate the existence of a defensive mechanism, for the emptiness relates specifically to the absence of the Diamond Will, which can only mean that its projection on the idealized figure is accompanied by its repression or splitting off. This defensive mechanism in the idealizing transference makes it difficult for us to accept that the idealization is simply a continuation or resumption of a natural developmental process; to do so would be to assume that some features of the process are inherently defensive, regardless of the environmental situation.

While we believe that childhood idealization differs from the adult version, it does seem that the latter develops from the former. As we saw in Anna's report, the childhood idealization may reflect a continuation of a real perception of essential reality, after what is perceived is no longer present. The idealization might also involve a reversion to an actual past perception of some of the real qualities of the parents. Perhaps, in some fleeting moments, one might have a real experience of a parent with the qualities of Diamond Will. Or perhaps he attributes the quality to a parent because he is still developmentally unequipped to experience it directly. If the process of idealization goes through its optimal development, the child will integrate his own Diamond Will; otherwise, he will develop deficient emptiness. At this point we leave this line of thought as a hypothetical, but interesting question that deserves additional research.

What is the relation between support and will?

Our perspective on will differs significantly from the conventional view. Will is usually associated with action, but we are seeing that in the context of spiritual work it implies the opposite: nonaction. Essential will is associated with action only in the sense that it provides the self with the confidence that allows it to persevere and to be patient. This insight becomes clearer as one experiences the various dimensions of will that manifest in the deeper stages of spiritual transformation. The Diamond Will clarifies this understanding in very specific details, in the utmost subtlety of inner actions. It is because of this precision, clarity, and subtlety, that we refer to the essential support as "Diamond" Will. This dimension of Essence supports the soul's identity with Being, not only by its presence, but also, very significantly, because its presence exposes the futility of engaging in activity to support one's sense of self. The "diamond" quality refers to the fact that this quality of presence is of a particular precise knowledge, a whole dimension of spiritual understanding. The presence of this quality teaches us that we do not need inner ego activity to support our true identity; in fact, the moment we reengage this habitual activity, we lose contact with the presence of the Diamond Will.

From this perspective, we come to understand that we may support ourselves to simply be not by doing anything, but by letting go of all inner activities towards that aim. The dimension of the Diamond Will provides guidance about the various barriers to this wisdom. It reveals, by its mere presence, how inner psychological activity is the primary barrier to simply being. It challenges all the false supports, all the activities and mechanisms that the self utilizes to gain support. The understanding that arises as we integrate this dimension of experience attains great subtlety and profundity. It includes the understanding of mental functioning and no-mind, timelessness, surrender and nondoing, and the ending of the search.

The idealizing transference is only one of the issues associated with the Diamond Will. The full integration of an entire dimension of Essence requires the resolution of many fundamental issues. Other issues which affect the integration of this aspect are ego activity and our various strategies for getting support. The student faces issues of

270   aloneness and autonomy and must work through many epistemological and cognitive questions. The realization of the Diamond Will
involves many experiences and insights, and ultimately gives birth to
a profound transformation of our view of ourselves and the world.

This full integration is not an easy feat. It requires a great deal of commitment and confrontation with the situation of the self. The wisdom
of nondoing is rarely attained in a complete way; most students develop
it only partially. To fully develop the wisdom of nondoing, which is to
absorb all the wisdom of the dimension of the Diamond Will, is to
attain permanent self-realization.

Kohut's belief that the self never becomes independent of the need
for external sources of support comes close to the truth, for it is rare
that an individual attains fully the wisdom of nondoing. Idealization,
and the dependence on external sources for narcissistic support, do not
involve only other individuals; we also use institutions, ideas, spiritual
notions, ideologies, situations, and activities as objects of idealization.
Only the truly self-realized individual can be herself while still perceiving everyone and everything in their true condition. Only she is
sufficiently comfortable with truth for it to be her only support.

Ultimately, the concept of support is inadequate to describe the
function of the Diamond Will. We cannot possibly think that Being
needs to be supported, for it is the simplicity and directness of what
is. So what do we mean when we say that the Diamond Will is the support for the Essential Identity? This is a profound question, and there
is no simple answer. We need to investigate the concept of support to
understand this situation. Support is one of those elements of experience that does not come to awareness unless it is lost. We conceive the
notion of support to explain our experience when support is missing.

Being is a unity, implicitly complete and perfect. When we engage
in inner ego activity to sustain and protect our sense of identity, this
activity blocks the experience of Being. It specifically blocks the
Diamond Will. Blocking any quality of Being constitutes a barrier to
full realization, because Being is a unity and does not exist in isolated
parts. When this particular barrier is removed, we first experience
Being in the aspect of the implicit perfection that had been blocked.
In its innate intelligence, Being manifests itself in the quality specifically

needed for it, Being, to reveal itself as the fundamental reality of the self. This manifestation makes explicit in experience the implicit perfection that was blocked.

Although the Diamond Will is a pure aspect of Essence (that has no equivalent in the conventional dimension of experience), we associate it with what is commonly called support. This aspect seems to be the prototype for the ordinary concept of support. This notion seems confirmed by the observation that we experience the need for support when the idealizing transference is disrupted, and working through the issues leads to the experience of support on the level of Being. While we recognize it as the true support, we see also that it is actually much more than support; it is a perfection of Being that remains mysterious regardless of how clearly and completely we know it.

It is in this sense that the Diamond Will is the support for the Essential Identity. The Essential Identity cannot stand on its own because it is only one of the perfections of Being. For it to stand on its own would mean that it can be isolated from the unity of Being. The Essential Identity is the perfection that represents the total identity of the self with this unity.

Diamond Will as a dimension

Diamond Will is what we call a *dimension* of Being. We use the word *dimension* to refer to a level or plane of Being, on which the various qualities of Essence appear in specific ways that differentiate it from other dimensions. Each dimension adds to essential aspects a new characteristic, universal to all aspects in this dimension. There is the dimension of objective Love, for instance, in which all aspects—Compassion, Clarity, Will, Peace, and so on—appear as manifestations of love. They retain their original qualities, like Compassion and Peace, but now all with the sweetness of Love.

The fact that the Diamond Will is a dimension of Essence means that integrating it is a much larger and more involved process than that of integrating a single essential aspect. As with other dimensions, the process of integration goes through two phases. The first phase is a matter of experiencing this whole dimension as a unit, as one manifestation. We experience it as a delineated form or structure of presence, very

272   intricate and rich with detail. It is basically the manifestation of all essential aspects together, forming one structure. Since each aspect has a unique color and affect, the structure appears to be composed of colored lights, dancing with blissful feelings. It is a self-luminous, latticed, crystalline structure, with brilliant, dancing colors inseparable from the blissful qualities, all held within a sense of power and solidity of presence. The sense of immensity and majesty is breathtaking, reminding us of the mother spaceship in the movie, *Close Encounters of the Third Kind.* Given that this breathtaking structure is the prototype, it is no wonder that in our transferences the idealized object is imbued with such perfection of power and beauty.

Experiencing Diamond Will elicits and clarifies all the major issues about support, particularly those of the idealizing transference. Other issues related to this dimension also arise, giving the student the opportunity to explore them.

A new phase of integration commences when specific essential aspects emerge singly or in combinations, experienced as aspects of support. In other words, Love, or Peace, or Kindness, or Intelligence, and so on, may arise as support. Each of these manifestations may bring up a specific issue about support.

For instance, the idealizing transference might be disrupted by what the student feels is an unempathic response from the teacher. If he takes this event to indicate the imperfection of the teacher's sensitivity and compassion, this means that he experiences the teacher as lacking the quality of compassion on the dimension of the Diamond Will, that is, as support. This typically will bring to consciousness the childhood situation in which the student felt that one of his parents did not compassionately relate to who he was. Issues arise about the need for the parent's compassionate support, with the associated object relations, emotional hurt, and other feelings. This exploration will lead to the deficient emptiness of support, which can then usher the student into the experience of true support.

In this context, the student's experience of support will include not only solidity and confidence—which indicate Will—but also qualities of warmth, gentleness, and loving kindness. He feels like a solid and immense mountain, a brilliant emerald mountain, with an exquisite

gentleness and a sacred sense of compassion. It is as if the immensity 273
has a heart of total empathy and deep consideration for the suffering
of the self, both his and others. His heart melts in exquisite warm surrender when he observes the effort that those around him are furi-
ously engaged in as they attempt to find themselves or to support
themselves. In this state, he cannot help but recognize that this search,
with all its activities, is both an expression and a perpetuation of the
deepest and most fundamental suffering that the self may experience.
He recognizes with clarity and exquisite kindness the futility of this
activity, and feels a deep spontaneous wish to be of help in alleviating
this suffering.

If he remains for some time with this compassionate manifestation
of the Diamond Will, the student may understand that he cannot help
by doing anything. This confronts him with his helplessness on a new
level. Accepting this helplessness with kindness, he may learn the wisdom implicit in the manifestation of Being he is experiencing, that his
contribution is his own presence, that he can support others by simply
being, and guiding them towards this Being.

This is an example of how an essential aspect is integrated on the
dimension of the Diamond Will, as a support for nondoing, and therefore, for simply being. It demonstrates how the qualities of the aspect—
in this case Loving Kindness—are completely intertwined with those
of support. It also demonstrates how this quality not only resolves the
issue about the need for kind support, but that it also reveals the knowledge and wisdom associated with it.

Each person has her own unique combination of psychological issues
related to her personal history, which create the need to integrate specific aspects as support. We saw in the cases above that Penny, for
instance, felt disappointed in me because she discovered that my clarity was not perfect, indicating she needed the aspect of Clarity as support. Martin discovered that for him an important aspect he needed
for support was Truth; for Donna, the needed aspect was Love, and for
Sam it was Intelligence, the aspect of Essence which is related to the quality of responsibility. Each individual needs to integrate the Diamond
Will as a whole dimension or structure, and also as the specific aspects
themselves, as they manifest in that dimension.

274   Three points are worthy of comment here:

1. It is clear from our discussion that support exists in various qualities. The child, or the student who is re-contacting his essential being, needs this support to be not only empathic and compassionate, but also needs support that is clear, strong, loving, calm, joyful, true, sincere, intelligent, and open, reflecting the need for the essential aspects of Clarity, Strength, Love, Peace, Joy, Truth, Sincerity, Intelligence, and Inner Spaciousness, respectively, as support. Kohut emphasized the need for the quality of Loving Kindness, which is associated with emotional warmth and empathic consideration, while Kernberg stressed Clarity. Now we see that many more qualities are needed to support the child's development of his true sense of self. This understanding may help us as parents to understand why our children idealize us, and help us to provide the true support they actually need as this need changes according to development and circumstances.

2. A teacher of self-realization can guide her students effectively only if she has integrated her own inner support. Her guidance and assistance are more objective and precise the more deeply she has integrated the dimension of the Diamond Will. This guidance can be most effective if she can manifest not only the structure of the Diamond Will, but also the various aspects, thus making it possible for her guidance and support to be precisely attuned to the needs of her particular students.

3. Kohut discovered several varieties of idealizing transference, but noted two basic ones:

   There are therapeutic reactivation of archaic states which hark back to the period when the idealized mother imago is still almost completely merged with that of the self; and there are other instances in which the pathognomonic transference reactivation concern much later points in the development of the idealizing libido and the idealized object. (Kohut, 1971, p. 55)

   This formulation is helpful when we discover that essential support is comprised of several levels. The two main levels correspond to the two developmental states Kohut mentions. The Diamond

Will manifests differently at several levels, with each level resolving the idealizing transference corresponding to it. We call the first level—which resolves the idealizing transference of the differentiated self—the Diamond Will, and the second level—which resolves the idealizing transference of the self still merged with the mother—the Merged Diamond Will. Our discussion so far has been of the first level of the Diamond Will, although some of the cases mentioned above, particularly Anna's, are representative of the Merged Diamond Will.

The different levels of Diamond Will correspond to different levels of essential identity. The first level corresponds to the Essential Identity, which is the identity for differentiated self. For most children, the idealized selfobject is the father, as we saw in most of the cases above. The next level of identity is related to experiencing ourselves as Being that is boundless and infinite. It is the self-realization of Being, on the cosmic level, where one recognizes Being, and hence, one's true identity, to be the undifferentiated unity of all existence. For most students, the childhood idealized selfobject relating to this realization is the mother of symbiosis, or more accurately, the mother of Mahler's dual unity. The next level of support, the Nonconceptual Diamond Will, relates to the identity with Being as a nonconceptual truth, and so on. This ultimately leads to the Nondual Diamond Will, which relates to the nondual presence as our identity, and this is the true self that transforms what we have called oral narcissism.

Our discussion can indicate only the general outlines of the issues and states of the Diamond Will. Since it is a whole dimension of Essence, it would take a book as long as this volume to investigate it in detail. The details are useful for students involved in the process of spiritual transformation, but are mainly necessary for the teacher of self-realization. Our appreciation of the enormity of this one dimension of Essence not only acknowledges the richness of Being, but given the fact that we must make intimate and thorough acquaintance with this dimension in order to truly transform narcissism and attain self-realization, allows us to appreciate the magnitude of the task.

PART 3

TRANSFORMATIONS

OF

NARCISSISM

U nderstanding narcissistic transferences allows us to investigate, in-depth, the narcissistic structures of the self. Inquiring into these structures and their manifestations in daily life and coming to see them as ego structures (rather than simply being identified with them), leads to their transformation. In our work, transformation of a psychic structure can include strengthening it, if that is what is necessary. But in the main, transformation involves the "thinning away" of such structures until they become completely flexible, and hence, transparent to essential presence. In Part II we saw this process from the perspective of the transformation of the structures that support the sense of identity. This process leads to the realization of Diamond Will, which enables the self to experience itself patterned by essential presence. We now feel intrinsically supported to be ourselves.

This process of self-realization naturally applies pressure on the conventional sense of identity. Issues arise which affect the central

278   narcissistic structure, that of self-identity. The transformation of narcissism consists largely of the transformation of this structure, leading to the realization of the Essential Identity. The increasing pressure on the structure of self-identity exposes its underlying vulnerability and shakiness. The student attempts to find ways to shore up his sense of identity, but can no longer turn so easily to idealization; he has seen through it. So he turns to mirroring selfobjects to help him preserve the integrity and cohesion of his capacity for self-recognition. This manifests as the need for mirroring, particularly in the mirror transference onto the teacher. Investigating this narcissistic transference in depth leads us to a thorough understanding of the sense of identity and its underlying structure. We become increasingly aware of the properties of the self-identity, which we have up to now taken for granted to be part of who we really are. This awareness begins to transform the self-identity, making it more flexible and realistic. So this structure becomes less and less opaque, until it is transparent enough to reveal the essential identity. This is the central process of the transformation of narcissism, which begins by observing and understanding the need to be seen and mirrored.

chapter 27

The Need to Be Seen

I n this chapter we will explore the mirror transference, which is the counterpart to the idealizing transference which arises in the student's process. The need of the typical student to be seen and appreciated by his teacher is part of his normal relationship with her. All people have this need in their important relationships. The mirror transference is a more intense manifestation of this normal need. It may occur in any significant relationship, but inevitably develops in the student in his relation to the teacher, as the narcissistic constellation approaches consciousness. He starts increasingly to feel the intense need to be seen, recognized, understood, related to, admired, and appreciated. He wants her to see him as special and unique. He wants the teacher to be accurately attuned and empathic to where he is. He comes to realize how much he wants her to give him special attention and love, and how sensitive he is to whether she is giving it to him or not.

This may manifest as an overt tendency to brag—openly or indirectly showing off his capacities and accomplishments, or as a passive sensitivity to the presence or absence of recognition and approval from the teacher. It may take the form of the outright demand to be seen and acknowledged consistently or in a special way, or as increased

280   sensitivity to imperfections in the teacher's perception of, and feedback to him. At this juncture, then, the needs of the student to be seen, related to, understood, valued, and admired as precious, special, and unique, with empathy and attunement, intensify in his relation to his teacher, and become the central thread in his process of understanding himself. He will usually also experience an intensification of these narcissistic needs in his various significant relationships, but it is in the relation with his teacher that he has the most favorable circumstance for understanding them.

Although these needs are generally not new in the student's experience, they can intensify to neurotic, even pathological, proportions. These manifestations are transitory, however, and so not actually pathological. With some guidance from the teacher the student is usually able to comprehend their meaning and thus, not completely identify with them.

Our understanding of the mirror transference reflects Kohut's and others' psychological theories, but differs from them regarding its genesis. Both Kernberg and Kohut hold the view that the mirror transference is the expression of the activation of the patient's grandiose self in the analytic situation, although they differ (as we have discussed) on the nature of this activation and on the origins of the grandiose self.

Kohut writes:

> In analogy to the cohesive therapeutic revival of the idealized selfobject in the idealizing transference, the grandiose self is therapeutically reactivated in the transference like condition for which the term mirror transference, despite its insufficient inclusiveness, will usually be employed. (Kohut, 1971, p. 106)

It would seem that the grandiose self that reappears has been split off, because the process of the gradual recognition of the actual limitations of the self—which facilitates the integration of the grandiose self into a more realistic self image—has been incomplete. Thus, the split-off or repressed grandiose self is retained in its primitive form, no longer accessible to external influence. It is then remobilized in the mirror transference as an attempt to resume the arrested development of the self.

This view addresses pathological narcissism, in which the grandiose self occupies a significant place in the structure of the self-identity. The mirror transference manifests, then, as the need for the grandiose self to be seen and admired. However, for most students in the process of self-realization we are describing, this is not the case; they are attempting to gain mirroring for their normal sense of identity, which is not grandiose. Thus, Kohut's view does not completely address the need of the normal individual for narcissistic mirroring.

Our understanding of the mirror transference as an intensification of the normal need for mirroring is an extension of our view of pathological narcissism as an exaggeration of the narcissism of everyday life. The need for mirroring is a completely natural phenomenon, which helps the self to integrate the various manifestations of the self, not only the grandiose self.

A poetic (but not actually metaphorical) way of describing the need for mirroring is that the human soul *feeds on light*. This light is awareness, the soul's clarity about itself. The self needs this nourishment for its growth, development and maturation. When our awareness about ourselves is opening, as in insight, at the moment of that insight there is a quickening, a movement towards integration and development. We also observe that when we don't understand, when we are not clear about where we are or what is happening to us, there is a lack of movement. The soul will not move from where it is until it completely comprehends, completely sees, where it is.

The soul is a living consciousness, a presence that is pure consciousness, which is characterized ultimately by pure transparency, pure clarity. The various qualities, capacities, and functions of this self will not develop completely until it is able to be those things consciously, with full awareness and clarity. So when we say that the soul feeds on light, we mean that developing a clear and objective recognition and perception of ourselves allows us to realize our capacities. Also, when a part of the self is not recognized, acknowledged, related to, and valued—when it is not positively seen—it will not develop. The element not seen might be a quality of Being, a dimension of mind or feeling, a certain capacity or a way of functioning. When any inherent attribute of the soul is not developed, the soul's overall development is not

282   harmonious. This highlights the importance of awareness, clarity, and self-recognition, all throughout life and not just in childhood.

The awareness that allows the self to grow optimally is a completely balanced recognition which implicitly embodies love, strength, compassion, appreciation, and joy. It is not enough simply to be seen; the self needs to be seen with all the essential qualities of Being. In other words, the self needs the kind of seeing that reflects its fundamental nature. This principle applies to other manifestations of the soul, such as emotions or intelligence. "Nature's imperative is, again, that no intelligence unfolds without a stimulus from a developed form of that intelligence." (Pearce, 1992, p. 115)

This complete consciousness characterizes the condition of self-realization, in which the nature of the self is seen and understood objectively and accurately. The Sufis think of the self as colorless; it attains the clarity that indicates both total transparency and completeness, for clear light includes all colors of the prism, symbolizing the various pure qualities of Essence. "The last stage is colourlessness, everything disappearing, and leaving the salik (seeker) in a state of fana (dissolution of the self-soul), the Transcendental wonder." (S.I.A. Shah, 1971, p. 218)

Buddhists call this condition "mirror-like awareness": The self is completely transparent to itself, can see and be itself fully, just like looking in a mirror. We then see things just as they are, without opinions, without projections, without ideas, without distortions: completely objective. When we realize mirror-like awareness, that transparency, clarity and complete colorlessness is seen at the same time to be complete perfection. This awareness makes us clear about ourselves, all the way to our true nature. So we are clearly and transparently cognizant of our condition at the moment. In the work of self-realization, the self regains its light, which is perception, which is awareness, which is clarity, which is understanding, which is consciousness. The inner journey is a matter of increased awareness, increased consciousness, increased clarity, increased perception, increased understanding, and increased knowledge, which inherently embody the spiritual qualities of love, compassion and so on, and the various faculties of functioning. Self-realization is the realization of the potential of the self with full awareness and appreciation.

The self feeds on light, and it does not matter where this light comes from. The self develops by becoming fully aware of the various dimensions of experience, but it does not matter how this awareness develops. It does not matter whether the source of this light is inside or outside, as long as the self comes to see and recognize itself. Whether we see ourselves directly or through someone pointing out the truth of the self to us, the result is the same: to quicken the soul's evolution. This observation can help us understand the need for mirroring.

What are the origins of the need for mirroring?

We have observed that the need for mirroring is based on the following three features of the process of the soul's development:

1. In order to develop, the soul needs, among many elements, to see and recognize itself.

2. It is immaterial whether this self-awareness and recognition results from directly seeing oneself or as a result of being seen by an external source.

3. In early childhood the soul does not possess the capacity for self-reflection. It does not see itself. This is an accepted fact in developmental psychology.

Therefore, the baby needs to be seen in order to grow because he is incapable of seeing himself. The only possibility, then, is to be seen from the outside. This expresses itself as the need for mirroring. The baby needs the environment to mirror him so that he can come to know himself, and for his soul to grow and develop. For this unfolding to occur completely and harmoniously, the baby needs reflection from the pure awareness which is the mirror-like awareness. He needs to be seen with the clear, objective light characterized by the pure spiritual qualities: love, value, openness, compassion, strength, intelligence, joy, satisfaction, peacefulness, and so on. So optimal mirroring is celebrative, appreciative, admiring, empathic, attuned, understanding, and relational, expressing the essential qualities of the mirror-like awareness. It is this awareness that is needed for the mirroring. If it is available then the self has the opportunity to mature naturally, spontaneously, fully, and perfectly.

284   For most of us, this quality of mirroring is rarely available. Even more rarely is it consistently available. In normal circumstances, our early mirroring inadequately reflects our true being. This inadequacy is the main environmental factor causing narcissism. Mirroring can be inadequate in two ways: It is either not available (or not available consistently), or when it is available, it is reflecting not the true nature of the infant but some more superficial aspect.

    In a reasonably healthy situation, the child receives clear and positive mirroring of certain parts of the self. Parents are selective about what they see and value, depending on their histories, their values, and their narcissistic identifications. Sometimes parents emphasize acknowledgment of the child's physical manifestations, sometimes the mental capacities, sometimes the emotional nature. Often, real features of the qualities of one's essential nature are appreciated. When the child is fortunate, one or both of the parents see these manifestations of her soul and appreciate, or even celebrate them. They are proud of her and lovingly admire her precious qualities and capacities. She might be liked and admired for being cute, for instance, or smart, or creative, or capable. A certain part of her is nourished by this loving light. This appreciation, recognition, support, and encouragement enable her to see these manifestations of her soul and to integrate them with a positive cathexis to her sense of identity. For example, this support is present when the child accomplishes certain tasks and the parent is seeing and appreciating her; the child is excited and the parent is sharing that excitement, and there is a joyful gleam in the mother or father's eyes. Now the child perceives, without thinking it, that the parent is actually seeing what she is doing and admiring her for it. This helps the child to reflect on her experience of herself and what she is doing. She now sees and knows this part of herself, which paves the way for its integration into her sense of who she is.

    The child might even be able to see this part of her self, but if the parent doesn't see it she will doubt its value, or even its reality. Mirroring, then, not only helps her see elements of her soul, but also confirms and establishes them as real and as her self. She is not hallucinating. Recognition confirms it, makes it real. Without the mirroring, it is difficult for the child to be her self, even if she is at a stage of development at which she can see her self.

What is mirror-like consciousness?

We call a certain kind of consciousness mirror-like understanding because it has no distortion or projection and is complete rather than selective. It is not mirror-like in the sense that it is dead, inert, or non-responsive; on the contrary, it has love, admiration, value and joyfulness, excitement and satisfaction. The developing self can recognize and cherish aspects of her self which are mirrored in this way and integrate them into her sense of identity. These qualities of the self grow in the light, into the light.

The manifestations of the soul that are inadequately mirrored remain in the dark recesses of unactualized potential. The child tends not to experience them as part of her self, or not value them. She might even view them as a threat to her connection to her parents. They do not become integrated into her sense of who she is, or if they do, the identification is conflictual. These elements of the self then fail to develop or become distorted. Thus, the development of the self as a whole lacks harmony and completeness, resulting in a general weakness of the identity.

The point of mirroring is not simply feedback; it is also acceptance and appreciation. The child needs to recognize her self in the manifestations of her soul, as precious and lovable. The need for mirroring is such a fundamental need of the self that when it is not satisfied she will try to get it one way or another, even at great cost to her self. It is as simple as that. She can't help but try to elicit positive mirroring.

Even though the situation creates an identity based on partial integration of the qualities of the soul where only some elements and dimensions of the soul are included, the developmental force inherent in the soul will always move towards completing its development. The soul will naturally desire experience of the excluded elements of the self. In adult life, this movement expresses itself in many ways, especially in the need for mirroring. This later need for mirroring is a direct expression of the hunger of the soul for light. More accurately, it is an expression of the soul's need to see, recognize and integrate the unintegrated elements of her potential. It is an expression of the inherent movement of the self towards self-realization, filtered through the veils created by early mirroring inadequacy.

286   The later quest for mirroring, after the self-identity is constructed, is always somewhat distorted by the distortions in the self-image. Our need for mirroring continues to exert pressure directly, as the normal need to be seen when we feel our known aspects are not seen, or when we are narcissistically insulted. But this need expresses itself also in the need for mirroring for the sense of identity itself; for the satisfaction of this particular need indicates to us that we are being seen and acknowledged. So we experience the need for mirroring as the need for the self-identity to be seen because we recognize ourselves through this identity.

There is a curious puzzle in the psychological understanding of this phenomenon. Why does the self need its identity to be seen if the identity has developed mostly through the integration of the elements of the self that were mirrored? The self-identity structure is constituted of the representations of the self that the self knows, partly because they were mirrored. Why is there a need for something to be seen when it has already been seen?

Our view is that this manifestation is a distortion of the natural need, which is distorted by its passage through the filter of the self-identity structure and its history of inadequate mirroring. The structure of self-identity is inherently vulnerable and shaky, and mirroring provides it with the cohesive glue that makes it feel more solid and real. As discussed in detail in Chapters 11 and 19, the identity is shaky because it is incomplete and distorted. The cohesion that results from the mirroring of the normal sense of identity is not lasting, so there results the chronic need for mirroring that we recognize as normal. Another factor affecting this need is that the self recognizes itself through the already established, normal sense of identity. Since we do not expect unknown elements of the soul to express their need for mirroring, we feel any need for mirroring as the need of the self-identity, and the deeper mirroring needs of these unknown aspects are subsumed by the mirroring of the normal identity. So the self-identity subverts the dynamic thrust toward development by appropriating the soul's energy to validate its own structure and reality. It's a case of mistaken identity. This is how life in the conventional dimension of experience becomes the living-out of patterns and programs

established in childhood, rather than an expanding and deepening
unfoldment of the soul's potential.

Only in the process of genuine development toward self-realization do we recognize the need for mirroring as the hunger of essential elements of the self for the light of awareness and recognition. Of course, for most students engaged in our work, this recognition is mixed with the need of the normal self for validation. The student will continue to identify with the normal self-identity structure, the transformation of which is a process that takes many years. However, as the process of self-realization puts pressure on this identity structure, exposing its emptiness and weakness, the student inevitably experiences increased narcissistic sensitivity and need for mirroring. It takes a lot of sincerity and precise understanding for the student to discriminate between the need for mirroring for the self-identity structure and for the real qualities of the soul.

Essence and mirroring

In the process of the work on self-realization, the student is learning to integrate deeper strata of the self, primarily the fundamental ground of the self, the essential presence. At some point, the need for mirroring becomes primarily the need to have mirrored the essence of who one is. This allows integration of essential presence into his direct experience of who he is, his true identity. The need for mirroring focuses on Essential Identity as the student is dealing with the issues of central narcissism, which is due to alienation from the Essential Identity. The need for mirroring and the mirror transference become most distinct and precise as the issues of central narcissism arise. The student is likely to experience the following issues:

- The need to be seen and admired, which is characteristic of narcissism in general, becomes more specifically the need to be seen as special and precious.

- It is accompanied by the need to be seen and recognized not only as special, but as unique. He wants his uniqueness to be seen and applauded, whether or not this uniqueness is specifically in relation to his qualities and existential traits.

288 • The more extreme his narcissistic alienation is, the more the need for mirroring is not only for specialness and uniqueness, but for grandiose conceptions of them.

These characteristics of the need for mirroring particular to central narcissism differentiate it from other issues in the spectrum of narcissism. They reflect the student's growing awareness of his need to recognize and realize the Essential Identity by having it mirrored to him, for it is the Essential Identity which is the essential aspect characterized by the feelings of specialness, uniqueness, preciousness, and grandeur.

• Sometimes the need for mirroring manifests specifically in the need to be seen for who he really is, in contradistinction to how he appears to be or what he does. This points to his increasing realization that he wants to integrate his true nature, his reality, his very beingness. In fact, he might actually feel the mirroring need for his being, for his existence, for simply being. The need for his essential nature to be mirrored cannot take a more explicit form.

chapter 28

The Mirror Transference

O ur interpretation of the mirror transference encompasses Kohut's view as a particular case of a more general situation. Recalling from Chapter 20 that the Essential Identity is the experiential origin of the grandiose self, the latter being a distorted representation of the former, we come full circle to Kohut's formulation that the mirror transference reflects the activation of the grandiose self in the relation with the analyst.

We can summarize our understanding as follows: The need for mirroring is a general need of the soul, necessary for it to recognize its manifestations and integrate them into its sense of identity. The mirror transference arises because of the activation of the elements of the self that were inadequately mirrored in the formative years. Since infants receive so little mirroring of their essential nature, when Essence is activated the mirror transference will be triggered. In any helping relationship and in spiritual work in particular, the mirror transference is primarily due to the activation of the Essential Identity. The more pathologically narcissistic the individual is, the more the mirror transference will express itself as the need of the grandiose self (rather than the Essential Identity) to be seen and glorified. Even in narcissistic pathology,

290   however, the mirror transference reflects the activation of the Essential
Identity. Since the grandiose self is the central representation in the
self-identity structure of the narcissistic personality, and since the deeper
need for mirroring of essential elements of the self is subsumed under
the mirroring need of the self-identity structure, in the narcissistic personality the grandiose self appropriates this desire for mirroring.[38]

Empathic mirroring

Even when a student is seen accurately, he will feel unseen if this particular structure, his familiar identity, is not recognized or acknowledged. Usually, a person is aware of only a part of what is going on with
him. He might be, for example, conscious of some of his thoughts and
anxieties but not of his anger, even though it is obvious to others.
Unaware of his arrogant and demanding behavior, he might think of
himself as a mistreated genius. So when his anger or his arrogance are
mirrored back to him, he feels hurt, insulted and not seen, because it
is not his anxieties or his genius that are mirrored. His center of awareness, which is associated with his familiar sense of self (see Chapter 10),
is located within a certain region of his structure, and he can thus
acknowledge only the feedback reflecting this region. Otherwise, he
experiences mirroring as a threat to this identity.

This phenomenon occurs in all kinds of relationships, particularly
between teacher and student. This is part of the difficulty with working with this constellation. For example, if the teacher thinks she has
a deep insight into the student's character and communicates it to him,
he may feel hurt about not being seen, although she is in fact seeing
him accurately. She is not acknowledging him exactly where he happens to be at the moment. She might be seeing deeper aspects of him
than he is experiencing himself, but he is not interested! He needs his
perception of himself to be mirrored.

The shakier or more limited is his sense of self, the more the student
wants that incomplete, vulnerable structure to be seen and validated.
The range of the landscape of his soul that he wants acknowledged, or
even can tolerate being seen, is very small. The less complete is the
identity, the more feeble it is, and the more elements of the soul it
excludes. When someone sees and acknowledges other aspects of his

soul, he experiences it as a lack of mirroring, even though these aspects do in fact need to be seen for them to become conscious. But the student is not ready for that deeper mirroring, and will tend to feel hurt and unsupported in this situation.

The less narcissistic the individual, that is, the firmer and more complete his sense of identity, the more an insight that is slightly off-center—the center that is marked by the identity—can be tolerated. He can easily stretch his awareness and become conscious of these other elements of himself.

However, when students in the process of self-realization develop a sensitivity that mimics pathological narcissism, creating a greatly increased need for mirroring—what is needed is a special kind of mirroring, empathic mirroring, which is reflection that is exactly appropriate for the particular individual at that specific time. This is a different kind of seeing than the mirror-like awareness. With the mirror-like awareness, we might see the totality of the person in his fullness and reflect that. But if the person is narcissistically sensitive, he will not feel seen by this reflection. He feels he is not getting what he needs, and in some sense he is right. What he needs is to be mirrored and supported in that particular place where his center of awareness—his identity—happens to be at that moment. If he is very narcissistically hurt or wounded, the most that we can do is to exactly reflect back what he says. He says, "I'm hurt." The teacher can say, "I can see you are hurt." If she says, "I see you are hurt because somebody didn't like you," he will feel hurt or angry because he might not know that yet, and will experience her feedback as a lack of empathy; he feels she is not seeing him. At this point he might start feeling that his sense of self is disintegrating. The teacher is adding something else, more than he can handle, even though it might be true, and it might be what he will need at some later point. But at this point he is not interested in the truth; he is interested in confirming his shaky identity, which happens to be his particular truth.

Empathic mirroring is not merely reflecting what the self presents to the observer; it is mirroring what the student is directly aware of and interested in. Empathic mirroring is attuned to where the student finds his sense of self. It is thus empathic to the specific narcissistic

292   needs of his identity at the moment and sensitive to the vulnerability and shakiness of this identity. Empathic mirroring makes the student feel that the teacher is aware of exactly where he is, that is, where his identity is situated, and is attuned to the narcissistic condition of this identity. This mirroring is not oriented towards the expansion of the student's awareness of himself, but rather, towards the support and validation of what he is aware of in himself at the moment.[39]

Kohut emphasized the need of the narcissistically wounded individual for empathy. "The precariously established self of the child (as revived in the analytic situation) depends for the maintenance of its cohesion on the near-perfect empathic responses of the self-object." (Kohut, 1977, p. 91)

The mirror transference expresses the general need for mirroring, but since every individual has some narcissistic wounding, and thus some degree of vulnerability in his identity, this need becomes intermingled with the need for empathic mirroring. The more narcissistically wounded the individual, the more the need is weighed towards empathic mirroring, with a tendency, then, to use the transference not for the maturation of the self, but for validation of the self-identity.

We are not implying that the need for empathic mirroring is not a legitimate need; the narcissistically wounded person definitely needs it for a modicum of balance in his emotional life. Even the student on a spiritual path needs it from his teacher, to have the support to experience himself fully and to develop trust in his teacher so that he can allow her to guide him. In the beginning of a student's process and at later junctures involving narcissistic crises, the teacher must be empathically attuned to the student in order to help him to withstand the rigors of the process of realization. Only rare individuals might be able to do without a minimum of empathic mirroring from the teacher.

Types of mirror transference

When discussing the mirror transference or the need for mirroring, we need to keep in mind that most of the literature on narcissism refers to empathic mirroring. This is primarily because most of the modern literature on narcissism focuses on the narcissistic personality disorder. Nevertheless, we find the formulations regarding the mirror transference extremely useful for our work. Kohut's classification of the types of mirror transference is especially helpful. Setting aside for the moment that Kohut thinks of the mirror transference as the reactivation of the grandiose self, we can consider his delineation of three forms of this transference, which manifest according to the stages of development to which the regression leads.

The first form Kohut describes is the archaic merger: "The analyst is experienced as an extension of the grandiose self and he is referred to only insofar as he has become the carrier of the grandiosity and exhibitionism of the analysand's grandiose self . . ." (Kohut, 1977, p. 114)

This is the most primitive type of mirror transference, where the object—the analyst, or the teacher in our case—is not seen as a separate individual, but as an extension of the self. There are no clear differentiating boundaries between self and object, and this nondifferentiated state is experienced in the narcissistic sector. According to Kohut, the object is felt to be important only as an extension of the grandiose self, like one's arm is important to one's body, and is expected to be subservient to the body.

In our work, where the normal sense of identity rather than the grandiose self is typically the center of one's narcissism, the merger mirror transference manifests as the need to perceive the teacher as inseparable from one's sense of self, to be in total agreement with the self, where this unit of undifferentiated self and object is experienced as special and precious. The mirroring is experienced, then, as a validation of this special identity between teacher and student. The more narcissistically disturbed student experiences this self-and-object unit similarly to the primitive grandiose self.

The second form of mirror transference is alter-ego transference or twinship. This is a less archaic form of relating, where the "pathognomic therapeutic regression is characterized by the fact that the patient assumes that the analyst is either like him or similar to him, or that the analyst's psychological makeup is like, or similar to, that of the patient." (Kohut, 1977, p. 115) There is a separation between the self and the object, and the mirroring is seen in the belief or confirmation of the belief that the student is similar to the teacher in one way or another. Again, we find this type of transference in the narcissism of

294 everyday life, where the likeness is not necessarily grandiose but is cherished in the same way.

In his later work, Kohut relates this type of mirroring to the intermediate pole of the bipolar self. He views the idealizing transference as connected to the ideals pole, the mirroring transference to the ambitions pole, and the twinship to the tension arc between the two poles, the area of skills and talents. "In later childhood we clearly see that it is the intermediate area of skills and talents—the girl kneading dough, the boy working with tools—that is the leading contact point in the twinship." (Kohut, 1984, p. 199)

The notion is that by performing a function near to and in the company of a selfobject, as in the case of a girl helping her mother knead dough or the boy helping his father make or repair something, the narcissistic structure related to the intermediate area (intermediate between the polar areas of ideals and ambitions) of skills and talents develops and becomes integrated.

We do not find in our work a consistent observation supporting this later position of Kohut in regard to twinship. However, we continue to find his earlier formulation—that twinship is a type of mirror transference—to be useful in our work. We regard the area of skills and talents as part of a different form of narcissism, namely, that of individuation narcissism.

The following case illustrates the need for twinship as a type of mirroring, as well as the other aspects of mirror transference:

We find Donna in the middle of her work on the narcissistic sector of her personality, alternating between idealizing and mirror transference in her relation to me.[40] In a session, she expresses her desire for a precious part of her to be seen, recognized, valued, and treated in a special way. In the course of our discussion, she understands that she is associating me with her father, and her early needs for mirroring from him. In exploring her recent relationship with me, and connecting it to her relationship with her father, she realizes that she feels that to have herself she needs to be inseparable from me, or be like me, or that I see her as she is. This brings in a great deal of sadness and hurt, and fear of losing my support. She tells me how much she admires my qualities of compassion and solidity, and admits that she likes it

that she has those qualities herself. She feels closer to me and more like   295
me. Understanding her need to be like me, which is to preserve her
sense of self, she starts feeling her own real compassion, which makes
it easier for her to tolerate the hurt and loss of the fantasy of twinship.
Then she starts feeling a soft and delicate presence, which she recognizes as the Essential Identity.

This theme continued for several teaching sessions, in which Donna's
need for mirroring manifested sometimes as wanting merging which
will make her feel safe and happy, sometimes as the direct need to be
seen and valued, and sometimes as wanting to see herself as similar to
me. These three types of relationships to me were ways for her to preserve her sense of self. The alternation of the three types indicates they
are all types of mirror transference, for she experiences all of them as
being needed to confirm her arising sense of Essential Identity.

The third form of the mirror transference is the most mature form
of activation of the narcissistic self, in which the teacher is recognized
as a separate and different person, but as significant only as an admiring mirror for the student's identity.

> In this narrower sense of the term the mirror transference is
> the therapeutic reinstatement of that normal phase of the
> development of the grandiose self in which the gleam in the
> mother's eye, which mirrors the child's exhibitionistic display,
> and other forms of maternal participation in and response to
> the child's narcissistic-exhibitionistic enjoyment confirm the
> child's self esteem . . . (Kohut, 1971, p. 116)

This is the mirror transference as described in this chapter, which
is the most prevalent type occurring between student and teacher. The
mirror transference in the narrower sense seems to dominate at the
beginning of activation for most students. The more primitive types
manifest later, as they are related to an earlier form of narcissism, the
oral form of narcissism. As these become understood and integrated,
the mirror transference reverts to the original type. We also find that
the more a student utilizes the two primitive types of mirror transference, the more difficult it is for him to heal the narcissistic sector of
his personality; these transferences reflect more deeply rooted disturbances of the self.

296 Defenses against the mirror transference

Although the need for mirroring is universal, the student does not always acknowledge it. He frequently defends against awareness of this need, so that even when he is acting it out he is unaware of the meaning of his behavior and might even vehemently deny it. A possible reason for such a defense is that he might want to be seen and admired, but he is afraid that if he is seen, people will see the part of him that he thinks is bad, and he wants what is good in him to be seen. This conflict can cause him to deny his need for mirroring. Even if what he wants to be seen is actually mirrored, this can bring up the older deprivations of this part of the self that was not seen and bring to awareness the hurt, anger, and depression about it. On a deeper level, to be truly seen for who he really is will bring to consciousness the inherent aloneness in the realm that wasn't seen. So he fights awareness of his need, even though he is always trying to satisfy it.

Narcissistic vulnerability distorts the natural need for mirroring, changing it from the need to be seen for who one really is to the need for mirroring of what he believes to be him. This makes the need for mirroring problematic, and thus, being seen is not always what is actually needed. For example, a person might be identified with a kind of hiddenness, and experience conflict when the need for mirroring manifests. The arising of the past hurt about not having been seen adds to the student's sensitivity. Also, the fear of unempathic mirroring can cause a student to defend against awareness of his need to be seen.[41]

The breakdown of the mirror transference

As long as the student feels that his teacher is empathically aware of him and mirroring him in an admiring or special way, he feels that she is supporting and validating his sense of self. This mirroring object relation is largely a fantasy in his mind, which is usually unconscious unless it is disturbed. He continues to bask in her positive light—whether real or imagined, which helps him to be open to seeing and accepting his exhibitionistic and grandiose tendencies. However, this equilibrium of his sense of self and self-esteem is precarious, as is reflected by his extreme sensitivity to any lapse or imperfection in the teacher's empathic mirroring. Now that he has established a mirror transference to his teacher, he is depending on her to shore up, confirm, and preserve the cohesion of his identity and its attendant self-esteem. He is extremely vulnerable to her, in a way that he might not appreciate until he feels some disruption in this idyllic condition. The shakiness of his sense of identity, his sensitivity to the absence or presence of perfect empathic mirroring, and his vulnerable dependency on the mirroring object (the teacher in this case) are reflected in the fact that what might appear to the external observer to be slight or even minute lapses in the mirroring cause extreme reactions of distress. Deep emotional hurt, tremendous rage, and an extreme loss of self-esteem are some of the elements of his reaction to slight inaccuracies of feedback from his teacher, or even her imagined absence or lessening of attention or approval from her.

The breakdown of the idealizing transference creates in the student a deep disappointment in the teacher, a devaluing rage towards her, and a feeling of loss of support. It is the supporting structure of his narcissism that is disrupted. The breakdown of the mirror transference, on the other hand, disrupts not what supports his identity, but the self-identity structure itself and its accompanying feeling of self-recognition. The integrity of who he takes himself to be is what is threatened at this point. Kohut puts it in his language: "Whenever the mirror transference cannot be maintained (in whichever of its three forms it has established itself), the patient feels threatened by the dissolution of the narcissistic unity of the self." (Kohut, 1971, p. 121) It is the structure of the self-identity, the specifically narcissistic sector of the self, that begins to dissolve when the mirror transference is disrupted, because it is this structure that needs mirroring for its continuing cohesion and stability.[42]

Kohut includes in the reactions to disruptions of the mirror transference, the regressions to states of the self that preceded the development of the cohesive sense of self, in other words, states of fragmentation of the self, and defenses against painful and frightening psychological conditions. As usual, however, his descriptions involve more pathological situations than we address with our students.[43] Kernberg gives similar accounts of such narcissistic disruptions, but his account reflects his view that the grandiose self is a purely defensive structure. So the

298   disruption which results when the mirror transference breaks down reveals the defended-against material and does not exactly lead to a regression to earlier and less integrated states of the self.[44] Kernberg's account highlights the reactions of rage and hatred, envy and fear, and the sense of emptiness and meaninglessness that we observe in the reactions of students to narcissistic disruptions.

We observe a much more orderly process of reaction to disruptions of mirroring, with a meaningful layering of affects, object relations, and states of the self. The various elements in the accounts of both Kohut and Kernberg seem to fall within a certain meaningful picture of the narcissistic structure which makes it possible for us to have a more precise understanding of the process of working-through and resolution. This understanding leads to areas of experience of the self not addressed by Kohut and Kernberg.

The most prevalent—and in most cases the first—reaction to the disruption of the mirror transference is that the student feels not seen, not understood, not approved of, not valued, not paid attention to in a way that he feels he wants and needs. In other words, at first the student feels the loss (real or imagined) of mirroring from the object. More exactly, he feels the loss of the mirroring selfobject, as the teacher is no longer perceived as such. This happens as he feels that the teacher's reflection, appreciation or understanding is imperfect. His perception of the loss of narcissistic supplies makes him aware of his narcissistic vulnerability, resulting in various degrees of dissolution of the narcissistic structure of self-identity, and the reactions to the loss and dissolution, along with the defenses against them. An example will be instructive here:

Beth has been working with the author for over three years. Her work is becoming focused on her narcissistic tendencies as she explores her problematic relations to men. She tends to become involved with men whom she can idealize, which supports her feeling of specialness and a larger-than-life sense of self. She ends up feeling devalued and hurt, but still unable to let go of the man. When she is with a man who is not markedly narcissistic, she tends to devalue him. Discussing her pattern of choosing narcissistic men, she recognizes that she needs such "brilliant and spiritually successful men" to feel she has an adequate mirroring for her sense of brilliance and reality. This causes her to feel a great deal of anger and hurt, reminding her of her relationship with her father, whom she saw as a brilliant and successful man, and for whom she was special. This turns into a feeling of hatred and meanness, but not yet in relation to me.

Slowly, however, she begins to complain that there is some sort of deficiency in the way I relate to her. Exploring it, we discover that she feels I don't treat her as special, as she believes I treat other students. She believes I don't love her in a way that makes me enjoy her freely, as I do with others. She wants me to treat her as special, the way her father did. This makes her feel that she is not important to me, not seen or valued by me, which brings up deep hurt and tears. She also starts seeing that she needs me to see her and love her as special for her to be able to have a sense of herself. She sees that she needs my mirroring to affirm the sense of real self she has been discovering.

Beth relates the weakness of her sense of self to the fear she tends to experience at night and to her need to tell me her experiences and feelings in such detail. As this shakiness of her sense of self is exposed, she begins to experience self-doubt, doubting the reality of her experience of herself, which makes her want my precise and detailed feedback about what she is experiencing. This doubt becomes connected to her childhood experience of her Essential Identity, which received no corroboration from anyone in her environment.

Beth's belief that I don't like her in a special way, and hence do not see and admire her, was difficult for her to see through and understand. It took several sessions, in which she went through many feelings of hurt, anger, and emptiness in relation to me, to her father, to men in general, and finally in relation to her mother. Her mother could not provide the kind of mirroring she needed. Before seeing that her feelings about me were mostly a transference of her relation to her mother, Beth explored her feelings that her mother was depressed in her attitude towards her and did not see her reality, her brilliance, and her aliveness. She did not relate to Beth with excitement and joy. Beth had to withdraw from her mother, which caused her a great deal of guilt. She then turned towards her father, who was more narcissistic but did give her some admiration and special treatment. She became

300   his special daughter. She liked the attention, but later saw it as problematic since it bound her to him in a way that made her future relationships to men conflictual and painful.

We can see from this example how the disruption or loss of the mirror transference reveals the underlying vulnerability of the self-identity
structure. The first reaction is that of feeling not seen or not seen adequately, when the teacher says something that is not precisely attuned
to the student, gives a reflection that is not totally accurate, expresses
an attitude that can be interpreted as not completely approving, or
behaves in any way that could indicate even a slight lack of empathy.
Sometimes it is a matter of saying or doing too much, sometimes too
little. At this point in the student's process, the vulnerability of the
narcissistic structure is so near the surface that it is waiting for the
slightest sign of narcissistic deprivation for it to explode into the scene,
with all its painful and conflictual object relations.

Working through the mirror transference

According to Kohut, just as the working-through process related to
the idealizing transference leads to the establishment and strengthening of one of the poles of the self, that of ideals,

> so is the primary goal of the working-through processes in the
> mirror transference the transformation of the grandiose self
> which results in a firming of the ego's potential for action
> (through the increasing realism of the ambitions of the per-
> sonality) and in a strengthening of realistic self-esteem. (Kohut,
> 1971, p. 175)

It is Kohut's idea that the establishment of a form of mirror transference is needed for this task. "The mirror transference in all its forms
thus creates for the patient a position of relative security which enables
him to persevere with the painful task of exposing the grandiose self
to a confrontation with reality." (Kohut, 1971, p. 191) This is one reason for Kohut's insistence on the need for empathy from the analyst,
so that the analyst will have an accepting and understanding attitude
towards the narcissistic manifestations of his patients rather than exert-
ing moral or educational pressures.[45]

Kohut's way of working with narcissism reflects his view that the mirror transference can be seen as a resumption of an aborted but legitimate developmental step, the integration of the developmentally natural grandiose self within an empathic and mirroring milieu. The mirror transference gives the person a chance to integrate the grandiose self that was hidden and denied in childhood, and hence remained in its original primitive form. So the working-through process is a process of completing an incomplete or arrested development of the self. Kernberg, on the other hand, views the treatment as a matter of dissolving a pathological defensive structure, the grandiose self, mostly through interpretation, and guiding the individual to come to terms with the defended-against intolerable object relations and their associated painful affects.

In our work on realization of the Essential Identity, it is this true identity that is ultimately mirrored by the teacher. However, in this process the student must come to see and understand the identity structure for the false identity that it is. This process reveals the structure to be inherently grandiose, since it is a substitute for the true identity. Thus, the student will need to completely work through all the issues surrounding the grandiosity of the identity structure.

chapter 29

The Empty Shell and Fakeness

Our approach to the working-through process reflects our understanding of fundamental narcissism as alienation from the deeper dimensions of the self. Exposing the unreality and incompleteness of one's normal sense of self is a necessary step toward the discovery and realization of these deeper dimensions. Although our understanding of narcissism informs our approach, in private teaching sessions we do not direct the student to experience particular states. The various states reveal themselves spontaneously in response to open-ended inquiry into the unfolding experience of the student. This process of working-through is the same as the process of realization of the Essential Identity. Some elements of this process are related to Kohut's view of the integration of the grandiose self and some to Kernberg's emphasis on uncovering and dealing with painful object relations and affects. A significant portion of the process relates to the understanding of the self-identity structure and its development, and the relationship of this development to the alienation from the essence of the soul.

We will now discuss this process in some detail, highlighting the major steps. The student goes through a sequence of experiences, realizations, or discoveries, that make sense as a series. Students seem to traverse these stages in a certain general sequence, although some variations in the order do occur. We will see that this series becomes comprehensible as we understand the structure of self-identity and its relation to the various levels of the experience of the self. The stages of working-through can be listed as follows. Each of these steps involves an arising awareness of a definite phenomenological element in the self-structure or an aspect of Being associated with elements of the true self:

1. Fakeness
2. The shell
3. The narcissistic wound
4. The great betrayal
5. Narcissistic rage, hatred and envy
6. Narcissistic emptiness, meaninglessness and pointlessness
7. Loss of orientation, center and self-recognition
8. Narcissistic shame
9. Narcissistic rejection object relation
10. Selfless inner spaciousness
11. Ego activity
12. Narcissistic depression
13. Helplessness and nondoing
14. Trust and the need for holding
15. The ego ideal
16. The holding loving light
17. The Essential Identity
18. Point-diamond, or essential self-recognition and resolution of the need for mirroring

As the student works through his ego identifications (the self-images that compose his self-representation), the structure of self-identity begins to be revealed as a psychic structure patterned by images from past experience. Further experience increasingly reveals the unreality and underlying emptiness of this central self-structure. The emptiness and meaninglessness expose the absence of fundamental truth in his normal sense of identity. He begins to realize that what he has been taking to be himself is actually a shell, devoid of any substantial reality or inherent richness.

304   At this point the student literally experiences himself as a hard shell (of various degrees of hardness depending on how defensive he feels) that contains nothing within it. The empty shell feels impoverished, insubstantial, and false. He feels hollow and vacant, as if his body has become a shell of tension with its insides sucked out of it.

We find Mark L. dealing with this painful realization of himself when he comes to his session, feeling a great deal of rage and envy of the teacher whom he sees doing what he likes to do and being authentic in it. He feels that he cannot authentically function on his own, comparing himself to the teacher and feeling incapable. Exploring his rage and feelings of inadequacy, he feels a hardness around his chest. Fear arises, which he tries to choke off because he wants to appear strong. As he sees through his defensive attempts, he becomes aware that the hardness around his chest conceals emptiness within it. He then remembers an incident with his father, a time when he stood up to him and asserted himself about something simple. His father could not tolerate his assertion and attacked him verbally. His mother did not help; in fact, she got angry at him in support of his father. He felt deeply hurt, wounded to the core, but he could not show it. He needed to appear strong. So he went numb in order to deal with the hurt and fear. He disconnected from himself, feeling that there was no support or approval for asserting who he was, and he did not want to lose the approval of his parents or hurt their feelings.

In this session Mark realized that incidents like this caused him to disconnect from himself and to appear different from his actual sense of himself. He then began to experience himself as a hard shell all around his body, not only around the chest. He felt empty, hollow, not present. However, the more he understood the situations that alienated him from his inner core, the sadder he felt.

For several months we continued to work with his sense of being an empty shell, exploring his relation to me, his father, and to people in his life in general. After three months he came to a session feeling distraught and rejecting himself. Exploring his self-rejection, we found that he had been feeling fake, phony. His rejection was an attempt to get away from this feeling of fakeness, which he then observed accompanying the state of the empty shell. He felt he was all fake, all his life was phony, had been a waste, and he felt despondent about the whole thing. The more he felt himself to be an empty shell the more he realized how fake he had been feeling. He felt not present in his experience, not present in his life and relationships to people. Also, the sense of the empty shell meant that the self he presented was a pretense, a make-believe self created for others to see and approve, like the pretense he had constructed earlier for his parents. He felt humiliated, ashamed and guilty, rejecting the shell in an attempt to get away from the sense of phoniness.

As I helped him to see that judging and rejecting his experience made it difficult to understand the truth of it, he managed to let his experience be, rather than trying to change or avoid it. His extensive experience doing inquiry, along with the trust he had developed in the teacher and in the process of investigation, helped him take the witness position rather than being totally identified with the particulars of his unfolding experience. This openness clarified how the sense of fakeness was a reflection of his realization that he had been living his life from the perspective of the empty shell, of an image of himself, rather than from his essential core. He saw then how this empty shell had been the center of his experience of himself for many years, that it was the reality of what he had been unknowingly taking himself to be.

Seeing that his normal sense of identity was based on this empty shell, and recognizing the development of this shell as the development of the concept of himself, he realized that the shell was composed of many self-images, many of which he had seen before, but a myriad of which were still waiting to be exposed. The more he felt the mental quality of the empty shell, the more he felt separate from it. Many fears and resistances accompanied this process, but Mark finally arrived at the experience of himself as a sense of "I am," witnessing the shell and its component images. He recognized himself as a brilliant point of light and awareness with an immense potential for experience, free and apart from any past experience or mental concept. He recognized the Essential Identity he had been alienated from and understood that it was exactly what was missing in the emptiness of the shell. This, of course, led him to other affects and memories and further understanding of himself.

306   This student's experience exemplifies the perception that the empty shell is simply the self emptied of its essential core. It is the self experiencing itself through the constructed self-representation and identified with that self-representation. It is the self experiencing itself through the mind, disconnected from its authenticity, its ontological truth, its actual presence, its essential nature.

In the language we have been developing, awareness of the empty shell is the direct awareness of the structure of self-identity when it is not being defended against. It is the structure of the self—patterned by the self-representation—which gives the individual his normal feeling of identity. It is very clear in the experience of the empty shell that experiencing ourselves through a representation alienates us from our essential core, and that identification with the self-representation and the feeling of hollowness are two aspects of the same phenomenon.

This shell, then, is simply the soul, structuring itself through the self-image. It is the self structured by the totality of all self-representations. It includes trying to be a certain way in order to be recognized and loved, but it also includes any image through which we define ourselves. Thus, the shell exists at several levels, depending on what dimension of identity we are aware of. Any definition of ourselves through an image, or through any concept, will at some point be seen as a shell. The moment we know ourselves through the mind, we become a shell. Even an image of the Essential Identity itself can become part of the shell. Any image, arising from any experience, even the experience of self-realization, becomes a shell if it is used by the mind to define who we are in the present. Any memory of Essence, or any spiritual experience, becomes part of the shell if it is used for identity. The shell is the self produced by the mind. It is a mental structure and not beingness in the now.

Understanding this about the shell helps keep us from becoming too discouraged in our process, for after we work through the shell it comes back! We may be liberated from some level of our old identity for some time, but then that sense of fakeness or hollowness will inevitably return. If we look closely at the shell at this later stage, we will see that it has different qualities; it might be softer or harder, have different characteristics or images in it. Some of the self-representations in this shell will be new, resulting from recent experiences, including experiences of Essence or spaciousness. Again the mind is structuring the self through memory. And again we are likely to experience an increased need for mirroring as we attempt to make this shell appear to be a true living identity, not just an image, not just an empty thing. We fear that we will die or disappear as we lose old identities, so there is an intense need for mirroring to confirm our very existence.

Another phenomenon illustrated by Mark's case history that when we finally understand the significance of the experience of the empty shell, we cannot help but see how phony we have been. Even if our self-representation is reasonably accurate, to be according to an image is a pretense; it is not the truth of simply being ourselves. Realizing this, we feel fake; we have been presenting ourselves to the world inauthentically. In a very real sense, we have been lying about who and what we are, both to the world and to ourselves.

In the process of working through our narcissism, we come to realize that to present an image of ourselves, instead of the immediate presence of who we are, regardless of how faithful it is to the original, is to be fake and to live a phony life. It is the life of the empty shell, a life without authenticity, without fundamental truth. This understanding of the sense of being phony that is universally associated with narcissism is more fundamental than that offered by the theories of depth psychology. It demonstrates that phoniness is inherent to the life of ego. It is not only a quality of pathological narcissism or what is called the "false self"; it is intrinsic to the experience of the self in the conventional dimension of experience. The fakeness is simply more obvious in pathological narcissism because the shell is more exposed.

The manifestation of the empty shell, with its attendant sense of falseness, tends to arise before the breakdown of the mirror transference, and hence is not dependent upon this breakdown. Becoming aware of the shell results from becoming less identified with the layers constituting the structure of self-identity. The totality of the processes in the work of self-realization leads to the revelation of the inner reality of this structure. So the empty shell may manifest before or during the breakdown of the idealizing transference, but more definitely after this breakdown and the consequent resolution of the need for

308   support. Several factors may affect the awareness of the empty shell. The breakdown of the idealizing transference destroys the main support for the self-identity structure. The arising essential support, in the experience of the Diamond Will, puts a pressure on this structure for it supports the true identity of Essence, and not ego structure. All these factors, plus the deepening working alliance with and trust in the teacher and the teaching, contribute to the accelerating exposure of the shell and its underlying emptiness.

Experiencing the empty shell is a major development in a student's process; it arises at several junctures in the process of resolving the narcissistic constellation. It is most intensely experienced around the breakdown of the mirror transference, because mirroring is the only major support left for this structure of the self. Although it is most intense just around the breakdown, it may manifest a long time before it, or even after it. It will continue to arise every time one recognizes the identification with a self-representation. It is the primary narcissistic structure and the main barrier to self-realization.

There are many resistances against experiencing and acknowledging the shell, some of which are: (a) fear of being nothing, or having nothing, (b) fear that if one looks deeply he will realize that he is not important, not significant, that he does not count, (c) fear that one really is just an empty shell, and (d) shame.

chapter 30

The Narcissistic Wound

T he process of working through narcissism reveals the vulnerability of the student's identity. As she consciously or unconsciously realizes her vulnerability, she tries to resort to the mirror transference in the attempt to preserve the cohesion and integrity of her familiar sense of self. In this phase, any disturbance of the mirror transference, or any indication of the loss of narcissistic supplies in any part of her life, will disturb the narcissistic equilibrium. The shell will be exposed and its very integrity will be threatened.

The awareness that the integrity of her sense of self is threatened may appear first as a vague feeling of dread. She may feel a general inexplicable anxiety. She may find herself preoccupied with catastrophic fantasies of being injured or harmed, even of fatal accidents. There is usually no rationale in her daily life for such feelings and thoughts, so she tends to dismiss them. She may become concerned about falling ill, and her fantasy might carry her to imagine extremes of illness and destruction with no apparent physical cause. She may start having nightmares about injury, illness, and death. Only an in-depth inquiry into these manifestations can reveal the underlying reasons for this existential dread. Then she can connect it to her work on

310   narcissism; the loss of narcissistic supplies is threatening her in a much deeper and more fundamental way than she believed possible.

Some students never clearly discriminate this feeling of dread because it is so vague and apparently unwarranted. In all cases, the consequences of the loss of narcissistic supplies are revealed more in specific object relations. When the student feels not seen or appreciated, not admired or treated in a special way by a particular important person in her life, she will experience the effect of the loss of mirroring on her sense of self. The first feeling is usually a sense of hurt, insult, betrayal, or loss. She is very sensitive at this point. The slightest indication of not being seen will evoke deep pain, intolerable anguish, endless tears about a bottomless grief. When investigated, rather than reacted to, this hurt reveals an emotional wound of staggering depth and profundity. It is difficult to tolerate at first, and she will tend to fight it off, to react to it and out of it. However, the presence of empathy and understanding, and especially the presence of kindness and compassion, make it possible for her to tolerate the hurt and thus feel it more directly and fully.

Here, we appreciate Kohut's emphasis on empathy and acceptance; a kind holding environment is necessary to allow the student to stay with such a deep wound. What is actually needed is the presence of compassion and kindness; these qualities are more fundamental than the presence of one kind of object relation or another. The aspect of Essence we recognize as Loving Kindness is the element of our true nature necessary for the self to tolerate the experience of emotional hurt. The more we are aware of the presence of Loving Kindness, the more our hurt can be uncovered and tolerated. This is like a natural law which we discover when we explore this particular manifestation of Being. The Loving Kindness needs definitely to be present in the holding environment, for instance, in the presence of the teacher. But unless the student herself has some realization of this kindness, it will be almost impossible for her to tolerate the deep hurt of the narcissistic wound.

Empathy and empathic mirroring are natural expressions of the presence of Loving Kindness. Loving Kindness is the warmth and openness of heart that makes it possible for us to be genuinely sensitive,

considerate, compassionate, and sympathetic, which qualities are the   311
basis of the capacity for empathy.[46] In the following report from Nyland
about some work in a small group setting, we see the need for the
warmth of Loving Kindness:

> *I felt this hole in my chest as a wound, a wound of hurt and sad-*
> *ness about the lack of compassion and attention from my mother.*
> *I felt like I was invisible to her. I felt I had never been seen by my*
> *mother. Feeling compassion for myself and feeling the hurt in my*
> *chest seemed to be the same thing. My head, also, became*
> *extremely empty, very spacey. I felt like I was floating, and there*
> *was a throbbing of sadness in my chest, that seemed to surround*
> *the emptiness, while the compassion was the catalyst.*

Experiencing the hurt for not being seen as a wound is not merely
a metaphor. The student actually feels wounded, not only in the emotional sense, but literally, almost physically, as is clear in Nyland's
report. The wound feels like a cut in the chest, as a gash, as if one's heart
were physically wounded. There is the physical sensation of a painful
cut, and this sensation of pain is inseparable from the emotional feeling of hurt. The emotion and the sensation comprise one state, an
emotional wound that feels like a rip which hurts emotionally.

This gash is not actually in the physical body; it is a cut in the shell,
a rip in the structure of self-identity. The shell is beginning to disinte-
grate as a result of the loss of the mirroring. The wound is the sign of
the threat to the cohesion of this structure. In fact, any narcissistic disturbance involves some level of breakdown in the structure of identity.

Unempathic or insensitive responses from the environment affect
the self like a stab of a knife. We actually feel stabbed, pierced, cut to
the core. We naturally feel great resistance to experiencing this wound.
We are terrified of falling apart, of losing the integrity of our sense of
self, of disintegrating and disappearing. No wonder we feel we need
mirroring for the preservation of the integrity and cohesion of this
self-structure. The glue that keeps this structure together is missing at
this point. This is literally true, almost physically true.

One might wonder why there is such a clear physical component
to the experiences described by students here. It appears that there
are at least three factors which affect the student's experience of the

312 self-structures as related to the physical body. First, as we have noted, Mahler's work on the development of self-identity clearly establishes that the body image is a deep structure in the self-representation. In fact, it is more or less impossible to have any experience of oneself in the conventional realm without a component of that experience being the identity with the body image. It is natural, then, that the student's experience of many states will involve a sense of how that state relates to the body image. It is normal in any alteration of experience for one's sense of one's body to change. When we feel confident or mature, we might feel taller, or more solid, compared with feeling small or empty or unstructured in the state of inadequacy. Thus, an experience like the narcissistic wound will evoke an actual body image.

A second related factor is that shutting down the flow of one's essential nature often involves actual blocks in the flow of physical energy in the body. Awareness of these blocks might feel like contraction, denseness or deadness—"my heart feels like a stone; my legs feel like wood; my head feels like a bowling ball"—or even complete opacity to our experience which can manifest as an inability to sense a certain part of the body at all—"I have no legs; my heart is numb; my head is blank." On a third, more subtle level, the block may be not so much in the flow of physical energy (which is of course never complete; blood flows, nerves function), but in the availability of parts of the body to awareness, or in the availability of the experience of essential presence in the body. Like a physical injury, the cutting or blocking of the flow of presence in the body causes pain, which is defended against in the normal course of conditioning, but the process of uncovering self-identity structures necessarily penetrates those defenses, and thus makes available the sense of pain resulting from what one can almost literally call a tear in the being of the self.

We usually experience embarrassment and shame when we begin to feel a narcissistic wound. Narcissistic hurt is a doorway to the insight that there is nothing to our conventional sense of self, that it is fake. We may feel ashamed of ourselves, deficient, worthless, not good enough, "found out" in our unreality. We might feel unimportant and worthless because we are empty of anything real and precious. Naturally, we defend against this wound.

Typically, the narcissistic wound arises when we feel not seen or appreciated for who we are; we feel the absence or loss of mirroring for who we take ourselves to be. This wound is connected with the original childhood hurt about not being seen or admired. At the deepest level, however, the narcissistic wound results from the loss of connection with the Essential Identity. The wound first appears as a rip in the shell, in the structure of the self-identity, reflecting the loss of a certain way that we recognize ourselves, often involving the dissolution of a certain self-image. As we experience the wound more deeply, we come closer to an awareness of the deeper loss, the severing of our connection to our Essential Identity. We see this clearly in the following report from Lynn W., who had been having a great deal of difficulty establishing her career even though she had finished her studies some time ago. It became clear that part of the difficulty had to do with not knowing what she really wanted and uncertainty about who she really was, which had been manifesting as a need for mirroring and support. The report describes a segment of work she did with the author in a small group setting:

> *I discussed feeling hurt, of which the original hurts happened when I was a baby. Now I just encounter situations that bring this up. I feel hurt for people always leaving me, and not seeing me. I was able to be objective and not reject the hurt feelings only for few seconds at the beginning. Most of the time I could not be objective about this hurt or my feeling angry because I was hurt.*
>
> *It was only when we followed the hurt/sadness back to a genuineness in myself that I could be more present and more objective with the hurt. It was as if once knowing or having a hint of what was behind say, a door, that I could see the door as a door rather than a barrier. That the hurt was something that had a purpose and could be followed somewhere meaningful that allowed me to be more objective and less judgmental about the pain.*

It was easier for Lynn to be with her pain when she realized that it had to do with the disconnection from a genuine part of her, which was abandoned in early childhood. This disconnection is the cause of the profound hurt and loss, the immense sadness and grief, associated with the narcissistic wound when it is deeply felt. Each time we lose connection

314   with an aspect of our Being, we are wounded, as if part of ourselves has
been cut out, even yanked violently out of us. The narcissistic wound,
however, is very different from other kinds of wounds, for example, the
wound of loss of other essential aspects such as Will or Love.

The typical process of working through narcissistic hurt is different
from that of working with the losses of other essential qualities.
Working with the disconnection from any aspect of Essence, we first
encounter an emptiness—what we have called a hole—and after the
emptiness we find a hurt; experiencing the hurt opens us up to the
essential aspect. Not so with narcissistic hurt; it's the other way around.
First, there is a wound which leads to emptiness. This makes the narcissistic wound more painful, often intolerable. When we allow the
wound, we experience it as a hurt with vulnerability. It's a vulnerable
kind of hurt. When we are in touch with this vulnerability, we are sensitive to any lack of attunement; it actually seems that we are vulnerable to the destruction of our structure; we can be devastated.

This is a very difficult place for the student; she is dealing with the
most sensitive of all psychic wounds. The more narcissistic she is, the
more untouchable is this place. We can't go near it without her reacting very strongly with rage or isolation or devaluation. She might be
able to tolerate feeling deep hurt and rejection, but when it comes to
the narcissistic hurt she will balk.

The unique quality of narcissistic hurt is that when it is allowed—
that is, not resisted—the rip in the shell will spread, and the hurt
becomes deeper and more extensive, until the whole shell dissolves,
which brings about the loss of the sense of identity. The student doesn't
just feel pain; she feels that if she experiences this hurt more deeply,
she will disappear. This threat of destruction is what makes it so hard
to tolerate, especially when it is first encountered.

Because this narcissistic hurt is a very difficult and sensitive place
for most people, at this juncture the student needs great empathy from
the teacher. This is when the student most needs the "emerald mountain," the aspect of Loving Kindness in the dimension of the Diamond
Will. She needs then the greatest empathic support, the greatest empathy, the greatest attunement, and the greatest sensitivity from the
teacher. The slightest thing could close down the student's experience

of this wound, or could bring in a reaction that closes it. The slightest lack of understanding, lack of attunement, or lack of consideration, and she will close down with some kind of reaction.

This is the main reason for the necessity of empathy, and not the reestablishment of the mirror transference, as Kohut believes. Empathic mirroring touches the student with the Loving Kindness of the teacher, which will help her to tolerate her own hurt and not close it down. It is not merely for the repair of the disruption of the mirror transference. This is a fundamental difference between our view of working with narcissism and Kohut's, which reflects our understanding that what is needed is not a confirming mirroring of the conventional self, but rather, the empathic holding of the unfolding of the student's experience, which is at this point in the stage of letting go of the structure of self-identity as the student opens up to her true identity. The difference we are articulating marks the bifurcation of the path of repairing the ego structure from the path of self-realization.

When the teacher can empathically support the student as she is feeling the narcissistic wound, and the student is able to tolerate it and feel it fully, it will deepen and expand, until the rip is complete and the cut becomes a total dissolution of the shell. The wound then becomes a window which can open up to a vast emptiness. This emptiness is the specific place of no self. This is what makes it vulnerable.

Experiencing the narcissistic wound completely, without defending against it, will lead to the dissolution of the shell, which is actually the awareness of the emptiness within it.

We sometimes refer to the narcissistic wound as the "emptiness wound." This wound opens us up to emptiness, to nothingness. It opens us to the nothingness of the dissolution of the self. No wonder it evokes such terror, which sometimes we feel as the fear of death. It is the ultimate fear of disintegration and disappearing. The vague sense of dread that we felt before we were directly aware of the wound becomes an immense terror, as the wound opens up to emptiness. It is here that we understand the existential dread and terror unique to narcissism.

However, when we understand the situation accurately, appreciating that we are opening up to a deeper experience of ourselves, and have the empathic support of the teacher, it becomes easier to surrender to the

316   process. The dissolution of the shell is actually a surrender of the self, letting go of our concept of self. The opening can then become an entrance into vastness, and into the fundamental presence and truth of the self. We see this process in another report, by James E., of some work he did with the author as part of his ongoing exploration into the narcissistic sector of his personality.

> *Working with you this time I felt more comfortable than in the past, much less scared. I felt more trust and I definitely experienced a deeper desire to understand myself. At times I felt a sense of not wanting to go into places and feelings completely. I experienced this feeling of journeying back, with hesitation and fear.*
>
> *I felt myself as an empty shell, impoverished, and saw my parents as nothing but empty shells. Letting go of support and feeling not seen felt sad. I felt hurt. Sensing the wound in my chest it felt very deep. I felt brittle, shaky and cold. I felt like a deep chasm without end, opening into cold space. I felt extremely sad. I felt not seen and not having any identity. The emptiness felt endless, almost forbidden. I understood my ongoing need for support, and for a mirror as something to give me a frame of reference.*
>
> *Then I began to experience my chest feeling full and warm, with a solid presence and substance. I felt alone, present without concern for identity. I felt like I filled space, or rather like I was the space itself.*
>
> *My understanding of the issues became clearer, but what seemed also important was the process, being able to tolerate the feelings and go into the places and feelings necessary to gain the understanding. This work helped me understand more my desperate need to get things from the outside, approval and admiration, the futile effort it is. I experienced a wonderful desire to understand myself, and the necessity of doing it.*

A primary element in resolving the narcissistic constellation is going through the narcissistic wound and understanding it precisely and objectively. It must be understood, not simply experienced. To understand it means to see how it is related to not having adequate mirroring. Our insight usually begins with seeing the narcissistic issues as they manifest in our present life circumstances, but generally goes on to remembering or re-experiencing the original childhood hurt. We recognize that the hurt is due to losing sight of what is genuine in us, of our precious nature, because it was not supported and mirrored in our early years. We feel hurt that the people in our environment did not see us, did not appreciate our truth, and were not attuned to our true nature. We feel hurt because being ourselves was not appreciated by those we cared about and depended on. As we become aware of this lack of mirroring and support for our true being, we might come to feel abandoned or forsaken.

chapter 31

The Great Betrayal

As we work with the narcissistic wound, we begin to understand its genesis in our lives. Feeling the emotions associated with the wound, and seeing its meaning, we begin to experience this hurt as a great betrayal, the betrayal of the self. Not being seen for what we truly are has led to a betrayal of this preciousness that is our essential core. We come to understand that we became false because the people in our early environment not only did not see and support our true self, but wanted us to be something else. They conditioned us to fit their idea of what we are or what we should be. The feeling of betrayal that accompanies our realization of this development is one of the ways we experience the narcissistic wound. We may experience the betrayal whenever we feel not seen or appreciated for who and what we are.

As this betrayal becomes conscious, we first see it as betrayal by the idealized or mirroring selfobject. This can be a teacher or friend, spouse or children, in the present time, or we might feel it connected to the past, to parents, teachers in school, or others. The realization of the significance of the betrayal may deepen the hurt, or it may lead to anger and rage. We feel let down, treated unjustly, abandoned, and left alone with our terrible pain. We experience the disruption or absence

of mirroring as a terrible betrayal, the most fundamental betrayal. This 319
is why we call it the "great betrayal." The most fundamental truth of
the soul has been betrayed and abandoned.

The more sincere we are with ourselves in this process, the closer
we come to a deeper and even more painful aspect of this betrayal.
When we are genuinely interested in the truth, the whole truth, we
realize with a greater sorrow that this betrayal from the outside is less
terrible than another betrayal: We come to understand that we have
betrayed ourselves. We realize that when our environment betrayed us
and abandoned us, with varying degrees of insensitivity, we felt alone
and abandoned, with no one relating to us. To be real meant being
isolated from the environment, living in another universe, a universe
not seen by our parents, not acknowledged by them, even not known
by them. We could not tolerate such isolation and abandonment. We
needed to relate and be related to; we needed contact, warmth, human
relationship. Since in the beginning we were capable of being our true
nature, and since those around us were unable to see and appreciate
this nature, our interpretation was inevitably to believe that to be real
means the absence of love, warmth, holding, security.

So we learned to pretend, to be like them, to join them in their world,
the world of lies, the world of the shell, the conventional world. We
became what they wanted us to be, what they paid attention to in us,
what they preferred in us, what made them relate to us. Through this
process of accommodation, we abandoned and rejected what they
could not see, the parts of us they did not relate to.[47] Since our essence
was the element they recognized or understood least, our essence was
the central element we disowned. We ended up abandoning and hid-
ing our most precious nature. We hid it finally even from ourselves;
most of us eventually forget it altogether.

As we begin to penetrate this forgetting, we see that we betrayed
ourselves, just as the people in our environment betrayed us. We chose
their company and approval over Essence. We recognize that this
betrayal is the deeper one, at the very roots of our disconnection from
our essential nature. We feel the hurt now as more terrible, the wound
a bottomless abyss of pain. There is great sorrow, regret, and sometimes shame, guilt, and self-hatred.

320   Sometimes we realize that we have sold out in other situations, apart from the experience of the narcissistic wound, but this realization may then reveal the narcissistic vulnerability. We see this in the case of Bill, who expressed in a group setting that he did not value the experience of Essence. We discussed this issue when he came to a private teaching session. He further expressed the anger and hurt he feels when other students value essential experiences. As he explained these feelings he began to remember his previous disillusionment and sense of betrayal in relation to a particular spiritual organization that he was a member of, in which he felt judged and not accepted. These memories brought about deep pain and bitterness; he remembered the shame of those times. The pain and shame became connected to his present condition; he felt that he gave up himself in that situation, and he had been doing the same in the present one, for the sake of safety. At this point he felt hurt, and realized that it was the pain of having betrayed himself by not fully being himself, because of his concern with safety and security. As this realization developed, he felt more present, with a great deal more sadness for himself. This session became the beginning of his inquiry into his narcissism, which resulted in his experiencing the empty shell a month later and exploring how it had developed as a result of the inadequate holding he received in early childhood.

Some students actually remember the precise time they made the conscious decision to turn away from Essence, and hence to betray themselves. The child saw that he could not survive in his environment without someone relating to him, even if only to a superficial part of him. He could not tolerate the pain of aloneness and the pain of not being seen, so he adopted a facade, an image that could be seen and supported. In time, the child identified so completely with the image that he believed it was all of him. Some students do not remember specific decisions or choices, just a gradual process of selling out, accommodating themselves to their parents and teachers, becoming what they were not, and turning into a normal self, which they now see is nothing but an empty shell. Very few do not forget their essential natures, but keep it secret, and feel alone with it. Like everyone else, they develop a shell that becomes their central identity.

Winnicott addresses the development of the false self:

When the mother's adaptation is not good enough at the start
the infant might be expected to die physically, because cathexis
of external objects is not initiated. The infant remains isolated. But in practice the infant lives, but lives falsely. The
protest against being forced into a false existence can be
detected from the earliest stages . . . the infant gets seduced
into a compliance, and a compliant False Self reacts to environmental demands and the infant seems to accept them.
Through this False Self the infant builds up a false set of relationships, and by means of introjections even attains a show
of being real, so that the child may grow to be just like mother,
nurse, aunt, brother, or whoever at the time dominates the
scene. (Winnicott, 1980, p. 146)

Although Winnicott is discussing the development of a pathology of
the self, the same picture applies to all normal individuals, when we take
into consideration the fact that the essential dimensions of the soul are
not recognized. Thus, if we apply Winnicott's definitions consistently,
what is considered a normal self is actually a false self. Winnicott understands the process as a seduction, which is an apt way of describing it,
pointing to participation on the part of the child, albeit unwilling participation. Thus, the sense of self-betrayal as this accommodation is
remembered.

The development of and identification with the self-representations
is of course not simply a result of the student turning away from her
essential self. Many other factors determine this development. However,
she has participated, wittingly or unwittingly, in the process of going
to sleep, of turning away from the aspects of her soul that her environment could not or would not recognize. She did it to survive,
because the loneliness and hurt were intolerable; nevertheless, she did
participate. Understanding her choiceless choice, her extreme dependency on her early caregivers, helps her now to acknowledge her part
in the betrayal and to feel compassion about the untenable position
she found herself in early childhood. The truth may help her now not
to deny such choices, which she is still making, but to understand the
situation. The understanding can bring warmth, acceptance and compassion, which will help her to stay with the pain, to feel it fully, and

322   to understand its significance completely, until it opens her to awareness of the emptiness of her false self, to the vastness that feeling this emptiness allows, and then to the preciousness she no longer need abandon.

She can now work through the guilt, self-recrimination and self-hatred that arises when she sees her betrayal of herself. As she uncovers and sees through these feelings, she can see more clearly how she is still betraying herself by not being authentic in her life.

At the deepest level, the wound is about having sold out. We begin by feeling betrayed by others through narcissistic insults; we realize the betrayal of our true nature by our parents; and ultimately we realize that, in our struggle for survival, we have rejected our own truth and lost our precious Essential Identity.

chapter 32

Narcissistic Rage

N arcissistic rage is a universal reaction to feeling unseen or misunderstood. When the mirroring selfobject fails to provide the desired admiration and empathy, the student not only feels hurt, but also angry and indignant. We will discuss three points in relation to this narcissistic reaction: what occasions its arising, its functions, and its specific characteristics.

Narcissistic rage might be a chronic feature of the self. For severely disturbed individuals, it is a typical mode of experiencing and expressing themselves. This hard rage is one of the main ways such individuals relate to the world; they easily feel slighted and unjustly treated, and are thus chronically angry and indignant, as if something to which they feel entitled has been taken from them. They are angry most of the time, and are quick to explode at the slightest signs of incomplete empathy or mirroring.

The normal individual will react in this manner only occasionally, in response to a gross lack of attunement. But when the student's narcissistic structure is vulnerable due to lessening identification with the personality structure (what we call "thinning away of the shell"), or due to the mirror transference, then the narcissistic sensitivity is close

324   to the surface, and this rage reaction happens more readily and more frequently.

Any disturbance to the narcissistic equilibrium—a failure in a life situation, loss of a coveted opportunity, or a humiliating defeat or encounter—may instigate this reaction. We encounter it most readily when there is a disruption in one of the narcissistic transferences. However, the situation that most singularly invokes intense narcissistic rage is a loss of or lapse in the mirroring response, and especially the breakdown of any form of mirror transference. It is a specific reaction to feeling slighted, not seen, not approved of, and not admired in a special way. In other words, it is a reaction to narcissistic hurt.

Narcissistic rage functions in two ways in relation to narcissistic hurt, and narcissistic vulnerability in general. It is a reaction to the hurt, from the hurt. The student feels deeply wounded and reacts out of this hurt with extreme anger. So we can see it as a normal reaction to hurt. However, it has special characteristics because the narcissistic hurt is different from other kinds of emotional pain. The fact that this wound is very vulnerable, and opens up to an emptiness signifying the dissolution of identity, imbues the reactive anger with an intensity and a hardness rarely seen in other kinds of anger. The reaction may actually precede the awareness of the hurt; the person will often experience the rage reaction and then, if at all, become consciously aware of the hurt. She perceives the failure of the selfobject and reacts to this failure directly with rage and indignation. Only on investigation, or after the rage has passed, does she realize that she has felt hurt and wounded. However, the rage may arise only after she has felt the hurt, and understood the loss of mirroring.

With more severely disturbed individuals the rage reaction is more likely to precede the awareness of the hurt. This points to the other function of the rage, that of psychological defense. The rage is used to avoid awareness of the wound, and the possible disintegration it may lead to. The more narcissistically vulnerable the self is, the more difficult it is for the student to acknowledge the wound directly, for to her this acknowledgment would mean weakness and defeat. It may take a lot of work and dedication for her to feel the hurt directly. The narcissistic rage functions to protect her from the awareness of her

vulnerability, dependency on mirroring, and the weakness of her sense   325
of self. When this issue is present, the student's trust in the teacher can
be an important factor.

What are the characteristics of narcissistic rage?

In narcissistic rage, a person reacts to the perceived failure of the
response of another person (a selfobject) with uncontrolled and irrational anger, defensiveness, negativity, devaluation, and meanness. The
reaction is more accurately termed rage than anger, because of its
uncontrolled and irrational features. It has several characteristics that
differentiate it from other kinds of anger and rage:

- It feels and appears irrational, for it is greatly out of proportion to
  the situations that provoke it. Also, when a person is in its grip, she
  does not feel any rationale for it and does not feel the need for any.
  She simply feels justified in her indignation. She simply feels she is
  in the right, without any interest in questioning what this right is.

- This gives the rage the quality of being uncontrollable or not easy to
  control. She does not feel the need to control it, for she is irrationally
  convinced she is justified. This reaction originates from depths of the
  self-identity structure which are not available to the conscious mind.
  This is why this rage is frequently acted out verbally and physically.

- This rage tends also to be acted out because, in addition to right-
  eousness and indignation, there is a sense of entitlement. The entitlement is part of the narcissistic manifestation, in which one feels
  entitled to be recognized and acknowledged as special and wonderful, and to be given privileges because of this specialness. So the
  indignation seems completely justified because one's sense of entitlement is not being honored. This is understandable when we consider that these feelings are felt towards the selfobject, who is
  unconsciously held as an extension of the self.

- The irrationality and uncontrolled quality make the person closed
  to others' responses or reasoning. She is not interested in what the
  other has to say, or what the other feels. She is only interested in
  expressing her rage and punishing the cause of it. She is convinced,
  without any thought, that she is justified. This is because the rage

326   is fueled by the underlying terrible wound, its true immediate cause, which unconsciously convinces her she is justified. In some sense she feels justified because she believes unconsciously that she is fighting for the integrity of her very existence.

- She is very sensitive to narcissistic insults, but the rage makes her unaware of this sensitivity. She is aware only of the insensitivity of the selfobject, and does not allow herself to see that her intense reaction indicates an unusual sensitivity and vulnerability on her part. This is the defensive function of narcissistic rage.

- This defense and denial of her unusual sensitivity to failures of the object leads to an attitude of blame. Since she sees insensitivity outside her she tends to blame everything on the selfobject, with a great deal of indignation.

- This blaming and defensive character of narcissistic rage gives it an isolating quality. It makes her insensitive to and unaware of the condition of the other; she does not care about the other's feelings and is not interested in knowing about them. This defensive schizoid feature of narcissistic rage isolates her from any true or meaningful contact or communication with the other.

- This schizoid quality is reflected in the actual energetic state of narcissistic rage. She feels, and is perceived by others as, hard and impenetrable, almost inhuman. It is an emotional hardness that feels almost metallic. It is as if the shell becomes as hard and harsh as cast iron with sharp aggressive spikes. The isolation is not only defensive and unfeeling, but also aggressive in that it is intended to punish the other as much as to defend the self.

- There is a meanness in this reaction, a desire to inflict pain, to get back, to avenge oneself for being slighted and humiliated. This meanness, along with the defensive and aggressive hardness, indicates the absence of kindness and compassion. It is as if the person cannot afford to feel any sensitivity, empathy or sympathy, for that would only expose the wound and the vulnerability of the self.

- Narcissistic rage is also characterized by a tendency to devalue the selfobject, an intense need to demean and insult him or her.

- Upon investigation, we discover an underlying motive of dissolving   327
  her wound by causing a similar wound in the selfobject who failed
  her. It is as if she is trying to displace her wound onto the selfobject,
  through an aggressive, indignant and punishing attitude.

The rage may turn into, or be accompanied by, a cold hatred that gives
her qualities of power, invincibility, and calculation. This hatred underlies the desire for vengeance, for wanting to inflict pain and suffering,
and for actually enjoying getting back at the person who failed her.

The rage and hatred may be accompanied, or even caused and fueled,
by envy. She envies the other for having the narcissistic success, the
acclaim, the qualities and skills that she lacks and covets. It hurts her
deeply to see others having and enjoying what she wants and does
not possess, and this hurt turns into rage and hatred, or is covered up
by them.

If there is to be any possibility of working through the narcissistic
constellation, with its impressive array of defensive reactions described
here, we must empathically understand these reactions of narcissistic
rage, hatred, envy, and jealousy. We must appreciate their defensive
function, observe the situations that occasion such reactions, and
explore their significance. This process can make it possible to fully
experience the narcissistic wound, and thus to open up to the emptiness that leads to the realization of the core of the soul. We may experience the narcissistic wound before the rage, but can experience it fully
and understand it completely only when we experience, understand,
and metabolize the narcissistic rage.

Kohut has been criticized by many researchers, including Kernberg,
for not emphasizing the role of aggression in the study of narcissistic
disturbances. "His analysis focuses almost exclusively on the vicissitudes of development of libidinal cathexis, so that his analysis of pathological narcissism is essentially unrelated to any examination of the
vicissitudes of aggression." (Kernberg, 1975, p 270) Kohut primarily
emphasizes narcissistic vulnerability and the need for empathy. On the
other hand, Kernberg sees the aggressive elements of narcissistic rage,
hatred and envy as central to the understanding and resolution of narcissistic disturbance. In fact, he considers the narcissistic transferences

328   as defenses against the object relations characterized by this aggression, and against the impoverished state of the self.

We agree with Kernberg when considering the severe pathology of narcissism, which one can consider a variety of the borderline condition. Such narcissistic disturbance is mainly what we have described as the oral form, and the narcissistic rage has an oral quality; these factors make aggression a central part of severe narcissistic disturbance. Kohut, on the other hand, seems to deal with less severely disturbed individuals, and he focuses on the central form of narcissism. So it makes sense that for Kohut aggression is less central. However, it is possible that Kohut does deemphasize the role of aggression because he believes it is important to reestablish the narcissistic transferences when they are disrupted.

In our work with normal (not severely disturbed) individuals, we find that dealing with narcissistic rage and hatred is necessary and important. If one does not deal with narcissistic rage, the understanding of one's narcissism cannot go very deep. Even with deep experiences of the Essential Identity, the resolution is not secure until one works through this issue. However, we do not conclude from this that aggression is central in the etiology of narcissistic disturbances, in the way Kernberg believes it to be. At least it is not central in the development of fundamental narcissism. The rage we have described in this chapter is simply one feature of fundamental narcissism. It is primarily a reaction to the perceived failure of the selfobject and a defense against narcissistic vulnerability.

chapter 33

The Great Chasm
and Black Space

————————————————————————————— •

When a student is able to deal with the narcissistic wound and the attendant rage, he can come to understand and accept the hurt. This allows him to be open to the essential quality of loving kindness and hence to develop a greater tolerance of this wound, which is felt as a rip in the shell of the self. As we have seen in some students' reports, the wound then expands and deepens, culminating in the experience of the dissolution of the shell. The experience generally proceeds until the student experiences no shell and no wound. There remains only an awareness of boundless emptiness, a nothingness that stretches out forever. The emptiness in the emptiness wound expands until its boundaries extend indefinitely. The emptiness within the shell is now completely revealed. We get a flavor of this experience in the following report by Beth, a student discussed earlier. This report is part of a letter she sent to the author, describing some of her experience in dealing with her narcissistic constellation in group, private sessions with the author, and on her own:

> *The work I have been doing internally has been around dissolving the narcissistic defenses of idealization and grandiosity. They are the defenses against feeling the emptiness underneath.*

329

330   *Through this next piece of work I experienced the emptiness as*
       of the shell of my ego. The identity of my ego is where all the
       images come from. I felt vulnerable, unprotected without this
       shell. That is when fear arose.

         I have been feeling depressed too. Depression aches, hurts, feels
       painful, pressure in chest. Depression wards off emptiness. Fear
       of feeling emptiness. Blank emptiness appears at some point.
       Emptiness feels different than other emptinesses I have experi-
       enced. A deficient emptiness, feels like loss, feels alone. There was
       absolutely nothing in this emptiness. Not hot or cold, no judg-
       ment, just neutrality, just is. This is what opened up to the vast-
       ness. But I felt a loss.

         When asked what was missing I heard from within, "me." My
       familiar sense of identity was not in this emptiness.

This emptiness is due to the absence of the shell, which we feel psychologically as the absence of the sense of identity. It is a feeling of a pervasive nothingness with an affect of deficiency, a sense that something
is missing. When we investigate this sense that something is lacking,
we discover that it is the feeling of identity which is missing. This
understanding is somewhat different than the accepted views in depth
psychology, where the emptiness is mostly seen as due to the absence
of internalized object relations.[48]

Our observation is that this emptiness indicates the loss of the shell,
the structure of self-identity, and its attendant feeling of identity. The
emptiness is specifically the absence of the familiar identity. This also
implies the loss of the internalized object relations that are part of the
identity structure, but it is specifically and centrally the loss of the
identity itself. We call this experience "narcissistic emptiness." It is
typically accompanied by a host of associated feelings, which are experienced singly or in combinations as one enters this emptiness. These
feelings reflect the various characteristics and functions of the ego
structure discussed in Chapter 10. Features of the narcissistic emptiness include the following:

• It is a nothingness that feels deficient. The sense of deficiency indicates the absence or loss of a psychic structure. This nothingness is
  actually a characteristic feature of the narcissistic disturbance in general.

It underlies the experience of the self in the conventional dimension   331
of experience in general, as well as in narcissistic pathology.

- When the deficiency manifests, there is no sense of self-recognition, indicating that the structure missing is that of the self-identity. The student defends against this because she does not want to lose her sense of self. When she does allow the emptiness, she will tend to feel that she does not know herself, or is somehow unable to know who she is. She feels she does not know herself. She has not lost her memory, nor does she fail to recognize her familiar physical and psychological qualities; there is merely the absence of the familiar identifying feeling of the self, which may have not yet been isolated in her experience.

- One way of experiencing this absence of the familiar sense of identity is to feel lost. The student feels lost psychologically, not knowing where she is and who she is. When she investigates this sense of being lost, she discovers that it means that she feels she cannot find herself, cannot find the feeling which gives her the sense of self-recognition. The lost feeling is part of the process of dissolving the structure of identity. When the dissolution is complete, the feeling is no longer that of feeling lost, but of having no self or no sense of identity.

- We saw in Chapter 10 that the sense of identity gives the self a sense of center, a center of awareness and action. We do observe that one feeling associated with the emptiness is that one has lost one's center, or does not have a center. This loss of center makes her feel that she does not know how to act, or more specifically, she feels: "I don't know what to do." The identity which has given her a center of initiative and the motivation for action seems to be missing. Kohut sees these motivations as ideals and ambitions, but rather than lacking motivation, it is more that the student needs to know who she is in order to take meaningful action. To know what she wants to do, she needs to know herself. This is a central factor in the sense of paralysis from which many extremely narcissistic individuals suffer. These individuals do not accomplish much in their lives; often they cannot find a job or decide on a career because they do not know what it is important for them to do. They do not know what is significant and meaningful for them because they are not in touch with who they are.[49]

- The loss of identity and center may also arise as the absence of orientation. The student feels disoriented; she does not know where she is, or what direction to take. This shows how identity gives the self the sense of orientation and meaningful direction of interest, intention and action. How can she know what to be interested in, what direction to take in her life, what to do, if she is not sure who she is?

- This absence of center and identity may also manifest as the absence of a meaningful purpose in her life. If she does not know what and who she is, then how can she find a real purpose to her life? This sense of purposelessness is a well-known feature of narcissistic disturbance, but it also arises in the process of self-realization as one recognizes the emptiness of one's familiar sense of self. From the perspective of self-realization, the life of the self in the dimension of conventional experience lacks a real purpose.

- This purposelessness may be felt as a sense of insignificance. She might feel she is not important or that her life has no real importance. Earlier experiences of not being treated as important may arise at this point, but with further investigation she will see that she feels she is not important because there is "nothing to her." She is empty, she is nothing, and this nothingness feels deficient, lacking in significance.

  This sense of insignificance which is encountered in the process of uncovering the narcissistic constellation points to an important component of the motivation for self-realization. Self-realization is inherently significant. When the student is in touch with her true identity, she realizes that she matters in a way that is independent from all object relations, because she is preciousness itself. When she is not realized, she will feel the absence of significance, and this absence can motivate a search for significance which can lead her to the process of self-realization.

- The sense of insignificance frequently manifests as low self-esteem and feelings of worthlessness. Narcissistic emptiness is closely related

to loss of self-esteem because the true origin of self-esteem is the   333
inherent value of our true nature.

- The lack of purpose may manifest as a meaninglessness that pervades
  her life and experience. This is a basic feeling associated with narcissistic emptiness, which sometimes precedes direct awareness of
  the emptiness. The implication is clear: Life is meaningless if one is
  not truly in it. There is no meaning or substance to her experience
  if she is not being herself.

- The meaninglessness is often experienced as pointlessness. When
  experiencing the narcissistic emptiness, the student frequently asks:
  "What's the point?" This is similar to meaninglessness and purposelessness, but is more specific, as will be seen shortly.

These associated feelings and reactions reflect the loss of one's identity—the familiar center of the self. They also reflect the absence of true
identity. The structure of self-identity is an empty shell because it is
empty of what is truly real. When we are focused on the loss of the shell,
whose dissolution reveals the emptiness, it seems that the loss of identity with the familiar self-structures is the "cause" of the emptiness. That
is also how it feels as a student is undergoing the process of losing identification with the shell. However, from another point of view, the dissolution has simply revealed the core absence which has always been
there, the absence of the Essential Identity. Often this perspective is also
part of the student's experience; particularly once the dissolution is
more complete, there is in retrospect a sense that one has always been
covering up this emptiness.

We have discussed how the development of the self-representation
creates the shell, and also disconnects the self from its essential core.
Now the dissolution of the shell reveals this disconnection. The emptiness reflects specifically the alienation from the essential core. The shell
can be seen as covering up this emptiness, but in fact, the emptiness
has always been there in the shell. The normal identity is the shell,
empty of essential nature.

This is the true meaning of narcissistic emptiness. Feelings of pointlessness, meaninglessness, purposelessness, absence of center, orientation, significance, and identity arise directly from the absence of

334   identity with the Essential Identity. In fact, the properties of center, identity, significance, purpose, meaning, and so on, are some of the experiential characteristics of the Essential Identity, the precious point of existence.[50]

Furthermore, since the Essential Identity is the identity of Being, the narcissistic emptiness has another, greater significance. Since the identity of Being is what gives the self the capacity to identify with Being in any of its aspects and dimensions, the realization of the Essential Identity is tantamount to the capacity to simply be. So narcissistic emptiness involves disconnection not only from the Essential Identity, but from Being as a whole. It is the absence of self-realization. It is the gap between our essential nature and who we take ourselves to be. It is the great chasm separating our experience in the conventional dimension of experience from the fundamental ground of the soul. It is the emptiness of narcissistic alienation itself.

Narcissistic shame

The narcissistic emptiness and its associated feelings are difficult to tolerate both because of its own phenomenological properties and because of the reactions to it. It is difficult for the student not to take it as an actual deficiency of the self and react accordingly—with judgment and rejection. We always find the student struggling with painful reactions to the emptiness as it is exposed. She feels deficient and inadequate, worthless and unimportant, weak and inferior, a failure, a loser, a nothing. She feels fake and unreal, lacking substance or value. She feels that she is a liar and a deceiver, an impostor. She feels her life has been a hoax, a waste.

These feelings and reactions bring up the most painful affect of them all, shame. The student feels ashamed of herself, embarrassed about herself; she wants to hide. The shame is a specific painful feeling of deficiency, exposure and judgment, all related to a sense of inadequacy in being oneself. What makes this shame specifically a narcissistic manifestation is that one feels inadequate in being oneself, or judges oneself as such. She judges herself as unable to be real. She feels also the emotions associated with the "great betrayal": she is a traitor to herself, she has sold out; she has been too weak and dependent to stand her ground.

Narcissistic shame is an intense pain related to social failure, failure   335
to be a true human being. It is a sense of being an inferior human
being, exposed to social judgment in the midst of severe disintegration
of the self. When experienced fully, the affect is very painful. The affect
itself has a disintegrating effect on the self.

The defenses against the shame and the other painful reactions to
emptiness make these painful affects difficult to experience fully, and
hence to understand completely. All of these painful affects must be
dealt with for the student to have a chance of transforming her narcissism. She needs to separate the state of emptiness itself from the
reactions to it. To do this, she needs to become aware of her judgments
of the emptiness and of her reactions. She needs to learn how to deal
successfully with these judgments, until they fall away.

Dealing with these judgments is primarily a matter of understanding and disengaging from a particular object relation. This is the object
relation between the empty and unreal self and a rejecting, critical,
and hateful object. The self feels empty, lost, and meaningless, and
projects on others the image of being critical, harsh, and rejecting of
her because she is fake and has failed to be an adequate self. She feels
helpless and impoverished, lost and worthless, and believes that others
hate and despise her for feeling this way. This is the narcissistic form
of a more general object relation, an object relation between a small
and scared self and a rejecting, hateful, and powerful object.[51]

In working through this very painful situation, the student needs to
realize that she is projecting her own criticalness, self-hatred, and rejection. She needs to see the totality of this object relation and understand
its genesis in her childhood. Only then can she disengage from this
object relation. This is not easy because it means learning to accept one's
sense of fakeness and emptiness without judgment, and to inquire
openly into its meaning and genesis.

If the student can achieve some openness to this experience, the
shame and the feelings of worthlessness and deficiency are not so powerful. She can then experience the emptiness without rejection or judgment. This is necessary to experience the emptiness as it is in itself,
free from the distortion of reactions and judgments. The full and direct
experience of the narcissistic emptiness allows the student to objectively

336   understand it. Only then does it become possible for her to understand that the emptiness is the absence of being herself.

Black space

When the student finally settles into this experience of deficient emptiness, allowing it without judgment, rejection or reaction, she sees that it is a state of no self, or, more specifically, no identity. When we fully experience this state of no identified self, it transforms naturally and spontaneously into a luminous vastness, a deep spaciousness, a peaceful emptiness.

We find Beth now dealing with her need for mirroring in her early relation to her mother. She comes to her session expressing judgment and criticalness of her narcissistic inner child. We discuss her mirroring needs which were not met in childhood. This reminds her that her mother was empty and depressed at the time when Beth needed her mother to be excited about her. Beth begins to feel lifeless, like cardboard. Then she feels angry at her mother, who made her this way because of her own emptiness. Realizing that her mother was emotionally a child, she starts feeling helpless and hopeless about satisfying her needs. This connects Beth with a very deep hatred for her inner child, the child of her childhood, for needing and wanting what she could not get. She understands now how she disowned herself in order to be able to relate to her mother. She rejected her natural need for mirroring because her mother could not satisfy it.

Beth comes to the next session quite identified with the rejection of her needy inner child. Through our investigation, she understands that she is now identified with the rejecting and hateful mother, who did not want her to have mirroring needs. She then begins experiencing the self she has been rejecting. She feels needy, and experiences herself as a hollow shell. Exploring the origins of this needy, empty self, she remembers herself as a child: alive and energetic, but needing somebody to be there for her. She still does not accept her old neediness. It takes her several sessions, going through oral need and rage, deep aloneness and loss, and so on, until she begins to get in touch with a deep depression.

She comes to a session feeling depressed and wanting to die. Her longing to be with a special man recurs, and she exhibits many kinds of resistances. Finally, she realizes she is feeling like an empty shell, but she is fighting awareness of it. Then she recognizes the rejection of feeling like nothing. Now she experiences the shell and Essence, side by side, but it becomes clear that her identity is with the shell. This clarifies her situation, that although she is in touch with the essential presence, she is still identified with the shell. She is still recognizing herself through an old image of herself. She does not like to see this, but the emptiness of the shell manifests more fully now, and as she settles into it, it transforms into a vast space, as she writes in part of her letter, quoted previously: "The ego identity was not in this emptiness. Then I looked and saw the emptiness open to the vastness of space."

The narcissistic emptiness sheds its deficiency and reveals its truth, as an emptiness that has no sense of self, but is spacious and peaceful. The deficient emptiness is actually nothing but this inner spaciousness, experienced through the judgment of deficiency. The state of no self is actually a pure manifestation of inner spacious reality, Being in its openness, we experience it as empty space, immaculate and pure, light and clean, empty of everything structured by the mind. However, the self reacts to the sense of no self in many ways—as a loss, as a deficiency, and so on, plus the associations, memories, and feelings that go with these interpretations. All this psychic content pervades the inner spaciousness so that we lose sight of its lightness, purity, immaculateness, and freedom. Instead, we feel it as deficient emptiness, dull and flat, heavy and dark.

Only when we allow this emptiness to be, without judgment or rejection, without reaction or opinion, does it shed its obscurations and reveal its inherent truth: the state of no self, the freedom and openness of our Being. We experience ourselves then as a luminous night sky, transparent and pure, light and happy, cool and virginal, deep and peaceful. An emptiness, yes, but a stillness, a silence, where we recognize the absence of the familiar identity as the absence of agitation.

This is black space, an inner spaciousness that manifests naturally when we accept the absence of self with no reaction at all. It arises when the self is free from identifying itself through representations. We experience freedom from the familiar identity and its structure. We experience ourselves without any structure, as openness, spaciousness, as boundless

338   and infinite space. Whenever we become free from our identification with any self-representation, we experience ourselves as free from the structure patterned by it. This always manifests as some kind of space, as an inner field that feels exactly like empty physical space, but it is a state of consciousness, a pure manifestation of Being. When the self-image is part of the self-identity structure—which functions to provide the self with the sense of identity—the space that arises is a black space, like the empty and starless night sky, or the depth of intergalactic space. When the self-image is part of the self-entity structure—which functions to provide the self with a sense of separating boundaries—the space that arises is clear, colorless space, like the clear space of daytime. The experience of black space goes through a deepening and a refinement, depending on the depth of the self-representations whose dissolution precipitates the experience. Our present discussion of the phenomenology of black space is general. (See *The Void* [Almaas, 1986], Chapter 6, for more discussion of the relation between space and self-image.)

In black space we are aware of the absence of the sense of self; however, we experience it not as a deficiency but rather as freedom and release. There is a sense of newness and coolness, of lightness and light-heartedness, of the absence of burden and suffering, and the presence of purity and peace. It is a nothingness, but it is a nothingness that is rich, that is satisfying precisely because of its emptiness. It is a direct sense of endless stillness, of pure peacefulness, of an infinity of blackness that is so black that it is luminous. It is a transparent blackness that is radiant because of its purity. This is not the experience of a self, an observer beholding the endlessness of space; rather, it is the experience of the self experiencing itself *as* the infinity of peaceful space. It is an infinite field of a conscious medium, aware at all points of it. The medium is totally at rest, with a stillness that is the same thing as the awareness of stillness.

chapter 34

Love in the Transformation of Narcissism

---•

The experience of black space is not immediately established as a permanent attainment because in addition to those we discussed in the last chapter, there are other barriers to this space. These usually present themselves after the full experience of inner spaciousness, but sometimes before it. The usual tendency is to fill the great chasm, the narcissistic emptiness, with whatever one can find. The ultimate filler is the formation of the shell, but the student will try anything to avoid awareness of this emptiness. We have discussed many of these fillers, the various reactions and object relations, the images and memories, the ambitions and ideals, the hopes and plans, and so on.

However, the direct encounter with black spaciousness magnifies a more subtle barrier against full awareness of the chasm. It reveals something ordinarily too subtle to see and too implicit to apprehend. It exposes, in clear relief, the activity through which this filling occurs, especially the activity through which the familiar identity perpetuates itself. In other words, the stillness of the inner spaciousness reveals the agitation which characterizes the activity of the familiar identity, what we have termed ego activity (see Chapter 8). In fact, the experience of the imperturbable peacefulness of the endless night sky not only

340   exposes this inner psychic activity, but tends to intensify it. The self
reacts to the stillness as a death, and intensifies its activity by which it
generates its sense of self-recognition. The ego activity becomes furi-
ous agitation and feverish inner obsessiveness.

The self-identity structure is a dynamic structure comprised not
only of self-representations, but also of inner activity (Kohut's tension
arc). This "dynamic essence of the self" is an automatic, compulsive
and incessant activity, which is mostly unconscious. We saw in
Chapter 8 that the main components of this activity are rejection, hope
and desire. Repeated experience of the stillness of black emptiness
exposes this activity as mental agitation, which now intensifies and
reaches feverish proportions, as an obsessive inner activity whose ultimate purpose is to perpetuate itself. It becomes increasingly obvious
that the details of this activity, the content of what the self rejects and
what it hopes for, are immaterial. What matters is the activity itself.
The notion of giving up this inner activity appears to the self as defeat,
a surrender to hopelessness.

The mental activity intensifies in an effort to avoid deep hopelessness
and helplessness, despair and depression. These feelings are part of a
narcissistic depression and deep hopelessness that the student feels about
being her real self. This heavy and painful state is characterized by iner-
tia, dullness, and self-hate. One feels existential hopelessness and despair
about the possibility of existing authentically, and about receiving support for one's authenticity. Alice Miller understands it this way: "Thus
depression can be understood as a sign of the loss of self and consists of
a denial of one's emotional reactions and feelings. This denial begins in
the service of an absolutely essential adaptation during childhood, to
avoid losing the object's love." (Morrison, 1986, p. 334)

The intense ego activity seems, at this juncture, like an alternative
to giving up hope and succumbing to this heavy hopelessness. However, some people get stuck in the narcissistic depression—not because
they cannot get out of it, but because it functions as a kind of a filler
for the narcissistic emptiness. It does feel like a heavy, sticky and thick
substance, which some students feel is more tolerable than the stark
emptiness. To be depressed is more acceptable than to be nothing at
all. As Beth states in another excerpt from her letter:

> *The depression came on to ward off the emptiness. As long as I was*
> *identified with depression nothing would move. From this arose*
> *fear of no protection from the emptiness, the emptiness of just is.*
> *There is nothing in the emptiness yet I hear a voice talking.*

Each student encounters this depression in the process of working through the narcissistic sector of the personality. Discovering that one has been living the life of the empty shell brings up a deep hopelessness about living an essentially authentic life.

This depression is not always differentiated from the emptiness. Furthermore, the depth and pervasiveness of this depression varies in different individuals when it finally becomes conscious.

The ego activity, the voice that still exists in the emptiness in Beth's report above, has a more comprehensive function, which is to perpetuate itself; this makes slowing it down extremely difficult. We get a taste of this difficulty in the following report from Mark:

> *In the meeting I asked about physical action and the activity of*
> *my mind, and mentioned that I did not know whether to do*
> *something or not because I thought it would just reinforce the*
> *basic inner activity. Then I realized from our work that the con-*
> *cern is the activity itself, to keep up the activity, and that I was*
> *wanting to do something out of rejection of what was happen-*
> *ing at the moment.*
>
> *When I saw that, the activity slowed down and I began to feel*
> *deficient, bad and ashamed about being deficient. I saw that the*
> *deficiency was what was behind the inner activity and that this*
> *activity was a rejection of the deficiency and an attempt to change*
> *it. The deficiency felt larger than I have felt before and I felt sus-*
> *pended. Then, after staying with the deficiency and relaxing my*
> *legs a pure experience of Being, Being without attributes,*
> *emerged. I felt complete for a second or two then I felt somewhat*
> *incomplete, and felt the incompleteness was about not knowing*
> *what to do with this sense of Being in my life.*
>
> *The activity of my mind began to increase again and the sense*
> *of pure Being became less, and the whole cycle began to feel that*
> *I just did not know what to do, and that was just a fact, and not*
> *a reflection of deficiency on my part. The activity stopped and*

the sense of pure Being came back more. Then I thought I had the answer now, became interested and desirous of holding onto it to be able to reenact this process. The activity began again.

You pointed out that we are not incomplete, that we think we are getting something but that is not the case. This insight seemed very significant and like the missing link. It made the whole situation look truly ridiculous.

Achieving a measure of freedom from this incessant ego activity is not easy; it requires a deep surrender. This letting-go requires several factors. One of these is learning what Mark says he discovered: that not knowing what to do in order to be is not a deficiency, for being is not a matter of doing anything. When there is nothing to do, then not knowing what to do is an objective situation and not an indication of a personal failing. When this happens, then the feeling of "I cannot do anything; I do not know what to do," which is the hole of the Diamond Will, transforms into the solidity of essential support, with the understanding that Being is the support for being (see Chapters 25 and 26).

The surrender also requires deep and unquestioned trust in truth and in reality in general. It requires an unusual faith or basic trust that if one suspends the activity, everything will be okay, that everything will be taken care of. For most people, this basic trust was eroded because of early parental treatment that failed to give the child the implicit confidence that she would be taken care of without having to manipulate for her environment to provide what she needed.

The inadequacies of the early holding environment made her feel that she cannot just relax and be; she has to take things into her own hands, and make sure that she will be safe and cared for. This orientation manifests in later life as a general distrust of reality. She learns to react instead of being, to manipulate things in an attempt to compensate for inadequate holding, as Winnicott observed some decades ago: "If maternal care is not good enough then the infant does not really come into existence, since there is no continuity of being; instead the personality becomes built on the basis of reactions to environmental impingement." (Winnicott, 1980, p. 54) This reactivity is part of the very structure of the self-identity; the fundamental distrust is one of the deepest motivations for the compulsive activity. Because the self believes that she can trust only her own activity, she is certain that it would be foolish and dangerous to cease this activity. Therefore, the prospect of the cessation of this activity tends to produce a tremendous amount of terror.

Another important factor in the ego activity is that the self is always striving to be a particular way, in order to achieve support. The primary image patterning this activity is the ego ideal. The self tries to approximate a certain ideal, in the hope that if she succeeds, she will be worthy of the support she needs. This ideal is never attained, but the self never tires of trying. Thus, effort is a chronic characteristic of the self-identity structure. This understanding of the ego activity of moulding oneself according to an ideal is similar—but not identical— to Kohut's formulation of the action arc of the self which is motivated by ideals. Our concept of ego ideal is borrowed from traditional ego psychology, but integrated into our conception of the self.

This lack of basic trust is fundamental to the normal identity. There is no sense that the deeper nature of the universe is good and loving. This basic distrust reflects the ignorance of the knowledge which arises only with self-realization, which is that Being is the fundamental ground of all existence, and that its nature is inherently benevolent. In religious language, this issue is understood as the lack of faith that God exists.

Universal love

As we explore the barriers to self-realization, we need to inquire into our basic distrust. This will take us into exploring our early holding environment and its effects on the development of our sense of self. Investigating the inadequacies of our early holding environment reveals the effects of these inadequacies on our particular self-identity structure. Working through this history, and illuminating the psychic structures it has created, leads finally to the awareness of the absence of basic holding. This absence is associated with a certain emptiness, the hole of a specific manifestation of Being. Learning to allow this emptiness finally ushers us into this manifestation of Being, which turns out to be a quality of love. It is a quality of boundless and gentle love, a delicate light experienced as the presence of softness, sweetness and

344   generosity. It is not exactly a personal kind of love. It is love for everything and everyone—universal love.

Its direct effect on the self is for her to feel lovingly held, as if cuddled in the infinitely loving arms of the universe. It also brings the perception that this loving, holding quality is intrinsic to the fundamental ground of all existence. The more she experiences this loving manifestation of Being, the more her basic trust develops, and the more her faith in reality is restored.

The issues of basic trust and the surrender that it engenders are not specific to the work on narcissism. However, some resolution of these issues is necessary for the surrender involved in slowing down and ceasing ego activity. The realization of this quality of love, which we call Living Daylight or Loving Light, resolves these issues. The presence of the Living Daylight helps us to let go of the empty shell, to allow the narcissistic wound and accept the narcissistic emptiness. This boundless, loving presence makes it easier for the self to relax and cease activity. One also comes to understand that it is this love which actually acts, and not the self. It is the melting action of this love that finally dissolves the ego activity.

Our discussion of the quality of Living Daylight is necessarily short, but it illuminates the deep dynamics underlying the activity which perpetuates the identity structure. We can see why the resolution of fundamental narcissism can come about only with a deep spiritual orientation. Realization requires a fundamental surrender of the self.

chapter 35

Realization
of the
Essential Identity

A s ego activity diminishes, it becomes easier to stay with and experience fully the selfless openness of the black space. The student can tolerate the absence of the familiar self with little difficulty and may even appreciate this absence. This sets the stage for the manifestation of the Essential Identity. The black space appears as the night sky where the Essential Identity may arise as a brilliant star in the pure darkness. A brilliant point of presence and awareness takes form in the endlessness of space, with the inner recognition: "I am here now." The student feels specifically *present*, as a singularity of presence, totally autonomous from all images, representations, or concepts of self. There is a new element in the experience: The sense of authentic identity is present, and it is experienced as oneself. One does not experience it, one *is* it. This development takes one to a new dimension of experience, as if one is experiencing things from the other side.

When one is completely being the Essential Identity, the experience no longer takes the form of being or seeing a point of light. The sense of size disappears, even the feeling of identity disappears. Self-realization becomes a matter of being, purely being, with an increasing understanding of what this means. There is a sense of simplicity and innocence, of

346   just simply being. It is not a matter of being oneself and knowing this by reflecting on the experience of oneself. There is no reflection on the state, no desire to analyze it. There is a sense of being alone, without the concept or feeling of aloneness. The aloneness is the perception of oneself as pure, undefiled and uncontaminated. There is lightness and freedom. The mind is quiet and sometimes without thought. This is a delicate state of the Essential Identity and is very vulnerable to obscuration by concepts and ideas. Concepts and ideas—even those of enlightenment and liberation—tend to obscure this state, even to eliminate it. Words cannot totally capture it. It is being prior to conceptualization.

More than all the discourses in the world, the clarity of this pure being illuminates the barriers against realizing it, gross and subtle. We begin to see that locating ourselves anywhere within the self-structure separates us from this simplicity. Any motive, any hope, any desire, any ego movement means identifying with the structured self, with the ego-self. Thus, any movement of rejection, choice, desire, motive, hope, preference, holding, grasping, trying or effort will separate the self from this simplicity of being.

The ego-self is always trying to approach the simplicity of realizing the Essential Identity (the point), but the more it tries, the farther it moves away from it. However, as the point, the student is aware of the ego self as if from the outside. It becomes possible for the first time to see and experience the normal self, the ego-self, from a vantage point totally outside of it. The student begins to have glimpses of the person he has been experiencing himself as, seen throughout his life, trying to free himself. He sees his virtues and vices, and understands—maybe for the first time—that this person has been doing all he could. He sees his purity, his effort, his confusion, his frustration, his dedication and his laziness, his sincerity and his blindness, his anger and his pain, his fear and his anxiety. As the pure presence of awareness and light, he perceives his ego-self as if in the third person. He recognizes himself as a compassionate and loving center, while the person who is the ego-self is doing everything in his power to approach and be this center. He sees how these attempts are inherently frustrating because they take him away from the true center.

He sees the ego-self as a center of sorts, but somewhat dark, like a dark cloud around the true center, which is a center of brilliance and

light. As he sees the struggle and the suffering of his ego-self, deep 347
compassion flows out of the purity of Being towards him. There is no
malice now, no hatred, no blame, no judgment, and no rejection. There
is only understanding, love and compassion. He can now understand
very clearly what really concerned his ego-self, what motivated his
thinking and feeling. He has only wanted to be accepted and loved, just
as he is, and has been trying everything to gain acceptance. He has just
wanted to be allowed to be, without hassle, without demands, without expectations. He has tried to live up to external ideals, in order to
gain acceptance. He tried to be pure, complete, good, and strong, but
none of it really worked. None of it could give him back his original
purity and simplicity.

This capacity to be the Essential Identity allows a kind of global
awareness and understanding of the hitherto normal experience of the
self. One can see the totality of the ego-self, with all its images, structures, object relations, ideas, feelings, plans, ideals, hopes, and patterns. It is not a matter of seeing all the specific details distinctly, but
of seeing the totality and knowing that it is the totality of the familiar
self, without completely delineating all the specific detail. The details
are in constant motion, some taking foreground for a while, then reced-
ing for another detail to take its place. There is the sense that the whole
personality is there, perceived by a center of awareness separate from
it, but totally compassionate towards it. This experience has a sense of
duality, but there is no duality in the way the self is experiencing the
Essential Identity.[52]

Then the student's perception may expand to reveal that the totality of the personality, with all its thoughts, feelings, hopes, desires, and
so on, is a part of a larger whole. It is an inseparable part of a universal network that includes all of his life, involving every person he has
any relation to. It feels like a heavy network of images, representations,
affects, and thoughts that pervades all his life, comprising an interconnected totality. It is a heavy, dark, and complicated network. He is
now experiencing the totality of his self-structure, seeing that it includes
everything and everyone his mind remembers and thinks about.

He experiences the totality of his personality as outside of him, separate from his pure being, but now as a continuity of a personal history.

348   He can see that the totality of his personality is not only continuous with all of the situations of his life, but also continuous with all of his past history. He sees that it is part of the continuity of this totality as a dynamic network of psychic structures.

If the experience continues to expand, the student recognizes that the network that comprises the totality of his personality is actually not separate from the totalities of all the people he knows and has known, and they in turn are connected to others, and so on. It becomes clear that his total personality is a part of a universal network that includes all of humanity, like a psychic network covering all the earth. This universal network includes all of human knowledge. Parts of the network are darker than others, with some brightness here and there. But it is generally dull and dark, heavy and complicated, in contrast to the simplicity, purity, and lightness of being the Essential Identity.

One comes to realize that all the spiritual knowledge of humankind is included in this network. This knowledge is the uppermost, subtlest, and brightest layer of this network, but nevertheless still dull and complicated. As long as it is knowledge in memory, it is not the presence of Being, and hence lacks the true luster of direct realization. He experiences all these teachings, including his own previous insights and discoveries, as artificial, external to the simplicity of being.

This perception may expand to reveal that this universal network is continuous with the totality of its past, which is human history. The student realizes that all of human history is alive and functioning through the minds and lives of present humanity. So his own psychological totality is inseparable from, and continuous with, the totality of the history of humanity.

He recognizes the immensity of the darkness he has been carrying all this time, of the tremendous weight that has been muffling his experience of himself. He appreciates, also, the extent of the task of self-realization, which involves becoming free from all this conditioning. Krishnamurti describes this perception eloquently:

> So our consciousness is not actually yours or mine; it is the consciousness of man, evolved, grown, accumulated through many, many centuries. In that consciousness is the faith, the gods, all the rituals man has invented. It is really an activity of

thought; it is thought that has made the content—behavior, action, culture, aspiration; the whole activity of man is the activity of thought. And this consciousness is the self, is the 'me,' the I, the ego, the personality and so on. (Krishnamurti, 1987, p. 32)

These perceptions may bring up new issues and psychological conflicts, expressing self-representations not yet processed, views and positions not exposed and clarified. One conflict that arises for most students at this time has to do with influence. Seeing the tremendous influence that is exerted on the mind by the totality of human consciousness may make the student want to escape this influence. The desire to be free becomes connected to old, unresolved object relations, especially those of separation and rapprochement, and manifests as the desire to separate and not be influenced by anyone or any teaching or situation. He might start wanting to isolate himself from people and situations he feels influenced by, like teachings, teachers, institutions, even family. He starts wanting his own mind, his own ideas, his autonomous way of viewing things, believing this will give him the freedom to simply be.

The narcissistic impasse

This can become a trap—what we term *the narcissistic impasse*—in which the student isolates himself physically or psychologically from situations or individuals that may be useful to him. This position indicates the absence of complete understanding of self-realization, the student thinking of it as a kind of mental autonomy. He is not seeing that the issue is not the influence of others, but how this influence is carried to the self. Regardless of how free his mind is, its very foundation—its concepts and words, its language and way of knowing—are all learned from the collective psyche. So there is no total freedom of mind as long as one is depending on mind for identity. More important, one must come to understand what Krishnamurti says above, that the problem is thought, that it is the mind that is the channel of influence. So freedom is not a matter of having one's autonomous mind, it is not a matter of freedom *of* mind, it is, rather, a matter of freedom *from* mind. Mind as knowledge from the past is the barrier,

350   even if the ideas and insights are totally one's own. Seeing ourselves from within and through impressions from the past is what separates us from the purity of simply being.

The narcissistic impasse is caused by confusing a phenomenological difficulty with a psychodynamic issue. The fact that experiencing the self through a self-representation alienates it from its ontological truth becomes confused with conflicts about separation involving a certain object relation.

Understanding this situation is important for self-realization. Whether one can work through it determines whether one moves from dual to nondual experience of essential presence. The student may start feeling that what he truly longs for is just to be himself, merely to be, without even caring to conceptualize what he is being. He just wants to simply be, and that is all. This clarity leads to greater realization of the Essential Identity, and greater differentiation in the properties of this experience. He experiences his essential nature in many ways now, expressing the various functions of this true identity.

Sometimes there is a sense of completeness. The act of being himself, which is not an activity, feels complete. The presence has no gaps. The center has no attitudes. It is just a complete existence, which is a perfect act of being. There is no familiar sense of self or no self, no sense of size or quality.

At other times he feels he is nothing, but a wondrous nothing. No characteristics, no perspective, no position, and no attitude. It is total freedom. This nothing feels like a fertile nothing, a potential for experience, any and all experience. In other words, the soul recognizes itself as pure openness to experience, the actual possibility for experience, the free potential for experience.

At other times, he experiences this nothing as a center of awareness, as only a witness, as perception without the sense of a perceiver. Mark reports his experience of this realization:

> *I asked about my issue of feeling lost in the crowd, my younger siblings transference onto the new students in the group and the anger at the old students. When I experienced the rage I realized I had been blocking my anger at my younger siblings. This cleared my head and I experienced myself as a bright point blending into*

awareness, but not lost in the crowd, or separate from it. There was no longer any issue. I became a witness, a center of awareness. It seemed amazingly simple and clear, and also that I have known this but have forgotten. The rest of the discussion made me realize how hard a time I've been giving myself for having issues. It was so obvious. I was surprised I hadn't seen it before.

The realization of the point can become so complete that one goes not only beyond mind, but also beyond time. The experience then is of the absence of time, of timelessness, or of time stopping. The presence is totally in the now without a hint of the past. One feels that time has ceased to pass.

One lives now in a wonderful universe of realization, insight, wonder, and profundity. Many perceptions arise and a continuity of being persists, but the experience that is the door to it all is when one realizes, "I am," without this being a thought. This "I-am-ness" is the primary experience of the Essential Identity that gives the self the capacity to experience Being, in any manifestation or dimension, in a nondual way. Then one can be love, can be stillness, can be luminosity, can be harmony . . .

Objective self-mirroring

The realization of the Essential Identity is not a complete resolution of the need for mirroring. We transcend the need for mirroring only when we recognize ourselves clearly and completely. In fact, our continuing curiosity about our experience—in this case, our experience of the need for mirroring—will naturally reveal what underlies it. We realize that we lack the complete capacity to see and recognize ourselves. In our work, this manifests as the arising of a certain dimension of Essence. Just as the resolution of the idealizing transference becomes the manifestation of the essential dimension of the Diamond Will, so the resolution of the mirror transference becomes the manifestation of a new plane of essential experience, which functions to give the self the capacity to see itself objectively, clearly, and completely.

This quality arises as the student continues to explore the narcissistic sector of his personality. It becomes more explicit as the student's understanding achieves increasing clarity and precision about this level

352   of self-realization. Further investigation into the issue of external influence, and an increasingly objective understanding about how experience unfolds, brings us to the understanding that to arrive at self-realization is not a matter of trying to get somewhere; it is not a question of working to actualize a specific state. If we engage in the process of self-realization from the perspective that there is an end-state to realize, we tend to interfere with the process. To attempt to generate or move towards a certain state indicates holding a particular conceptual position. Not only will this tend to force the unfoldment of the self to go into directions that might not be appropriate at the moment, but it is this very attitude which underlies the development of self-representations. To work on self-realization by attempting to move towards a certain state implies that we have some concept of what this state is, which will influence our experience of ourselves according to that view. This is bound to create a veil of conceptualization between ourselves and our experience of ourselves, which then blocks the condition of self-realization. We cannot go about working towards self-realization by taking a position that negates it.

What is left for us then is only open inquiry into our experience. We can only engage in a process (which is not a technique) of finding out where we are. Finding out where we are is a matter of recognizing the self in whatever state one happens to be in. It is not a matter of manipulating the soul into some state, but rather, of being clear and fully present in whatever state the soul happens to be presenting itself in.

This open inquiry requires that certain capacities or understandings have been developed. These capacities are revealed as the specific teaching of the new essential dimension.

• Freedom from the need to fixate on any state. This freedom arises from objective and full understanding of the nature of realization. There is no concept of an end-state and no psychic structure; any psychic structure is a fixation on some state of the soul. In other words, one is free from the need for fixed structures and ideals, including spiritual ideals.

• Detachment from comparative judgment. We are not interested in comparing our state to other states and judging whether it is acceptable or not. We engage in no measurement of our arising state with the ideals of any system, our own previous experiences, or the experiences of others. We need total, nonjudgmental acceptance of whatever state of soul may arise.[53]

- Engaging in any activity—ego manipulation or spiritual technique—in order to put oneself in one state or another can only lead to disconnecting from where one is, which is bound to lead to alienation from presence, for presence is always now. So at this point we need to forget about the conceptualizations of whatever teaching or system we have been following. This is the meaning of the Zen koan, "If you meet the Buddha on the road kill him." We also need, at this point, to cease any practice or method that includes any effort, orientation, aim, or position. Some theistic traditions call this stage "surrender to God's will" (in contrast to surrender to God). Traditions which use meditation as the primary spiritual method call it "nonmeditation."[54]

- The approach becomes finding where one is—that is, what happens to be the manifestation of the soul at the moment—and inquiring into it. We simply follow the thread of where we are. This acceptance spontaneously reveals the various facets and dimensions of the soul as a result of the evolutionary optimizing force inherent in the dynamism of our Being. This is the process of spontaneous unfoldment of the potentials of the self naturally revealing its ultimate wholeness. This is a celebrative and appreciative participation in life as the revelation of the mysteries of Being.

- The insight that specifically invokes the manifestation of the new dimension is that of seeing, in one's experience, that freedom from influence does not happen through control of one's experience or circumstances, but by surrendering to where one is. Where we are is how Being is manifesting itself in the presentations of the self. We discover that what we want is to be truly where we are, whatever Being is presenting in our experience. Joy arises now, as the heart is fulfilled and brimming with the sweetness of love.

At this stage, seeing where we are transforms smoothly into the state of self-realization with objective awareness of ourselves. There is the presence of the point (Essential Identity) and the nondual experience of it; the point is present within a clear and transparent medium. We

354   know ourselves as a transparent and clear presence, crystalline in its clarity and precision, the center of which is the blinding brilliance of the Essential Identity. The presence is totally clear, totally devoid of any obscurations; it is sharp, vivid, and rich, with inherent luminosity. This is the mirror-like awareness, which is now inseparable from the presence of the Essential Identity, but in a faceted and precise diamond-like form. There is a precise, clear, and objective seeing of oneself inseparable from the simplicity of being oneself. Seeing where one is and following the thread of one's unfoldment is the teaching of this manifestation of Essence.

This manifestation of Essence is a whole dimension which manifests as a diamond-like clarity, with the various colors and qualities of the essential aspects. The clear, crystalline medium manifests itself both in a colorless form, indicating clarity, and also colored with the rich hues of the essential aspects. As we become clearer about this self-aware, clear presence as it manifests as and through the essential aspects, we come to understand the various elements needed in mirroring.

We do not simply need to be seen; we need to be seen with admiration, kindness, appreciation, love, precision, clarity, joy, excitement, and so on. These needs are totally met when we start seeing ourselves with these qualities, reflecting the presence of these essential qualities in the mirroring awareness. The clear medium then appears with the beautiful yellow of Joy, reflecting seeing ourselves happily; or with the soft pink of Love, reflecting seeing ourselves with sweetness and love; or with the emerald green of Loving Kindness, reflecting seeing ourselves with kindness and sensitivity; or with the deep amber of Value, as we see ourselves with appreciation and esteem; or with the brilliant ruby red of Strength, reflecting seeing ourselves with excitement and aliveness; or with the rich apricot color of Fulfillment, reflecting being fulfilled by seeing ourselves; and so on.

The crystalline medium of the presence continues to be clear, transparent, and sharply-faceted, at the center of which is the brilliant point of existence, pervaded by the varying colors reflecting the various qualities of Essence.

Only the realization of this dimension of Being will completely resolve the need for mirroring.[55] This dimension also clarifies why we

need to be seen with appreciation, sensitivity, love, and so on, for we 355
need to realize this richness of our Being. It is our potential and our
human inheritance, and it is our unconsciously-felt right, which we
usually experience as entitlement. Our potential beckons to us, and at
the beginning this beckoning appears as our need and our sense of
entitlement.

BOOK THREE

——————————— • ———————————

FORMS OF NARCISSISM AND DIMENSIONS OF REALIZATION

THE DEVELOPMENTAL
SPECTRUM OF
NARCISSISM

E very individual suffers from a degree of narcissistic disturbance, and this disturbance typically includes all forms of
narcissism. The forms we enumerated in Chapter 4—oral,
central, individuation, and oedipal narcissism—telescope
together as total narcissism, reflecting alienation from the deeper strata
of the self and expressing the vicissitudes of this alienation throughout its various developmental stages. We observe in general that a student will manifest all the forms of narcissism, but that she will tend to
suffer from one of its forms more than from the others. We also notice
that the issues regarding forms of narcissism alternate in predominance in each student's process. So the student will work on one form,
and as she arrives at some understanding and resolution of it, it will
recede, and another form will dominate her experience, while at all
times her particular difficulty is somewhat apparent. For example, she
may suffer mostly from oral narcissism, so its particular characteristics are always intensely present even though other forms might

360   dominate her experience some of the time. So at one time the characteristics of oedipal narcissism might dominate her process, while those of oral narcissism are still easily discernable to the experienced observer, underlying and mixed with those of the oedipal form.

Only when the student's specific narcissistic difficulty has gone through some healing transformation will the other forms manifest in a clearly delineated way. The other forms will now be seen more clearly, opening the way to their eventual transformation.

At all times, however, the characteristics of fundamental narcissism, the alienation from the core of the self, can be seen to underlie all these manifestations. The need for idealized and mirroring selfobjects, exaggerated self-reference and entitlement, grandiosity, propensity towards slights and hurts, superficiality and fakeness, and the tendency towards narcissistic rage and devaluation, will always be discernable whenever she is dealing with narcissism.

What is the relation between fundamental and central narcissism?

The characteristics of fundamental narcissism are most clearly and specifically seen when central narcissism dominates the student's experience.

Central narcissism indicates the alienation from the Essential Identity. Since this aspect of Essence functions as the true identity, it is what gives the self the capacity for being its essential presence. Since the disturbance of this capacity is what underlies the fundamental narcissistic characteristics, it is clear that these characteristics will be most clearly manifest when central narcissism dominates experience. More specifically, the alienation from the Essential Identity disturbs the capacity of the self, in general, to be its essential core. Therefore, it is paramount to work on central narcissism to accomplish any deep transformation in fundamental narcissism. This is why central narcissism is our primary focus in this study. In reality, the work on central narcissism is the most fundamental and necessary work needed to be done on narcissism.

Frequently, a student needs to work on her predominant form of narcissism before she can approach her central narcissism; but she will not be able to effect any deep transformation in it before tackling central

narcissism. So the general pattern of the process of working on narcis-
sism is that the student will do some work on the predominant form,
then address central narcissism deeply, and after that, return to the first
to be able to understand it more completely. This is the general orientation of the process, but we do find variations and deviations from
this pattern.

Experience is rarely so orderly or definite, so our inquiry always
includes some mixture of fundamental narcissism with the manifestations of the form dominating a person's present experience. So, in
some sense, we are always working on central narcissism, regardless
of what form we happen to be focusing on. We have given a detailed
account of the manifestations of central narcissism, and the process
of working through it, and now we will address the manifestations of
the other forms of narcissism. Our discussion will be short, for our
attempt is merely to give the general outlines of the work on, and
understanding of, these forms. For other relevant materials the interested reader can consult the references we list.

chapter 36

Individuation Narcissism

I ndividuation narcissism is associated with the lack of development of what we call the "Personal Essence." This is a manifestation of essential presence in which—like Essential Identity—we experience "I am," but here, the emphasis in experience is more on the "am" than on the "I." It is a presence of fullness, substantiality and well-being. I am, as personal presence; I experience myself as a person, but this person is not patterned by self-representations. The Personal Essence is the presence of the self as a person, a human individual with unique qualities and capacities. This person is an ontological presence of pure consciousness.

In contrast, the sense of being a person in the conventional dimension of experience is determined by self-images based on our experience of the body and of object relations. We have discussed Mahler's descriptions of the development of the normal sense of being a person, in which the ego structure is constructed through the process of separation-individuation. According to Mahler's model, the sense of being an individual is the outcome of the development of the two ego structures—self-identity and self-entity, as we see in the following passage quoted by Marjorie T. White:

'The task to be achieved by development in the course of the
normal separation-individuation process is the establishment
of both a measure of object constancy and a measure of self
constancy, an enduring individuality as it were. The latter
achievement consists of the attainment of the two levels of the
sense of identity: (1) the awareness of being a separate and
individual entity, and (2) a beginning awareness of a gender-
defined self-identity. . .' (White, in Morrison, 1986, p. 162)

Thus, the ordinary sense of being a person is the experience of the
self patterned by the structures that give it the sense of being an individual entity with a particular identity.

The Personal Essence, in contrast, is the sense of being a person
independent of ego structures. It is the awareness of presence quali-
fied by personhood. This sense of personhood is independent of one's
personal history; it is a direct recognition of a pure form of Being. This
form of Being feels personal, and gives the self the capacity for immediate personal contact. It is an individuated experience of presence,
arising from the unique development of the self into a person with
essential qualities that provide the self with various capacities, skills,
and talents. It is the integration of the development of the self on the
essential dimension. The Personal Essence, then, is the essential counterpart to the sense of individuality that Mahler describes as being
established through ego development.[1]

From the perspective of self-realization, the Personal Essence is the
individuation of the soul. When the self is alienated from this form of
Being, it is narcissistically disturbed in relation to individuation, rather
than in relation to identity only, as in central narcissism. Thus, there
are narcissistic disturbances in relation to the sense of being an
autonomous individual, in the integration of the unique individual
qualities of the self, and in the integration of its capacities, skills, and
talents. The development of individuality, qualities, skills, and talents
is not necessarily absent; rather, the integration of this development
into one's sense of identity is disturbed. Issues of self-esteem related
to this development are significant in individuation narcissism. This
narcissism is an important element of the disturbances of individuation, but not identical to them. Individuation narcissism manifests as

364   the need for support for individuation, and as the need for mirroring of one's skills and capacities, and as grandiose ideas about one's qualities, skills, talents, and accomplishments. One is narcissistic in relation to one's competence and capacity, as well as in relation to one's sense of being, as we see in the following report by James E., which we presented in Chapter 10:

> *It became clear that identifying with my personality and my self-image as lacking capacities was a matter of having an identity. Seeing myself with capacities I felt without identity, not being able to recognize myself as I have always known myself, and feeling like nothing. The feeling of being like a donut was one of contraction attempting to create capacities around an emptiness.*

Seeing and acknowledging his capacities made James feel the loss of identity, because his identity excluded them. His capacities were not mirrored with excitement and appreciation; instead, he was seen as lacking capacities, which caused him to develop a deficient sense of identity. He had no sense of connection to feeling capable. This sense of capacity is one of the qualities of the experience of the Personal Essence, as we see in the continuation of his report:

> *My experience of being nothing, without identity, was at first frightening. I began to experience making contact with you. I began to feel in my belly a strong, warm sense of being substantial, with substance of my own. I felt as if capacity came from this state, this place inside me, and without effort when needed. I feel love along with these feelings.*

James began to experience the Personal Essence, first in the quality of contact, but then more definitely as a strong and warm fullness, "*a substance of my own,*" indicating the autonomy of Being. Then he had the insight that this presence connects him with the sense of capacity. It is important to see here that he felt the fullness of presence as the source of capacity; thus, that capacity was not integrated into his sense of self through a representation. This report illustrates how we can experience individuation on the essential dimension.

James's case illustrates one particular dynamic of individuation narcissism: The inadequacy of mirroring and support for an able and competent sense of self leads to the disconnection of his identity from 365 his capacities. There are other dynamics which generate individuation narcissism, as we will discuss shortly.

Since this narcissism is related to individuation, when the student experiences the lack of this quality, the empty shell will feel like it lacks the sense of individuality. The student will realize that his usual sense of being an individual is really an empty shell.[2] This empty shell will be exposed when his autonomy, or his capacities, are not mirrored adequately, or when he feels they are not, if, for example, the mirror transference is disturbed. Then he will feel narcissistically hurt and might resort to narcissistic rage. But allowing the hurt and the sense of betrayal will reveal the emptiness underlying his sense of being a person. Allowing this emptiness will make it possible for his Essence to arise, as we see in James's report above. The essential presence that arises will not be the Essential Identity with its singular radiance, but rather, the Personal Essence with its fullness and roundedness.

Since the empty shell associated with this form of narcissism is the structure of the ego individuality which develops through the process of separation-individuation, the history of individuation narcissism can best be seen in the terms of this process. In fact, some psychological researchers view narcissism in terms of specific disturbances of the process of separation-individuation. These are the researchers who base their work on Mahler's theories. This body of understanding is most appropriate for exploring individuation narcissism, even though they think of it as addressing narcissism in general.

These researchers believe narcissism results from disturbances of the process of the child's separation from the mother. For instance, the mother's inadequate response to the child's developing autonomy—intrusiveness, for example—might interfere with individuation, as we see in the following passage from "A Narcissistic Defence Against Affects and the Illusion of Self-Sufficiency," a paper by Arnold Modell:

> We have observed that in our patients with narcissistic character disorders, there is probably a disturbance in the process of the development of the self vis-a-vis the child's relationship to its mother. Although the specifics of the environmental trauma will vary, we have observed that the trauma results in

the need to defend the sense of the separateness of the self against the intrusiveness of the mother. (Morrison, 1986, p. 296)

This reflects Mahler's understanding that the sense of being an individual with unique capacities and qualities develops as the child separates from his mother, resulting in separate self-representations, indicating separation from the original state of fused-self-with-mother. This fused condition of the self, characterizing the symbiotic stage of development in the first few months of life, is seen as the milieu from which the child separates as he develops his autonomous sense of self.

Modell's understanding of narcissism focuses on the precocious development of the individuality, where the child develops a sense of capacity before he can actually manage the separation. In other words, he believes narcissistic disturbance is related to growing up too soon, before the child is able to do so emotionally.

> The human child, as is true of all primates, is dependent upon the mother to protect it from the dangers of the environment so that the perception of the mother's unreliability must have profound consequences. We suggest that it leads in some patients to the formation of precocious separation from the mother which is supported by fantasies of omnipotence. (Morrison, 1986, p. 297)

Precocious development that alienates one's capacities from one's sense of self is another dynamic in the development of individuation narcissism. Our observations seem to corroborate Modell's, but only in relation to individuation narcissism, and not to narcissism in general.[3] We find that in this form of narcissism, grandiosity is used as a defense against the sense of inadequacy and deficiency that underlies the precocious development, as illustrated in the following report by Jordan D:

> *My work Saturday night put a lot of things together for me. I have been bouncing back and forth between feeling inadequate, afraid, deficient, etc. and grandiose, manic, like I could do anything I wanted. Both of these poles are painful. I have been aware of all the energy it takes to maintain the illusion that I am the best, most advanced, most together, etc. Both feelings of inadequacy and of grandiosity lead me to compare and judge.*

The sense of inadequacy characterizes the emptiness connected with   367
the absence of the Personal Essence, while feeling adequate and mature
characterizes its presence. In time, Jordan's work led him to see how
his relation to his father and mother led him to separate prematurely,
helping him understand this narcissistic manifestation as an expression of his precocious development. However, he was not able to go
very deeply into this exploration until he first focused on his central
narcissism, then returned to issues of individuation narcissism. This
process involved many difficult states and life conflicts, but as his capacity to experience the Personal Essence increased, he managed to develop
the personal life of work and family that he had always desired.

Arnold Rothstein emphasizes the role of separation anxiety in the
development of narcissism: "Secondary narcissistic investment is a
defensive response of the ego to the signal of separation anxiety stimulated by the perception of a state of separateness." (Morrison, 1986,
p. 308) He views narcissism as the result of not being loved consistently for being oneself, but admired only for one's performance. This
unempathic mirroring leads to the separation of one's capacity from
one's sense of self, reflecting individuation narcissism. Rothstein thinks
of the self both as self-as-object and self-as-agent, reflecting both entity-
hood and functioning, indicating individuality. In Chapter 10 we discussed how the structure of self-entity is related to functioning and how
it gives the self the sense of separating boundaries needed for the sense
of being an individual entity. Rothstein describes his view of narcissism most clearly when he relates it to the self-as-agent:

> A healthy narcissistic self-representation is one in which the
> 'self-as-agent' is comprised, in part, of memory traces of being
> loved consistently and empathically. This experience has
> allowed the 'self-as-agent' to develop an internalized expecta-
> tion of being loved primarily for himself rather than for his
> performance. (Morrison, 1986, p. 314)

This describes our own view of another dynamic involved in the
development of individuation narcissism, in which the form that
the self becomes alienated from is a presence inseparable from one's
functioning.

368   Gertrude and Rubin Blanck base their view of narcissism on the work of Mahler and her colleagues. Their perspective relates narcissism and narcissistic disturbance to the stages of the separation-individuation process, thus developing a model that unifies the various dynamics underlying individuation narcissism. The main thrust of their view is that narcissistic disturbance is a specific outcome of disruptions to the task of self-organization in the various stages of ego development.

> With specific reference to narcissistic features, those which are familiarly designated as grandiosity, magical omnipotence, and the like are now more accurately thought to be behavioral manifestations of unfulfilled developmental tasks, as clinical evidences of phase and subphase inadequacies. (G. and R. Blanck, 1974b, p. 50)

The idea is that the ego-self, which they see as an organizing process, develops through several phases, those of symbiosis, differentiation, practicing, rapprochement, and on-the-way-to-object-constancy (see Mahler et al., 1975). The child encounters different developmental tasks at each of these phases, such as separating from his mother, developing a self-image, internalizing an integrated image of mother, and so on. Success in dealing with the developmental tasks of each phase results in the increasing cathexis of the self-representation with positive value, indicating healthy development of the self in the narcissistic sector. They write: "Then we may speak of narcissism as positive cathexis of whole and relatively stable self representations. . . . The very experience of adequacy, that is, optimal fulfillment of the developmental purpose, adds to the sense of self-valuation." (G. and R. Blanck, 1974b, pp. 58–59)

It is significant that they consider "the very experience of adequacy" important for narcissistic health. This reflects their emphasis on functioning in the developing self. Functioning is again a characteristic of the Personal Essence, as contrasted to the Essential Identity. The Essential Identity brings a sense of authenticity, reality, being oneself, spontaneity, being a center of initiative and awareness, and so on. The Personal Essence, on the other hand, is related to qualities of integration, competence, individuation, autonomy, capacity, personal love, and so on.

The Blancks discuss the development of narcissism from phase to   369
phase in the process of separation-individuation, seeing this development as one line of two; the other line is the development of object
love. This enables them to elucidate the balance needed between these
two lines of development, thus resolving a long-standing debate about
the relationship of narcissism to the development of object relations:

> Self esteem, if sacrificed in favor of excessive valuation of the
> object, will remain fixated in primitive form while organiza-
> tion, now skewed, will proceed nonetheless toward distur-
> bances in identity formation. If the imbalance is in the other
> direction, narcissism will grow in exaggerated form at the
> expense of capacity to love and will reflect, in adulthood, its
> infantile distortions. (G. and R. Blanck, 1974b, p. 179)

We agree with this formulation, with two reservations. First we see
the Blancks' view, like that of others like Modell and Rothstein above,
as addressing only one form of narcissism—individuation narcissism—
and not narcissism in general. Thus, their understanding is useful in
our work of self-realization when the student is dealing with individuation narcissism. However, we believe that the Blancks' view is not
only inadequate for understanding the other forms of narcissism, but
would probably be misleading if used exclusively to understand them.

The other reservation is our general one regarding psychological
theories of narcissism, namely, that this view does not address the issue
of alienation from Being as the cause of fundamental narcissism. The
failures in meeting subphase developmental tasks which contribute to
the development of individuation narcissism also contribute to this
alienation. It is this alienation, specifically from the Personal Essence,
which is at the root of this form of narcissism.

This distinction is not simply a matter of theory. If the alienation
from Being is not addressed, then this narcissism cannot be transformed; it can only be ameliorated. Its fundamental transformation is
equivalent to the integration of the Personal Essence, to the degree of
self-realization. Only when the student is able to experience himself as
the Personal Essence can we say that individuation narcissism has been
transformed. This is a resolution of a spiritual nature. It is not only a

370   matter of developing a sense of individuation with a capacity for relating with others. It is not only a matter of establishing a stable sense of autonomy with realistic self-esteem. It is a matter of fundamentally knowing oneself as an authentic presence of Being, which feels personal and human, and whose self-esteem springs from the fact that this presence is its own value.

This realization requires the integration of the Personal Essence, as discussed in *The Pearl Beyond Price* (Almaas, 1988). As part of the process of integration, one must address the narcissism related to the Personal Essence, until one is able not only to permanently experience it, but is able to *be* it in a nondual manner. This is the coemergence of self-realization and individuation. It is a very subtle state in which we experience the Essential Identity and the Personal Essence as one manifestation of presence. We are the fullness of the personal presence, but our center is the brilliant preciousness of the Essential Identity.[4] We are capable of living a personal life as a human being, with competence, dignity, and maturity, but our center and source is the timeless preciousness of true nature. We are in the world, but we never leave the transcendent depths of Being.

chapter 37

Oedipal Narcissism

O edipal narcissism is a continuation of individuation narcissism, in the sense that it concerns the integration of further qualities and capacities of the self into the identity. We delineate it as a separate form of narcissism for two reasons. First, it originates in a distinctly separate development stage, the oedipal stage of psychosexual development, between the ages of three and six years. Second, we discriminate this form of narcissism because it involves alienation from the essential presence that arises at the oedipal stage, which is different from the quality of Personal Essence that dominates in the rapprochement phase of the separation-individuation process, and which is related to individuation narcissism.

Our understanding of oedipal narcissism relies heavily on that of Kohut, who accepts the primary elements of the oedipal complex as formulated by Freud,[5] but views its development differently. He believes that the grossly sexual impulses, the genital lusty possessiveness, the exaggerated destructive and competitive impulses, the murderous hatred, and the intense fear of retaliation, or castration anxiety, all result from narcissistic insult to the child's developing self in the oedipal phase. He calls these constituents of the classic oedipal complex disintegration

372   products, which arise from the disintegration of the self as a result of the parents' gross lack of empathy during the child's oedipal stage. Kohut contrasts this situation with what he calls the "normal oedipal" situation, in which:

> If a child enters the oedipal phase with a firm, cohesive, continuous self, he will then experience assertive-possessive, affectionate-sexual desires for the heterogenital parent and assertive, self-confident, competitive feelings vis-a-vis the parent of the same sex. (Kohut, 1977, p. 230)

In other words, if a boy arrives at the oedipal stage narcissistically healthy and relatively uninjured, he will naturally begin to feel sexual feelings of a tender nature towards his mother and healthy confident competition with his father, and vice versa for the girl. What happens at this point depends on the reaction of the parents.

Kohut assumes that it is natural for the parents to react to the sexual desires and the competitive rivalry of the child with some sexual stimulation and counteraggression. However, how they handle the child's feelings will depend on how comfortable they are with them and with their own feelings. They are empathically attuned, supportive, and adequately mirroring of the child's developing self if they respond to this development with pride and joy. The child's sense of self will be confirmed by this attuned response, and he will experience a similar pride and joy in his own sexual development, which helps him integrate into his identity, with self-esteem, his gender, his maleness. Kohut puts it this way:

> If the little boy, for example, feels that his father looks upon him proudly as a chip off the old block and allows him to merge with him and with his adult greatness, then his oedipal phase will be a decisive step in self-consolidation and self-pattern-firming, including the laying down of one of the several variants of integrated maleness. (Kohut, 1977, p. 234)

Kohut further believes that a boy who is exposed to the responses of psychologically healthy parents does not experience a significant degree of castration anxiety during the oedipal phase. (Kohut, 1984, p. 14) The parents' response to the child's growing self is unhealthy when the parents cannot establish an empathic bond with him, tending to look at his oedipal feelings in isolation, rather than as a natural expression of his developing self. They might interpret his behavior as abnormal and as alarming sexuality and hostility, rather than as expressions of assertive affection and competition. So the father may respond with dismay, judgment, rejection, anger, or outright hostile competition. He may punish the child, or admonish him to behave, making him feel bad and guilty, or terrified. Or he may completely ignore the signs of his son's developing self due to his own narcissistic preoccupation. The father may even withdraw, feeling unable to handle the situation. He may be permissive, allowing the boy to feel that he can win his mother, failing to set the appropriate boundaries that his son needs to feel mirrored and to feel guided in terms of sexual expression and appropriateness. The mother may react with irritation, awkwardness, alarm, withdrawal, pretending not to notice, or with rejection, criticism, or even anger. She might instead react not only with approval, but also with encouragement, or with covert—or even overt—seduction. Kohut describes these unempathic responses when he writes about the child's real fears in the oedipal phase, stating that:

> The girl's primary oedipal fears are of being confronted by a nonempathically sexually seductive rather than affection-accepting paternal selfobject or by a competitive-hostile rather than pridefully pleased maternal one. The boy's primary oedipal fears, on the other hand, are of being confronted by a nonempathic sexually seductive rather than affection-accepting maternal selfobject or by a competitive-hostile rather than pridefully pleased paternal one. (Kohut, 1984, p. 24)

Kohut believes that these fears transform into the intense fears of the classic oedipal complex—seeing these latter as secondary—as the child's focus shifts from his deeper narcissistic needs for empathic selfobjects to concerns with psychosocial tensions. Rather than integrating his assertive affection and competition, and realizing his gender identity, he is now narcissistically injured, and thus, he loses the joy in his oedipal development. His sense of self is weakened and perhaps even disintegrated. In other words ". . . whether the parental pathology is expressed openly or covertly, the child's self becomes fragmented,

374   weakened, and disharmonious and his normal nonsexual affection become grossly sexual and hostile." (Kohut, 1984, p. 24) Kohut views this development as the cause of the pathological oedipal complex, and believes that this latter phenomenon is the attempt of the self to organize the fragments resulting from the primarily narcissistic injury.

One reason we find Kohut's view of the oedipal complex convincing is that, in most of our students, we do not see the extremes of sexual desire and hatred characteristic of the classic oedipal formulation. What we find is closer to what Kohut refers to as the feelings of the normal oedipal phase, although there are some differences that we will discuss shortly. Our understanding of the development of oedipal narcissism, then, is that the oedipal self becomes weakened and distorted in the absence or inadequacy of appropriate mirroring and support. The self develops without integrating the qualities and capacities that emerge at this stage of development, or it develops with distortions that impel it to compulsively and unsuccessfully seek mirroring and supportive selfobjects for these manifestations of the self.

The following are some important observations regarding the oedipal stage, its narcissism, and the relation to the self's development:

- *Freud and his work has been under attack from various quarters in recent years. Whatever the validity and reason for such attacks we find that the oedipal situation is a real one for the development of the self.* We find Kohut's formulation more consonant with our observations, but this changes the kind and intensity of the emotions, and some of their meanings, but it does not change the basic object relations of this triadic situation. The heterosexual child does experience some kind of desire for the parent of the opposite sex and competitive feelings toward the parent of the same sex. The feelings are not as grossly sexual or aggressive as Freud believed, but the complex of feelings seems to still emerge at this stage. In our work with students, since it is open and open-ended inquiry, we do not go seeking out or looking for signs of the oedipal stage. What we find, however, is that students do encounter this complex of object relations and affects at some point in working on their self structure. It does not happen at the beginning of the inner journey, and in fact this complex begins to show itself after the student has gone

through a great deal of metabolism of childhood material. The situations and conflicts of the separation-individuation process seem
to emerge much more readily than those of the oedipal complex.
When these are metabolized to some extent, and the student has
achieved a greater stability of autonomy and individuation, the feelings of the oedipal situation begin to emerge. And the feelings seem
to mostly connect with narcissistic considerations, specifically the
need for mirroring or support for one's erotic-passionate-loving
feelings. This is actually the reason we have discussed individuation
narcissism before oedipal narcissism in this book. Another important observation is that individuals differ in the intensity of their
oedipal feelings. For some it is intense and problematic; for others
the feelings arise but do not have much charge or intensity. It would
seem that the importance and intensity of the oedipal complex
depends a great deal on one's history with one's parents, supporting Kohut's view of this developmental stage.

- *Our observations support Kohut's conclusions that sexual seduction is
  significant in generating oedipal narcissism.* The more gross and
  intense the seduction is, the greater the narcissistic wounding to the
  self. The seduction can be purely emotional or quite indirect, and
  yet still have far reaching consequences on one's erotic and sexual
  identity and life. The impact is obviously greater when the seduction is gross and physical, but in both emotional and physical erotic
  seductions, the child is bound to feel compelled, conflicted, ashamed,
  and guilty, in ways that tend to last a life time. The child always ends
  up feeling used and abused, and such early sexual abuse has a radical effect on the development of oedipal narcissism and to the development of the self in general. The distortions in the oedipal self as
  a result of the psychodynamic disturbances pale in comparison with
  the alienation from the depths of the self that result from the dissociation the child resorts to in response to such trauma.

  It is well known that early sexual abuse, especially incest, and
  physical abuse as well, create havoc in the psychic equilibrium of its
  survivors and become a major source of suffering and conflict in
  their lives. Sexual and physical abuse confront the child with so
  much pain, and such intolerable conflicts, that typically the child

376 shuts off the whole situation from awareness. Whether there is amnesia or only emotional isolation, there results a dissociation from deep experience of the self in general. "Unable to remove herself physically from the abuse, the creative child victim finds other ways to leave. Frequently this leaving takes the form of 'separation from the self,' or 'depersonalization.'" (E. Blume, 1990, p. 82)

Since essential presence is the core depth of the self, it must be dissociated from, or it will tend to expose the painful events of the abuse.[6] So early abuse is a specific cause of the alienation from the core of the self, and hence leads to the development of narcissistic disturbance. Early abuse, including sexual abuse, causes not only oedipal narcissism, but other forms of narcissism, depending on when it occurred.

• *Oedipal seduction and abuse have devastating effects on the developing self, but mostly on the erotic and passionate self, and creates immense difficulties for the persons' adult intimate relationships.* The individual will generally find it difficult to recognize and appreciate appropriate behavior and boundaries in the erotic, sexual, and emotional spheres in relation to others, will tend to be too permissive or too rigid, too seductive or too aggressive, sometimes develop pornographic tendencies, or other variants of sexual distortion. One of the worst effects is a long lasting sensitivity and vulnerability, and a predisposition to wounding and disruption in erotic and passionate relationships, that makes it quite difficult and problematic to have and sustain a long term intimate relationship. This means that the disruptions of the oedipal stage influence the development of the self not only in terms of the specific qualities of this stage, but also in the development of object relations in general, especially in completing object constancy to the stage which includes erotic, sexual, and passionate adult relationships. In other words, the narcissistic disruptions of the oedipal stage make it difficult for the self to harmoniously integrate the essential qualities of passionate love, appreciative love, and the sensuous contactful features of the Personal Essence.

• *The child needs a model for being a man or a woman and for sexual identity in general.* For a child to grow up feeling value and pride in his or her sexuality and gender, affirming and supportive mirroring

is very important. This mirroring depends not only on the response   377
of the selfobjects, but also on their own state of being. The boy is
confirmed in his maleness by having a father who is happy and
proud of his own adult maleness, and the girl is supported in her
femaleness by interacting with a mother who values her own adult
femaleness with pride, joy, and pleasure. We agree with Kohut's view
on female sexuality when he explains some of the cultural stereotypes of femininity, by saying that:

> . . . the girl's rejection of femininity, her feeling of being cas-
> trated and inferior, and her intense wish for a penis arise not
> because the male sex organs are psychologically more desir-
> able than the female ones, but because the little girl's selfobjects
> failed to respond to her with appropriate mirroring, since
> either no idealizable female parental imago was available to
> her, or that no alter ego gave her support during the child-
> hood years when a proud feminine self should have estab-
> lished itself. (Kohut, 1984, p. 21)

Our present culture lacks true models of sexuality, both feminine
and masculine. Neither the female nor male popular stereotypes are
true representations of femininity or masculinity. It is sufficient to
consider the male and female idols in the movie industry and in the
music scene, and the most popular personifications of men and
women in the mass media, to see the utter confusion and the sense
of loss from which the culture as a whole is suffering when it comes
to the sexual self.

The absence of true models of sexuality has been extending to
the home environment, where the differences between men and
women, masculinity and femininity, are becoming increasingly
blurred in our contemporary Western culture. The attempt at finding economical and social equality between the sexes, even though
necessary and important, is frequently carried to excess in areas
where the differences are necessary. It becomes difficult sometimes
for the child to know what are the unique characteristics of being a
man or a woman, when more and more things are becoming uni-
sex. It seems that our culture is still quite a distance from achieving
true equality and parity between the sexes that can retain the unique

378   and valuable differences that make a man a man and a woman a woman. We are passing through a period of confusion regarding maleness and femaleness, which might be necessary before a new and higher but true social organization is achieved. We do not see how this can happen if we do not consider the essential qualities and their impact on the sense of femininity and masculinity.

Some elements in the women's movement are attempting to redefine the meaning of femaleness, but we do not notice much success. This is understandable because redefinition requires a rediscovery, and this is possible only by going very deep into the sense of self. Redefinition cannot happen through a political or a social movement; it must be the outcome of a deep transformation, of the realization of the erotic gender-determined self. This is basically a spiritual discovery.

Hormones and genes are fundamental in this regard, but it is our essential presence and its qualities that give us the possibility of subjectively and personally knowing what is real and authentic in our own experience and feelings of identity. Only when we can experience the qualities of our true nature throughout our body, including our genital and erotic regions, can we truly recognize what is masculine and what is feminine, and what it is like to be a man or a woman. We also recognize that there is a whole field of research that is waiting to be tapped, that of the relation of essential aspects and qualities to hormones and enzymes, that may shed a new kind of scientific light on the question of femininity and masculinity.

• *The fifth observation brings us to the point at which we differ from Kohut in our understanding of oedipal narcissism.* Kohut thinks of the self in the oedipal phase, as characterized by assertive affection and competition. We find this to be true, but there are other qualities and levels of manifestation of the oedipal self which are very significant. Kohut seems to underemphasize some of the other significant properties of the oedipal self, probably due to his attempt to relate the classic Oedipus complex to his psychology of the self. He seems to actually lean further away from the classic position in his later writings; he describes the feelings of the self in the oedipal phase, in *How Does Analysis Cure?* (Kohut, 1984), in a way that makes the phase more tender and loving than it appears in his early 379 writing, *The Restoration of the Self* (Kohut, 1971).

Our repeated observations indicate that the oedipal self is not only assertively affectionate and competitive. It is a sexy self, in the sense that the affection it experiences has a primary pleasurable, sensuous, and erotic quality to it. It is true; there is sweetness and softness, the appreciative affection of love. The assertiveness, however, manifests as passion, as consuming and ecstatic love. This Passionate Love does not differentiate between desire and appreciation; it is an intense excitation, both consuming and sweet. There is softness and gentleness, but there is also an exquisite lusty passionateness. It is the lusty, erotic, sexy, sensuous, ecstatic love of life. It is a matter of being lovingly and passionately turned on to life, and deeper still to the truth of the mystery of our Being. It is not necessarily genital, and is generally not genital in early childhood, but it can be, and is appropriately so in adulthood.

- *The oedipal self combines both tender-affectionate and passionate-erotic feelings and qualities in the same experience.* It unifies the heart and the genitals in one feeling state. This level of optimal development of this aspect of the self was explored by many, including Wilhelm Reich, in *Character Analysis* (Reich, 1945), and by Otto Fenichel, in *The Psychoanalytic Theory of Neurosis* (Fenichel, 1945). They believed that this development is necessary for maintaining a viable intimate relation between two individuals, and its absence is an indication of classic neurosis. We need some degree of resolution of oedipal narcissism in order to sustain a thriving sexual-intimate couple relationship.

Falling in love

Recognizing and appreciating the nature of the oedipal self and its narcissistic disturbances brings us a powerful understanding of the phenomenon of falling in love. The characteristics of this form of self, both the sweetness of love and the ecstasy of passion, are exactly what the individual in love enjoys. To be in love is to be swept by an ecstatic love, in which the sweetness of appreciation and affection cannot be separated from a passionate desire to be one with the beloved. We feel

380 full, alive, sexually stimulated, and vigorous; we behold the beloved as beautiful, luscious, sexy, and extremely desirable. We feel tender and selflessly loving, but also turned on, excited and full of life.

We need intensely for this love to be seen, appreciated and reciprocated. Unrequited love causes us extreme frustration, also deep narcissistic hurt and disappointment. It exposes the disturbances of oedipal narcissism. A common narcissistic element of being in love is exclusive preoccupation with the beloved at the expense of other areas of one's life. The lover has extreme hopes for a level of fulfillment that goes beyond merely the reciprocation of love; he deeply entertains the hope for complete narcissistic gratification, which will enable him to spontaneously be himself with deep, orgiastic abandon. In other words, the lover's desire is not only the reciprocation of his passionate love, but the realization—through the support and mirroring in this reciprocation—of his oedipal self.

Depth psychology tends to view the qualities of falling in love as determined mostly by idealization of the beloved and grandiose images of the self. This is partially accurate, but this depends on our view of the oedipal self. We saw in our exploration of central narcissism that idealization and grandiosity are remnants of memories and intuitions of authentic potentials of the self, of essential qualities the self has not yet realized. We believe this is also the case with the phenomenon of falling in love. The qualities the lover sees in his beloved are partly her actual essential qualities, but she cannot completely embody them. The fact that the lover is seeing qualities of the beloved which she herself has not completely realized may allow us to view the lover's feeling as based on idealization. However, this is at most a partial explanation. Part of what the lover beholds in his beloved is a projection of qualities of his own oedipal self; his longing to merge with the beloved is partly the desire to regain the lost connection to the vigor and aliveness of his oedipal self.

The transformation of oedipal narcissism makes it possible for falling in love to be a fulfilling and fulfilled experience. Kernberg writes about the effects of narcissism on one's love life:

> Complete absence of sexual interest in women in the severely
> ill patients; the frantic search for sexual excitement and sexual

promiscuity, linked with an incapacity for establishing a more permanent relationship, in less severe ones; and a limited capacity for transitory infatuation in still milder cases represent the spectrum of narcissistic pathology of love life. (Kernberg, 1979, p. 195)[7]

Some measure of resolution of oedipal narcissism is necessary for falling in love to happen at all. A greater resolution allows the individual to actualize an enduring intimate relationship based on being in love. Unless one has dealt with his oedipal history and arrived at some realization of his oedipal self, one's love life will be contaminated with his narcissistic needs and vulnerabilities.

The last of our considerations concerns our main contribution to the understanding of oedipal narcissism. The self that is realized when oedipal narcissism is transformed is not the self patterned by the development of a psychic structure, accruing from experiences at the oedipal phase, as Kohut believes, but a specific essential form, a presence of Being inseparable from love and passion. We recognize ourselves as a presence that is full, sensuous, vigorous, vibrant, alive, erotic, flowing, beautiful, and youthful. We recognize ourselves as this quality by directly being this vigorous and passionate presence. The passionate love, the vigor and sensuousness, are not attributes of this sense of self; they are its very substance. One is a vigorous river of aliveness, passionately in love with life and truth. This river is an actuality, a tangy flow of presence, a consuming continuity of Being.[8]

Our description of the oedipal self might induce the reader to wonder whether it possesses any maturity or responsibility, for the qualities discussed so far might be construed as fine for the adolescent years, but not for adulthood. However, the qualities of the oedipal self are definitely desired or experienced by responsible adults in appropriate situations. They are appropriate and even necessary elements of a harmoniously developed self. The mature self has the competence, responsibility, and integrity specific to the individuation self and also the qualities of authenticity, reality, and preciousness specific to the central self. In other words, the self-realized individual has integrated not only the oedipal self, but also the Personal Essence and the Essential Identity. At any given moment, his predominant experience of himself might

382   be the timeless transcendence of the Essential Identity, the competent fullness of the Personal Essence, or the sensuous passionateness of the oedipal self. He can also experience all three simultaneously, with varying degrees of differentiation. What he experiences as himself will depend on the life situation he finds himself in, as the qualities of his soul emerge in appropriate responses to the situations in his life.[9]

chapter 38

Oral Narcissism

O ral narcissism is related to disturbances in what Freud called primary narcissism. In terms of our consideration of self-realization, oral narcissism results from disturbance of the original equilibrium of the self which we have termed primary self-realization. This corresponds to the initial phases of early development coinciding with Mahler's autistic and symbiotic stages, or Freud's oral stage of psychosexual development. We have termed it "oral narcissism" because of the predominance of oral needs and concerns. It underlies all other forms of narcissism because it is the earliest in development. Thus, it colors the manifestations of later developments. When oral narcissism is the dominant form for a particular individual, her narcissism telescopes all the four forms, with the oral characteristics dominating the picture. We find Kernberg's formulations most useful in addressing this level of narcissism.

Oral narcissism is characterized by a primitive quality and intensity of emotion that are associated with borderline disorders. Since the child's experience in infancy is undifferentiated, the two lines of development—those of narcissism and object love—are not yet differentiated. This situation eliminates the possibility of clear differentiation

384   between narcissism and the borderline conditions. This explains why Kernberg tends to view narcissism as a form of borderline structure, for oral narcissism is inseparable from other disturbances of the self at this early stage.

Kernberg views the grandiose self as a pathological development in the service of defense against a primarily borderline weakness, but he also acknowledges that it provides the individual with a kind of identity.

> The integration of this pathological, grandiose self compensates for the lack of integration of the normal self-concept which is part of the underlying borderline personality organization. (Kernberg, 1975, p. 266)

In other words, the self-structure of the narcissist consists of a pathological grandiose self that defends against, and compensates for, an underlying borderline weakness. So it is a specific form of borderline organization.

Our view is that oral narcissism does include borderline weakness, but this is because it develops from the oral stage, which is characterized by primitive manifestations usually associated with borderline organizations, and not because it is a form of such organizations. However, this is a moot point because of the absence of differentiation in this developmental stage.

Kernberg views the grandiose self as a structure that defends against very primitive, terrifying, and conflictual object relations.

> The patient's efforts to hold on to his grandiose self, and to avoid acknowledging the analyst as an independent, autonomous person, consistently reveal his defense against the intense envy, against the feared relationship with the hated and sadistically perceived mother image, and his dread of a sense of empty loneliness in a world devoid of personal meaning. (Kernberg, 1975, p. 287)

He observes that in most cases these individuals had a narcissistic mother who was chronically cold, but overprotective.

In most of our students, the grandiose self that becomes exposed is not generally the major structure of the self. However, we do observe

that if the work of inquiry progresses very deeply, each individual will
eventually encounter oral narcissism with its intense envy, hate, hunger,
devaluation, and rage. This does not ordinarily indicate a deep pathology, but reflects the fact that each self in the conventional dimension
of experience—each self patterned by ego structures—is fundamentally narcissistic, and this narcissism always includes some degree of
oral narcissism. The oral narcissism which arises in the process of spiritual development reflects fundamental narcissism in the oral stage and
relates to the processes in the very early part of life which contributed
to alienation of the self from its essential core.

The intensity and the degree of uncontrollability of the arising manifestations depend on the degree of disturbance in early childhood, but
the quality and flavor of these manifestations are common to all ego-
selves. In general, it is difficult to penetrate and transform oral narcissism, and this difficulty does not depend only on the degree of
disturbance. The primitive nature of the affects and object relations
that emerge, the vagueness of experience and structure that reflect the
undifferentiation of this early stage, and the deep compulsiveness of
the impulses of this form of self, combine to make this work subtle,
difficult, and of long duration. This work penetrates to the deepest
strata of the structure of the self, addresses areas of the self that—under
normal circumstances—are obscure and hidden, and deals with fundamental questions regarding self, life, drives, needs, and impulses.

However, we do observe the layering of object relations that Kernberg
describes. First, there is the initial defensive and compensatory layer
of either devaluation or idealization, which Kernberg attributes to the
identification with, or projection of, the grandiose self, respectively.
This initial layer does not necessarily involve a pathological self; rather,
the student seems to resort to idealization, devaluation, or grandiosity, or any combination of these, to defend against the underlying layer
as the latter begins to intrude into conscious experience.

Kernberg describes the second layer as consisting of "a more primitive, pathological object relation centered around narcissistic rage and
envy, fear and guilt because of this rage, and yet a desperate longing for
a loving relationship that will not be destroyed by hatred." (Kernberg,
1975, p. 274)

386   What we find is a group of object relations centered around power-ful aggression, rage, and hatred on the one hand, and intense instinc-tual and animal-like devouring desire and wanting on the other. The student experiences herself as an instinctual animal organism, some-times as an intensely emotional infant, and sometimes as a more prim-itive structure like a powerful and primitive animal—a leopard or panther. She feels either rageful and hateful, wanting to destroy the selfobjects that failed her, or she experiences a deep, lustful, powerful, and devouring hunger and wanting. The selfobject she perceives is either a person, a group, or the whole world. The hateful-destructive object relation is usually reversed at the beginning; so she first projects her power and hatred onto the object, feeling that she is small, weak, helpless, generally good, but paranoid and terrified of the all-bad power-ful looming object.[10]

Transformation of this object relation through precise understand-ing of its meaning and etiology leads to the integration of the aspect of essential personal Power. One then experiences oneself imbued with natural power, an amazing fullness that feels both alive and forbid-ding. This is the power of the primal self of the oral stage, which was distorted by frustration of the attempt to gain the orally fulfilling nar-cissistic support and enhancement in early childhood.

The other major object relation involved in oral narcissism is that of a hungry, libidinal, and devouring self, that feels full of life and vigor, passion and desire, uncontrollably wanting an object that appears to it full, luscious, yummy, and totally desirable. The resistance against this early oral object relation is due to the fear of destroying the object by devouring it, and deeper still, the fear of frustration in the event the libidinal object is unattainable. This resistance frequently appears as a defense against dependency, which manifests as devaluation of the object, and not feeling one's neediness. Another form this resistance assumes is that of creating relationships in which the other experi-ences the narcissist as full and desirable but unavailable.

When the resistances dissolve and the object relation becomes con-scious, one's experience of oneself ranges from being a hungry and desirous infant to a sense of being a primitive, instinctual, devouring organism. There is passionate love suffused with devouring desire.

This is not an easy object relation to transform, and its significance   387
is not restricted to the question of narcissism. It underlies some of the
fundamental attitudes of the personality, and its transformation
requires the exploration and clarification of object relations in general. Fairbairn has conceptualized this object relation as the relation
between the libidinal ego—which is a split-off part of the self—and
the exciting and frustrating object. This libidinal ego is the underlying oral self that needs to be transformed in the resolution of oral
narcissism. It is not what Freud called the id; it is a primitive structure of the ego-self.

> The 'libidinal ego' also differs from the 'id' in that it is con-
> ceived, not as a mere reservoir of instinctive impulses, but as a
> dynamic structure comparable to the 'central ego', although
> differing from the latter in various respects, e.g., in its more
> infantile character, in a lesser degree of organization, in a smaller
> measure of adaptation to reality and in a greater devotion to
> internalized objects. (Fairbairn, 1984, p. 106)

The transformation of this libidinal object relation usually takes the
student into a deep experience of the self, in which he feels integrated
with his essential heart. He then feels full and fulfilled, juicy and sati-
ated, with the qualities of the heart aspects, those of Joy, Love,
Contentment, Value, Satisfaction, Nourishment, and so on. He feels
his heart full of wonderful tastes and textures.

The understanding, clarification, and transformation of this group
of object relations is a complex process, fraught with difficulties, terror, rage, pain, frustration, deprivation, and so on. The passionate-
devouring object relation is deeper and more basic than the
aggressive-destructive one; in fact, the latter may be understood as a
reaction to the frustration of the desire in the first. Kernberg believes
that the self at this level of object relation is the deepest self-structure
defended against, and he describes it as "a hungry, enraged, empty self,
full of impotent anger at being frustrated, and fearful of a world which
seems as hateful and revengeful as the patient himself." (Kernberg,
1975, p. 233) This is a combination of the two selves of the above two
object relations. But it can be seen more accurately as the self revealed

388   through the clarification of the object relations. It is the beginning of
seeing the narcissism underlying these object relations—the emptiness that underlies the devouring hunger—which is at the heart of
both the frustration and the rage.

The student understands at this point that this hungry, empty self
is the deepest psychodynamic source of his selfishness, self-centeredness, self-seeking, exploitativeness, cruelty, heartlessness, and compulsive need for narcissistic supplies. This self views these supplies—
the admiration, acknowledgment, recognition, support, love, success, acclaim, applause, and the rest—as a kind of food it needs to
assuage the gnawing hunger and to fill its painful emptiness.[11] At this
point, as the underlying emptiness of the self begins to manifest, the
student might experience the usual narcissistic meaninglessness and
emptiness of life and existence. He feels empty and meaningless, but
also experiences the whole world as empty, devoid of warmth and
nourishment. Persisting with exploring these manifestations, he discovers that for this self, meaning is food, or a full stomach. However,
this food has a narcissistic quality to it. Before he actually experiences the emptiness, he feels hungry, and observes that he tries to
assuage his hunger with narcissistic supplies. He tries to fill himself
with acclaim, applause, admiring mirroring, adoring support, and
idealizing love, with recognition, appreciation, and approval, but
goes about it with the uncontrollable hunger of a famished soul. He
can never get enough; his satiation is transitory and his fullness can
only be short-lived.[12]

This phenomenon clarifies in a very striking manner why narcissism is primarily a matter of connection to the self, and only secon-
darily a question of object relations. Why is it that when the self feels
hungry and empty, due to oral deprivation, it resorts to narcissistic
supplies to assuage this hunger? Why does the self try to fill its oral
emptiness with supplies that are intended to shore up and enhance
the sense of self? It would seem that if the emptiness is due to inadequacy of nourishment or love, it should seek these. But it does not;
instead, it seeks tirelessly for feedback that will help it to feel a stable
and cohesive sense of self, for interactions and situations that support
its feeling like a whole and integrated self. Clearly, the emptiness is not

the absence of nourishment, love or warmth, although the absence of these might be important in the genesis of this emptiness.

The obvious conclusion is that deprivation and conflictual object relations in the oral stage affected the child in such a way that he lost his inner core. Early experiences of frustration and abandonment, lack of attunement and adequate support, or intrusiveness and hostility, disrupt the integrity of the child's self in such a way that he loses his connection to his core. This loss of core is the specific narcissistic disruption. It is what accounts for the character of narcissistic strategies to regain connection to it.

We have arrived at this understanding of the emptiness within the hungry self through a sustained inquiry into the nature and origins of the above object relations and a host of others. This inquiry takes the student back to his earliest experiences, especially with his mother. He finds himself dealing with his early life experiences, with the question of maternal care, with his real hunger and its frustrations, with his oral need for love, warmth, holding, and safety. He confronts the effects of early deprivation, physical and emotional abandonment, inattunement to his needs, and intrusiveness into his field of experience. He experiences the wounding, the betrayal, the rage, the hunger, and finally, the emptiness. It is a specific narcissistic emptiness, a gnawing and dry emptiness. Sometimes the student feels that his mouth is dry, his stomach empty, and his body stiff and lifeless. When he perseveres with this condition, he will begin feeling the specific empty shell of oral narcissism. This empty shell does not reveal itself until he goes deeper into understanding the hungry and empty self. Then he will experience himself as an empty bag, a flaccid, empty stomach sack. This empty bag, which is the self devoid of its living core, becomes a hungry, angry, and empty self when he reacts to the emptiness with orally-determined feelings. The state of the empty stomach is most clearly revealed when he can accept the emptiness and learns not to react to it with anger, frustration or hunger.

The empty bag is a deeper structure than the hungry self; thus, we differ from Kernberg, who believes in the reverse. Kernberg approaches recognition of the oral empty shell when he points out a level of the oral self that he believes is less regressed than the hungry self. After discussing

390   the latter, he writes: "On an even less regressed level, the available remnants of such self images reveal a picture of a worthless, poverty-stricken,
empty person who feels always left 'outside,' devoured by envy of those
who have food, happiness, and fame." (Kernberg, 1975, p. 234)

It is possible that Kernberg believes this level of self is less regressed
than the hungry self because he views the object relation level of the
hungry self as primary; also, the hungry self engages in what seem to
be extremely primitive object relations. In any case, it is our observation that the worthless, poverty-stricken, and empty self is the deeper
of the two structures. It approaches the experience of being an empty
bag. This bag or shell has several characteristics that distinguish oral
narcissism from other forms. It includes the characteristics of the empty
shell of the three other forms of narcissism: It feels fake, empty of significance and authenticity, reflecting central narcissism; weak and incapable of functioning, reflecting individuation narcissism; and lifeless
and impoverished, reflecting oedipal narcissism. In oral narcissism,
the presence of all these elements does not indicate a telescoping of the
several levels of empty shell, for this earliest and most primitive narcissistic state cannot be reduced through analysis to the three types of
shells. Under investigation, this state reveals an important characteristic of the primal self, the self in the oral stage. A case vignette will
begin to illuminate this characteristic.

Jane has been dealing with a new level of emptiness and meaninglessness. She has already done a lot of work on central narcissism, and
some on oedipal and individuation narcissism, as part of her ongoing
process. Exploring the meaninglessness takes her to an object relation
of feeling small in relation to a big destructive force. This leads her to
experiencing herself as a kind of a devil-animal, which resolves to a
sense of power that makes it possible for her to be herself. It takes her
some time to begin to accept the instinctuality of her arising sense of
self. In a later session she works with feeling that she doesn't belong,
and with her experience of shame and embarrassment about this. She
then encounters some sadness and longing. She remembers parts of
her early life where she lived in a foster home, and felt lonely. Then
she starts feeling small and regressed, vulnerable and wounded. She
cries. She then feels a desire to be connected, but feels guilty about

wanting that. She feels she is not supposed to want me, nor her father or mother. She understands the conflictual early object relations that make her feel this way. This brings up a new resistance, which she feels as a kind of cocoon all around her, which makes her feel disconnected.

Jane arrives at the next session and reports that she has been feeling very hungry for some time. She has been experiencing intense wanting, with greed and aggression. She misses what she calls "co-creation," and wants it in a devouring way. When I inquire what this means, she starts feeling that she wants some kind of wholeness. She feels she wants a sense of totality and completeness. She feels hungry and empty, and when I inquire about what will satisfy her, she says feeling whole. This brings up her sense of body boundaries, and she feels the restriction of her self-entity structure. This leads to other experiences of presence and boundlessness.

We see here that after she felt the emptiness and meaninglessness Jane started experiencing the oral hunger for self. The self she felt she lacked was a sense of totality and wholeness. This brings us back to the question of the characteristics of the primal self.

In his description of primary narcissism, Freud noted that the original condition of the self is a sense of perfection and equilibrium. Hartmann pointed out that this condition lacks differentiation between the various elements of the self, describing what he called the "undifferentiated matrix," which refers to the experience of the neonate as a unified whole, without differentiation between body and psyche, ego and id, inside and outside, and so on.

Some self psychological researchers have understood that narcissistic disruptions in the oral stage lead primarily to the loss of wholeness of the self. The Jungian analyst, Schwartz-Salant, conceives of the situation as that of the child losing his Dionysian foundation for an object world that is ruled by an Apollonian I-Thou clarity.

> It is a stage in which there is a consolidation of opposites, but a loss of wholeness, the Dionysian wholeness of body and mind. . . . But it loses something in the process: it loses a part of its soul, and an experience of soma that it was born with. It becomes at least somewhat disembodied, schizoid. (Schwartz-Salant, 1982, p. 144)[13]

392   But what is this Dionysian wholeness? How is it experienced? Schwartz-Salant uses archetypal psychology, including Greek myths and mythological figures, to give some sense of it, but refers to it also as the union of the ego (normal self) and the divine child, characterized primarily by joy: "The two parts of the emerging Self, the part with an archetypal link and the older part, carrying all the residual elements of a process that has never successfully unfolded, unify in the analytical vessel through dealing with the erotic energies of the transference." (Schwartz-Salant, 1982, p. 165) We do observe this unification taking place as part of the recovered wholeness, but the wholeness implies a great deal more.

Wholeness

The self that emerges in the transformation of oral narcissism is a presence that feels whole and total. It feels like the presence of a total completeness of being ourselves. We feel a sense of purity, of clarity and lightness, that seems to exclude nothing. We feel as if all of what we are is present, but all comprising one indivisible whole. There are no parts; all of our feelings, thoughts, and movements appear as colorful manifestations within, and inseparable from, this pure and innocent presence. At the same time this presence has a deep sense of dynamism, as if it is in constant flow and transformation. This flow and transformation is the appearance of the changes in the manifestation of this presence.

The self realized through the transformation of oral narcissism is a dynamic wholeness. It is the integrity of oneself that includes all of one's qualities and dimensions of experience. The life of this presence is the flow of qualities of Essence, which emerge according to the demands of the situation, without being separate from the presence of wholeness.

The wholeness of the primordial self implicitly includes all aspects of Essence, present in an undifferentiated way. The aspects differentiate sometimes in response to situations, but even when an aspect is manifesting explicitly, we feel whole and complete.

The disruption of the self in the oral stage can best be described as the loss of wholeness. By losing contact with the primordial presence, the self loses the element responsible for a sense of wholeness. This loss

is like the loss of the glue that maintains the cohesiveness of the experi-   393
ence of the self. This cohesiveness is not that of an ego structure, but
of the primordial wholeness, where everything is an indivisible presence, that contains mind, but is not structured by it.

This is why, at this juncture of work on self-realization, students feel
the need for their wholeness to be seen. The narcissistic wound appears
whenever one is seen partially. In other words, if only some of one's
qualities and capacities are seen and mirrored, but not others, she will
tend to react narcissistically, with hurt and rage. In fact, the need for
this specific kind of mirroring is one of the most certain indications
that we are dealing with oral narcissism. It indicates the disconnection
from wholeness.

At this level of self-realization, the presence of the self is nondual,
and thus primordial, or prior to concepts. In the transformation of the
other forms of narcissism, the realized self is clearly separate and different from the normal sense of self. There is always a duality between
the familiar experience of the self and that of essential presence. We
are identified as the familiar self which can experience the essential
presence only in a dual way, as a subject experiencing an object. In the
realization of the Essential Identity, the situation is reversed; it is true
that then we experience this presence in a nondual manner, in other
words, we are the essential presence, but we perceive the familiar self
in the third person. Duality persists, as we are aware of the distinction
between the normal manifestation of the self and the essential presence. We are the essential presence, but feel separate from the other
manifestations of the self—separate from thoughts, feelings, activities, and the body. We still experience all of these, and actually experience them with a much greater aliveness and vividness, but they remain
separate from our sense of identity.

The primordial presence, on the other hand, is nondual in all
respects. The sense of wholeness means all dimensions of the self—
the conventional and the essential—constitute one indivisible whole.
We experience everything as presence, including thoughts and feelings. We are a presence coemergent with the body; the body feels like
a part of this presence. This is also true of images, feelings, and activities. At this level even the ego structures, with their images and object

394   relations, are seen to be part of this presence. We are aware of these
structures of internalized images, but they appear as less luminous
patterns within the overall presence. There is one presence, whole,
continuous and homogeneous, clear and transparent. Within this pure
presence appear many colorful and exquisite forms, but they are manifestations of and within the same presence. These forms are the various essential aspects, the natural manifestations of the flow of Being.
But there also appear a different kind of forms, patterns of light, texture, and color. These forms have various degrees of vividness and
luminosity, some transparent and vivid, some dull and thick. These
are the thoughts and feelings, and also the body and its sensations.
Generally speaking, continuing to be present in this condition tends
to clarify and purify the areas of dullness and thickness. The process
of clarification occurs naturally and spontaneously, but is aided greatly
by inquiry and understanding, because there are always areas of the
self that remain obscure and unconscious.

So the fundamental ground is the pure presence, and it is this which
we experience as our true identity. This development is the pure experience of the soul in complete identity with its true nature. The self
becomes the open, flowing experience of soul, aware of its true nature
by simply being it. The soul knows itself as primordial presence. This
presence is the very substance and existence of all the forms appearing within it; hence, we experience all the forms, all dimensions of
experience, as part of our sense of self, without separateness. This is
not a matter of a lack of differentiation, since one can discriminate
forms within this changing presence. It is rather the absence of separateness and duality. This is the wholeness of primordial presence,
where the purity of Being is the fundamental fabric, and all other
dimensions and elements are the patterns in this fabric.

Persisting in this condition of primordial self-realization, we realize
that even the concept of self begins to lose its meaning and significance.
The ordinary sense of self, familiar for many years, falls away slowly, to
be replaced by a sense of freshness and nowness of experience, as ever-
new forms and modes of experience appear and disappear. There is no
more need to recognize ourselves through an old, familiar sense of self,
for self-recognition is spontaneous and inherent in the primordial

presence, as its own mirror-like awareness. It is a minute-to-minute   395
recognition of ourselves as the ongoing mirror-like awareness of the
unfoldment of presence, inseparable from its beingness. Self can only
be the nondual presence that continues unfolding as an expression of
its own dynamism. But then this is inseparable from, and nondual with,
the totality of all presence, which is all of appearance.

Contrast this transformation with Kernberg's formulation of successful therapy: "If they are treated successfully, they come to realize
a deeper and more meaningful life, and begin to draw from sources of
strength and creativity in their newly developing world of internalized
object relationships." (Kernberg, in Morrison, 1986, p. 241) Kernberg
understands the meaninglessness experienced in oral narcissism in
terms of object relations: "The loss of the world of loving and loved
internal objects brings about the loss of meaning of the self and of the
world." (Morrison, 1986, p. 290) Our view is that the narcissistic meaninglessness is a reflection of the loss of what gives the self meaning, the
presence of the fundamental truth of the self and the world, which
returns us to an awareness of our wholeness when we experience the
presence completely and fully.

The loss of this wholeness is equivalent to the loss of contact with
all the aspects of Essence. This explains why the empty shell that is due
to the loss of the primal self feels like the shells of all of the other forms
of narcissism combined. The primal self is the wholeness that implicitly includes the qualities of the true self of all later stages, in an undifferentiated way.

From this perspective, we can understand the manifestations of oral
narcissism as the expression of the self identifying itself with the oral,
deficient, and empty self, the self that feels itself as an empty, impoverished bag, because of the loss of its core, its inherent essential richness. The empty, hungry self is the experience of the self patterned by
the structure that develops as a reaction to the disturbances of the primal self. This empty self then relates to the world in an oral way, trying to regain its earlier perfection and wholeness by devouring and
possessing the exciting objects that it believes are the sources of acclaim,
admiration, and idealization. The underlying image of this exciting
and desirable object is the full and luscious breast of the all-good

396   mother. And we agree with Kernberg that the "lack of an integrated self is also characterized by chronic feelings of unreality, puzzlement, emptiness, or general disturbances in the 'self feeling' . . . as well as in a marked incapacity to perceive oneself realistically as a total human being." (Kernberg, 1975, p. 316) We would only substitute "wholeness" for "integrated self" and understand the "total human being" to mean the "total completeness of human Being."

Our account of oral narcissism and the process of its transformation is by necessity very brief; we have left out many important details. One such detail is the transformation of the deficient narcissistic emptiness of this form of narcissism to its corresponding inner spaciousness. This is a significant process that clarifies the most subtle aspects of narcissism, and also illuminates the functioning of the normal self. We will discuss this process in the next few chapters, utilizing for this exploration the understanding of certain transcendent dimensions of Being.

DIMENSIONS
OF
SELF-REALIZATION

We have investigated the development of fundamental narcissism throughout the various stages of the development of the self. And since fundamental narcissism is the direct expression of the alienation from the fundamental truth of the self, its true nature and core, its transformation results in the self-realization of various manifestations of this essential core. More succinctly, the resolution of fundamental narcissism is equivalent to the self-realization of Being.

Full self-realization means the complete realization of the fullness of Being. By fullness of Being, we mean Being in its totality and completeness, including all of its dimensions and aspects. This is finally realized in the resolution of oral narcissism as the self-realization of nondual presence. This attainment is so profound and radical that no book can do it justice. Our discussion of oral narcissism only alludes to what is involved in this realization. To truly appreciate the scope of this attainment, we need to have—among other things—a more

398   thorough grasp of the phenomenology of Being, of its richness and subtlety, and of the profound implications of understanding these.

In other words, the experience of nondual presence includes subtleties and nuances we have not yet attempted to elucidate. In fact, these added dimensions, apparent in full self-realization, can be seen to be related to some specific transformations of fundamental narcissism. More accurately, the full self-realization can be understood as the deepening of the transformation of central narcissism, until it merges with the transformation of oral narcissism.

We are referring to the fact that the realization of the Essential Identity makes up only the first step in the resolution of central narcissism, and that central narcissism emerges again at deeper levels of experience. Its resolution at these levels leads to the self-realization of deeper dimensions of Being. The progressive self-realization of deeper and deeper dimensions of Being, indicating the increasing subtlety in its appreciation, finally culminates in the realization of nondual presence, which is the wholeness of the self, experienced in its primordial original condition.

This allows us to envision central narcissism as possessing several levels, each associated with the alienation from a certain level of essential identity. We believe these levels of central narcissism are best conceived of as related to stages of development extending from the beginning of life to about sixteen months of age. In this way, we begin with oral narcissism and end with the central narcissism associated with the Essential Identity. We suggest this only as a helpful framework that has emerged from our investigations, but we do not know with certainty whether these levels of central narcissism originate each in a specific and different developmental stage, or are all expressions of one stage. We do observe, however, in the work of self-realization, that these levels emerge in a certain progressive order, and that this progression coincides with increasing manifestations of oral characteristics in the arising associated structures of the self. We also observe that the levels of Being that emerge are inclined towards a deeper and more complete nonduality of experience.

Conceptualizing levels and dimensions of Being is inherently problematic, and there is a great deal of disagreement and debate between the various spiritual traditions regarding it. Some traditions, like that of Buddhism, deny the existence of such levels, conceptualizing the view that we are either aware of the true (Buddha) nature or not, and that levels can only be in the fullness, or limitation, of our experience of this true nature.[14] Other traditional teachings, like those of the Kabala, or Sufism, conceptualize the view that Being manifests in various and delineated levels—reminiscent of the dimensions of Being in neoplatonic philosophy—each real and objective on its own level.

Our view, which reflects our experience, is that Being is inherently a unity, a nondual presence that contains no levels, but that it can manifest itself in levels and dimensions experienced as true and objective in their own sphere of experience. In other words, experience indicates that Being manifests itself in various degrees of subtlety and completeness, and these manifestations appear as levels and dimensions of Being, objective and valid on their own levels. More accurately, experience indicates that Being can and does manifest in different levels and dimensions, but that upon analysis of these experiences, we can see they are merely different degrees of subtlety of the experience of the same nature. We do not take the position of accepting either experience or analysis as the final arbiter of ultimate truth, and hence, find no incentive to engage in this ancient debate. We find that each view has its own merits in terms of the work of self-realization, and thus we use them appropriately depending on the degree of maturity of the student.[15] More specifically, we find in our work with students that the perspective of levels and dimensions is helpful most of the time, but that the perspective of a true nature transcending all experience of levels becomes most helpful at the deepest stages of work.

For the purposes of our present study, we will take the view that the Essential Identity actuates the shift of identity from the conventional dimension of experience to that of Being, but that Being is realized in stages that reflect increasing subtlety of its phenomenological properties. These stages appear, then, in actual experience, as the realization of different dimensions of Being. In other words, what the student learns about the nature of Being as he progresses through these stages, is increasingly more accurate, although he experiences himself realizing distinct dimensions of Being.[16] More precisely, Being reveals its subtleties of

400   experience in a discontinuous manner that makes it readily possible to view this experience as of delineated and distinct dimensions.

The pattern of experience in the realization of each of these dimensions follows the one we have discussed for the Essential Identity. The student deals with the idealizing and mirror transferences, now on a more primitive level of experience, which exposes an empty shell. Investigation of this newly arising empty shell, which reflects a deeper strata of the self-identity structure, leads to the experience of a deeper narcissistic wound, with its associated rage, betrayal, and so on. This then activates earlier object relations and leads to the narcissistic emptiness associated with the alienation from this dimension of Being. This culminates in the arising of this dimension and its self-realization. We experience our identity now as this manifestation of Being or as Being with new phenomenological properties. So we see that the process is a recurrence of the same process as that involved in realizing the Essential Identity with some differences that reflect the new properties of Being. Therefore, we will discuss these processes only to highlight the differences, which can be seen as further transformation and resolution of central narcissism. We will also confine our discussion to only a few of the dimensions of Being, the most significant in understanding the overall process of resolution of narcissism and the realization of Being.

chapter 39

Pure Being

---•

I n the realization of the Essential Identity, it is useful to discriminate the self-identity from the self-entity; it is specifically the
former that replaces the Essential Identity as the sense of self-
recognition. However, Being will challenge all structures of the ego-
self, and self-realization will challenge not only the self-identity
structure, but all structures that support it or are related to it. The
most significant of these is the self-entity structure. This structure supports the identity in many ways. It becomes increasingly challenged as
Being reveals its more profound dimensions.

This aspect of the process manifests initially as the arising need
for more primitive forms of idealized and mirroring selfobjects. Specifically, the student recognizes his need for a merged relationship that
provides support and mirroring. He begins realizing his need to depend
on the selfobject, to know his experience of himself, and to value it.
So he expects the teacher, or significant others in his life, to know how
he feels and to satisfy his needs, without him having to communicate them himself. This exposes the need for the merged mirroring
selfobject, which may also manifest as seeing the selfobject as an
extension of himself, which has no value or existence independent

402   from him. He becomes hurt and enraged if the selfobject does not act
        solely to please and serve him, if she acts in an independent way that
        neglects his needs or does not make them her only concern. The
        absence or loss of this merged selfobject allows him to feel an empti-
        ness characterized by the lack of a sense of identity and by loneliness.
        In this state, he feels the loss of both himself and the other; he is lost
        and also lonely, indicating the loss of both mirroring and the merged
        connection.

        The need for idealization manifests as the need for a dual unity in
        which both individuals are positive objects; it is also important that they
        share the same qualities and interests. The student idealizes both the
        selfobject and the connection with her. It is important that they agree
        on everything, so he tends to disregard disagreements and differences
        to avoid experiencing a severe disruption in his relation to her and a loss
        of self and support. Disagreement by the selfobject, her expression of a
        difference—or his observation of it—will make him feel betrayed and
        disappointed. He feels abandoned when he perceives that the selfobject
        is different from him or not an extension of him. Understanding this
        transference manifestation leads to the realization of the Diamond Will
        on the merged dimension, in other words, the presence of essential sup-
        port in the absence of a differentiated self. The differentiation between
        the mirroring and idealized selfobjects becomes difficult at this point
        because the self in the merger transference is an undifferentiated self
        where the self and the object are not clearly differentiated.

        A certain shell arises at this level of the process; it is reminiscent of
        the fakeness and emptiness experienced in dealing with the Essential
        Identity, but there are significant differences. We experience the fake-
        ness not only in ourselves, but everywhere. We feel fake and empty,
        empty of anything real and significant, and we also feel that every-
        thing around us is empty and lacks fullness. We first feel the empty shell
        as a contraction around the body, as a membrane that separates us
        from the rest of the world, reflecting the structure of self-entity. Further
        investigation reveals that the shell is not really separate from others—
        it is an extension of a larger and universal shell that includes everyone.
        When we finally experience the shell completely, we feel like part of a
        universal shell that includes the whole universe. In other words, we see

that what we have been seeing as the world—both animate and inanimate—is actually empty and devoid of fullness, nourishment, or significance. This reflects the loss of the nondifferentiated self, the state of the soul in which the self and the object world are not yet differentiated in experience.

This shell is not only our personal empty self, but the perception of everything as empty and devoid of substance. We perceive that the whole world is only an appearance; everything is only a shell that has no inner truth or reality. Our empty shell is part of a larger shell that includes everything. There is nowhere to go; a painful and deficient emptiness is everywhere. This stage is difficult to go through, especially when there is no experienced guide who can hold the experience as a legitimate part of the process of self-realization.[17]

The student alternates between experiencing herself as an empty shell and feeling the whole of the universe as empty of truth and fullness. She is now most vulnerable to disruption of mirroring. Understanding the mirroring she needs at this point sheds light on the self that needs to be mirrored, as we see in the case of Anna, who has been dealing with the issues of this level of central narcissism. She comes to a session feeling enraged at her friends and colleagues. Upon investigation, we find out she is angry because they do not see her as the most special of all. She realizes that what she expects is unrealistic, but she can't help feeling she is the most special person around, and feels a deep hurt and tremendous rage when anyone behaves in a way that does not reflect that. Anything that challenges this conviction deeply insults and angers her. She realizes that although she does not usually feel this way, she can see now that this has been an underlying conviction that has been unconscious, but which influenced how she felt in relation to others. In other words, although she usually does not feel she is the best and most special, she understands now that it does explain many of her feelings, attitudes, and actions.

She recognizes and understands the narcissistic qualities of her rage, and how the rage is partly an attempt to defend and protect a certain preciousness that she is aware of in herself. Before we continue with our discussion of Anna's experience, we need to reflect first on some of the points her experience raises.

The first is related to the sense of specialness, which we have seen to be connected to central narcissism. As the Essential Identity, we feel ourselves as precious, unique, and special. There is no need to be the most special, for we are unique in our specialness. But the need for specialness changes as we go deeper into the investigation of central narcissism. When we deal with the universal shell, the specialness one seeks involves being not only unique, but also being the best. We need to be the most special, more special than anybody else. So whenever one is not treated as the most special, a narcissistic wound manifests. More precisely, when we do not feel special, a certain narcissistic wound arises, but when we do not feel we are the *most* special, another, deeper, narcissistic wound appears. The first reflects the alienation from the Essential Identity, and the second, the alienation from a deeper true self, which we will discuss shortly.

The narcissistic wound that arises has all the characteristics of the wound of alienation from the Essential Identity, but feels more profound and has other differentiating characteristics. The wound feels like a deep hurt, a very teary sadness, but we do not generally experience this sadness and hurt as differentiated from the deficient emptiness. We feel an emptiness permeated with sadness, a vast nothingness that pervades the whole world. This nothingness is pregnant with hurt. There is hurt, a sense of wounding, a sadness, but also a compassionate warmth that pervades the emptiness. Thus, when we experience the narcissistic wound at this level of narcissism, it is indistinguishable from narcissistic emptiness. It is as if the wound opens up and pervades the emptiness, inviting the quality of loving kindness, which we experience now as boundless and infinite. This allows the sadness to become deep and profound, as if the wound goes through the depth of the universe. We feel as if tears drown all of reality. The wound feels like a very deep and boundless emptiness, filled with tears and pervaded by compassion. These phenomena hint at the specific properties of the true self which is about to manifest, but also show that the narcissistic wound at this level is the same as the chasm that separates the self from this dimension of Being.

Remaining in this emptiness, and not resisting or reacting to it, clarifies the nature of the sadness and loss. Sometimes the sadness becomes

a deep longing for the dissolution of our separateness from everything.   405
We feel what seems to be the deepest and most expanded longing, from
the depths of the universe, a longing to lose our personal boundaries
and to be part of the whole. Thus, this longing is for the dissolution of
the self-entity structure, which is the barrier to the currently arising
dimension of Being. At this point in our process we are identified with
Being, but the boundaries of the self-entity structure seem to limit us
from experiencing our Being in a more profound and expanded way.

We return to Anna, and follow the unfoldment of her experience in
that particular session, where she understood this level of her central
narcissism. She now experiences the deep wound with its profound
emptiness. She realizes that she never expected this experience to be
held by anybody. This insight leads to the feelings of lack of holding
and support. She feels hopeless and empty. However, remaining with
the wound and emptiness, she starts to experience a new sense of presence, a sense of purity of Being, that she recognizes to be who and
what she is. When I inquire into the specific details of her experience
of presence, she says that she feels that she does not end at the boundaries of her body, that she extends indefinitely. She experiences a pure
presence, boundless and infinite, and containing everything. She
expresses this experience by saying: "Everything is mine. I am the center
of the universe. Everything is in me."

She recognizes now that what hurt her before was people not seeing
and recognizing the truth of the boundlessness of Being. In other words,
not seeing the boundlessness of Being means not seeing her, because it
is her very identity. This also explains why she wanted to be the most
special. Recognizing that Being is actually infinite and not bounded by
any partitions has profound implications. One important one is that
Being is the ground of everything and everyone. In other words, there is
only one indivisible Being which is the nature and Essence of everything.

Here, we know ourselves as a presence totally pure and completely
real. It is so pure it has no qualities; it is just the fact of beingness experienced as an ontological presence. This presence is clarity, lightness,
transparency, all ineffable and precious in an undefinable way. It is so
ineffable that it feels both empty and full simultaneously. There is the
sense of being wide awake, with fresh awareness and lucid perception.

406   In this manifestation of Being, we know Being in its purity, before differentiation and discrimination, before labeling and reaction. There are no differentiated qualities, but nothing is missing. We experience a completeness. It is as if all the qualities are present before differentiation. This is one of the first things we discover as we go through this level of narcissism. Before this discovery, our experience of Being takes the form of one of its differentiated manifestations—like love, intelligence, or even identity—but now we know ourselves purely, before recognizable and conceptualizable qualities.

The other important discovery we make at this point is the one that Anna had, which is that Being is inherently boundless. We experience this purity of presence as pervasive and infinite, and see, also, that it underlies everything. We come to see that pure Being is the essence and true nature of all manifestation, not only of the self. Further, we experience Being not only as the essence of everything, but *as* everything. It constitutes not only the core of everything, but the very substance and fabric of everything. It is a medium inside every object, outside it, and in between the outside and inside. It makes up the very substance of the form, not only what fills it. It is both the essence and the boundaries of all forms. So Being is the nature, essence, and substance of all physical objects, all mental objects, and all experienceable manifestations. It is the body, the feelings, the thoughts, the actions, the sounds, the sights, and the meanings. Being is everything.

At this level of realization, we come also to perceive the unity of all manifestation. Since Being is an indivisible medium (not composed of parts), it follows that everything makes up a unity, a oneness. There is one existence, as opposed to two, or many. It is merely an infinite presence that possesses a pattern. This pattern is everything we perceive, including all persons and objects. So everything is connected to everything; there exist no separate and autonomous objects or persons.

Another discovery is that we see this unity and oneness as our very self and identity. We experience: "I am everything. I am everyone, the bodies, thoughts and feelings of everybody, inseparable from all objects. I am the ground, essence, and source of everything."

No wonder we have been longing for the dissolution of the separating boundaries; the self intuited that the arising manifestation of

Being is boundless and infinite. And no wonder we need to be seen   407
as the most special. Pure Being is the most precious thing in reality
because it is the preciousness of everything in reality. It is most special because it is the precious ground of everything that is special. In
fact, it is what ascribes specialness to anything. This is the reason some
students experience the narcissistic need as to be seen as the most
special person.

The self knows unconsciously, or we could say intuitively, that its
identity is the boundless pure Being, but it is still consciously identified with being a separate entity. So even at this level of work, there are
often big issues. For example, when this manifestation is arising, and
the student is feeling that she is the "most special" or the "only special"
one, when anyone else is treated in a special way, she feels hurt and
wounded. So she knows she is the most special because she is the purity
of Being, but becomes grandiose when she attributes this specialness
to her conscious identification of herself as a separate individual. Clearly,
the way to work with the situation effectively is not to judge her narcissistic need as grandiose and unrealistic, but to discover in that need
information about the true self from which she feels alienated.

The narcissistic wound that arises here is for not being seen as the
source of everything, of all knowledge, understanding, love, value, preciousness, meaning, and existence. We are hurt about not being recognized as this supreme manifestation of Being, the one most worthy
of love and admiration. It also reflects our own incapacity to see our
true pure nature, as we are not yet realized at this level.

At this juncture, we understand that believing that we are separate
individuals, or autonomous entities, rather than recognizing ourselves
as the oneness of all existence, creates alienation from pure Being. To
take oneself as ultimately a separate and autonomous person creates
the supreme wound, which appears as an abyss, an abysmal chasm, that
alienates us not only from our true nature, but also from everybody
and everything. This is the supreme betrayal, and the beginning of
endless suffering.[18]

We also understand, here, the cosmic shell as the experience of the
world devoid of its true nature, the infinite pure Being. Looking through
the representational world, we see only a world devoid of Being.

The quality of infinity and omnipresence of the identity at this level of experience eliminates duality. We experience Being not only as our true nature, but as the nature of everything. This means it is also the true nature of the ego-self. The pure presence of Being is the underlying ground both for aspects of Essence, and for structures of the ego-self. Both become seen as particular formations within the presence of pure Being.

At this level, the movement from the duality between Essence and personality is different from that involved in realizing the Essential Identity. In the realization of the Essential Identity, the student experiences the personality in the third person, as if from the outside, as the totality of the suffering individual. She experiences herself as a center of awareness and presence separate from the individual person, relating to that person with compassion, love, and understanding. Or she experiences herself as a personality aware of the Essential Identity as an essential presence, characterized by the feeling of identity. There is duality in this experience.

In the process of realization of pure Being, the alternation is not between the personality and presence, but rather, between duality and unity. In duality, the student experiences herself as the totality of the ego-self, the personality, separate from the presence and resistant to it. She also experiences and understands it by being it. She experiences the movement of her ego-self directly, in all its details. She experiences it from within, in its totality, with a specific understanding of the nature of its functioning. This is in contrast to the experience of the personality in the dimension of the Essential Identity, where she experiences it from the outside, as the other who is struggling and suffering. In the dimension of pure Being, her understanding of the nature of suffering becomes more specific and complete.

The result is that the personality is not necessarily transformed in the self-realization of the Essential Identity; there is only the shift of its identity. The complete realization of pure Being involves a process of purification and clarification of the personality, until there is no difference between it and the purity of Being. The final outcome is the condition of unity in which we experience the personality (the ego-self) as an inseparable manifestation of pure Being.[19]

chapter 40

Nonconceptual Reality

R ealizing the omnipresence of Being allows the experiences of unity and oneness of existence. As we stay with this process, however, we continue to realize ever more profound implications of the truth of our identity with pure Being. The next steps in the relentless evolution towards complete clarity and precision continue to expose deeper and subtler dimensions in the experience of the ego-self. Being continues to reveal its reality more forcefully, and this brings back the ego-self; the latter can still restructure itself because of the lack of understanding of some of its subtler underpinnings. The self-identity structure reappears at this point as yet another empty shell, with even deeper elements illuminated.

The empty shell appears at this time, as specific tensions around the head, indicating the concentration of the structure of the shell at the head. The student feels he is an empty shell, and his head is the thickest layer of the shell. Thinking becomes obsessive and speedy, and the empty shell feels more and more dry and abstract. Slowly, with patient inquiry into this manifestation, the student begins to realize the mental nature of the empty shell. He begins to see quite directly, and in lived experience, how his sense of self originates in his mind, how his familiar

410   identity is a product of a mental network that is perpetuated by a mental process. He can see sometimes how mental his experience of himself and the world has been, even when he is quite emotional or physical. The more he understands the mental quality of his life and world, the more he begins to feel empty, meaningless, superficial, and dry. The mental shell becomes emptier and flimsier when he begins to see how he used ideas, mental postures, and concepts to define himself.

This insight reveals that the identity of the ego-self has not only developed through the integration of early object relations, but that this process of internalization and integration has depended on the conceptualization of the elements of experience. Patterning of the ego-self depends on concepts that form the ideas and images which compose the self-representation. Thus, the familiar sense of identity is totally dependent on concepts. This understanding exposes how the student has been using her mind, in the form of concepts, to support her sense of self. Seeing this undermines a very deep and basic support for the structure of self-identity, and she begins to feel the absence of grounding and the sense of emptiness, that signify the absence of support. When investigated fully, this new level of emptiness leads to the realization of the Diamond Will on a new level, a nonconceptual level of experience.

This development thins away the mental shell and further exposes its dry emptiness. As we have seen, the narcissistic wound will arise whenever there is a lapse of mirroring. At this stage, the student experiences this lapse whenever she feels the pressure to conceptualize her experience of herself so that she can be seen and recognized. When anyone defines her with words or concepts, or expects her to manifest herself with words and concepts, she experiences the loss of the mirroring self-object.[20] This activates the narcissistic wound, the hurt and sadness of her alienation from her Being. At this level, the hurt is activated by any identification with a mental structure, sometimes by any conceptualization of her experience of herself. This is a deep and fundamental hurt that underlies all experiences of the ego-self, any experience of self in the conventional dimension of experience. It is very subtle and cannot be contacted without the capacity to experience the warmth of compassion on a very deep level, beyond thought or concept.[21]

At this point in the student's process, the narcissistic constellation   411
alternates with the experience of herself as the unity of pure Being.
The newly challenged dimensions of the empty shell tend to disconnect her from identity with presence, which is now the purity of Being.
However, the manifestation of Being that is pushing towards conscious
experience is deeper, or subtler, than that of pure Being. This leads to
the experience of the oneness of Being as part of the mental shell, a
surprise to the student who has settled on this dimension of Being as
the ultimate experience. This is a very significant insight that sheds
more light on the nature of Being.

The student may experience the shell at this point as the oneness of
everything. More accurately, as the shell, he experiences himself inseparable from the oneness of everything. The nature of the shell is clear
presence, and it contains all phenomena. But he begins to experience
the totality of the world—which forms a oneness—as external to himself, as if his identity now is deeper than this unity of existence. He
finds that the experience of oneness is still conceptual, or more accurately, there still remain subtle concepts in his experience of Being,
which now make him include it as part of his mental shell. He realizes
that he still adheres to the concepts of world, oneness, existence, and
so on, or more precisely, that these things are actually concepts. He
penetrates his reification of Being, unity, and oneness.

This precipitates the movement of the student's identity into a subtler manifestation of Being, a totally nonconceptual realization of true
nature. He experiences himself now as nonconceptual reality, beyond
all mind and concepts, beyond all specifications and recognitions. He
cannot even say whether he is being or nonbeing, absence or presence.
Existence is negated, and this negation in turn is negated. His recognition of himself negates both negation and affirmation of any attributes,
which is a much more profound experience of Being than that of pure
Being. There is now no definite sense of any concept, reality, thing, or
manifestation. He is both existence and nonexistence, not existence and
not nonexistence. He is both self and not self. This is a very paradoxical manifestation of Being, beyond any conceptualization.[22]

This experience is boundless, but it does not feel as clear as presence or fullness. It is like experiencing the inside of all of the universe

412   as a totally clear and completely transparent, crystalline medium. There is no iota of obscuration or impediment, just an infinity of transparent clarity. There is a stunning sense of awakeness, intensely fresh and new. When there are no concepts in our recognition of ourselves, nothing is old; everything is the pure freshness of suchness, the intensity of eternity that has no concept of time.

The recognition of ourselves has no mental elaboration; it is the totally pure being of transparent crystalline clarity. There is a solidity of presence, an infinite immensity that feels at the same time absolutely empty and nonexistent. We know our nature as the most solid and fundamental ground of all appearance, without this nature taking on any sense of fullness or substance. It is a totally solid, complete absence, which shatters the mind with its cool transparency.

In this manifestation there is no sense of individual or self, but no sense of their absence, for either would be a concept. Everything seems to be part of this immense clarity, which is totally itself, without it needing to be conceptualized. All objects and persons appear as part of this transparent clarity, pervaded with it, constituted of it, but only as transparent patterns in this nameless reality. Thus, duality is transcended before it is even conceptualized.

It is suchness, pure suchness. We cannot say anything about it. We cannot say it is self, we cannot say it is not self, we cannot say it is God, we cannot say it is the universe, we cannot say it is a person, we cannot say it is not a person; the moment we say anything, we are within mind. If we use any concept here, even the concept of purity, simplicity, or whatever, we are within the mind, and we are blocking that which cannot be named.

The only thing that is there is consciousness. But consciousness here is not exactly a concept; it is just the fact of consciousness. We are not unconscious, that's all. There is consciousness, but there is no one who is conscious. Here, we are going into the true nature of Being, the true nature of God, or the true nature of the universe, before any mind, before any conceptualization, before any specification, before any differentiation, before we can experience or say anything; so this pure consciousness is beyond experience, beyond mind, beyond concept, beyond all these things.

We realize that we are the suchness, but we don't feel that, "I am the 413 suchness"; there is just suchness, and we don't even say there is suchness.

This nonconceptual awareness is truly radical. While it does not affirm any concept, neither does it negate or deny any concept. To negate is to affirm and to affirm is to negate, for in both cases a concept is present. This reality is prior to any concept, and hence, possesses no presupposition whatsoever. Purity of Being is now nonconceptual, so it is complete, and recognized as the fundamental reality of all experience.

Many lucid insights appear. The reality of the self is beyond concepts, so thinking about it, conceptualizing around it, or remembering it, is bound to make it into an object. Conceptualizing automatically creates a shell, a mental representation. The mind tends to remember experience, to think and talk about it. This can become an attempt to hold on to the experience for the purpose of self-recognition, for identity. There is also the concern that if we do not remember and think about any experience of self—including that of presence—we will lose connection to it, not realizing that presence of Being is fundamental and is independent of memory and mind. We don't realize that it isn't going to go away if we don't strive to remember it.

Unless there is complete spontaneity, we create a shell, so on this level of realization, communication and functioning, including thinking, need to be totally spontaneous. Otherwise, functioning relies on ego activity which depends on conceptualizing the self. In this dimension, we learn that our realization must be totally independent of conceptualization, that our experience and life proceed apart from what we think. We also learn the danger of adhering to any view or conceptualization about the nature of reality and self-realization. We learn to be masters of concepts: Since we recognize our beingness beyond any concept, we are free to create any concept to communicate.

In this dimension of Being, much learning and experience are possible, but we are discussing only the bare minimum necessary to understand how self-realization resolves narcissism at this fundamental level. We will mention one more important feature of this dimension of experience: The clarity and transparency of this manifestation challenges the very deep obscurations inherent in the structures of the ego-self. It exposes some of our most basic, cherished attachments about

414   life and world. These attachments are difficult to transform, since they have deep, entrenched roots. Their transformation confronts us with our primitive oral deprivations, needs, and impulses, and therefore with the issues of oral narcissism, specifically with the libidinal ego. We perceive that the attachments originate from this primitive structure of the ego-self.

The nonconceptual nature of the arising presence, which is appropriate for understanding these preverbal issues, teaches us about nonattachment, and clarifies that attachment cannot be completely dissolved unless we realize the nonconceptuality of all of existence. We learn that those things we are attached to are ultimately nothing but concepts, and that what is fundamentally precious is beyond all such concepts. It is the suchness of our very beingness.

chapter 41

Absolute Truth

---•

U nderstanding our attachments and realizing the nonconceptual reality of true nature does not resolve our narcissism
completely. The empty shell returns, revealing even more
primitive levels of its structure, which alienates us again from identity
with Being.[23] The object relations that manifest at this juncture are
mostly the oral type, and the ego-self is the oral libidinal self that
becomes aggressive when it is frustrated. There are different levels of
this primitive structure, as we saw in our discussion of oral narcissism.
The self at this point manifests as more dynamic and alive than usual,
full of impulses, desires, and passions. There is a distinct animal instinctuality to its experience, and a very robust and vigorous emotionality.
In some sense, this is the first time that the student experiences herself in a fully emotional and physical way and recognizes a self that is
the ground and source of all of her emotions and impulses.

The normal experience of the ego-self is much more mental than
we realize, in the sense that we may experience emotions and impulses
but feel them to be vaguely related to a sense of self. Now, however,
there is no vague sense of self or identity; we know ourselves intimately
as a living, vital, animal organism, imbued with clearly instinctual,

416   primitive, and powerful drives and impulses. The primitiveness of the structure means there is very little representation left in the self, mostly a sense of entitihood with very early and simple object relations. So there is a more direct experience of the quality of presence imbued with animal and primitive energies and drives.

At this point the shell does not always feel like a rigid boundary, but is teeming with aliveness and pulsing with desires. There is a distinct dynamism to the experience of the self, but as an instinctual and primitive force, it is loosely structured and poorly channeled. The impulsiveness and uncontrollability of the libidinal ego and its passionately overwhelming nature can dominate the student's experience here.

The student generally finds this transformation exciting and promising, especially if she has had mostly a schizoid kind of personality. Hence, it might take a lot of experience, sincerity, and discrimination for her to begin to feel this sense of self as dystonic to her well-being and to see that it alienates her from her essential nature. If she remains sincerely dedicated to her inquiry, she finds that the instinctual drivenness characteristic of her libidinal ego makes her less transparent to the purity and subtlety of essential nature. She sees now that these instinctual drives tend to fixate her consciousness and direct it in a certain prejudiced direction, which clouds her clarity. These drives confuse truth with falsehood and disorient her in her quest for self-realization. The drives, especially the primitive oral ones, tend to orient the self outward, towards promising objects, and away from itself and its beingness. This outward orientation is one of the most basic and stubborn characteristics of the libidinal ego and becomes one of the main barriers to self-realization. Self-realization involves emotional and spiritual self-sufficiency, while the libidinal ego is totally governed by the attitude that all goodness and nourishment come from outside, as if one were an empty stomach.[24] This outward orientation, coupled with insatiable hunger, automatically disconnects the self from the stillness of its beingness, leading to narcissistic alienation.

This situation necessitates working through the oral object relations discussed in Chapter 38. Confronting the various narcissistic hurts and reactions, and then learning not to identify with the drives, finally reveals the inner truth of the libidinal self as an empty bag: a thin, weak, soft,

vulnerable container that is hungry and deprived. Both the inside and   417
outside feel empty. The student experiences here the mere entitihood
of the ego-self, the bare bones of the structure of self-entity, which at
this point is all that is left for the self to use for identity.[25] She may also
recognize that this bare minimum of structure is the center and source
of all attachments, emotional reactions, and instinctual impulses.

The features of this denuded ego-self that remain are negations, or
deficiencies. The student feels withdrawn, weak and inadequate, empty
and impoverished.[26] She feels vulnerable, lacking any strength or positive qualities. Frequently, she will feel this structure as a sac around
her physical heart, and feel the heart empty and lacking. She begins to
feel not only that she is insignificant, but that she is nothing and has
nothing. She feels that she, as the ego-self, is nothing but a container
that contains nothing. There is no sense of existence or presence, just
the experience of the bag, a mere boundary around an emptiness.

The libidinal wanting may return at this point, but it can have a different aim. If she is not bound by her habitual beliefs, the student might
come to realize that she longs to disappear, to gently vanish, to be no
more. She experiences a very deep weariness, and a teary subtle longing, that sometimes becomes powerful and passionate, to simply fade
away, and not to leave any trace. She finds the notion of absolute cessation sweet and dear to her heart. She feels that not to be, not even to
know that she is not, would be the final release from a life of striving
and searching. She contemplates not being, not knowing that she is not
being, and not remembering that she ever has been, as some kind of
ultimate, albeit obscure, fulfillment of her heart. It is as if she senses that
only not being will bring contentment, and a peace beyond peace.[27]

This gentle disappearing will actually come to pass if the process
takes its course. She will have the experience once in a while—especially when she is relaxed and mentally unconcerned—of feeling herself disappearing. There will be a gap in consciousness, a cessation of
all sensation and perception, without falling asleep or unconscious. She
knows this because, when she comes to, she feels quite rested but also
indescribably clear and fresh, as if her soul has been washed of its heaviness and conflicts. She feels lucid and totally care-free, light and totally
light-hearted. No sleep ever rejuvenates her this much. It is as if not

418   only her body, but her very self and soul have been renewed. She does not remember what happened because absolutely nothing has happened. There was absolutely no content of experience.

This is the beginning of tasting the absolute depth of her Being, although the encounter is still limited. She still needs to understand and let go of the subtle vestiges of representations. This transpires in many ways. One of the most significant ways is to follow the narcissistic emptiness related to the approaching depth of Being. The student feels empty and impoverished. If she manages not to reject, judge, or react to this emptiness, she begins to realize how impoverished she actually is. She feels devoid of significance or value, of Essence or substance; she feels that she has only attachments. She begins to feel that she has to let go of everything because she does not possess anything. She has to let go of her attachment to relationships, pleasure, comfort, security, knowledge, Essence, realization, enlightenment, ego, self, suffering, and so on. Holding on to any of these attachments simply means resisting awareness of the poverty of the denuded shell of the self. She realizes she needs to let go of having—or let go of the belief that she has—a position, a place, recognition, fruit of work, accomplishment, contribution, knowledge, even state or development. She needs to let go of everything if she is not going to spend the rest of her life fighting the emptiness of her shell. This activates deep grief, very deep sadness and tears. The emptiness becomes a vast black ocean of tears.

The student realizes that in identifying with the ego-self she truly has nothing, for everything comes from Being. As the ego-self, she is fundamentally poor, totally indigent, devoid of all possessions and qualities. This state is very profound; by this point, too, the student is coming to the insight that this is the intrinsic condition of the ego-self, and is not particular only to her personal situation. The state has a sense of having nothing, feeling nothing, being nothing, and perceiving nothing. It can easily shift to the state of cessation (the disappearing), but it can go further.[28]

The state of poverty, which some traditions call "mystical poverty," is the expression of the transformation of narcissistic emptiness into true inner spaciousness, a profound void now penetrating the shell due to the shell's almost complete denudement. As the self is letting go of its representations of itself, which feels like the surrendering of everything she believed she possessed, she becomes increasingly transparent to the presentations of Being. She experiences a new profundity of true emptiness—black space—but it is reflected through a slight vestige of psychic structure, the concept of entity. So she feels this emptiness as the poverty of her sense of self.[29]

As the student remains in this condition, surrendering all manipulations and desires, this profound emptiness dissolves the remaining vestiges of structure, and propels her into the full and direct experience of this deepest of all voids. But she then discovers that this most profound inner spaciousness is also identical to the absolute depth of all Being. She has arrived home; her poverty has been the doorway.

Although the process of transformation of narcissism at this level is similar to the general process of going through any level of fundamental narcissism, it has some differentiating properties which reflect the level of the true self being realized. The sense of poverty of the shell is an indirect reflection of the truth of this depth of Being. The deficient narcissistic emptiness specific to this stage is nothing but the associated inner spaciousness, experienced as deficient because of some subtle defensiveness on the part of the self. The presence of the thin membrane of the shell indicates an attachment to a vestige of structure, which means that there is a subtle resistance to the inner spaciousness. When this resistance is abandoned, the emptiness is experienced in its true condition as the most profound of all voids.

However, because of the characteristics of the true self approaching conscious experience, this profound spaciousness is not differentiated from the related true self. The inner spaciousness turns out to be not only an emptiness, but at the same time a facet of this depth of Being, inseparable from it, actually nondual with it. More precisely, the inner black spaciousness at this level of self-realization is coemergent with the level of Being realized. Holding on to the belief that the separate self possesses anything, even existence, is a resistance against this absolute depth of Being; this resistance makes this depth appear to the self as a deficient emptiness characterized by impoverishment. Surrendering all positions and concepts of self, the student discovers the absolute depth of her nature. The transition is very subtle; it is a matter of

420   asserting self or not. But the difference is profound: It is the difference between being an impoverished self lost in the universe or being the inexhaustible vast depth of Being. Or as a Buddhist might see it, it is the difference between samsara and nirvana. We can see this transition to lie at the root of narcissism: In one direction lies fundamental narcissism and in the other lies self-realization. Self-assertion results in samsara and selflessness leads to nirvana.

This realization goes beyond cessation to the realization of selflessness, which is equivalent to the realization of the absolute truth of Being. An avalanche of perceptions and insights arises at this point; here we will note a few that are most relevant for our understanding of the transformation of narcissism and its relation to self-realization.

- The state of poverty is the emptiness within the libidinal ego. We experience it as a state of deprivation and insufficiency due to the oral fixation on emptiness as lack of nourishment. This makes us want to move away from it and to seek fullness from outside. This extroverted orientation is one of the first, basic ego attitudes that disconnect the self from its inherent inner richness. Turning toward external objects as sources of fulfillment is the oral fixation of the self on a mode of operation natural and necessary in the first year of life, a fixation that patterns the self in such a way that it alienates it from its inner core. Actual and severe deprivations and disruptions in early infancy will clearly deepen this fixation and give it a distorted character, but this basic fixation develops in all infants because of their total dependency. This patterning is a basic structure of the ego-self.

- This extroverted orientation coincides with the development of object relations and the object-seeking drive characterizing the libidinal ego. Thus, the self becomes deeply impressed and patterned by the concept of relationship, which means that it is always relating to an object. This pattern becomes an impediment to self-realization, for the self tends to objectify Being and relate to it as an object. The structure of object relations is experienced as relating, and becomes a ground for the development of attachments. These attachments in turn become barriers against the capacity to simply be. This does not mean relating *per se* is problematic; but to use relating to define identity is.

- At this level the shell tends to dissolve by turning into hot tears, initially because of the depth of grief of losing the self and its possessions; but ultimately the grief is about the self's loss of contact with the depths of its Being. The dissolution into tears typically manifests as a disappearing, sometimes with intensity and passion. The passion is a deep love for the state of cessation, which turns out to be for the absolute depth of Being. The passionate intensity is sometimes due to the dissolving action of this depth of Being. The dissolution might be experienced as a passionate annihilation of the self by the powerful love of Being, as self and Being connect in a passionate love towards each other. More accurately, we frequently experience the closing of distance and the dissolution of duality between self and Being as the gravitational pull of a passionate, ecstatic love, that annihilates the self into the depth of Being, evoking the analogy of lover and beloved.

- This becomes an intense encounter when the student experiences the dissolution in the heart. She becomes aware of the shell as a membrane around the heart, where she feels the heart as the emptiness and the sense of poverty. As she accepts the poverty, the inner emptiness in the heart transforms into inner spaciousness, which is the absolute depth of Being. She recognizes she has been a lover and now has found her beloved, the true fulfillment of her heart.[30] She feels that what she beholds now in her heart is what she has been searching for all her life. Her heart has found many lovers, but never one so perfect as this. She has always been searching for this beloved, but has seen him in one object or another. They were all idols standing between her heart and its true beloved, distracting her even more as they drew her closer. They were all veils, and now the beloved has been unveiled.

  The depth of oral longing is simply a reflection of the deepest longing of the heart for its ultimate beloved. One has mistaken the libidinal exciting object of the oral stage for the true beloved, thus embarking on a never-ending journey of estrangement. By turning outward for fullness, the soul disconnected from her inner Being, then sought it in outside objects.

- One issue that tends to arise at this point is guilt. We frequently feel the turn towards the inner depths of Being as a turning away from the world, as an abandonment of the world of manifestation and experience. This can bring up what has remained of our rapprochement conflict, but deeper still, it brings up guilt for abandoning the world. Abandoning the world can be understood at this level as abandoning our mother, the deepest object for the libidinal ego. This brings up deep anguish and guilt, with a torrent of tears and sorrow. We are actually turning away from all objects, including mother's internalized image, and towards the depths of our Being. There might also be conflict, fear of separation, and fear of loss. Some students report sleepless nights, turning restlessly in one's bed, not being able to feel warm, as if one's skin has lost all comfort and warmth.

The passionate love for truth can be so powerful that it dissolves all these barriers with clear and discriminating understanding. Now, the student might find herself turning completely towards the depths, into her heart, the window to the mystery of Being.

• What she beholds now bedazzles her, enchants her, and fires her passionate love. She beholds a luminous vastness, an infinite depth so black it shines. The depth is so profound that it shatters any possibility of mental comprehension, and the luminosity so magnificent that it ricochets in her heart like brilliant lightning. She feels as if she is looking into the very essence of God, into the absolute purity of Essence, into the very center of the universe. It is the most beautiful sight she has ever beheld, dazzling her with its clarity and radiance. It is so black that its blackness luminates with brilliance. Its black and radiant beauty is so powerful that it annihilates her with an ecstatic, passionate abandon. She loves to give up all self and to totally disappear into its mysterious depths. She feels that nothing else deserves to be seen and loved, and thus she recognizes the deep source of her need for mirroring.

The beauty of this depth is majestic, radiant with a crystal brilliance that bedazzles her and makes her forget all else. She feels passionately shattered, lovingly dissolved, and deliciously annihilated.

• She feels she has arrived home, the original place from which she had strayed. She has been lost without knowing from what, searching without knowing for what, and now her search has ended and she is resting at home. At this point we understand narcissistic alienation as a movement of leaving the place where we belong—the only place where the self can totally rest—with its heart completely fulfilled. We might literally feel that we have been in exile, estranged from our home, never feeling at home. We see now why we could never before feel totally at home, for until now we had never experienced being totally at home.

- The student may also come to understand that the love might be passionate and consuming, sweet and heavenly, but even that will tend to separate her somewhat from her beloved, for it relates her to it instead of totally disappearing into it. This only deepens her love to the point of totally annihilating all self-recognition. This precipitates the self-realization of the absolute truth of Being, where she becomes one with this dazzling mystery, totally identified with this luminous, crystal black vastness.

  The student realizes at this point that she is infinite and boundless, a vastness that has no end. It is as if she becomes the vastness of intergalactic space, seeing that this absolute blackness has a crystalline purity and clarity which make the blackness shimmer and glitter with indescribable brilliance. Her mind explodes into absolute clarity and brilliance, her heart a vastness of annihilating intimacy and bliss, and her body a shimmering which is the appearance of the totality of the universe.

- She perceives the universe, in all its multiplicity and richness, as a beautiful appearance, as a brilliantly colored robe that she wears. She finds herself to be the immensity of the mysterious blackness, with the universe as the colorful pattern of her radiance. The totality of the universe is a unified oneness, but more than that. Oneness is a poor concept to describe such sheer beauty. She recognizes all of appearance, all that appears to perception, as the brilliant luminosity of the mysterious black vastness.

- She recognizes that it feels mysterious because she cannot determine its nature, which is absolutely indeterminable. She feels total solidity, a crystalline diamond solidity, but at the same time recognizes that she is absolutely nothing, that she is absence itself. The absolute truth of Being is absolute existence which is at the same time

424   absolute absence. It is the source and essence of everything, but at the same time it is total openness, an absolute absence of any weight or substance. The fact that it is absolute nonexistence gives it its annihilating power. The self feels annihilated because it discovers that its absolute essence is total absence. There is actually no annihilation, only the realization of the selflessness of Being, whose absolute essence is totally ungraspable, completely beyond definition. This indeterminacy is experienced as a paradox of being and nonbeing, existence and nonexistence, neither and not neither.

- The quality of absence inherent in the Absolute, its utter sense of openness and emptiness, is what makes the associated level of the shell feel like poverty. More precisely, the mysterious emptiness—which is a sense of indeterminacy and wonder when experienced clearly—is interpreted through the veil of the shell as a deficiency and lack. It is the source of all richness, but the fact that it feels like nothing makes the denuded self approaching it feel that it is poor and indigent.

- We can have endless, amazing understanding in this absolute essence of Being; we can describe some of its qualities; but we never feel we have described it because it is inexhaustible.[31] It is the source of all qualities, all possibilities, and all potential; but when we experience it directly we find absolutely nothing. It is a delightful nothing that dazzles and releases. In other words, it is the unmanifest source of all manifestation. From this source, everything appears as itself, originating from this unfathomable emptiness, but nothing becomes anything.

- This luminous, crystalline vastness is absolute stillness, total peace, and complete silence. It is total stillness that is the richest of textures, stupendous silence that speaks more loudly than anything else, and complete peace that is the source of all manifestations. It is an absence that—by its sheer absence—becomes solid peace. But at the same time it is simplicity itself—not simplicity of mind, but of pure experience. Any ego activity is perceived with utmost clarity as a jarring and jagged energy.

- Perhaps the best description of this state is that it is absolute and total intimacy, for we are directly in touch with the inmost of everything

we experience. This sense of intimacy has an exquisite gentleness to   425
it and a melting softness. Its smoothness makes the finest silk seem
rough, and its texture the softest of all velvet gross.

- We may recognize it as the self, but there is no feeling of "I," identity, or self. This recognition has no conceptual quality. There is only
  the direct and clear perception that it is none other than one is. It
  is both the self and the nature of the self, but also of everything. It
  is the perception of the beingness of oneself without the feeling of
  oneself. One knows it is oneself because it is oneself. There is nothing else that is oneself. This realization is sometimes referred to as
  absolute subjectivity or realizing the absolute subject.

  The Sufis refer to this reality as the "divine essence," the essence
  of God, but also as the final nature of all existence. They use the
  Arabic word *dhat* to refer to it, which means self, identity, nature,
  and Essence all at the same time. The closest English equivalent of
  this term is the word *ipseity*. In the experience of ipseity, the absolute truth of Being, duality ends as we perceive that the identity and
  nature of everything, including ourselves, is inseparable from everything. Everything is the radiance of absolute ipseity, just as light is
  the radiance of the sun.

- Everything appears in a state of flux and transformation, as a oneness inseparable from its manifestations. We perceive the universe
  as a dynamic unity of appearance. However, there is no "I," no sense
  of self, and no center for this perception. There is perception without a perceiver, all taking place within the immense mystery of absolute Being. It is as if the black vastness manifests the perception as
  its own luminosity.

  This clarifies how perception always has an "I" except at this stage.
  We become aware that there has been a continuous and incessant sense
  or feeling of self or "I," that was present in all experiences up to this
  point. Now there is experience and perception of experience, without
  being related to an "I." More accurately, any experience is a manifestation of "who I am," without "who I am" feeling attached to "I."

- This realization has fascinating consequences. We feel as if reality has
  two sides, front and back, the Shakti and Shiva of Kashmir Shaivism.

426   The front is the totality of the dynamic universe, and the back is an absence. In fact, as it develops, it becomes even more mysterious: There is only a front; there is no back. We know then that there is nothing more behind or underneath this vastness; in some sense it is ultimate. There is nothing behind it because it has no back.

• We feel utter spontaneity, where each thought, word, and activity arises before there is any recognition. We merely witness the expression happening, and recognize it only after it happens. We are so much at the source of all expression that we can only perceive our expression as it manifests. This complete spontaneity can be quite disconcerting at the beginning because we feel no control over what we do or say.

• The complete spontaneity is due to the fact that, in this condition of self-realization, there is absolutely no self-consciousness. We only see our front; there is no back to look back to, and hence, there is no possibility for us to look inward or backward towards ourselves. In fact, if we attempt to look back and reflect on the source of our manifestations, we encounter nothing. There is only a gap of consciousness or perception. We look back, and the first thing we become aware of is our looking outward towards the world of manifestation. There is no "inner" to the absolute truth, for it is the inner of the inner, the inmost of the inmost. There is only the possibility of looking to the front, or outward, which is inseparable from the manifestation of experience.

This clarifies the observation that one of the main sources of narcissism is the self-reflective capacity of the normal self. More precisely, one of the main characteristics of narcissism is self-consciousness, an outcome of the normal self's capacity for self-reflection. It is only at the level of the Absolute that this characteristic disappears. It does not disappear at the earlier stages of self-realization, not even at the level of nonconceptual reality because there is always consciousness when we reflect. The ego-self hangs on to this consciousness, even nonconceptual consciousness, by self-reflection. In the experience of nonconceptual reality, we perceive pure consciousness when looking backward or inward. In the experience of the Absolute, consciousness disappears when we attempt to reflect. The experience then is not self-consciousness but cessation of all consciousness.

We could say that in the self-realization of the absolute truth, our 427 front is the perception of phenomena, which is the same as the phenomena, and our back is total cessation. The quality of this depth of Being, whose nature is total cessation, dissolves self-consciousness. This eliminates the last element which supports narcissism.

- We notice that our need for mirroring decreases radically and rapidly. We need less and less recognition and reflection. We find any reflection or mirroring a burden, a redundancy. The desire for mirroring becomes a habitual trace of a bygone need, although this trace might last a long time. If the need arises, it can only mean that we have objectified the absolute truth. How can absence need mirroring or support?

- At the beginning it seems that the Absolute is something very distinct from everything else, but when our experience matures we realize there is nothing but the Absolute. Everything that happens is a manifestation of the Absolute. Everything is the Absolute, but with a form. So wherever we look we see the Absolute. In the experience of cessation, everything disappears; then, everything reappears as a manifestation of the Absolute, as the luminous awareness of the Absolute.

chapter 42

Nondual Presence

———————————————————————————

T he full transformation of oral narcissism requires not only the
self-realization of the greatest depth of Being, the absolute
truth, but the wholeness of Being, the nonduality of its depth
with all manifestation. This is not exactly a matter of realizing a new
presentation of Being, but of the integration of all levels in one unified presentation. This is a place of utmost subtlety, and the various
spiritual teachings take different positions about its meaning. It is a
question of what the ultimate truth is, which is related to the ultimate
state of realization posited by each teaching. Different traditions
embrace varying positions about what exactly is the ultimate truth
and variations in what ultimate realization entails.

The Sufis, for instance, take the view that the Absolute is the
unmanifest essence of divinity and that it transcends all manifestations. However, they do consider that the ultimate realization is to
become part of the fabric of this reality. The Sufis do not usually
attempt to analyze its nature beyond seeing it as a mystery, the source
and ultimate nature of all manifestations, a bedazzling majesty and
indescribable beauty. Their focus is not on analyzing its nature, but
on becoming so totally suffused by it that one becomes the legs by

which it walks, the eyes by which it sees, and the tongue by which 429
it speaks.

The Sufi formulation of this realization is not much different from other traditions, but some other traditions focus more on what it is. The analysis of its nature confronts us with the question of what non-duality means, and it is at this point that many traditions differ. Advaita Vedanta, for instance, posits the Absolute as the ultimate truth, but also as the ultimate realization. One realizes the Absolute as one's true identity, totally beyond all manifestations, but containing them within its mysterious vastness. The emphasis is on the transcendence of the world, including the body and mind. One becomes the immense solidity of the Absolute, totally still and inactive, while dispassionately witnessing the play of all phenomena. He witnesses all phenomena as the dynamic transformation of a cosmic and boundless consciousness, which consciousness arises in his silent immensity as a surface phenomenon. In the vastness of his silence, the world arises in all its multiplicity, but all the world is made out of a conscious presence, a presence which is a consciousness that can reflect on itself. So the world—with its fabric of consciousness—is the surface shimmering of the immensity of the absolute truth, forming only an onion-skin thin layer on its infinite depth. The fabric of conscious presence which is the world is inseparable from the Absolute, within it and part of it, but it is qualitatively different from it. This is like a body of water whose surface (or a bubble within it) is tinted by a color which differentiates it from the body itself, without separating from it in any way.

The question of duality and nonduality is not so obvious in this state of realization. It is all the Absolute, so there is no duality, but there is a differentiation between the Absolute and the manifestation, which can be seen as duality. However, it is not the duality of the ego-self, where there is a subject autonomous from an object. The subject in this realization is the Absolute, but the object, which is the surface manifestation, is an inseparable part of it. So we may say there is duality only in perception but not in reality. This realization seems to be the one taught by the late Nisargadatta Maharaj:

> As Absolute, I am timeless, infinite, and I am awareness, without being aware of awareness. As infinity I express myself as

430   space, as timeless I express myself as time. Unless there is space
           and duration I cannot be conscious of myself. When space
           and time are present there is consciousness, in that total man-
           ifestation takes place and various phenomena come into being.
           (J. Dunn, ed., 1985, p. 72)

Nisargadatta indicates here that in the self-realization of the Absolute
there is consciousness of experience only when we witness manifestation. When we turn to the depths of the Absolute there is no experience; there is cessation. Nisargadatta recognizes the absolute truth as
pure awareness, but he also says that pure awareness needs something
to manifest in order to be aware. The Absolute is the witness, but the
witness cannot witness itself because there is nothing to witness then.
This is a very interesting characteristic of the absolute truth. The fact
that it is awareness takes us to the Buddhist view of reality.

The Buddhist schools have different views of ultimate truth: Some
posit emptiness, and some nondual presence, to be this ultimate. The
schools that posit emptiness as the ultimate truth seem to understand it
in a way similar to our description of the Absolute. More accurately, they
discuss emptiness the way we recognize the absence, simplicity, and non-
determinacy of the Absolute. These schools posit this understanding to
be the unqualified, ultimate truth. The primary origin of this view is the
Prasangika school of Madhyamika, as we see in the following passage:

> The Prasangika are very careful to emphasize that as well as
> things not being truly existent . . . and not arising . . . they are
> also not not truly existing . . . and not non arising. . . . Such
> positions are equally unsatisfactory, because if true existence
> does not exist, then neither can its opposite, not true existence,
> since that only has meaning in relation to existence. If simi-
> larly there is no arising there is no nonarising. In this way they
> make sure that all concepts, positive and negative, are negated
> and that nothing is asserted in their place. In other words the
> Prasangika system is beyond any mental grasping whatsoever
> . . . (Tsultrim Gyamtso Rinpoche, 1986, p. 70)

Some Tibetan schools of Buddhism posit that emptiness is different from the consciousness that realizes the emptiness. Usually the

consciousness is what is called "clear light," which is reminiscent of our   431
description of pure Being and nonconceptual truth. For instance, the
Dalai Lama says:

> The treatment of the object, emptiness, as the view and also
> of the subject, the wisdom consciousness, as the view is not a
> unique feature of tantra but is similar to the Middle Way
> Autonomy School's presentation of emptiness as the ultimate
> truth and the mind realizing emptiness as a concordant ulti-
> mate [this being accepted by both the Old and New Translation
> Schools]. (Dalai Lama, 1984, p. 208)

In other words, emptiness is the ultimate truth, and it can be realized
by a pure consciousness. This is similar to the view taught by Nisargadatta
Maharaj, except that there is a reversal of subject and object. The common Buddhist view of emptiness as ultimate truth does not understand
it as awareness. In fact, awareness is seen as the marriage or coemergence of consciousness (clear light) and emptiness. This can be seen as
a realization that awareness indicates clear light to be inherently coemergent with emptiness, or that clear light is inherently empty. These schools
equate this realization with the ultimate attainment:

> When this mind of vajra-like concentration overcomes the
> very last obscurations preventing omniscience at dawn you
> become a fully awakened buddha. At that time your mind of
> clear light realizing emptiness becomes indestructible and con-
> stant . . . (Kelsang Gyatso, 1982, p. 221)[32]

Here, the final realization is a state where clear light and emptiness are
inseparable. However, these schools, like that of the Dalai Lama's
Gelugpa, posit that emptiness itself is the ultimate truth. We see this
perspective in the following quote from the above book on Mahamudra, aimed at criticizing the other schools, mainly the Nyingmapa,
which do not take this view:

> They think the ultimate nature of the mind is its clarity and
> cognition free of conceptualization; they do not realize that the
> ultimate nature of the mind is the non-affirming negation that
> is the mere absence of the inherent existence of the mind.
> (Kelsang Gyatso, 1982, p. 141)

432   The other schools, especially that of the Nyingmapa, in their highest teaching—Dzogchen—view the ultimate truth as a nondual presence that is both clear and empty. They view emptiness as only a facet of the ultimate truth. They understand nondual presence as pure awareness, as we see in the following words from one of the original masters of Dzogchen:

> [The state of pure and total presence] is equally praised by all teachers who have been the light of the world. . . . Non-conceptual, ever fresh awareness, supreme and indestructible, is, moreover, also this very [state of pure and total presence]. (Manjusrimitra, 1987, pp. 55–56)

The emphasis of these schools is not on emptiness, but on Buddha nature or Buddha mind, *bodhicitta*, which they understand differently from the other schools, as Kennard Lipman writes in his commentary on Longchenpa, the main Tibetan writer on Dzogchen: "In dzogchen, bodhicitta refers to the natural state of the individual; it is synonymous with the state of total completeness and sheer presence." (Longchenpa, 1987, p. 69) We have already encountered the Tibetan term for this pure nondual presence, *rigpa*, which literally means the fact of knowing and luminosity of consciousness:

> It is basic knowledge (rig pa), clear light ('od gsal), the fundamental innate mind of clear light (gnyug ma lhan cig skyes pa'i 'od gsal) which is the final status (gnas lugs) of things. (Dalai Lama, 1984, p. 208)

Rigpa, or pure nondual presence, becomes both ultimate truth and ultimate realization, but the emphasis of the teaching is on the nonduality of experience where the presence is totally nondual with all manifestation. We do not experience ourselves as witnessing phenomena, but as the presence which is the very substance of all phenomena. The ultimate truth is awareness, as in the teaching of Nisargadatta Maharaj, but awareness here is not different from the conscious presence that is the very nature and ground of manifestation. There is no duality in perception, and there is no witnessing transcendent to manifestation.[33]

All that is has me—universal creativity, pure and total   433
   presence—as its root.
How things appear is my being.
How things arise is my manifestation.
Sounds and words heard are my messages expressed in
   sounds and words.
All capacities, forms, and pristine awarenesses of the buddhas;
The bodies of sentient beings, their habituations, and so forth;
All environments and their inhabitants, life forms, and
   experiences;
Are the primordial state of pure and total presence.
(Longchenpa, 1987, p. 32)

The idea is that rigpa is the fundamental, ultimate ground, so it is present in any state or manifestation. The various states, manifestations, and changes are only the play of this ground, transient colorations and forms of the basic presence. This indicates that rigpa has a dynamic characteristic that makes it always in a state of flux and transformation. However, the self-realized individual will always be aware of the basic presence, with its clarity and emptiness, coemergent with the manifestation:

There is not a single state which is not this vast state of presence.
It is the site and home of everything. (Longchenpa, 1987, p. 49)

This realization, then, is a state of wholeness, in which all of our manifestations are seen to comprise our presence. The body, thoughts, feelings, actions, and perceptions are all manifestations of this pure presence. They are all presence, displaying its richness in a dynamic dance of manifestation.

Nondual presence is what arises as the wholeness of the self when oral narcissism is transformed; hence, it is not only the realization of the Absolute. Or so it seems. There is a subtlety here which will be useful for us to understand.

Nondual Absolute

It is our observation that most of the translated Dzogchen texts (and to a slightly lesser degree, the Mahamudra texts) on nondual presence

434   describe it in a way that can qualify it as either pure Being or nonconceptual reality. Both these levels of manifestation of Being are characterized by awareness which is both presence and openness. Pure
Being feels like a presence that is inseparable from the sense of total
lightness and openness. It is both fullness and nothingness. This paradoxical quality is even sharper in the experience of nonconceptual reality, where we feel it as a presence that is at the same time an absence.
The emptiness here is much more than the nothingness of pure Being.
It is so empty that it is actually a total absence.

The experience of the Absolute is similar to that of nonconceptual
reality, with an important difference: In looking towards the depths
of presence instead of towards manifestation (that is, focusing the
attention on the quality of presence rather than on the forms and colors that it displays), we find clarity characterized by absence in the latter and cessation of all perception in the former. The experience of
nonconceptual reality is like clear, colorless light, while the Absolute
has more a sense of clear, black light. The blackness of the Absolute is
not a color, however; it is the absence of perception. It is cessation. So
the experience of the Absolute is even more paradoxical than that of
the nonconceptual dimension.

The teaching of Nisargadatta Maharaj leads one to believe that the
self-realization of the Absolute can only take the form of being aware
of oneself as an unchanging, vast subject, witnessing phenomena without being involved in it. However, this is not the case. We can experience the Absolute as presence totally nondual with its manifestations.
In other words, all phenomena can be experienced as the display of
the Absolute. Everything is the Absolute, not only arising within it and
as part of it. We could say here that this puts the Absolute within the
category of rigpa or nondual presence. However, there is a subtle difference, even more paradoxical than what we have seen so far. One
perceives that everything is the display of emptiness, that the ultimate
state of everything is the Absolute. All phenomena appear as a substantial, dynamic presence, but when we investigate this presence, we
do not find it. In other words, everything appears as a phantasmagoric
display of dazzling brilliance without ever existing.

Tarthang Tulku, an original and creative visionary and explorer of   435
the nature of Being, expresses this beautifully, using the word *openness* instead of *emptiness*:

> The presence of appearance as Being is such that only the most paradoxical language can express it. Presence is, yet open—like a drawing in the sky. . . . What there is is entirely open in a way that sustains an undimmed radiance, an infinitely textured radiance that is magic. (Tarthang Tulku, 1977, pp. 296–207)[34]

All phenomena appear as a majestic, colorful display of pure presence, but when we investigate the essence of this presence, perception ceases. At the same time, the presence is sheer clarity, a lucid and fresh awareness. In this experience there is only emptiness, but emptiness is awareness, which is transparent clarity. However, the clarity is dark, making it ever clearer, like the way intergalactic space is more transparent than the sky in daytime, although it is pitch darkness.

Clarity is an inherent property of the Absolute; awareness is the luminosity of emptiness. This delineation is slightly different from that some Dzogchen teachers imply; it means that clarity is a facet of emptiness (the Absolute), and not vice versa. Awareness is sometimes seen as the ultimate, equated with emptiness whose radiance is clarity. Some ancient Dzogchen masters seem to imply that clarity is inherent to emptiness, giving emptiness a greater weight, as we see in the nondual realization of the Absolute. They view awareness itself, then, as the radiance of emptiness, giving emptiness an ultimacy very near to that posited by most other Buddhist schools. We see this clearly in the following passage by Padmasambhava, one of the most ancient teachers of Dzogchen, where he refers to emptiness as "the Essence":

> Your own awareness is inherently knowing, inherently clear, and luminously brilliant.
> When it arises, it is called the Bodhichitta, 'the enlightened mind.'
> Being without any activity of meditation, it transcends all objects of knowledge.
> Being without any distraction, *it is the luminous clarity of the Essence itself.* [emphasis added] (Reynolds, 1989, p. 18)

436   The situation is subtle, but we are trying to clarify these distinctions because whatever view we take will be reflected in personal experience. The different views put forward by various spiritual researchers reflect their personal experiences, which indicates that experience accommodates all of these views. We may experience nonduality in many ways.

Our observation is that nonduality is the experience of many levels of presentation of Being.[35] We can experience nondual presence that is pure Being, or the nonconceptual reality, or the absolute truth. Also, on any of these levels there is a continuous gradation of dominance of presence or clarity on the one hand, and emptiness on the other. One can experience mostly the fullness of presence or the openness of emptiness, without losing the other quality. This is most clear in the case of the Absolute, where we experience this crystalline emptiness coemergent with pure Being or nonconceptual reality. Then we can experience a nondual presence that is a pure presence of fullness, or a nonconceptual clarity, totally inseparable from the crystalline voidness of the Absolute. We then know ourselves as the Absolute, which is total cessation, but which manifests clarity by its sheer radiance. This clarity changes from a fullness and solidity to the most subtle shimmering. In all these transformations of radiance there is a constant, the mysterious Absolute Essence. The Absolute is unchanging, but its radiance is in a constant state of dynamic transformation. The radiance is not apart of the Absolute, but totally coextensive with it. So the Absolute is the absolutely unchanging, while it never ceases to change.

This coemergence or coextensiveness of the Absolute and its radiant clarity is what ultimately ends the need for mirroring. The radiant clarity is the mirror-like awareness, and the Absolute is the ultimate depth of Being. So depth and awareness of depth are inseparable. We know the depth of our Being in the very fact of simply being.

This experience of the nondual Absolute is a wonderment. Everything appears more clearly defined, more three-dimensional, more textured, but also transparent and luminous. Everything makes up a nonconceptual unity, multifaceted and multidimensional, but glittering brilliantly as if made out of diamonds. At the same time, the whole appearance is a presentation of the Absolute, so it is all a projection of an unfathomable depth that bedazzles with its scintillating mystery. And we are this. Sometimes we are individuated—but inseparable—expressions of it.

We have pursued this discussion of the subtleties of nondual presence because the complete transformation of narcissism requires the full self-realization of this level. Full self-realization now appears to be not only the realization of nondual presence, which is needed for resolution of oral narcissism, but the realization of the nondual Absolute.

Many seekers of spiritual development come to believe that having profound experiences, like the ones discussed above, is enough to bring about total liberation. This is a vestige of the oral self, believing that one good nursing is all that one needs. The situation is much more involved; permanent realization requires a great deal more than the arising of the experience of self-realization. The difficult work is that of the clarification of the self from all rigid ego structures, and this does not happen automatically by the mere experiencing of the state of self-realization. We need to become aware of the various ego structures and their associated affects and desires. We need to understand them to the extent of completely seeing their mental nature, and hence, their lack of ultimate reality. We need to see, understand, and be released from, the various misunderstandings, tendencies, and attachments of the self that orient it away from its inherent endowments and cause it to stand in its own way. This is a deep, slow process of maturation, but it is greatly aided by the arising of various experiences of self-realization. As the student clarifies the various structures of the self, Being—in its various manifestations—becomes a permanent center of experience and eventually the constant ground and fabric of the self.

Nondual absolute presence can become the constant condition of the self, but this cannot be arrived at by pushing the self towards it as if it is an aim or achievement. We stand in our own way when we judge and reject our present experience and try to manipulate ourselves into posited heights of realization. Such attitudes and efforts will only disconnect us from ourselves, and as we have seen, this disconnection is the hallmark of narcissistic alienation. We need from the beginning to respect our humanness, to appreciate our immediate experience, and

438   to learn to simply be where we are. It is in the gentleness and acceptance of relaxing where we experientially find ourselves, and the openness to the present manifestation of our Being, that makes it possible for us to sink deeper into our nature. This open acceptance can express itself in a lighthearted curiosity about ourselves and our experience in the world, inviting the depths of our Being to reveal themselves naturally and spontaneously. When this becomes our way of life, the various human situations we find ourselves in will become the context for our unfoldment, revealing the riches of Being as the natural maturation of our humanness.[36]

THE ESSENTIAL IDENTITY

IN

SPIRITUAL TRADITIONS

Awareness of the essential aspect of Identity, the radiant point of light, is not unique to our work. This experience is familiar to many spiritual teachings, traditional and modern, Eastern and Western. Many of these teachings appreciate its importance for self-realization and spiritual liberation, even though they may differ in their understanding of the way it is important. The centrality of this aspect, in the overall process of spiritual development and maturity, is appreciated by many teachings. Its realization is the primary turning point in the journey towards ultimate reality; specifically, this realization is the primary step towards integrating the soul into ultimate reality, the absolute nature of Being.

Each teaching posits a final or absolute ground of Being that forms the irreducible simplicity of true nature. We refer to this ground as the absolute dimension of Being. The understanding of this ultimate true

440   nature of the self and everything differs in subtle ways from one teaching or philosophy to another. In Christianity, it is the father who is the inscrutable darkness; in Kabala, it is the *ain* (nothing) or *ain sof* (infinite); in Sufism, it is the divine Essence; in Buddhism, it is emptiness (*sunyata*) or Buddha nature (*tathagatagarbha*); in Taoism, it is the Tao or the nothing; in Vedanta, it is the Brahman or absolute self; in Kashmir Shaivism, it is Shiva; and so on. The spiritual quest becomes that of the soul integrating this ultimate nature as its inner nature, source, and sometimes its identity.

The realization of the Essential Identity becomes the primary step towards this ultimate integration; hence, most spiritual practice is devoted to this realization. This is because many of these teachings understand that this point of light and presence is the direct expression of the absolute nature in the world of time and space. Some see it as the reflection of the Absolute in the body, or in the individual soul or self. Some see it as the God within, or the inner divine spark. Hence, this point of light or presence functions as the bridge towards the realization of the absolute nature, or the union with it, depending on the conceptualization of the particular teaching.

This is similar to our view and understanding of the process of spiritual development and the role of the Essential Identity in it. We have explored this in detail in previous chapters, so we will recapitulate it briefly here, to help us situate our work in relation to other spiritual teachings. In our view, Being has a final, irreducible simplicity that we call the Absolute or absolute dimension. It is the original nature of everything, the source of all manifestations (see Chapter 41). Everything arises out of this ground and ultimately returns to it. This ground is totally mysterious and indeterminable, but implicitly contains all the perfections of spiritual nature. It manifests these perfections in a differentiated and explicit way within the soul as the essential aspects. So each aspect of Essence is a differentiated manifestation of an inherent, implicit perfection in the Absolute Essence, each explicitly expressing a specific quality and function. Each aspect serves to provide the soul with a quality and function needed for her life, development, and maturation. But centrally, each aspect reveals one of the perfections of the Absolute in the experience of the individual soul and its role in the relationship of the soul to the Absolute.

The aspect of Truth, for example, functions in helping the soul to 441 discriminate between truth and falsehood, and hence guides her in her life and development towards greater and deeper truth. The deepening experience of Truth opens the soul to the ultimate truth, which is revealed to be the Absolute. In other words, the aspect of Truth reveals itself ultimately to be simply the manifestation of an implicit perfection inherent in the Absolute: The Absolute is absolute Truth. It is the absolute and final truth of the soul and everything else. Therefore, the aspect of Truth functions to provide the soul with the capacity of discrimination necessary for her life and development in the world, but also, and at the same time as it does that, it connects her with the Absolute, revealing it as her ultimate truth.

The Essential Identity functions similarly to other aspects, with the dual function of providing a capacity necessary for the life and development of the soul and connecting her to the Absolute in a specific way that reveals the nature of this connection. The essential aspect of Identity, the point of light and presence, provides the soul with a center and identity necessary for her life, which will at the same time ultimately connect her with the Absolute, as her final and absolute identity. The Essential Identity is the implicit perfection inherent in the Absolute that explicitly expresses in the individual soul that the Absolute is not only ultimate truth, but also ultimate identity. It is the Absolute as identity manifesting within the individual experience of the soul.

Therefore, since full self-realization requires the realization of the Absolute as one's ultimate identity, the realization of the Essential Identity becomes the primary and most important fulcrum towards the completion of the spiritual journey. Realization of the Essential Identity is the expression of the realization of the Absolute, as reflected in individual experience, within the world of space-time. The Essential Identity is the spark of the Absolute within the individual soul, and since the central process of spiritual development is self-realization, its realization begins the realization of the Absolute.

We will explore in the next two chapters how some spiritual traditions view this process and how they go about accomplishing it.

chapter 43

The Stillpoint
in Christianity

•────────────────────────

T he Essential Identity is seen in Christianity as the inner spark,
the stillpoint of the soul, well-known from the writings of St.
Augustine, St. Thomas Aquinas, St. John of the Cross, and
others. We will explore the Christian perspective by discussing the
experience of a contemporary Christian contemplative, Bernadette
Roberts, who has written several books describing her inner journey
and her understanding of that journey, situating it within the larger
contemplative tradition in Christianity.

Roberts describes her realization of the Absolute, in *The Experience
of No-Self*, and presents a description of her process as an expression
of the Christian contemplative path, in *The Path to No-Self*. She
describes her process of transformation as consisting of six phases, the
six phases of the unitive life. For Roberts, the first phase marks the
entrance into the dark night of the spirit, "where we have no choice
but to go down into the depths of our nothingness where, at rock bottom, God eventually reveals Himself and discloses to us the rootedness of our existence in Him." (Roberts, 1985, pp. 9–10) It is clear here
that she had first to go through the nothingness of the familiar self, as
we have described in preceding chapters, and that going through this

nothingness does not lead to a new self-structure, but to rootedness 443
in a spiritual dimension. It is characteristic of Christian writers, and
all writers adhering to the theistic traditions, to conceptualize the arising of certain spiritual realities within them as an experience of God.
Roberts conceives of her essential connection as the rootedness of her
existence in God. It is significant that it is her "existence" that she recognizes as rooted in God, for essential presence is our true existence.
Roberts's perspective corresponds to our view that all aspects of Essence
are expressions of the Absolute Truth.

Roberts's experience becomes more relevant for our exploration
when she describes this experience of rootedness: "Thus having trav-
eled through the bottomless void of our being, we eventually come to
rest in a deep union with God—the abiding stillpoint at the center of
being." (Roberts, 1985, p. 10) In other words, the union with God is
the experience of the stillpoint, which she recognizes to be the center
of being. This means that the unitive life begins, for Roberts, with the
experience of this new spiritual center. It is important to see here that
this is the experience of Essence and not yet its realization. She is experiencing essential presence from the perspective of the first kind of experience of Essence, still dualistically according to our perspective. This is
clear in the following passage: "From here on, when looking deep into
the center of being, we no longer see a self but see God instead. . ."
(Roberts, 1985, p. 42) In other words, there is a subject looking at an
object, God, as the stillpoint.

This is even clearer in the next passage, where Roberts tries to establish that it is not true that our true self is God:

> The proof of this is that, despite seeing only God at the cen-
> ter, we nevertheless retain the feeling of selfhood, or 'I am,'
> because the eye looking inward—that which is aware of the
> unitive center—is the subjective, witnessing pole of self-
> consciousness. (Roberts, 1985, p. 43)

The sense of duality in experience is clear here, but it seems to us
that Roberts believes that the feeling of "I am" is coming from the subjective pole of the self. In our understanding, and assuming that by
"I am" she means both being and identity, this is not exact; what is

444   happening here is that she is beginning to recognize that the stillpoint is her essential self. The sense of "I am" is the recognition of the affect in the experience of the essential presence, as we saw in previous chapters and as we will also see in the writings of other authors. This is clear when she goes on to say: "Thus, although we no longer see self at the center, we still retain a feeling, or sense, of personal selfhood." (Roberts, 1985, p. 43) In our view, she is not discriminating exactly what is happening because of her doctrinal position that God and the self are not the same. We do not take the view that the individual self is God, but that the stillpoint, the God within, functions as the ontological ground, true center, and identity of the self. This again brings us to more agreement with Roberts, for she discovers this truth in the second phase of her process: "What I called 'myself' was the totality of being wherein God was the center." (Roberts, 1985, p. 71–72) It is also clear that here, her conception of the self is similar to ours, as the actual, total self.

These are subtle considerations, about which various traditional teachings are not in complete agreement. They become clearer as we go on. We have seen so far that when Roberts goes through the emptiness underlying the conventional experience of self, she arrives at a spiritual reality which is termed, in Christian writings, the *stillpoint*. She recognizes this point as the center of herself and as the union of self and God. This gives her a great experiential certitude which forms the backbone of her unitive life and what comes after it. Her experience unfolds in relation to this new center of self:

> From this point on, we have continuous access to this stillpoint of our existence to which all aspects of being must now conform, so that no movement of mind or emotion can rob us of its silence or move us from this center. (Roberts, 1985, p. 10)

Many processes ensue in relation to integrating her mind and life into this new center of life. She uses contemplation, service, and prayer. Describing this phase, she relates her experiences to well-known prayers in the Christian contemplative path: "Life at the bottom is much like the description of the prayer-of-quiet, which is said to be a state of interior silence in which the will is one with God." (Roberts, 1985, p. 32)

This continues until after the third phase, where she has an experience of disappearance of the inner God. This turns out not to be a loss, but a further transformation that reveals the inner center as more specifically the Essential Identity, the point of light:

> Whether from shock or disbelief, I watched this disappearance in complete stillness, without a single response. It was a long time before it dawned on me that God had not really disappeared, but instead had only gone underground, and remained as a pinpoint of light. (Roberts, 1985, p. 115)

It is interesting to point out that Roberts had no reaction to the disappearance of the inner God; then her insight arose, along with the appearance of the point. This corresponds to the understanding we presented in earlier chapters that for the Essential Identity to arise, one needs total openness and no reactivity. This experience develops Roberts's understanding of what her true self is and of what its relation is to God and Christ:

> After that, however, the point of light seemed to explode and become all of this human form but the external husk. I saw how God was indeed my very life and breath, and that Christ, as the true self, was the inner strength, the will-to-God, the essence of the new man. . . (Roberts, 1985, p. 116)

It becomes clear to her that her true self is the self whose life and breath is God. In our language, she discovered that her true self is the self that is filled with her true nature, the essential presence. This is what we call the soul, even though we recognize that the self is always the soul. This is because one recognizes the self as the soul only when one experiences it inseparable from its essence, the ontological presence. Then one recognizes the soul as a living presence. The point is the expression of the Absolute in the self, so it is the source of all essential qualities, like strength and will. As Roberts experienced it exploding, she had the experience of her self being filled with Essence, which she then recognized as the true self.

The view Roberts takes from this experience is that the soul is the Christ and the point of light is the Holy Spirit:

446   When the pinpoint of light, the Holy Spirit, exploded outward, Christ was revealed as the true subjective self, the vessel whose center was the Spirit, the Spirit which remained as the object of interior vision—Christ's own vision. (Roberts, 1985, p. 116)

We do not necessarily take such a view, partly because our language and conceptualizations are different from those of the Christian faith; we are also aware that not all Christians take this view. This remains, however, the perspective from which Roberts and others understand their experience as it relates to Christian metaphysics. What is important for our discussion here is that she recognizes that the point of light, the Essential Identity, is the center of the self. She also recognizes that both the soul and the point are manifestations of ultimate being.

> As the human manifestation of God, Christ is more subjective to us than the Holy Spirit, which has no human manifestation, and therefore remains as the objective stillpoint, or light at the center. Thus, despite their unity, Christ as the subjective vessel and the Spirit as its objective interior focal point are two different experiences of God. (Roberts, 1985, p. 116)[37]

Further experiences and processes take Roberts towards the realization of the Absolute, the "Father" in Christianity. She understands this happening through the death of the unitive self, the Christ contemplating the Holy Spirit, a death she relates to the Cross and the resurrection.

> As stated elsewhere, death of the unitive self is the death of both God and the self as reflective objects of consciousness, followed by the birth of God as pure subjectivity, God's own way of knowing all that exists—the Eye seeing itself. It is this transition between God-as-object and God-as-subject that takes place between Cross and Resurrection. (Roberts, 1985, p. 121)

Roberts's experience corresponds with our observations in several ways, for instance, the fact that the movement from one dimension of identity to another always begins with some kind of loss, a death of identity with the previous dimension. (See Book Three, Part II.) What is interesting for us is that the realization of the point, as the inner Holy Spirit, functions as the stepping stone for the realization of absolute nature:

> The mature unitive stage is a recapitulation of Christ's life, a 447
> life that lead to his death, an unusual death in that it was more
> than his physical dissolution; rather it was the type of death
> that led to the resurrection—the eternal vision beyond self.
> (Roberts, 1985, p. 120)

Roberts's experience of the nature of God is similar to our description of the Absolute: "God is not a looming power, but total, absolute silence." (Roberts, 1985, p. 193) What strikes her most is that in the realization of this dimension of Being, self-consciousness, or the self-reflective property of the self, is absent. We have described this phenomenon as part of the experience of the Absolute. Roberts refers to this as the experience of no-self; this experience of no-self turns out to be a nondual experience, which she conceptualizes as the unity of Christian Trinity:

> In this breakthrough, we also realize the Oneness of Christ,
> Father and Spirit, three distinct, non-interchangeable aspects
> of the Godhead. There are no such things as greater or lesser
> aspects of God; the three act as one, and to finally see how this
> works is what the no-self is all about. (Roberts, 1985, p. 195)

Roberts then reiterates how the unitive state leads into this realization: "The unitive state runs into the state of no-self; it is the means by which we come to it." (Roberts, 1985, p. 195) This corresponds to our understanding of how the soul's realization of the point becomes the entry into the boundless dimensions of being, culminating in nonduality.

chapter 44

The Atman
in Hinduism

●──

I t is interesting that the realization of the essential point as the center of the self prompts the unfoldment of Bernadette Roberts's experience to deeper dimensions, even though she never seems to understand its function as identity. Some Sufis take the point of light to be identity, when they say that the dhat (identity) is a star. The understanding of the Essential Identity as the inner identity, as the true experience of "I am," is more developed in some branches of Hinduism, where the point of light is recognized as the Atman, the essential self. Vedanta, a nondual teaching of Hinduism, employs methods of inquiry into the nature of the self. Asking oneself the question, "Who am I?" was the path of the great teacher Ramana Maharshi, who lived in India at the turn of the century. Some Vedantists regard the point of light as the essential "I am," the true and essential identity, and believe that its realization is the necessary step towards the realization of the Absolute, the Brahman. We see this very clearly in the work of the late Sri Nisargadatta Maharaj, one of the most well-known and respected contemporary teachers of Vedanta.

Sri Nisargadatta recognizes the point of light as the center of the self, the ground of the soul: "At the root of my being is pure awareness, a speck of intense light." (Nisargadatta, 1982, p. 180) He views it as the true and essential self, and understands its importance not only for self-realization, but as the essence of our humanity.

> That which makes you think you are human is not human. It is a dimensionless point of consciousness, a conscious nothing; all you can say about yourself is: 'I am.' You are pure being-awareness-bliss. To realize that is the end of seeking. You come to it when you see all you think yourself to be as mere imagination and stand aloof in pure awareness. . . (Nisargadatta, 1982, p. 316)

Nisargadatta's understanding of the point of light as Being is very precise and definite in this utterance, as is the observation that it is the true "I am," the essential self-recognition of Being. He is also very clear that the method of its realization is a matter of seeing through what we take ourselves to be, which we have been calling the self-representation. He refers to the point as a conscious nothing, seeing it as the witness, as we described in the experience of Mark in Chapter 35. He states this even more clearly:

> The witness is merely a point of awareness. It has no name and form. It is like the reflection of the sun in a drop of dew. The drop of dew has name and form, but the little point of light is caused by the sun. (Nisargadatta, 1982, p. 399)

This is a beautiful description of the relationship of the Essential Identity to the self and the Absolute. The drop of dew is the self, which has a name and form, while the sun is the Absolute, where the light is its awareness. The point is the reflection of the sun in the drop of dew; the Essential Identity is the manifestation of the Absolute in the individual soul.

The understanding that the point is the manifestation of the Absolute in the individual soul is nowhere clearer than in Nisargadatta's following statement: "You are always the supreme which appears at a given point of time and space as the witness, a bridge between the pure awareness of the Supreme and the manifold consciousness of the person." (Nisargadatta, 1982, p. 64) And: "Look within and you will find that the point of light is the reflection of the immensity of light in the

450 body, as the sense 'I am'. There is only light, all else appears." (*Ibid.*, p. 392–393). It is very clear in the following statement that by "the light," he means the Absolute, for he describes it in a similar way to how we understand it: "By itself the light can only be compared to a solid, dense, rocklike, homogeneous and changeless mass of pure awareness, free from the mental patterns of name and shape." (Nisargadatta, 1982, p. 34) (See *The Pearl Beyond Price*, p. 468 [Almaas, 1988].)

Nisargadatta understands the point to represent the Absolute in even more fundamental ways, by seeing it as the source of our experiences of the world:

> Know yourself as you are—a mere point in consciousness, dimensionless and timeless. You are like the point of the pencil—by mere contact with you the mind draws its picture of the world. You are single and simple—the picture is complex and extensive. Don't be misled by the picture—remain aware of the tiny point—which is everywhere in the picture. (Nisargadatta, 1982, pp. 451–452)

He describes the Essential Identity as simple and timeless, qualities we described in Chapter 35. He also sees that it is more fundamental than our picture of the world, what we have called the representational world.

Nisargadatta goes further, asserting that Essential Identity is the source of the universe, and not only our picture of it, again because the Absolute is the source of everything:

> As the tiny point of a pencil can draw innumerable pictures, so does the dimensionless point of awareness draw the contents of the vast universe. Find that point and be free. (Nisargadatta, 1982, p. 389)[38]

The understanding of the indestructibility and invulnerability of the point is clear in the following:

> When you realize yourself as less than a point in space and time, something too small to be cut and too short-lived to be killed, then, and then only, all fear goes. When you are smaller than the point of the needle, then the needle cannot pierce you—you pierce the needle! (Nisargadatta, 1982, p. 466)

Nisargadatta appreciated the importance of the point for liberation, as is clear in the following statement, in which he discusses the role of awareness and of God: "Yet all this is secondary to the tiny little thing which is the 'I am'. . . . False ideas about this 'I am' lead to bondage, right knowledge leads to freedom and happiness." (Nisargadatta, 1982, p. 62) He regards the realization of the point as the way to realize the Absolute, as the stepping stone towards ultimate realization.

> The sense 'I am' is the manifestation of a deeper cause, which you may call self, God, Reality or by any other name. The 'I am' is in the world; but it is the key which can open the door out of the world. (Nisargadatta, 1982, p. 199)

And again:

> Go deep into the sense of 'I am' and you will find. . . . Ask yourself whence it comes, or just watch it quietly. When the mind stays in the 'I am', without moving, you enter a state which cannot be verbalized but can be experienced. (Nisargadatta, 1982, p. 2)

In the following statement, Nisargadatta describes his experience of going from a manifestation of the self as anger, to the point of consciousness, to the Absolute silence:

> I may be furious, pacing the room up and down; at the same time I know what I am, a centre of wisdom and love, an atom of pure existence. All subsides and mind merges into silence. (Nisargadatta, 1982, p. 88)

We can find more detailed and technical knowledge about the Essential Identity in some of the Hindu yogas. An example is raja yoga, as taught by Swami Saraswati, and described in his book, *Science of the Soul*. Referring to the Essential Identity as the soul, he writes:

> The abode of the conscious Atman [soul] is this body made up of material elements, and is likened to a castle. There are three parts of this castle: the physical body, the astral body, and the causal body. (Saraswati, 1987, p. 11)

The self in this yoga is seen as composed of three bodies: the physical, which includes two sheaths—the body and the energetic-emotional

452   dimension; the astral, which includes two sheaths—the mind and intellect; and the causal, the bliss sheath that has several levels. The practice is to train and refine the awareness until it is able to penetrate to the Atman at the center of the bliss sheath, whose location is the physical heart. The yoga consists of four limbs: restraints, observances, postures, and breath control. These prepare the aspirant for the deeper limbs of the practice of yoga, which consist of training in concentration and contemplation, culminating in absorption or *samadhi*. There are kinds and levels of samadhi, but the idea is to attain one-pointedness that is free from the conceptual mind, that can penetrate to the depths of the self.

The Atman, referred to in this text mostly as the *jivatman*,[39] the individual true self (to differentiate it from the universal self), is understood as giving life and consciousness to the totality of the self in its five sheaths:

> This conscious being, though itself very small, of the size of an atom, yet gives life to the five sheaths and sustains the three bodies. It is as if a stream of water gushes from the centre of a lake and sends its waves to the banks. (Saraswati, 1987, p. 224)

The jivatman is conceived of as residing in the very consciousness-stuff (chitta) of the self, the medium of living presence constituting the nature of the soul. The chitta is located in the region of the heart at the center of the chest.

> It sustains Jivatman as well as all the Samskara-s, Vasana-s and Smriti [memory] in an unmanifest or seed form. Because of its contact with Atman it has special luminosity and is very active; it appears to be ever conscious. . . . It is the revealer of the nature of Jivatman. (Saraswati, 1987, p. 109)

Even though it is a luminous consciousness, the chitta becomes patterned by the entitihood of the ego, just as we have described the structuring of the soul by the self-representation:

> This small Chitta becomes so luminous, so bright due to luminosity of Atman, and becomes so coloured by the idea of ego, that although it is not impossible, it is certainly difficult to separate—to pick out the minute subtle Atman—in this ego-coloured luminous Chitta. (Saraswati, 1987, p. 126)

The idea here is that in the advanced stages of yoga, the aspirant penetrates to the luminous chitta, but it is still difficult to discriminate the Atman that resides in it because of its coloration with the ego principle. It is necessary to discriminate the Essential Identity from essential presence in general.

Through the development of the discriminating consciousness to the essential level, one becomes able to discriminate the Atman in the chitta: "Then, in the gentle light of Sattwa, there shines Viveka Jnana or discriminative knowledge which shows the difference between Chitta and Atman." (Saraswati, 1987, p. 239) The Atman is recognized as a point of light and consciousness, as the Essential Identity:

> From the point of view of size in this creation, the orb of Atman, the soul, is smaller than an atom, and from the point of view of subtlety it is similar to Brahman. . . . This Jivatman or individual soul exists in the form of an extremely subtle point or dot. (Saraswati, 1987, p. 208)

And in another passage: "In the innermost centre of the orb of Chitta exists Atman, the self, like a living spark, radiant and beautiful." (Saraswati, 1987, p. 221)

The discrimination of the jivatman from the chitta becomes a matter of understanding the "I am" precisely and completely. The sense of self in the "I am" disappears; there remain no concepts, not even the concept of "I" or "am." This is similar to our description in Chapter 35, where we saw the need to be without any concept, without any self-reflection. This is the self-realization of the Essential Identity where one simply is, without knowing what one is. In this yoga, Saraswati understands this state as that of experiencing the Atman without the ego principle. In other words, the sense of "I am" that one has in the experience of the Atman, is due partly to the ego principle. One experiences the Atman as brilliant white when it is still nondifferentiated from the chitta, but as it becomes discriminated it loses its "I-am-ness" and attains its subtlest form.

Saraswati writes, after describing the process of purification of the chitta, developing it to its sattvic (clear light) nature:

> Having gone beyond this, one sees a tranquil ocean of pure white luminous light resembling a crystal. This is the expansive

454   nature of Chitta, the mind-stuff, and at this time there is no
wave or agitation in the Chitta. Then one realizes the subtlest
Jivatman, the individual soul, which is incomparable. In the
transparent tranquil lake of the Chitta in its Sattwik state,
Jivatman, described as the subtlest of the subtle, is seen.
(Saraswati, 1987, p. 223)

Using our language, the soul needs to be purified to total transparency, until it becomes clear and lucid. This, of course, necessitates
the penetration and clarification of all obscurations of the soul, whether
of psychodynamic, structural, or phenomenological origin.

This reveals the Atman in its purity, as a diamond-like spark, rather
than a shining spark:

This luminous, gentle, diamond-like spark of the soul is
enveloped by the apparel of Chitta which is snowy-white and
radiantly luminous. Jivatman that shines like a spark is still
seen as not different from Chitta, being wrapped up by a part
of the Chitta. (Saraswati, 1987, p. 223)

This clarifies a particular aspect of our understanding regarding the
realization of Essential Identity. The realization of any essential aspect
beyond mind and concepts means the objective understanding of this
aspect of Essence. To be objective about it means to see it from its own
perspective, independent from mind. This objectivity always reveals
the aspect in a diamond-like form, giving the experience clarity, precision, and sharpness.

When we become objective about the Essential Identity, the point
of light, when we recognize it just as it is, it appears as a diamond point.
This is an amazing perception, unexpected and unimaginable in the
conventional dimension of experience. We behold the Essential Identity
as a faceted point of light. There is then a certainty about our identity,
without this having anything to do with a conceptual or self-reflective
knowledge. This objectivity, however, is not related to the color the
point manifests itself in. Saraswati seems to think that only the colorless diamond point is the pure Atman. In our understanding, what
makes our experience of the point objective is its diamondness, its
facetedness, and sharpness.

The diamond point may appear in any color, each representing a par-   455
ticular essential quality, each appearing for certain situations and functions; each is an objective perception of the point. One way the
diamond point manifests is as the clear quality. It is then just as
Saraswati describes it, a diamond point of transparent, clear light.

APPENDICES

C.G. Jung
and the Spiritual
Dimension of Self

———————————————————————— •

Jung was one of the first Western depth psychologists, and the first psychoanalyst, to appreciate the spiritual dimension of the self and to construct his psychology to include it. Our view of the self is similar to Jung's, yet we look at the self from a different angle, with a very different emphasis. This creates significant differences in psychology, methodology, and orientation. His view of the self is that it is an archetype:

> the archetype of wholeness and the regulating center of the personality. It is experienced as a transpersonal power which transcends the ego, e,g., God. (Schwartz-Salant, 1982, p. 181)

This definition says something useful about the self, particularly with respect to the understanding of the self as a wholeness which is related to the regulation of the personality. However, the concept of archetype is oriented towards a level of abstraction and imagery, and hence the products of the various levels of the imaginative capacity, that our approach does not emphasize. This is due to Jung's conception of the self as an archetype, where archetypes are:

460   irrepresentable in themselves, but their effects appear in consciousness as the archetypal images and ideas. These are universal patterns or motifs which come from the collective unconscious and are the basic content of religions, mythologies, legends, and fairy tales. They emerge in individuals through dreams and visions. (Schwartz-Salant, 1982, p. 180)

This perspective orients research and experience towards archetypal images and ideas, as they appear in dreams and visions. In contrast, our approach emphasizes the actual phenomenology of experience, and we take the perspective that emphasis on images and dreams, legends and mythologies, will tend to keep the investigation on a more conceptual level. Our approach is guided by the understanding that, although the spiritual dimension of the self transcends all products of the psyche, it can still be experienced directly and concretely. When it is directly apprehended, it is recognized as an ontological reality, the most important element of which is its phenomenology, that is, the quality of its actual perceived existence.

For example, when a student perceives the image of a rose in the heart, our focus is not as much on what the rose symbolizes, but on the actual feel and sensation of the rose. The experienced texture of the rose, the color and its brilliance or depth, the scent (if it is available to perception), the taste, and so on, give us much more information than the symbolism. This phenomenological exploration keeps us in touch with the actual lived experience, while looking for symbolism and meanings tends to take us away from it. Our interest is in the very consciousness that is the fabric and substance of the rose, of which the rose is only an incidental—although certainly meaningful—form.

The question of symbols and their place and function in our inner life is a deep one, but here it is sufficient to say that our perspective does not rely to any appreciable degree on the use of symbolism. One may look at symbols differently from the conventional sense, and one may view the appearance of things as pointing to something deeper when this appearance is experienced in a vibrant and living way. In this case, the symbol is not standing for something else, but is revealing a deeper reality. An example is experiencing an unusually beautiful and alive woman, where we feel and see that she reveals and brings out, in

some very real way, the beauty of existence. We can say she is a sym-   461
bol of the beauty inherent in reality, meaning that she embodies this
beauty and reveals it in such an obvious and striking manner that we
cannot help but see and appreciate not only her beauty, but all beauty.

This understanding of symbolism is part of some traditional spiritual systems, like the Tibetan or the Sufi. The Sufi tradition follows the
Islamic view, as spelled out in the Quran, which understands everything in existence to be an *a'ya* or sign, a symbol of God, in the sense
we are discussing. In other words, every manifestation points beyond
itself, to its creator and source. To actually see in this way requires a
refined and highly developed perception, in which one can actually see
and feel how they are actually external appearances of a deeper mystery, which they not only hide but also reveal.

We may find this understanding of symbolism in some of Jung's
work, or the work of some of his followers. Nevertheless, it is not the
most widely accepted understanding in the writings of Jung and his
followers. This is why we differentiate our work from Jung's, based on
this different emphasis on symbols.

There are other elements that differentiate our work from Jung's.
Although Jung seems to address the same self that we are studying, he
addresses it in a way that leads to other areas of investigation than
those we are interested in. His approach makes it seem as if one cannot know the wholeness of the self directly, and that one cannot experience its spiritual essence in an immediate way, or that one cannot know
its ultimate meaning. He writes:

> It is easy enough to say 'self,' but exactly what have we said?
> That remains shrouded in 'metaphysical' darkness. I may
> define "self" as the totality of the conscious and unconscious
> psyche, but this totality transcends our vision; it is a veritable
> *lapis invisibilitatis.* Insofar as the unconscious exists it is not
> definable; its existence is a mere postulate and nothing what-
> ever can be predicted as to its possible contents. The totality
> can only be experienced in its parts and then only insofar as
> these are contents of consciousness. . . . All that can be ascer-
> tained at present about the symbolism [of the self] is that it
> portrays an autonomous psychic fact, characterized by a

462   phenomenology which is always repeating itself and is everywhere the same. It seems to be a sort of atomic nucleus about
whose innermost structure and ultimate meaning we know
nothing. (C. Jung, 1953–1979, pars. 247, 249)

There is much in this passage that corresponds to our view of the self,
and much that does not. The reader will have a good idea about these
as we proceed with presenting our understanding of the self. The above
passage postulates the self to be primarily of a psychic nature, and not
of a spiritual nature, because spiritual nature is basically an ontological and phenomenological reality, the realization of which reveals the
usual experience of the psyche to be fundamentally delusional.

If our comments here do not give Jung's work its rightful due, that
is partially a reflection of our limited familiarity with it. Some of his
followers might have different understandings, and there are probably various developments from his work that might be more in harmony with our approach. This is also the place for us to state the reasons
behind the fact that we have not utilized Jung's contributions given the
fact that we share with him the appreciation of the spiritual dimension of the self. It is actually this commonality between us that primarily
mitigates against us using his work more in our perspective. He has
his own original view of the spiritual dimension, with its own unavoidable idiosyncrasies, and this view entails a wealth of concepts regarding the common psychic experience of the self. This creates a whole
metaphysical and metapsychological system, a particular logos. Our
perspective—or logos—of the spiritual dimension is also an original
one, but quite different from that of Jung. Jung's conceptualizations
are inappropriate for our approach to the spiritual work of self-
realization, except perhaps peripherally. Our understanding of spiritual experience is different from his, at least in terms of emphasis.

It is significant also to realize that Jung was primarily a psychologist, and his work was primarily to create a psychology. Even though
his psychology appreciates the spiritual dimension, it is still primarily a psychology. This differentiates it from a view that is primarily
spiritual, where the direct spiritual experience and the spiritual realization function as the ground from which a psychology emerges.
Our approach is primarily spiritual, and our interest is centrally in

self-realization; hence, we use psychological knowledge only because   463
it is useful in our work.

We also do not agree with many of Jung's ideas, particularly with respect to their accuracy regarding actual spiritual experience. His concept of the self and his perspective on spiritual realization have already been criticized by the proponents of some traditional spiritual teachings. But this is not the main reason we do not use his work. Regardless of its correctness, objectivity, or completeness, the important factor is that his work is based on a different view of the spiritual dimension and its relation to the everyday experience of self than our work is.

Thus, rather than trying to square our understanding with Jung's, we have come to use psychological knowledge that is available in other schools of depth psychology which do not include the spiritual dimension. In this way, we can remain with the purity of our understanding and experience of the spiritual dimension and create concepts that connect them to the psychological knowledge that are appropriate to such understanding and experience. So we use the findings of Freudian psychoanalysis, ego psychology, object relations theory, and self psychology, amongst others, integrated with our view of spiritual development. At the same time, we appreciate Jung's work as more complete than the Freudian perspective, primarily because it integrates the spiritual dimension.

Our discussion of this discrimination in perspective does not reflect an intended creation of a new understanding. Our view, understanding, and experience developed in a natural way, spontaneously integrating the psychological knowledge we found useful, without making conscious differentiations between Jung's work and that of the other, more Freudian, schools of depth psychology. The notion of archetypes, and Jung's general approach, simply did not seem helpful for our spiritual experience as it was unfolding. His analogical, symbological, and mythological approach does not correspond to the kind of phenomenological precision and immediacy our experience and understanding demanded. His approach is primarily symbological, and ours mostly phenomenological. This does not indicate that we believe his approach is invalid, or that we have no appreciation for his work.

464   Our work includes the concept of structures of essential reality, which can easily be confused with Jung's archetypes. This confusion leads to significant misunderstandings; thus, arises our effort to clarify the question of our understanding relative to Jung's.

appendix B

The Ultimate
Nature of Self
in Spiritual Traditions

M ost schools of philosophy and spiritual teachings share our understanding that the fundamental dimension of the self, its ultimate nature, is Being. There are subtle differences between the various teachings regarding how Being is conceived of and how it is described. Many traditions conceive of Being as ontological or nonconceptual presence. But some schools, such as the Hindu tradition, conceive of true nature as pure consciousness. There is actually no difficulty between this view and that of presence because presence is the essence of pure consciousness; expressed in a different way, when consciousness is experienced in its purity, it is experienced as presence, the ontological and phenomenological reality of consciousness.

Some schools say that spiritual Essence is some kind of light. This again does not create any difficulty with the view of presence. Presence is nothing but the presence of spiritual light; spiritual light can be experienced as a fundamental reality, which has an ontological property. The ontological property of spiritual light is presence, where light and presence are not two separate things. By spiritual light, we do not mean the common experience of seeing light in one's psyche. The spiritual light we are referring to is the fundamental light of consciousness and awareness.

466   Some will leave the spiritual Essence undefined and merely refer to it as spirit. An example of leaving the ultimate truth undefined is that of the teaching of Kabala, in the concept of Ain or Nothing:

> The value of AIN is that of the Middle Pillar, or the exact Nil-point between extremities of polarities. It is the absolute Stillness in the midst of motion, the never encompassing Ever. It is the essence of God. We are only playing with words in attempting to describe the indescribable. (Gray, 1968, p. 225)

But how is spirit experienced? It is ultimately presence. What about the traditions that say that spirit is love? The same is true: love is experienced as presence. Spiritual love is definitely not an emotion.

Most levels and schools of Buddhism believe the ultimate nature of the self is emptiness. The matter becomes more subtle here because emptiness or void seems to be the opposite of presence. Our concept of presence corresponds with the Buddhist concept of Buddha nature (Tathagatagarbha), which is conceived of as the ultimate nature of the self and everything else. There are subtle differences between the various Buddhist schools in terms of what exactly is the Tathagatagarbha, but it is generally conceived of as a nonconceptual wisdom mind; a consciousness of pure truth not dependent on any conceptual elaboration.

> All the teachings of Mahamudra and Maha Ati and the whole of the Tantra are about this non-conceptual Wisdom Mind and the means of realizing it. . . . It is also called the non-dual Wisdom Mind (Jnana), Clear Light (prabhasavare) Nature of Mind and Dhatu (spacious expanse or element). Elsewhere it is called Dhatu and awareness inseparable, clarity and emptiness inseparable, bliss and emptiness inseparable. It is also called the Kharmata and the Tathagatagarbha. (Tsultrim Gyamtso Rimpoche, 1986, pp. 76–78)

Some Buddhist teachings, such as Mahamudra, view Buddha nature as the unity of clear light and emptiness, so it is asserted that:

> when the mind is in tranquil equipoise, there emerges a union of awareness and void that is vivid, transparent, and unblem-

ished. This is the nonconceptual awareness of intrinsic real- 467
ity. (Takpo Tashi Namgyal, 1986, p. 78)

But this again will be the experience of presence, in a very subtle and deep dimension of its realization, because it is thought of as something that truly exists. "It can be said to be the only thing that has absolute and true existence." (Takpo Tashi Namgyal, 1986, p. 76) Other teachings, like Dzogchen, think of the ultimate nature to be directly presence, whose essence is emptiness.

The following verse from Padmasambhava, one of the first principal teachers of Dzogchen, shows that emptiness is inseparable from clarity, and this inseparability, intrinsic awareness, is presence:

> This intrinsic awareness is free of the eight extremes, such as
>   eternalism and nihilism, and the rest.
> Thus we speak of the Middle Way where one does not fall
>   into any of the extremes,
> And we speak of intrinsic awareness as uninterrupted mind-
>   ful presence.
> Since emptiness possesses a heart that is intrinsic awareness,
> Therefore it is called by the name of Tathagatagarbha, that
>   is, 'the embryo or heart of Buddhahood.'
> (Reynolds, 1989, p. 21)

This is the same as the truth of Mahamudra and the other Tathagatagarbha schools. It is what we call primordial or quintessential presence.

Presence can be experienced on many levels of subtlety and refinement. It can be experienced as the presence of light, the presence of consciousness, the presence of awareness, the presence of love, the presence of clear light, or the presence that is the nonduality (coemergence) of consciousness (or light) and emptiness. Even emptiness, as conceived of by the Theravada and some of the Mahayana schools of Buddhism, can actually be experienced as presence. But then we move into very subtle domains of discrimination, where emptiness is described as neither being nor nonbeing.

That presence and emptiness form a unity, besides being opposites, was also recognized by some of the Western philosophers, as in the case of Hegel:

468   Nothing, if it is thus immediate and equal to itself, is also conversely the same as Being is. The truth of Being and of Nothing
is accordingly the unity of the two: and this unity is Becoming.
(Weiss, 1974, p. 119)

We hope that this note will suffice to clarify our view that the experience of the spiritual and true essence, and the nature of the self, is
presence.

Levels of Conceptualization

————————————————————— •

Does spiritual experience lend itself to precise discrimination?

It is our understanding that experiential, or experience-near, concepts can arise directly from the immediate perception of the phenomenological characteristics of the actual, present-centered manifestations of the self. Discrimination within many different categories of experience is a capacity that everyone possesses and a skill that can be developed. Those who have not developed discrimination in a given area might either view those who do as having mysterious or magical capacities, or might dismiss the discriminations as invalid. Discrimination of subtle psychological and spiritual experience is, of course, often subject to the latter response.

However, we can identify many areas in which certain people have developed precise discriminating abilities that seem impossible to those who lack them. On a physiological level, a person who is diabetic can learn to discriminate the subtle subjective effects of differing levels of blood sugar, so that he knows with some precision when he needs to eat or to take an insulin shot. The athlete knows when his body is "on" for a certain challenge. Anyone can learn to become very precise about what

470   emotions he is experiencing. People with dangerous physical tasks learn to monitor their alertness. An artist or a musician learns to discriminate very well the internal states necessary to create or perform certain things; these states may not be comprehensible to an outsider, but people within the same field develop whole structures of concepts to describe these very precise, subtle internal states involved in certain activities and states of being. Another example is the discourse within any religion. The Christian contemplative can describe many different internal states relating to prayer, the "distance" between the self and God, and many degrees of being open or closed to certain kinds of experience. The Sufis discriminate hundreds of different possible states of internal experience, associating them with stages of the path of transformation.

    Clearly, the capacity for discrimination can operate in all dimensions of experience, including those usually relegated to the "spiritual." This is contrary to the view that spiritual experience is incapable of precise discrimination.[1] *The capacity of the self for discrimination originates from the dimension of full self-realization.* The experience of primordial presence, the primary experiential element in full self-realization, is not an experience of something vague or unrecognizable. When a person has any deep spiritual experience for the first time, it is not uncommon to experience a sense of vagueness, a lack of recognition, and the sense that one can't label or communicate the experience. This condition is transitory; it reflects both unfamiliarity with the new experience, and the incompleteness of the realization. The full realization integrates all dimensions, as we have already described, including one's thoughts and emotions. In this state, the consciousness is operating simultaneously on the nonconceptual and conceptual dimensions, except that the latter is not the familiar conceptual world.[2] It is rather a dimension of experience that is intrinsically discriminated, a clear and sharp discrimination of the phenomenological characteristics of experience, as the precise and crystal clear delineation—in the felt experience—of patterns, qualities, colors, and meanings. This clearly perceived discriminated pattern of experience arises in coemergence with a nonconceptual dimension of pure presence. This experience of self-realization is more complete than the experience of nonconceptual consciousness alone.

This understanding is expressed in the advanced stages of realization in Buddhism. This tradition describes the experience of self-realization as the coemergence of awareness and appearance, where awareness is the nonconceptual consciousness or presence, and appearance is the fully and clearly discriminated patterns in perception, of all content of experience. "The term 'coemergence' means the spontaneous coexistence—from the very beginning—of the characteristics of things or phenomena and their intrinsic reality or inherent emptiness, as you could say that rock sugar and its sweetness coexist, or fire and its heat coexist." (Takpo Tashi Namgyal, 1986, p. 223) (In Mahamudra, emptiness is seen as inseparable from awareness.)

In Tibetan Buddhism, this crystal clear discrimination in the experience of full self-realization is called the wisdom of discrimination, one of the five primary wisdoms (awarenesses) of the Buddha, the enlightened manifestation of "amitabha dhyani Buddha."[3] This dimension of discrimination is not the operation of the personal mind, which cannot be free from its concepts, contaminated by the misunderstanding, obscurations, associations, and prejudices stemming from a personal history whose conditioning and emotional reactions determine perception. The spiritual dimension of discriminating wisdom is the direct perception of the self-existing and real discrimination in the actual premises of experience. It is free from the influences of the past, uncreated by the individual mind. The discrimination is not of abstract ideas, like the ideas of democracy or achievement, but of the concrete givens of experience. It is like the perception of the wetness of water. We can experience the wetness, know precisely what it feels like, although we might not conceptualize it with a word. The quality of wetness exists in perception, whether we have a mental concept of it or not. This is clearly the case in infancy, before the development of conceptualization. To stay with this example, the discriminating perception of wetness does not disappear in self-realization; in fact, we experience it with a much greater vividness and precision than in the conventional dimension of experience, because of the complete intimacy and immediacy of the nondual consciousness. We can then give such discriminated perception a label, like "wetness" or any other word, and this label refers to an experiential or experience-near concept. It

472   is the same with water itself, which is not a concept constructed by mind, but something that exists independent of our minds, already present and ready to be isolated by mind, although the word itself exists only in our minds and our speech. In this book, we will call such a perceived discriminated reality, like wetness or water, a "universal concept."

This dimension of discrimination, the precise discrimination of the ontological pattern in perception, is what has been referred to as the "nous" or "first intellect" in Neoplatonic and Hellenic philosophies, the "logos" in some schools of Christian theology, and "the total or universal intellect" in Sufi ontology, as we see clearly in the following passage that describes such fundamental discrimination as theophany, according to the Sufi school of Ibn Arabi:

> Without confusing the theophanism of Ibn 'Arabi and the emanationism of the Neoplatonists, we may say that the figure which corresponds to the Nous of the Neoplatonists (First Intelligence, supreme Spirit, Muhammadic Spirit, Archangel Gabriel) presents the precise structure which determines the theophanic precedence of the Feminine. (Corbin, 1977, p. 340)[4]

In this dimension, we not only perceive discriminated phenomena, we recognize them. This is well known in neoplatonism, in Plotinus's concept of "nous," the higher mind or intellectual principle, where knowledge and being are identical:

> Hence we may conclude that, in the Intellectual Principle itself, there is complete identity of Knower and Known, and this not by way of domiciliation, as in the case of even the highest soul, but by Essence, by the fact that there, no distinction exists between Being and Knowing. (Plotinus, 1991, p. 241)

For example, we might not only experience crystal clear transparency in our consciousness, but also recognize it as clarity. The recognition and the experience are almost the same thing. The recognition of clarity is prior to the word of clarity, which encapsulates the concept of clarity. A baby knows that he is hungry before he learns the word and discriminates the concept of hunger. He will know that he needs food, just like the individual who is in the experience of self-realization knows that his perception is now more precise and penetrating than usual.

This discriminated and discriminating property of the essential dimension, and of the essence of the self, makes it possible for us to recognize the many forms in which presence manifests. This capacity is a reflection of the wisdom of discrimination, of the nous dimension of presence. Our understanding is that the capacity of discrimination exists fundamentally on the ontological dimension of presence, and it remains the same property or capacity in other dimensions, but we do not see its reality because we have lost contact with presence.

In the experience of self-realization, this property gives the self a capacity for discrimination of such precision and sharpness that is inconceivable in the conventional dimension of experience.[5] This element of the essential dimension contributes to its aesthetic quality, the beauty and indescribable majesty of essential manifestations. The view of the structures of manifestation in all its dimensions, perceived through all the modalities of perception, is breathtaking.

How close to immediate experience can we make our conceptualizations?

Because of the complete immediacy and intimacy of the state of self-realization, discrimination in the dimension of presence is totally experiential. This intrinsic discrimination can become the source of experience-near concepts. It is the absolute limit on the conceptualization as experience-near.

The closer our experience is to the dimension of primordial presence, the more experience-near is it possible for one's conceptualization to be. This gives the already useful psychoanalytic concept, "experience-near," an unexpected precision that helps us understand and appreciate how far from experience-near are the concepts that dominate conventional experience. The precision of discriminating wisdom also makes possible a continuous range of experience-near conceptualizations, and provides a general way of assessing the degree of nearness. So experience-nearness of our conceptualizations of the self, and its manifestations, depends on how near to the inner core of essential presence is our felt experience.

474   The nearness to experience is determined not only by the distance of abstraction from the lived experience, as the concept is ordinarily understood in psychoanalytic thinking, but also by the distance of the experience from the primordial presence. This is because experience is relatively abstract on all dimensions of experience except for that of primordial presence, since these dimensions are characterized by the lack of complete immediacy in the experience as a result of the intervening veil of mental concepts.

This is a significant issue for understanding the status of any knowledge, but it is useful specifically for our present study of self-realization and narcissism, since narcissism itself is due to the distance of our experience of ourselves from fundamental ontological presence. This returns us to our earlier observation of the impoverishing effect of the lack of appreciation of the deeper spiritual dimensions of the self on the prevailing psychological theories of narcissism. Putting this simply, our conceptualizations of the self, and of its manifestations and difficulties, are bound to be limited by the limitations of our experience of the self.

Essence and Narcissistic Libido

———————————————— •

We find slight differences between the various psychoanalytic researchers' definitions of narcissism. There is general agreement that "healthy narcissism" is a matter of the cathexis (energetic investment) of the self-representation, but the various theorists disagree on the kind of energy involved in this cathexis or investment. This disparity in definition seems to reflect the divergence of various authors' areas of focus in terms of narcissistic characteristics and manifestations. The classic definition, developed from Freud's original writings about narcissism, is that this energy is what Freud termed libido, an energetic term with instinctual and primarily sexual connotations—hence the definition of narcissism as the libidinal investment of the self (self-representation).

Kohut believed that the energetic charge in this cathexis is not the libido of Freud, but a specific energetic quality specific to narcissism, which he termed narcissistic libido. He believed that an important difference between his conception of narcissism and that of the ego psychological (classical) view relates to the quality of charge in the cathexis:

> Narcissism, within my general outlook, is defined not by the target of the instinctual investment (i.e., whether it is the

476   subject himself or other people) but by the nature or quality of the instinctual charge. (Kohut, 1971, p. 26)

The difference Kohut is pointing out, which is a significant one, is that investment of the self with erotic (sexual) libido means one will be in love with oneself, which refers to the original definition of Freud. Freud adopted it from Havelock Ellis, who was investigating some sexual aberrations that involved being in love with one's own body. This is the popular understanding of narcissism, which does reflect some of its characteristics.

Kohut's view focuses on different characteristics of narcissism, which have to do with a specific relationship to whatever object (selfobject) is narcissistically cathected, but where the in-love quality is only one aspect of this relationship. The main quality of this relationship, determined by narcissistic libido, is that the individual expects to have a certain kind of access to, and control over, the narcissistically cathected object.

The expected control over such others (self-object) is then closer to the concept of the control which a grownup expects to have over his own body and mind than to the concept of the control which he expects to have over others. (Kohut, 1971, pp. 26–27)

Kohut's focus clarifies the specific narcissistic need of the individual to experience the narcissistically cathected object as behaving according to how he exactly wants him to; that is, the object is important primarily to serve the individual's self. This is why Kohut refers to the narcissistically cathected object as a "selfobject."

Applying this definition of narcissistic investment to the cathexis of the self-representation, then, implies that healthy development of narcissism is equivalent to a firmly established self-concept. This is an important point, because a healthy, normal individual feels secure in her sense of self and identity, while the more narcissistically disturbed is the individual, the more insecure she is about her sense of self and identity. When this view of narcissistic investment is applied to the cathexis of other people, we start appreciating the quality of the individual's narcissistic need for their support. She needs them basically to support and shore up her sense of self and identity.

In other words, the classic definition of narcissism emphasizes the self reference involved in one's narcissism, while Kohut's view of narcissistic libido expresses the narcissistic need underlying this self reference, in other words, one's deep need for the structure of the self-concept and the psychic structures that support it.

Gertrude and Rubin Blanck, on the other hand, emphasize a different area of narcissism with respect to the quality of charge involved in narcissism. They focus on the form of narcissism we have termed "individuation narcissism," using primarily Mahler's theory of separation-individuation in formulating their understanding of normal and pathological narcissism. They see narcissism as a component of ego development, which goes through its own vicissitudes as the sense of being an individual self is established through the stages of separation-individuation. They speak of "narcissism as positive cathexis of whole and relatively stable self representations" (G. and R. Blanck, 1974b, p. 58), which corresponds to the general psychoanalytic definition. However, their view of this cathexis is different; they do not see it as instinctual, but emphasize that it is an affective investment, meaning it has to do with a feeling tone about oneself. They write:

> Mahler describes sound secondary narcissism as the result of acquisition of healthy self regard. This does not represent libidinal self connection, but rather an affective state in which the self representations are cathected with value. (G. and R. Blanck, 1974b, p. 55)

The Blancks emphasize the fact that narcissism is closely allied to self-esteem and its regulation. For them, normal development of narcissism not only involves the firm cathexis of the self-representation, but also, "with this development, a sense of enduring self-esteem comes into being." (G. and R. Blanck, 1974b, p. 58) In other words, the narcissistically normal or "healthy" individual has a stable sense of valuing himself. And since the Blancks view this development as an important part of the development of the ego through the separation-individuation process, they consider the adequate fulfillment of the child's needs in the various subphases of this process as a primary requirement for it (for development of a self-concept accompanied with value). As the self grows, to accomplish its developmental purpose (i.e., to be an

478   individual with a sense of identity through the process of separation-individuation), the child's needs change from one subphase to another, depending on the particular characteristics of each subphase. For instance, the child needs to be almost completely dependent on the mother in the symbiotic phase, but needs her to support him to be more separate from her in the differentiation subphase, and to delight in his explorations and discovery in the practicing period.

> The very experience of adequacy, that is, optimal fulfillment of the developmental purpose, adds to the sense of self-valuation. But the affective experiences which accompany the main developmental purpose contribute significantly to accumulation of self-esteem or to pathological narcissistic formation. (G. and R. Blanck, 1974b, p. 59)

In our perspective, these differences in the views of cathexis amongst the various authors are not significant; rather, they are useful for clarifying different aspects of narcissism.

Part of the reason for the divergence of various authors' views of narcissistic cathexis, and the sense that they have fundamental differences, is that the concept of cathexis is not precise. It is an experience-distant concept, and it is not clear to what experiential categories it refers.

In our understanding, when used to define narcissism, the term *cathexis* refers to the fact that one experiences one's self-concept as inseparable from oneself. It highlights the intimate integration of this self-concept. It becomes easier to understand if we think of it in relation to the integration of the sense of identity. Cathexis, then, means the integration of one's identity. We term this integration, in our work, self-realization. In other words, the "cathexis of the self" is a psychoanalytic concept that approximates our concept of the "realization of the self." Our view includes a detailed understanding of what is required for the attainment or development of self-realization. Self-realization requires the establishment of inner support, which manifests as a specific dimension of Essence, the Diamond Will, which is constituted of many qualities of presence. These qualities are related to the aspects of Love, Value, Strength, and so on. The Essential Identity needs to be supported with the presence of Love, Value, Strength, and so on, for it to be integrated. In psychoanalytic language, the self needs to be supported in order to become firmly established; this support manifests as different forms of cathexis of the self. From this perspective, Kohut's emphasis reflects his focus on the general need for support; the classical (Freudian) emphasis reflects the focus on the specific need for Love as support for the self; the Blancks' emphasis reflects the focus on the specific need for Value as support for the self. This is a simplification of our view, which includes a detailed knowledge of the narcissistic need for support and the spectrum of qualities needed for supporting the self in its self-realization. Other qualities needed for support are, for example, Nourishment, Kindness, Intelligence, Integration, and Will. However, Value (related to self-esteem) and Love (related to libido) are the most obviously dominant and prevalent ones.

The Bipolar Self
and Ego Structure

●————————————————————————————

I t is not clear from Kohut's writings whether he views the bipolar
self as a representation or not, but it is obvious from his definition that he views it as a psychic structure. We have discussed
briefly how prevalent psychoanalytic thought is not definite about the
difference between a representation and a psychic structure, and
unclear whether there even is a difference. We have tried to clarify the
difference by understanding a psychic structure as a structuralization
of the substrate of the self by the imprint of a representation. The relationship between a structure and the representation that gives it its
particular characteristics is like the relationship between a sculpture
and the form of the sculpture, or between a building and its blueprints.
In the case of a marble sculpture of a horse, for example, the structure
is the sculpture in its totality, and the representation is the abstract
form of the horse. It is the abstract form of the horse, the image of the
horse, which structures the marble to form it into the sculpture of a
horse. In this way, the structure and the representation are inseparable, although they are not identical.

We have also seen, for instance with Kernberg, that most psychoanalytic writers use the two terms interchangeably. So it becomes

difficult to understand when someone—for instance, followers of Kohut—says that the bipolar self is not a representation. For if it is a psychic structure, as Kohut defines it, then even if it is not a representation, it is still formed by a representation. It develops through the integration of representations of impressions of previous experiences. As far as we can tell, he never defines psychic structure in any new way to differentiate it from the accepted meaning in psychoanalytic writings, and he is definitely familiar with this meaning. So we can only assume that he means it in the usually accepted way as a configuration of the self that is determined through the impact of a complex organization of representations.

Kohut described the bipolar or nuclear self as a psychic structure that develops from structural building, and this makes it a metapsychological concept, not in the sense of whether or not it is part of the ego, but that it is built through a similar psychic process, as object relations theory views the building of ego structures. It is more accurate to think of Kohut's formulation as an alternative object relations theory, or more precisely, an alternative psychoanalytic developmental theory of psychology. His concept of the bipolar self is mostly a self-representation, and in fact, he does refer to it as a (supraordinate) concept of the self, except that he emphasizes its specific content (ambitions and ideals), instead of the fact that it is a representation, an organization of structures related to the ambitions and ideals.

Another view of the bipolar self in which it is not a representation is given by Greenberg and Mitchell: "The self is no longer a representation, a product of the activity of the ego, but is itself the active agent." (Greenberg and Mitchell, 1983, p. 353) However, the authors here are not differentiating between a representation and a psychic structure, but instead, between an ego structure and a self structure, where, in classical psychoanalytic thinking (as in ego psychology), it is the ego structures that have the functional role, while in Kohut's "psychology of the self" it is the self structure that has such a role. So what the authors are pointing out is that the bipolar self of Kohut is not only a representation, but also an active agent.

This means that the bipolar self is the actual self, or more accurately, a certain structured segment of the actual self, for it is the actual self

482   which is the functioning self. Although Kohut, by this view, is emphasizing the functional property of the self—an emphasis that has it own advantages—this does not change the fact that he is defining it as a psychic structure, which is ascribed a particular form and characteristics through a representation.

We discuss this functional property of the bipolar self in Chapter 7, but we want to show that it is of the same character as ego structures, for all of these structures are forms of the substrate of the self. Attributing the functional capacity to the ego or the self is not that significant for us, even though it might be significant to psychoanalytic theorists. After all, the ego structures are parts of the self, for the self is the totality of the consciousness of the individual.

There is one sense in which it is significant that Kohut gives the self a functional property, for it indicates his greater appreciation of the self as the actual dynamic self and his greater distancing of his psychology from the representational aspect of its structure. But we must not forget that he still views it as a psychic structure, of which the representation is an important and necessary component. We are emphasizing this point because it is central to understanding how his view of self and narcissism relates to our own.

The Optimizing Force
of Being
in the Self

R ecognizing that presence manifests itself in various qualities
and forms which are constantly changing, reveals that Essence
is not static, but is in constant transformation. Being is dynamic. This dynamism manifests the richness of Being, inherent in us as
the potentialities of ourselves, and because this nature is our nature, it
moves our experience towards greater optimization. In other words, the
dynamism of Being impels and guides the self towards a greater revelation of its potentialities, towards manifesting its primordial wholeness. So it is an evolutionary force that moves the self towards greater
clarity, luminosity, creativity, depth, expansion, individuation, richness, and so on. In his discussion of Dzogchen, Guenther describes this
optimizing thrust of Being as possessing two inseparable components:

> A fundamental property of Being's mystery is what is termed
> its communicative thrust. . . . This is itself a process in which
> there is an inextricable relational functioning of two modes.
> The one termed the operational mode (thabs) names the auto-
> regulative nature of Being's communicative thrust, thereby
> indicating that this thrust is entirely due to Being's intrinsic
> dynamics. The other mode, termed appreciative discrimination

484   (shes-rab), names the cognitively and aesthetically accessible nature of Being's thrust. Although analytically separable into two modes, functionally these modes operate as a coherent, unified process. (Guenther, 1984, p. 5)

Guenther goes on to elaborate the various facets that this thrust presents, operating to optimize it: "All of them operate so as to ensure optimization of Being's communicative thrust." (Guenther, 1984, p. 5)

This optimizing force is felt as an inner pressure to complete the task of bringing about the development of the self to its ultimate possibility, that of primordial wholeness, but also as an inner guidance towards this task of completeness. This manifests, starting in early childhood development, as the developmental thrust, recognized differently by different researchers. Mahler, for example, conceptualizes it as separation-individuation and C. G. Jung as individuation.

Kohut had a notion similar to that of the optimizing thrust to explain his developmental theory of narcissism, a notion he borrowed from B. Zeigarnik. He used it to explain that narcissistic transferences reinstitute themselves as the attempt of the self to correct its defects, the defects that manifest in its defective psychic structures.

The new explanation is based by Kohut (1977) on the Zeigarnik effect (1927). . . for which Kohut postulates some kind of inner motivation of underdeveloped structures to resume their development when given the opportunity; the energy behind this motivation has nothing to do with Freud's instinctual drives, and the origin of it is not explained. (Chessick, 1985, p. 167)

Chessick assumes this force to be a sort of biological growth force. In our view, the Zeigarnik effect is a way of conceptualizing the optimizing thrust of the dynamism of the self. This dynamism of the self appears in the initial stages of the development of the self, partially in the form of the establishment of psychic structures. The essence of this dynamism, which is directly perceived in spiritual development—although present in early childhood development—is the essential flow of presence as it transforms its qualities and properties. This is the reason we view Essence as the true agent of transformation, as we discuss in our book, *The Elixir of Enlightenment* (Almaas, 1984).

It is this ontologically given, and spontaneously functioning, evo- 485
lutionary dynamism of the self that we see driving human psychological evolution, which is experienced directly in self-realization, but lost
sight of in the experience of the ego-self. The dynamism of Being drives
the evolutionary thrust of the self at all stages of its development, but
it is also the dynamic center and source of any activity and creativity
in the state of self-realization. The loss of direct contact with this essential dynamic center manifests, then, in the development of ego-activity,
or as Kohut terms it, the tension arc, which derives its energy ultimately from the dynamism of Being, but functions in ways that disconnect it from Being. The overall development of the self is always
governed by the evolutionary dynamism of Being. Human individual
activity is, however, primarily governed by the ego activity of the bipolar
self, or the center of the conventional self, but occasionally by the direct
experience of the dynamism of Being. For the latter to happen, the self
must be able to experience itself free from the influences of the past,
in other words, be able to simply be. This requires the resolution of
the narcissism of everyday life.

Understanding and Experience

The common view of *understanding* is that it is basically an intellectual comprehension of some content of experience, perception, or thought. It is usually an insight or idea that can occur after an experience has ensued.

We use the term *understanding* in a specific way that is particular to our view. By *understanding*, we mean the insightful awareness of our experience. There is immediate contact with the particulars of our experience—both inner and outer—plus the comprehension of this content, a comprehension that is part of, and inseparable from, the immediate experience. Hence, it is not merely an intellectual comprehension, although such comprehension forms part of it. Since the insight is part of, and inseparable from, the immediate experience, it does not have the abstract quality characteristic of intellectual comprehension.

We generally use the term with this specific meaning, and occasionally in the common sense, as intellectual comprehension. The intended meaning will be clear from the general context, but we indicate which sense we mean in the cases where the context does not show it.

The understanding and view developed in this book is part of a larger body of knowledge, the Diamond Approach℠, which is a modern

spiritual teaching that uses psychological understanding for spiritual 487
development. Self-realization is an important and necessary step in
this teaching, as it is in any spiritual development.

Gradual and Direct Approaches to Self-Realization

———————————————————————

The Diamond Approach^{SM} involves a gradual realization of Essence, a process that includes many subprocesses. It is possible for self-realization to occur as a one-step event (which occasionally occurs for students involved in the Diamond Approach^{SM}). This occurrence, termed sudden or direct realization, is the main focus of some traditional teachings, such as Zen and Dzogchen.

These teachings emphasize experiencing of self-realization directly. They do not work with the process of the integration of specific aspects of Essence. In fact, Dzogchen and many other direct approaches do not even conceptualize the possibility of experiencing Essence in particular aspects. In Dzogchen, Essence is formulated as "rigpa," a complete and total presence that includes its dynamism and the richness of its manifestation, without going into the particulars of this richness. The method, then, is the direct experience of this total and complete presence, as we see in the following passage:

> There is not a single state which is not this vast state of presence.
> It is the site and home of everything.

So remain in this which cannot be constructed or taken
    apart.
Here it is not necessary to progress gradually or to purify
    anything.
(Longchenpa, 1987, p. 48)

That this is not an easy experience to have, let alone to permanently realize, is reflected in the fact that Dzogchen views its teaching to be appropriate only for individuals with superior endowment or preparation. This practice is referred to as a practice for Buddhas.

One way of seeing the difficulty is to realize that the direct experience of "rigpa" means the penetration of all the barriers against full self-realization. This means that one needs to resolve all the issues related to the realization of the various aspects and dimensions of Being, plus the narcissistic issues of self-realization, in order to penetrate to "rigpa" (nondual presence). Otherwise, these issues will arise as barriers to this experience, or as a result of one managing to have a taste, for instance in initiation. In the latter case, all the issues will arise en masse, undifferentiated and hence, unclearly. In most circumstances the practitioner has no way to deal with these issues all at once, partly because there are so many of them and partly because it is impossible to differentiate them under such conditions. This differentiation is necessary in order to use understanding to resolve the specific issues for discrimination depends on it. Narcissism, and its various manifestations, will be part of what arises, but it will be obscured because of the simultaneous presence of all other issues and disturbances.

In other words, the direct methods, like those of Dzogchen and Zen, regardless of how powerful they are, do not have a place for understanding, especially the psychological understanding of the self. Therefore, it is our understanding that they are effective only for the few fortunate individuals with an unusual endowment and/or an unusually harmonious and balanced development of the self. A great deal of preparatory work is necessary for most individuals before they can possess the capacity to experience self-realization and retain it as a permanent condition.

The integration of the aspects of Essence, which we have described as supporting self-realization, may be seen as such preparation.

490 However, in the Diamond Approach^{SM} in particular, this work is not only a preparation, but a partial realization. In other words, elements of self-realization are present in the initial stages of integrating essential presence. So self-realization occurs, then, as a completion of development, and not only a result of preparation. What usually occurs in the Diamond Approach^{SM} is that very precise understanding about particular issues is possible. This understanding leads to the experience of specific pure manifestations of Essence. Essential experience is not complete self-realization at this point, but it is far more accessible because it is much easier to deal with a particular segment of self-structure than with the whole thing. This experience deepens and expands as more and deeper segments of the self are precisely understood, until it reaches self-realization. One encounters the issues of narcissism specifically at the transition to self-realization, although they also manifest occasionally and generally as part of the personality of the individual.

NOTES

Book One Notes

―――――――――――――――――――――――――――――――――――― •

1.   Western philosophy has been, in great measure, the study of Being. Although the ideas of the various philosophers originated primarily in their personal experience and appreciation of Being, the abstraction of philosophical language has made Being seem to be mostly an abstract idea. Being became more experiential and immediate for the existentialists, for example, Martin Heidegger, but it has always been seen as the fundamental truth of experience throughout the development of Western philosophy. Hegel, for instance, understood Being as the fundamental truth beyond mediation, as the beginning of experience and consciousness:

> Pure Being makes the beginning: because it is on one hand pure thought, and on the other immediacy itself, simple and indeterminate; and the first beginning cannot be mediated by anything, or be further determined. (Weiss, 1974, p. 114)

2.   We are implying here that the extent and consequences of this mediation of past experience can be perceived and understood in the experience of self-realization, before full and permanent self-realization. We differentiate between the experience of self-realization and the

493

494   permanent establishment of this experience. Self-realization is not a
       matter of having a certain experience of true nature and then living
       under the influence of its memory, nor is it a matter of having this expe-
       rience which then automatically lasts indefinitely. The usual situation
       is that an individual working on self-realization begins to have this
       experience occasionally, at the beginning of a process, and then more
       frequently. It becomes permanently established only slowly and with a
       great deal of work. The condition of self-realization is also comprised
       of many degrees of freedom, and many levels of subtlety, which will be
       discussed in some detail in this study.

            3.   More detailed and different treatments of Being and presence
       can be found in our previous books, particularly *Essence* (Almaas, 1986),
       and *The Pearl Beyond Price* (Almaas, 1988).

            4.   What about identifying with the physical body, the emotional
       nature, or the mind? This is the usual situation, but is actually the same
       as identifying with a psychic content. As will be discussed in detail in
       later chapters, the experience of our body, feelings, and mind is pat-
       terned to an enormous extent by our previous experiences of ourselves.
       This has been amply explored and demonstrated by developmental psy-
       chology, especially by object relations theory. We do not elaborate on
       this point here because it involves a subtlety that is not possible to address
       before establishing further precepts.

            5.   The difference between identity with presence and identity with
       images or constructs in the psyche is that identity with presence does
       not involve exercising any capacity of the self. It is not a matter of an
       activity of the psyche. It is a matter of simply being. On the other hand,
       psychic activities of various kinds are employed in identifying with a
       mental content, like those of memory, imaging, and so on.

            6.   We have so far used the terms "essential presence" and "primor-
       dial presence" interchangeably, but there is actually a slight difference in
       meaning. The presence which is the essence of the self can be experienced
       on many levels of subtlety, or dimensions of spiritual experience. It is
       always presence, but we refer to it as essential presence, on any of the
       spiritual dimensions, to point to its truth as the inner ontological core of
       the self. By primordial presence, on the other hand, we mean the deepest

level of the essential presence, what is referred to in some traditions as nondual presence. This primordial presence can be experienced as the true nature of the self only in the experience of full self-realization.

We will use the terms "essential presence" and "primordial presence" interchangeably when the distinction between the two meanings is immaterial. However, on the occasions in our discussion where we focus on one of the two particular meanings, we will discriminate the meaning.

7.   We understand that this view presents the individual used to situating her identity in the conventional dimension of experience with many, and quite possibly insurmountable, difficulties. Yet we need to give as accurate an account of our view of self-realization and the self as possible if we are to convey an appreciation of the comprehensive understanding of narcissism we intend to propose. We ask our kind reader for patience; in the appropriate places in our study we will connect this view with the usual perceptions and concerns of the conventional dimension of experience.

8.   We are aware of the various and conflicting psychological (mostly psychoanalytic) theories regarding self and identity, and we will explore the most prevalent ones in terms of their relation to our view of the self. Some researchers equate self with identity, some differentiate them, and some do not even have the concept of identity. In fact, some psychoanalytic researchers, such as Kohut, attribute narcissism to difficulties in the experience of the identity of the self, as we do, but call it self. It becomes confusing, then, when the problems of identity are used to understand the self in general.

9.   This is not completely true, but it is a good approximation. Actual conceptual memory traces are not retained until certain cognitive and mental functions develop. However, the self can retain impressions before the development of verbal memory. Some experimental research indicates that infants can retain some information nonverbally, through what is called "Representations of Interactions that have been Generalized" (RIGs). Daniel Stern, a professor of psychiatry, relates some of these experiments and their findings to support his theory of the emerging of a core sense of self much earlier than is usually believed in object relations theory. He writes:

496   We do know that infants have some abilities to abstract, aver-
       age, and represent information preverbally. . . .
          RIGs can thus constitute a basic unit for the representation
       of the core self. RIGs result from the direct impress of multi-
       ple realities as experienced, and they integrate into a whole
       the various actional, perceptual, and affective attributes of the
       core self. (Stern, 1985, p. 98)

One property of the self that becomes apparent in the work of self-
realization is that its consciousness can be impressed directly, like the
toy "silly putty" can pick up ink from newspaper cartoons. It can
begin to develop the rudiments of fixed forms before the capacity for
the usual kind of verbal memory develops. What Stern, above, calls
RIGs, seems to be a way of conceptualizing this property of the self
in a scientific language that can be checked experimentally. We find
this property of the self to be independent of age, but much more
available in the early years due to the original fluidity and openness
of the self to impressions. Although this impressionability never disappears as a property of the self, it decreases in later years due to the
dominance of the fixed ego structures which tend to inhibit further
impressing.

This means that the infant has already developed rudiments of relatively fixed forms from its prenatal experience. This patterning has been
documented as emotional and physical fixations that can sometimes be
released by some forms of therapy. Laing writes about patterns formed
in prenatal life: "Prenatal patterns occur in postnatal life. These prenatal patterns occur again and again in dreams, phantasies, feelings, in
the schema and image of the body, in visions, in the most ordinary states
of mind." (Laing, 1982, p. 111) There is a growing body of research and
literature about prenatal experience and the forms it creates in the postnatal experience of the self.

This subject matter is relevant to the general exploration of the self
as soul, which we will leave for a future study. Here, the important point
is that although there are already some relatively fixed forms in the self
of the infant, these forms are rudimentary, largely fluid, and relatively
few, and not yet sufficiently integrated to seriously impede the infant's
capacity to experience himself in a direct and immediate fashion. There
is definitely some effect, which depends on the prenatal history of the

particular infant, but in almost all circumstances, it is negligible. To the   497
extent that it is a significant effect, we can easily, for the purposes of our
thesis, shift the experience of primary self-realization to an earlier time,
perhaps to the prenatal period. It is definitely the case that prenatal
experience is largely characterized by primary self-realization, but it is
a safe assumption that, although there is a reduction of the wholeness
and the perfection after birth, primary self-realization typifies the
infant's experience during the first few months of life.

10. In primary narcissism the infant is capable of little differentiation between the self and other, inside and outside, thus calling it "primary narcissism" does not imply isolation from the environment. In fact,
the absence of differentiation reflects one of the main attributes of the
full experience of self-realization. This is the perception of the oneness
of Being, in which the primordial presence is experienced not only as
one's personal inner nature, but as the nature of the totality of existence. One experiences oneself as part and fabric of the one infinite
presence which is the totality of the universe, or as this totality itself. In
this development there is no differentiation, or more precisely, no separating boundaries, between one's usual manifestations and boundless
presence.

11. Margaret Mahler and her collaborators developed the current
most widely accepted theory about child development. Her theory
includes the notion that the neonate's experience is undifferentiated,
and does not yet include the sense of a separate self or other. The sense
of a separate self develops gradually in early childhood, within the interaction with the environment, particularly with the mother. The self
develops through the creation of internalized images of oneself and the
other. These images, or more accurately, representations, become integrated into overall structures that finally give the individual the sense
of being a person with a sense of identity and unique characteristics.

Mahler calls this process of the development of ego structures the
separation-individuation process, and assigned to it several stages,
according to her experimental-observational studies of children with
their mothers. The first stage is the autistic, in the first few weeks of life,
in which the neonate does not yet have any relationship with a significant other. The second is that of symbiosis, characterized by the neonate
experiencing itself within a common boundary with the mother, where

498   it is not separate from her, but in a dual unity with her. The next phase is that of differentiation, starting around seven months of age, where the baby starts experiencing itself as separate from the mother. This phase is the time when the self starts establishing representations of a separate self and other. The next is the practicing period, from twelve to eighteen months, when the child begins discovering and exercising its unique capacities and functions. The next is that of rapprochement, between eighteen and thirty-six months, where the toddler vacillates between moving towards autonomy and returning to closeness to mother and dependence on her. In the last phase, which begins at three years, but lasts throughout the life cycle, the sense of autonomous individuality develops with its twin achievement of object constancy. The latter is the capacity to experience another human being, originally the mother, as an autonomous individual in his or her own right, with unique qualities and functions. (See Mahler et al., 1975.)

12. We can define "spiritual" more precisely at this point. The spiritual dimension of the self is its ontological presence, its essential nature. In fact, what we have termed Essence is what the various philosophies, religions, and spiritual teachings have called spirit. So we see that spirit is not something otherworldly and ephemeral; it is actually our fundamental nature, the ground and ultimate truth of ourselves.

Spiritual development means, then, the discovery and integration of our essential presence in our experience of ourselves. And since this presence is ultimately nondual and forms the ground of our wholeness, spiritual development can also be seen as the movement towards wholeness.

13. "Experience-near" is a concept we borrow from psychoanalysis; we find it useful in classifying concepts in general. The idea is that concepts can arise in relation to two major sources. They may arise in relation to a lived experience, like the concept of "burning" to describe what happens when we put our hands in fire. But concepts can also arise in relation to theoretical considerations, like the concept of "intrapsychic" relationships, to refer to the interactions between two psychic structures in psychoanalysis, as in interactions between the ego and the superego. The concept "intrapsychic" arises only when we have the theoretical model of the psyche as having different parts, as Freud did in creating his structural theory.

The first kind of concept is then referred to as experience-near, 499 because it is nearer to actual experience. The actual situation is not so clear cut, and conceptualizations arise in response to a continuum of considerations with various degrees of nearness to lived experience. So concepts can be more or less experience-near, depending on how close they are to lived experience.

14. The account of the self in Buddhism that we find most useful for our investigation is that of the eight consciousnesses:

> They are the operations to which we give the generic term 'consciousness.' There are five perceptive functions coordinated with five sensory capacities and their domains. These five functions, however, are not adequate to account for the full range of consciousness . . . . The sixth function, or formative operation is termed . . . (in Sanskrit manovijnana). . . . Another (seventh) operation concerns the fact that all perceptions are related to a center which, like the perceptions themselves, is an event and not an abiding entity. This central event is affectively toned and accounts for the fact that all perceptions are constituted against a background 'mood' which then sustains them and gives them the specific ego-centeredness of consciousness. This operation is termed . . . (in Sanskrit klistamanas). . . . The eighth operation is what may be called the genotype of conscious life . . . (in Sanskrit alayavijnana), constituting the 'inherited program of instructions' . . . (in Sanskrit vasana), which control the development of an individual. (Guenther, 1984, p. 229)

We find this view most useful in the latter stages of self-realization, and not so useful at the beginning or middle. This is due to the way that Buddhism conceptualizes the various dimensions of experience of the self, which is quite unique to this teaching. Buddhism views the final and ultimate nature, that of primordial presence (Tathagatagarbha or Buddha nature), to be the only true and real dimension. All other dimensions of experience are viewed as delusional, not in the sense that they do not exist, but that they are distortions of the dimension of Buddha nature, of various degrees and types of distortions. We believe that this perspective, although possessing a great deal of truth and power, will be experienced as alien and invalidating by the Western individual. The Western mind is the product of a long history of a

500   specific view of the self that recognizes that it has many planes of experience, each with its own truth and valid cognition. This history dates back to the ancient Hellenic philosophers, through Pythagoras (who learned much from Pharaonic Egypt), Socrates, Plato, the Neoplatonists, the various spiritual and mystical schools that synthesized this view with the religious teachings of Judaism, Christianity, and Islam, to some of the well-known philosophers like Kant, Hegel, Schopenhauer, and Heidegger. A clear example is the view of the Sufis, whose teachings are said to synthesize the Neoplatonic system with the spiritual teachings of Islam.

15. This area of psychology, unique to modern depth psychology, makes it possible for us to investigate the self through a new type of psychological insight, due mostly to the discovery of psychodynamics by Freud.

Psychodynamic understanding involves comprehending the conscious manifestations of the self in terms of the influence of unconscious forces. The conceptualization of the unconscious by Freud, his view of it and how it influences our conscious experience, made it possible for us to understand how early childhood experience survives in the self: as repressed memories which continue to influence and determine to a large degree our experience of ourselves and our lives. His view of the dynamic interaction between the unconscious and conscious experience provided, also, ways of accessing the material hidden in the unconscious, thus initiating a whole methodology of psychotherapy. We use psychodynamic understanding in our work, integrated with our expanded view of the self, not for psychotherapy, but for understanding and revealing the nature of the self, not only of the psychological dimension which is the area of focus of psychoanalytic theory, but in addition, the spiritual dimensions of experience. This gives us a psychodynamic way to investigate the various dimensions of experience, some of which have been accessible only, and mostly, so far, through meditation, yogic exercises, prayers, and so on.

16. Hartmann writes:

> Mental development is not simply the outcome of the struggle with instinctual drives, with love-objects, with the superego, and so on. For instance we have reason to assume that this

development is served by apparatuses which function from the   501
beginning of life. (Hartmann, 1939, p. 24)

17. Most object relations theorists, for example Kernberg, make no explicit distinction between ego psychic structures and organized systems of images. We can theoretically make a distinction between the two because the self, or its psyche in this case, includes both the mental content of thoughts and images, and affects, drives, sensations, functions, and so on. It is difficult to make this distinction clearly within the current conceptualizations of depth psychology because, although some writers have made attempts, depth psychology does not yet have a concept of the actual psychic consciousness (substance or material), the substrate that forms the experiential ground for all experiences of the self. This substrate can be known directly only in spiritual experience, and its perception makes it possible to distinguish clearly between psychic structure and organized systems of images.

Psychic structure can be seen, then, simply as the structuralization of the substrate or consciousness, the ground of experience of the self, under the impact or imprint of the organized systems of images. Image is a content of organized memory, but structures the substrate of the self in the present. We will explore this question in greater detail in a future book about the self, but it suffices for our present study to see that it is possible to make the above distinction.

18. The distinction between structures of the self and mental structures of memories is ordinarily immaterial for the concerns of object relations theory because the field of study of this theory, and depth psychological research in general, consists only of experiences in the conventional domain of the self. This dimension of experience is formed by the imprint of organized systems of images (based on memories) on the substrate of the self, as we will see shortly, and hence such systems are usually not found separate from psychic structures. In other words, in the conventional domain of experience, mental systems (of memories and images) exist as the structuring imprint of the psychic structures, and hence inseparable from them. Therefore, there is normally no need to distinguish the two in discussing the experience of the self. The distinction is important in theory and for the work of spiritual development, for the latter involves developing the capacity to experience the self free from the influences of memory.

502   The fixation of these representations in the mind is called "internal-
        ization." As more of these representations accumulate, which means as
        more memories are retained and fixed, there begins a process of orga-
        nization of these representations. This organization of internalized
        object relations is the task of the separation-individuation process, which
        ordinarily culminates in the development of self and object constancy.
            According to Kernberg, the process of internalization and organiza-
        tion of object relations occurs through different mechanisms, depend-
        ing on the stage of development. He groups them in three categories:
        introjection, identification, and ego identity.

> Introjection is the earliest, most primitive, and basic level in the
> organization of internalization processes. It is the reproduction
> and fixation of an interaction with the environment by means of
> an organized cluster of memory traces implying the three com-
> ponents of the units of object relations. This process is a mecha-
> nism of growth of the psychic apparatus. (Kernberg, 1979, p. 29)

Kernberg then relates this definition of introjection to the mechanism of identification: Identification is a higher-level form of introjection which can only take place when the perceptive and cognitive abilities
of the child have increased to the point that it can recognize the role
aspects of interpersonal interaction. (Kernberg, 1979, p. 30)
    Thus, identification is like introjection, except that the object relations
internalized are on a more developed level. The object is seen as a person
with a specific role—for example, the role of protecting or mothering—
rather than just as a vague object that is needed. These internalized roles
are expressed later in development as traits of character and personality.
In other words, this internalized repertoire of roles becomes organized
into a cohesive self-image through which the child at the end of development interacts with his environment. Kernberg puts it this way:

> Since identifications imply the internalization of roles as defined
> above, behavioral manifestations of the individual, which
> express one or both of the reciprocal roles of the respective
> interaction, become a predominant result of identification; the
> behavioral manifestations of introjections are less apparent in
> interpersonal interactions. (Kernberg, 1979, p. 31)

(See our book, *The Pearl Beyond Price* [Almaas, 1988] for a more
detailed account of this process.)

19. There is general agreement that "healthy narcissism" is a matter   503
of the cathexis (energetic investment) of the self-representation, but the
various theorists disagree on the kind of energy in this cathexis or investment. (See Appendix D.)

20. It is the implicit view of most psychological researchers that
this development is not only normal, but allows for the spontaneity
and creativity of the self. This view implies that, although the self's
experience is formed greatly by the self-representation, the latter is
not necessarily rigid or inflexible in the healthy and normal individual, but can change and accommodate new impressions from experience. The self-representation develops mainly in early childhood, so
its major building blocks and characteristics are already laid down
quite early on, but it continues to change, to some degree, by integrating new impressions. In fact, the self's capacity for creativity,
spontaneity, humor, and even transcendence, is considered to be the
outcome of the harmonious development and cathexis of the self-
representation, or alternatively, of the resolution of the narcissistic
disturbances, which amounts to the same thing. (Kohut, 1971; and
Masterson, 1985)

This is a complex and subtle question, for how can the experience of
the self which is formed so much by a self-concept built mostly in the
first few years of life be creative and spontaneous? It is nevertheless true:
The self-concept is built mostly in early life, and the individual can be
spontaneous and creative, especially when the development is harmonious and the representation is firmly cathected. This does not mean,
however, that we understand how this happens, for it is understood in
the experience of self-realization that spontaneity and creativity, and
even the capacity for enjoyment, are reduced and hampered in the presence of any concept of the self, especially if that concept comes from past
experience. The capacity for enjoyment, creativity, spontaneity, and
transcendence comes from the self's spiritual nature, its essential presence, for it is this presence that is totally free and intrinsically spontaneous, and transcendence is nothing but fully experiencing this fact.
Also, as we have seen, we are cut off from this core nature when our experience comes through the accumulations of the past. At the same time,
the self-representation is the accumulation of the past, integrated and
synthesized in an overall concept.

504   This shows that there is still no understanding of how the harmonious development and cathexis of the self-representation allow creativity and spontaneity. It is our understanding that there is the need both for a deep experience and understanding of self-realization on the one hand, and a more precise understanding of the development of the self-representation, its relation to the self, and the process of cathexis, on the other, if we are going to approach such complex, deep, and subtle questions. We made an attempt at such understanding in our book, *The Pearl Beyond Price*, when we discussed the integration of the ego's identification systems (which are the units constituting the self-representation) into Being, the essential presence, as the final step in the process of metabolism of experience. The main insight was that any component self-representation (or any identification system of the ego) can go through a process of clarification by seeing exactly the actual truth of the experiences which were the source of it. This way, the self-representation loses whatever defensive element it has had, and this makes it more transparent to the essential presence and its pure qualities. This transparency is the mature and developed level of what is referred to as the lack of rigidity, the flexibility, and mature tolerance or openness of the self-representation that has developed and matured harmoniously. This transparency exists, of course, in degrees, depending on how truthful or defensive is the content of the self-representation.

In our understanding, this transparency accounts for the possibility of creativity, spontaneity, and so on, of the self in the presence of the self-representation. At the same time, the capacity for creativity and spontaneity increases with the increasing transparency of the particular self-representation, reaching its fullness and completeness at the point of self-realization. This is the point of complete transparency of the self-representation, which is the same as the complete metabolism of the experiences that originated it, which is identical to the self-representation's integration into the presence of Being. This is the direct and full experience of presence, which means there is no more representation of the self. So the full development of creativity and spontaneity coincides with the total absorption of the particular self-representation into Being, or, in other words, with its annihilation as a mental concept.

What does this mean, then, about cathexis? Can we call such complete integration—to the point of the elimination of mental representation—cathexis? This was not the intention of the psychologists who

coined this concept, and we will not go further into this question here.   505
However, in this study we will give another account, from a different
perspective, of how creativity increases with the firmer cathexis of the
self-representation.

21. This is probably the main reason it is difficult for depth psychology to differentiate clearly between a mental image and a psychic
structure. Depth psychology focuses solely on the dimension of conventional experience, which is inherently incapable of differentiating
the self from the self-concept.

22. The experience of fragmentation occurs in some stages of spiritual development. In the deeper stages it loses its threatening and terrifying character. This is partly due to the increasing insight that it is an
image that is fragmenting, not oneself or one's body. Also, the individual increasingly attains the capacity to be the self without the self-
representation. So we can experience the self and the self-representation
separately. And since we can see directly that it is not who we are that
is fragmenting, but some representation of who or what we are, there
is more equanimity about the experience.

23. At this point we might ask whether there could be development
of the self without the development of the self-representation, in other
words, how can childhood self-realization not be lost? As far as we can
see, the development of the self-representation as part of the normal
development of the self is unavoidable for many reasons. One of these
is that the needs of the self are never perfectly satisfied, so there are
bound to be narcissistic disturbances. We will discuss this issue further
in our exploration of the development of narcissism; our understanding is similar to many of the prevalent views of childhood disturbances
to our narcissism, except that it includes consideration of the disturbance
of development of specific essential qualities of the soul.

A second and more fundamental reason is developmental; the way
the cognitive and perceptual faculties develop in childhood makes it
unlikely for the child to develop with full self-realization. By the time
the child has developed her cognitive capacities to the degree needed
for the recognition of self-realization, the self-representation will have
developed. This makes the development of the narcissism of everyday
life an unavoidable element in the development of the self.

506   However, this does not mean this is, or has to be, the ultimate development, a truth attested to by the various spiritual teachings, and experienced in self-realization. The self can develop, although usually not
initially in childhood, without that development being a development
of the self-representation. This is a difficult thing to envision psychologically, for this development has to do with the spontaneously arising and developing pure forms of presence, the manifestations of the
ontological creativity and richness of the deeper potentials of the self.
The self becomes spontaneously patterned from within, completely
independent from the self-representation, and as a natural response of
the self to the developing circumstances of life. We have given an account
of part of this process, the part that has to do with the essential individuation of the self, in our book, *The Pearl Beyond Price* (Almaas, 1988).

24. The concept of the narcissism of everyday life is not identical to
the concept of normal narcissism used in psychoanalysis, although there
is a great deal of overlap between the two. They both recognize the
cathexis of the self-representation. Normal narcissism involves relatively
minor disturbances in the experience of the self, so that the self is in a
state of relative harmony. The notion of the narcissism of everyday life,
however, implies the presence of subtle but profound disturbances in
the experience of the self. It also implies that the normal harmony of
the self is far from the harmony that is possible in the condition of self-
realization.

The normal narcissism, defined as the firm cathexis of the self-
representation, is usually referred to as secondary narcissism—a practice
initiated by Freud and followed by later theoreticians—to differentiate
it from primary narcissism, the original perfection and harmony of
infantile and uterine life. Secondary narcissism becomes the healthy or
normal development of the self after the loss of the symbiotic union
and its bliss. Although primary narcissism is also defined as the cathexis
of the self, the self here is not a self-representation, but the actual self
of the symbiotic phase, or as Annie Reich describes it: "Infantile narcissism consists in the cathexis of the self at a time of incomplete ego
differentiation and insufficient delimitation of self and object world."
(Morrison, 1986, p. 45)

Primary narcissism is normal narcissism in infants. This concept corresponds more to our concept of primary self-realization. In other words,

we do not see subtle disturbances in the experience of the self here, as 507
we do in secondary narcissism.

25. This understanding provides a clear explanation for the phenomenon of the aggravation of the usually normal narcissistic manifestations in some stages of spiritual development, for in these stages we are in the process of becoming aware of how, and how much, our self-representation alienates us from our essence.

It is insights and perceptions like these that support our thesis that narcissism is fundamentally due to the alienation from essential presence, the ontological ground of the self, and that pathological narcissism is a distorted exaggeration of this fundamental narcissism. We have not attempted to give clear conceptual support for our thesis because it is a result of many observations and insights whose source is direct experience and not theoretical considerations. The conceptual framework will develop and its inner consistency will reveal itself as we discuss the various elements and issues of narcissism and self-realization. It is the total picture, its nearness to actual lived experience, and its capacity to illuminate a wide range of observations, which support our main thesis.

Our view also shows that what the spiritual teachings call the main barrier to spiritual realization—the ego, or what some traditions simply call the self—is nothing but the self-representation, and not the system ego, per se, or the actual self. Depth psychology has rendered a great service to spiritual teachings by providing a clear definition of the form of the self that is the main barrier in the spiritual path.

26. This is an important methodological difference from the psychotherapeutic approaches founded on depth psychology, based on a difference of view regarding the origin and meaning of narcissistic emptiness. Psychotherapeutic methods do not usually focus on the impartial experience of emptiness because such emptiness is considered a manifestation of psychopathology, in this case a weakness or loss of a self-structure. Focusing on the emptiness is thought to intensify pathology, that is, to weaken the psychic structure instead of supporting or strengthening it.

This might be the case if the sense of emptiness is chronic, or if the ego of the particular individual is not strong enough to be able to reestablish itself easily for purposes of functioning. This is not the case in Pia's situation, or in the usual situations we find in our work. For emptiness

508 arises frequently in the work of self-realization due to the fact that the latter is primarily a training in developing the capacity to experience the self without a structure based on past experience. So, in our method, full experience of the arising emptiness is not only attempted, but is an important step in the process of reconnecting with essential presence.

However, even in the case of psychopathology, narcissistic emptiness is an expression of disconnection from the essential core of the self. Since our work is not oriented towards the treatment of psychopathology, we do not know whether the direct confrontation of emptiness is a useful approach in such cases. It might not be, and the correct approach might very well turn out to be the building of psychic structure through one method or another. The result, even when it is the overcoming of psychopathology, will most definitely be a building or strengthening of a psychic structure that will function, at least in part, to cover up the underlying emptiness. In other words, this emptiness does not disappear totally when the structures of the self are established securely, even though it disappears from consciousness. The emptiness of the empty shell will be more effectively driven out of consciousness, and the shell will be stronger and even more resilient, and it will not be experienced consciously as a shell, but as the normal sense of self. This might be necessary in the treatment of psychopathology, for it will transform pathological narcissism to the narcissism of everyday life, but a different direction is needed if we want to resolve the narcissism of everyday life. We will see in our further exploration of the self-representation that it is always an empty shell, for it is devoid of Essence, its true ontological presence.

27. It is an exhilarating and exciting journey when a person with pathological narcissism (or any pathology that restricts or denies the emotions, feelings and their vitality) begins to open up emotionally and to learn the freedom and spontaneity in this maturity. A whole universe opens up, a universe of qualities, meanings, new modes of relating, and a new maturity and expansion of the self. Something similar happens when the self opens up to its essence, except that the experience now has a vividness, a depth, a profundity and openness that was not only unavailable on the emotional realm, but hardly conceivable. The richness and the sense of realness in the essential realm of presence eclipse the emotional experience, in all of its heights and depths, in ways not conceivable by us until we actually have the direct taste. This direct taste

will immediately show us how limiting is the life based on emotional
maturity (to the exclusion of the essential realm) and why it remains
narcissistically incomplete.

28. These expressions indicate that what Kohut calls the bipolar self
is not the actual self, at least not the total self, and that what he calls the
personality is probably the closest concept he has to it. The actual self is
the totality of the self that contains all its parts and sectors. So we can
assume that he considers the bipolar self to be the center of the self, a view
that will be illuminating for our further study of the self-representation.
In other words, it seems that he thinks of the bipolar self as the central
part of the overall self-representation, even though he thinks of it as a
supraordinate concept of the self.

29. If the self were an energetic continuum, it would be similar to
the self as it manifests in self-realization. We experience presence in self-
realization as permeating all of the self's sectors and manifestations as
an alive and energetic continuum, the way protoplasm permeates all
parts of the body, constituting their inner core. The self experiences
itself as the unfoldment of presence, as a flow of essential forms, or, in
other words, as a dynamic essence. It is interesting, in light of this, that
Kohut thinks of the tension arc of the bipolar self as "the dynamic essence
of the complete, nondefective self." (Kohut, 1984, pp. 4–5) But how can
a psychic structure—which is either a representation or at least formed
by a representation, or an activity based on it—be the essence of the self?
One possibility is that the "essence" is of another structure; in this case,
in his expression, "essence of . . . self," both "essence" and "self" refer
to psychic structures, one more fundamental than the other.

The other possibility, in case "self" here means the bipolar self, is that
"essence" is not actually a psychic structure but a different kind of manifestation of the self—in this case, the tension arc, which is some kind
of psychological activity. So the tension arc is the dynamic essence of
the bipolar self. This indicates that the essence of the psychic structure
of the bipolar self is a psychological activity.

It is clear from this discussion that Kohut's later definition of the self
is problematic, for it is not clear whether his continued use of the concept of "psychic structure" is according to the classical usage or not
because he says that the nuclear self is not a depth psychological concept, but at the same time he calls it a psychic structure.

30. Most depth psychological views of the self unfortunately fall into this trap, defining the self from the viewpoint of psychopathology, and hence limiting it, at best, to what is termed normalcy, which only refers to the conventional realm. In most cases, the views of the self reflect the disturbances the researchers are attempting to study. It is our position that we need a view of the self which is comprehensive and inclusive of all possible manifestations of experience, not only the pathological and "normal," but also the unconventional and rare. Only this can provide us with a complete and objective basis from which to view distortions and disturbances.

31. Kohut makes the same criticism of the concept of normality, as part of his defense of his views on the baby's natural endowment. We quote him here for we find his statement relevant for our discussion:

> In this context it behooves us to ponder C. Daly King's state-
> ment that the 'average may be, and very often is, abnormal.
> The normal, on the other hand, is objectively, and properly, to
> be defined as that which functions in accordance with its
> design' (1945, p. 493). We may or may not choose to use King's
> definition of normalcy, and we are also free to dispense with
> the value-laden principle of normalcy altogether. Still, if we
> need to choose a baseline from which to measure degrees of
> deviation, King's concept strikes me as a very felicitous one for
> this purpose. (Kohut, 1984, p. 212)

We find this argument acceptable, but in applying it to Kohut's definition of the self, we see that even though his definition may reflect the average condition of the self in our times, it does not necessarily reflect the truly normal condition of the self. This may produce unexpected difficulties, especially if we are interested in understanding the true and natural normalcy of the self, and in restoring it by treating deviations from it.

Here, we are not questioning the usefulness of Kohut's work for treating narcissistic disorders, but pointing out that Kohut's conceptualizations of the self might not reflect his immediate experience and understanding of it, at least, not the totality of this experience. We have seen this to be the case with some other writers on narcissism.

32. In the deeper stages of self-realization, and especially in the experience of primordial nondual presence, the flow of presence is

completely coemergent with action. Action flows out completely insep- 511
arable from presence, for the body and mind are inseparable manifestations of presence. In some sense, there is no such thing on this
dimension as action, for there is only the continuity of presence, as a
discriminated and patterned flow. Some of these patterns we ordinarily call actions, some we call feelings, and some we call states, but they
are all nothing but presence, the expression of the never-ending creativity of presence. In other words, action here is ontological creativity.

The notion of presence as a center of initiative and action breaks
down on this level of experience, for the center is completely inseparable from, and in fact totally coemergent with, the totality of the self.
There is much more depth and implications of this view, but this is not
the place to expand upon it. We have given a brief account of the inner
flow of the self in relation to action and creativity in order to discuss
Kohut's notion of the tension arc more completely.

33. There is, of course, more to the creative activity of the true painter
than the influence of past experiences. There is, for instance, the spontaneous creativity of something truly new. There is also the true creative
impulse which is not a matter of attaining something determined by past
experience, but is an actual and natural expression of the true unfoldment of the self. The painter might be so creative that both his creations
and the source of his creativity are outside of time, and hence, outside
of his personal history. This was Immanuel Kant's view of artistic creativity, discussed in his *Critique of Judgments.*

These are the marks of genuine creative artists, but then they are in
touch with a source in the self that is not a result of personal history.
This source can only be the essential core of the self, which is free from
the experiences of the past. There is no ideal here leading the painter;
the activity is an expression of the dynamism of Essence, and is not
emanating from ego-activity, the psychological activity of the center of
the conventional self. When creativity reaches this degree of genuine-
ness, it is not a product of the psychological activity of the bipolar self,
but rather the expression of essential experience.

Kohut explains this artistic creativity with his tension arc, but we do
not see how this is possible. The tension arc is dependent on ideals that
are based on psychic structures, structures that developed from past
experiences. These will tend to crowd out and impede the genuine

512   creativity, for they are the product of time, while the essence of genuine creativity comes from a timeless place. The usual situation, however, is that the creative painter is impelled by his bipolar self, its ambitions and ideals, but he is capable—at least occasionally—of letting go of this center of his self, and allowing himself to be touched by his essential core. This occasional essential taste is then taken over by his bipolar self and is fit into his ideals and ambitions. So there is a mixture, we believe, in most creative productions, of the activity of the ego-self and the dynamism of Essence. This is because most artists are not self-realized, and the experience of self-realization can only be, if an artist is fortunate, an occasional spark that informs and initiates her or his creative work. But the true creative spark (artistic inspiration) can come only from the essential core, which is beyond personal history, and hence, beyond any of the held ideals of the artist.

Kohut is probably aware of this situation, but conceptualizes the whole process in terms of basic ambitions and ideals, which are based on psychic structures laid down in early life. It seems that Kohut actually has a taste or appreciation of the true essential source of genuine creativity, but fails to include it in his theory because his conceptualizations exclude the spiritual (essential) element. Possibly this taste is part of the reason for his lack of emphasis on the structures themselves and his focus on what he calls the "flow of liberated narcissistic libido." His unacknowledged appreciation of creativity as transcending psychic structure can also be seen in an early statement about creativity, where he relates it to primary narcissism, the infantile stage of perfection. "Nevertheless, I believe that the creative person's relationship to his work has less in common with the expanded narcissism of motherhood than with the still unrestricted narcissism of early childhood." (Morrison, 1986, p. 75) Of course, Kohut is not thinking here of essential presence, but of early childhood narcissism which precedes the establishment of psychic structures.

It is our view that there is much more to the human self than is recognized by Kohut and the rest of the psychoanalytic theorists. A human being is a much more interesting and exciting phenomenon than is allowed by these theories. These theories tend to close the doors to the inexhaustible mysteries, what the ancients symbolized as hidden treasures, lying at the depths of the self: the sources of delight, creativity, fulfillment, and transcendence. One of the purposes of our work is to understand

some of these theories from the perspective of the hidden treasures, and   513
hence, see their relationship to them. This then can function to open up
our present psychological knowledge to the infinite depths within us.

34. The simple animal desires (like hunger or sexual drive) are not
dependent on previous experience and not based on psychic structure;
hence, they are not part of the psychological activity of the psychic center of the self. They can become part of the latter, or influenced by it, as
frequently happens, but then the desires are not the simple animal ones,
but are based on previous experience, and on one's ideal images and self-
images. Then they are part of the psychological activity of the center of
the self, and definitely imply a rejection of the present condition or state
of the self. This is obvious in the case of the feeling of hunger whose function is primarily to assuage an emotional difficulty, as in the situation
of overeating, and in the case of the sexual drive when it is primarily
intended for the relief of some difficult psychological state—for instance,
a need for intimacy.

35. It is widely accepted in depth psychology that the sense of being
a separate entity does not exist for the infant, but develops as part of
ego development. The original state of the self of the infant is that of an
undifferentiated matrix, where the various components of the self's
experience, taken for granted by the adult, like mind and body, self and
other, are still not experienced separately.

36. Kernberg views the loss of separateness (loss of ego boundaries)
in psychopathology to be either a fixation at, or a regression to, the symbiotic stage of Mahler's separation-individuation process, and his stage
2 of the development of object relations in ego development, where the
self has not yet developed a differentiated and separate self-representation.
He writes:

> Stage 2: Normal 'Symbiosis' or Stage of Primary, Undif-
> ferentiated Self-Object Representations. . . . Pathological fixa-
> tion of or regression to stage 2 of development of internalized
> object relations is clinically characterized by the failure in—or
> loss of—the differentiation of ego boundaries, which is char-
> acteristic of symbiotic psychosis of childhood (Mahler, 1968),
> most types of adult schizophrenia (Jacobson, 1954), and depres-
> sive psychoses (Jacobson, 1966). (Kernberg, 1979, p. 60)

514   37. Identity is also easily delineated in some forms of psychopathology because the failure to develop it is part of the reason behind the development of such psychopathology. In fact, this is what prompted Mahler and her colleagues to conceptualize this structure and to study its development. She writes: "Concern with the problem of identity arose from observing a puzzling clinical phenomenon, namely, that the psychotic child never attains a feeling of wholeness, of individual entity, let alone 'a sense of human identity.'" (Mahler, et al., 1975, p. 11)

38. Here, the question may arise: Where does the self get its capacity for identification in infancy before the development of the self-identity? The point is that identification is one of the ego functions used in the beginning of ego development, in the process of developing the self-identity. So if the self-identity is what functions to give the self the capacity for identification, as we are asserting, then where does this capacity originate? Depth psychology, as far as we know, does not address this question in any significant manner, except for the fact that ego psychology considers identification to be an innate capacity of the self, present in the beginning of life as one of the apparatuses of primary autonomy, which are some of the constituents of the undifferentiated matrix.

We find this view to be inadequate for our purposes. Our observation is that identification is a process that occurs simultaneously with the presence of the feeling of identity. Whenever there is identification with any of the content of the self, there is a feeling of identity, and vice versa, at least under normal circumstances. So if it is difficult for us to accept at this point that the self-identity is what provides the self, in the conventional dimension of experience, with the capacity to identify, then it suffices at this point to recognize the intimate relationship between the two.

39. Usually, there is a general sense of being a person, an individual with a sense of self or identity. However, we know that this is only the surface phenomenon. At deeper levels of the personality, there are many self-images, with definite traits, organized in a particular structure that gives the feeling of an overall self-identity.

Different life situations bring to the surface different self-images and their corresponding object relations. This determines the changing of moods, emotions, states of mind, and actions throughout a person's life, and even throughout a day. It is understood in object relations theory that although the self-representation is an overall integrated self-concept that includes all the units of self-representations, an individual experiences himself, at each moment, from the perspective of a component self-representation, or a larger integrated unit that has in it more than a single component unit. Kernberg relates how, in the process of psychoanalysis, as the patient goes deeper in understanding his mind, there first manifests the general overall self-images and their corresponding object relations, but that as the process deepens, the more specific constituent sub-self-images become expressed in the analytic situation. He writes in a paper about psychoanalytic technique:

> Here, in the course of the psychoanalytic process, the development of a regressive transference neurosis will gradually activate in the transference the constituent units of internalized object relations that form part of ego and superego structures, and of the repressed units of internalized object relations that have become part of the id. (Blum, 1980, p. 211)

Thus, transference occurs, in object relations terms, when past object relations are activated. However, it is not only in analysis or psychotherapy that these small units of object relations are activated. It happens for everyone, at all times, and simply becomes apparent under scrutiny. As Freud first emphasized, in *The Psychopathology of Everyday Life*, such transference is a normal everyday occurrence, not an isolated instance in analysis.

Of course, all this occurs in the context of the overall sense of self constituted by the sum of the integrated representations.

40. This overall world of the self-representation is termed by Sandler, "the representational world," which develops as part of ego development, from the myriad images of the various human objects in childhood experience.

> Thus, self and object representations, culled from a multitude of impressions, constitute a network of concepts and enduring images, a 'representational world' which provides the basic organizational framework for the child's experience. (Greenberg and Mitchell, 1983, pp. 373–374)

516   So, the self's experience of itself is patterned by the integration of early object relations, and also its experience of the world at large.

41. The idea here is reminiscent of Castaneda's notion of the "assemblage point" which determines the realm of experience that the individual is aware of. In his writings, Castaneda gives an account of a teaching transmitted to him by a Yaqui Indian, Don Juan. An important part of this teaching is that a human being is psychically some form of consciousness, in the shape of an egg, that has many bands of different psychic wave lengths, so to speak, called emanations. These bands represent different experiential realms, and an individual experiences the particular realms associated with the bands in which the "assemblage point" is located. In the words of Don Juan:

> 'The next truth is that perception takes place,' he went on, 'because there is in each of us an agent called the assemblage point that selects internal and external emanations for alignment. The particular alignment that we perceive as the world is the product of the specific spot where our assemblage point is located on our cocoon.' (Castaneda, 1984, p. 115)

The "assemblage point" functions primarily to locate the experience of the self by shifting attention to the particular bands, this way functioning similarly to the self-identity. We do not believe that the concept of "assemblage point" is identical to that of the self-identity, but we do think it is related to it. Our understanding of the Essential Identity is the aspect of the self that most corresponds to Castaneda's "assemblage point."

42. The notion of physical location is applicable here. The identity not only locates the body in space and time, but it also locates the sense of self in the body. It is not unusual, and definitely not accidental, that, as is most explicit in the case of young children, one will point someplace in the body when using the pronoun "I." It is significant whether one points to the head, to the chest, or to the body in general, for these could be indications of the realms of experience one identifies with: mental, emotional, or physical, respectively. This is, of course, not a definite indication, for the location might, and generally does, change from one time to another. This indicates that the psychic structure of

self-identity can be experienced directly, and that it is something that can be located in space, and also that it can change location.

All this may sound strange, but these observations can be corroborated in some of the experiences we encounter in spiritual development in which the various psychic structures are revealed to their bare-bones fundaments and where they can manifest in a concrete manner unfamiliar to normal experience. We will discuss some of these manifestations as they become relevant to our exploration. It suffices for our present discussion to understand that identity locates the experience of the self in whatever dimension of experience the self-representation conceptualizes. This last observation is consistent with depth psychological formulations, and with common sense experience.

43. The observations that the center of perception can shift position, and that this center of perception is inseparable from the feeling of identity, both corroborate the observations in the previous note that identity has both a spatial location in inner experience, and also a locus that can shift. But this then brings up the question of what accounts for this spatial locus and movement of identity. Exploring this question will take us far afield at this point, but we can say that a psychic structure can be experienced directly and concretely as a spatial, but not physical, form. If this seems far-fetched, contemplate how inner emptiness can be experienced as a phenomenological voidness, an actual (almost physical) sensation of nothingness, a psychic impression of the same category as that of experiencing a psychic structure having a spatial (almost physical) form.

44. We need to differentiate the condition of the diffusion of the observer, as defined in meditational practices, from the absence or weakness of the observer in some forms of psychopathology. In this latter case, it is the lack or distorted development of one of the ego functions, that of being a somewhat detached center of observation. This is not a state of boundless awareness, but of being so involved and identified with the particulars of experience that one cannot merely observe them. So it is a condition of total identification that usually indicates a regressive state, while the diffusion of the observer in spiritual experience is a state of total disidentification with any content of experience.

45. It is possible that Kohut does not view identity as we do, as a psychic structure of the self, but is mentioning it more as the feeling of

518   identity. This implies, however, that he views identity as the self's feeling and recognition of itself—the affective tone expressing a psychic
structure —as has also been conceptualized by Jacobson and Mahler.

46. The main rationale behind this conclusion is not the content of
our discussion comparing the bipolar self to identity, but the fact that
he views narcissistic disturbances to be related directly to problems of
the bipolar self, as well as the fact that we see that narcissism is related
basically to problems of identity.

47. It is our understanding that it would be extremely difficult to
possess this precision about identity without the help of perception and
experience available only in some of the stages of spiritual development.
Precise details about identity and its experience included in our view
come in a large degree not only from essential experience in general, but
specifically from the experience and understanding of identity on the
dimension of Essence. Essential Identity, as we refer to it, allows an
unexpected precision and exactness in both experience and understanding, especially in relation to identity.

48. We can visualize the self and its structures in other ways. One way
to understand the relation between the two structures and how they are
integrated is to envision the self as a balloon with a certain colored
design. Each individual is one such balloon. They are all entities because
they all have separate boundaries. Each has an identity which distinguishes him or her, which is a unique colored design.

49. Since identity is what situates individual awareness in one dimension of experience or another, its absence may manifest as a sense of
unreality as if one were a ghost without much substance or grounding.
One is not present then, in some important way, in any dimension of
experience.

50. The importance we are placing on being as precise as possible in
terms of understanding the specific structure responsible for narcissism
stems from the fact that the disturbances of the overall self-representation
express themselves not only in narcissism, nor even in the borderline
conditions, but in all psychopathology and in all psychic conflict. It is
also important for our view about spiritual development, where there
is a need to deal with many kinds of issues. All of these issues can be

traced to the self experiencing itself from within, and through, the over- .519
all self-representation. So to be able to be specific, and hence precise, about particular issues, we need to be specific and precise about the particular substructures of the overall self-representation. We find a great help for this specificity in the great discriminating capacity inherent in the dimension of Being.

51. In terms of the spatial metaphors we have used, we can say that the borderline individual is like a sphere with shaky, unstable boundaries, which may become deformed or even fragmented, distorting its identity.

52. It is not necessary to this discussion to postulate that it is the self-entity which is the structure responsible for the execution of action. For our perspective regarding the difference between the underlying structural origins of narcissism and the borderline conditions, it is sufficient to see that it is the total self-representation that is the structure responsible for the execution of action because it is this overall structure, in our view, that is disturbed in the borderline conditions.

53. This is actually not so surprising an observation as it might seem, when we appreciate what it means. It is understood that even the most psychologically healthy individual will have some vulnerability to narcissistic insult and injury. Each of us has limitations on how much deprivation of external support, mirroring, recognition, or admiring attention is tolerated before we react with narcissistic rage, hurt, or loss of identity. Kohut goes so far as to include in his perspective that it is normal and healthy for us to always need external narcissistic support and mirroring reflected in the lifelong need for selfobjects. His view of psychological health in the narcissistic sector includes the belief that we never transcend the need for the support of selfobjects, and that maturity means only that the form of relationship to these selfobjects changes, so only the quality of need changes from archaic to more mature forms, but it never ceases to be a need for the self. This is clear in the following passage, where Kohut describes the meaning of cure, which brings about health:

> True, psychological structure is acquired through psychoanalysis and the self becomes more firm. But this increased firmness does not make the self independent of selfobjects. Instead,

520   it increases the self's ability to use selfobjects for its own suste-
           nance, including an increased freedom in choosing selfobjects.
           (Kohut, 1984, p. 77)

This means the self will always need external supports to shore up its identity, which means that the identity has a weakness and vulnerability that cannot disappear in the conventional dimension of experience.

In our view, this is true only in the conventional dimension of experience, for it does not apply to the state of self-realization, in which the self no longer needs external supports to shore up the sense of self. So both normal experience and the formulations of depth psychology, at least in Kohut's case, correspond with our view that the self-identity, in the conventional dimension of experience, possesses a fundamental weakness and vulnerability. Most of us take this fact actually to be normal, and never question it, while in reality it is only the expression of our incomplete experience of ourselves.

54. It is possible for us to experience Essence as a presence, while still maintaining our identity, but this is not the experience of self-realization. Self-realization means we are not only experiencing Essence, but experiencing it as our inherent nature. More specifically, we may experience Essence and still identify with the self-representation, but this is experiencing Essence as an object, while the identity remains as the subject, which is possible, and constitutes the first step in the process of integrating Essence. Self-realization is the next step, where we not only experience Essence to be our true nature, but also, and more significantly, experience it as ourselves, as our very identity. This is simply being, which we have described as identity with the presence of Being. We are being presence, which includes no conceptualization or representation.

55. Because of this fact, developing the capacity for disidentification becomes the aim of many spiritual practices and techniques. One way of developing this capacity is the gradual freeing of identity from the various component self-representations. This may involve, for example, techniques of surrender or confrontation of one's personal characteristics, beliefs, and limitations, or methods for awareness and understanding of them. The idea is to become aware of the manifestations of these representations for the purpose of letting them go, or ceasing to hold onto them.

Another way to develop the capacity for disidentification is to do it directly, by paying attention to the process of identifying and working towards not going along with it. This involves observation of oneself and not going along with the identification with the various observed manifestations of self. An example of this practice is the Buddhist vipassana meditation, where one works to be aware of the manifestations of one's mind without reacting to them or engaging them. Another teaching that uses disidentification as a central practice is that of Gurdjieff. He speaks in the following excerpt from a talk about identification and self-remembering—a concept that approximates becoming aware of the real self: 521

> Identifying is the chief obstacle to self-remembering. A man who identifies with anything is unable to remember himself. In order to remember oneself it is necessary first of all not to identify. (Ouspensky, 1949, p. 151)

We use a form of self-remembering in our approach to disidentification, but we also use discriminating understanding to bring about greater distance of identity from the various self-representations. This practice of understanding—which is our central method for the work on inner realization, and not only restricted to developing the capacity for disidentification—requires that we bring to consciousness all the self-representations which are used for identity and that we then gradually (or sometimes abruptly) disidentify from this mental content by understanding it as representations. At the beginning, we see through the more superficial identifications. These are the chronologically later representations which were internalized after the development of a relatively stable sense of identity. They generally involve some content connected with modeling oneself after one or both parents. At this level we deal especially with object representations established in the development of the superego. Working through these identifications usually removes the repression against some of the deep feelings about the parent with which we identify. The letting-go of these identifications then brings to light the actual personal relationship to the parent, revealing the real emotions of the relationship.

An example is the working-through of the identifications which function to repress the castration and oedipus complexes. A girl, for

522   instance, typically manages her oedipal feelings by finally identifying with her mother, so that she becomes like her—rather than a rival to her—for the father's affections. When this identification is exposed, the oedipal feelings of rivalry with the mother will emerge and must be dealt with.

This process continues as the self-representation manifests its component representations that date progressively to earlier times of identity formation. This process strengthens the identity by working out the various difficulties and conflicts in these earlier representations, leading to its greater flexibility and freeing it from the rigid identifications with those representations. This process becomes extremely subtle, and it resembles psychotherapy less and less as very early and primitive identifications are confronted.

56. A certain degree of the development of this capacity for disidentification must be part of the curative effect of psychotherapy, where the distance from the particular conflictual content is not enough to allow essential presence, but sufficient for the amelioration of conflict and suffering. This is most likely the case when the psychological difficulty is due to the presence of painful or conflictual self-representations and their affects. These self-representations (or representations of internalized object relations) do not usually totally disappear; rather, the individual becomes increasingly disidentified from them. The same thing, of course, happens in the initial phases of spiritual development.

57. We are, of course, aware that frequently some individuals, especially some of the followers of a particular teacher or guru, will continue to believe the teacher is fully realized and rationalize away his disturbed behavior, partly because of their personal needs, but also because they do not understand the situation. This is due to the wrong view, promulgated by some writings and individuals, that spiritual development means one is either enlightened (realized) or not. So some individuals find it easy, as a result of this wrong view, to dismiss the aberrant behavior of the spiritual teacher because they witness the truth and value of the teacher's state and understanding and can only conclude that he is enlightened, and that they merely do not understand his behavior.

Some individuals have developed another and more subtle rationalization, due to this wrong view, which is the belief that one can be enlightened but neurotic. This is the view, of the "sick gurus," that takes it to be

possible that one can be fully realized (enlightened) but still exhibit aber- 523
rant and neurotic behavior. This view also reflects an inaccurate understanding of what self-realization is, assuming that self-realization can be
an attainment separate from the structures of the self, where there can be
full realization that does not influence one's neurotic structures.

It is our understanding that spiritual states, in general, require disidentification from psychic structures, normal or neurotic, and that self-
realization, in particular, means the absence of these structures, at least
in the duration of the experience, as we have discussed in very specific
details. Full self-realization—enlightenment—requires the complete
and final dissolution of all psychic structures. There cannot be neurotic
manifestations in full self-realization, because any neurotic manifestation must be the expression of some psychic structures, which, by their
representational nature, will limit the realization. So what is called a
"sick guru" must be an individual who is spiritually developed but not
fully realized or enlightened.

This understanding, besides illuminating the nature of spiritual realization and protecting its purity, may help us to see the imperfections
in a spiritual teacher's realization without having to rationalize them
away or to devalue him or her completely. This way, we may retain the
objectivity that we need to help us appreciate what we can learn from
a particular teacher and what we cannot. The situation of spirituality
in the world is not such that we need a fully realized and enlightened
master—a Buddha, a Lao Tzu, or a Christ—for us to receive guidance
in our spiritual quest. The situation is not unlike others, in most fields,
where we find teachers of various degrees of competence and maturity,
and the student needs to find the ones who can help him or her best.

58. We discuss the notion of absorption in *The Pearl Beyond Price*,
(Almaas, 1988) in some detail. It basically means that a representation
will lose its defensive properties, including the subtle ones of holding
on to any particular content, to the extent that it becomes totally transparent to the presence of Essence. When this condition occurs, the representation becomes absorbed and does not exist as a representation
any more. What remains is a condition of the self that indicates its greater
development due to the absorption of the wisdom acquired from the
experiences that generated the representation to start with. The learning remains in the transformation of the self and not as content of

524   representation. Whatever mental information survives will not be used in any fundamental way for self-recognition.

59. The reader might be interested to know that we do not know this condition of final and ultimate realization from direct experience, for the author does not consider himself to have attained permanent full self-realization. This condition of full enlightenment is clearly necessary for direct knowledge of what it is. Our discussion of it is based, out of necessity, on some experience of the state of full self-realization, on the deduction from such limited experience and other experiences and understanding of general spiritual development, and from the insights of individuals acknowledged as having reached such attainment.

60. It is clear here that the ego or self which is annihilated in "ego death" is not the ego of depth psychology and it is not the actual self. It is specifically the self-identity. The death of this identity merely means that there is no barrier or resistance to the presence of Essence. There is no need to uphold an identity based on a psychic structure that is bound to have some rigidity for the simple reason that this psychic structure is based on a representation, and that the representation is based on past experience. This might prove to be irrelevant to the arising dimension of presence, but it is an irrelevance that is bound to function as a measure of inflexibility. Ego death also implies the total freedom from the overall self-representation.

This condition does not necessarily mean there will be no more self-representation or identity; it means that this representation does not pattern the experience of the self and that the identity is not experienced as oneself. The self is the presence of Essence itself, and when the identity is present in experience, it is perceived to refer to a superficial manifestation of oneself.

61. Buddhism, especially in the Theravada school, terms this condition "emptiness of self" or "no self" (anatma). The teaching here is that the self does not ultimately exist, in other words, does not possess a truly independent existence, but is merely a conceptualized existence. The self here refers to identifying oneself as an independent entity continuous in space and time. So the "no self" of Buddhism refers to the truth that both senses of self, that of entity and identity, are only mental creations.

This actually corresponds with the understanding in depth psychology, as we have discussed.

The experience of emptiness reveals the underlying unreality of the familiar sense of self, which coincides with not identifying with it. In other words, as the sense of self is exposed to be based on a representation, and hence does not possess an ontological truth, the identity dissolves.

62. We call this fundamental narcissism "the narcissism of everyday life" for no conventional self is ever free from it. However, this may bring up the question of how this dissolution of identity is related to the condition of fragmentation or disintegration of identity, which is, under normal circumstances, a manifestation of pathological narcissism. The main difference between the "death of the self" in self-realization and the disintegration of identity in pathological narcissism is that the former is a developmental achievement based on the greater strength and flexibility of identity, while the latter is a developmental difficulty resulting from an extreme weakness and brittleness of the identity. There is no sense of the normal self in both conditions, but the former is a state of equanimity of the self for being fully itself, so fully itself that there is no need for self-reflection, while the latter is a painful and deficient state of the self, where it feels disconnected from its depth and fullness. The former is a state of self-recognition not based on any representation, for it is recognizing what is actually present, while the latter is a state where there is no self-recognition of any kind.

An important difference is that the state of ego death in self-realization is free from all representations, while the condition of a disintegrated or lost identity, although it lacks a coherent identity structure, is still a condition of the self patterned by self-representations. The situation of a disintegrated or lost identity is a condition where the patterning of the self remains, but remains in an incomplete, distorted, incoherent, and defective state. It is the existence of incomplete and distorted psychic structures which accounts for the pain and deficiency, and not merely the absence of identity. In pathological states of narcissism, the absence of identity only manifests an already present distortion, or a greater deterioration of it.

63. This chapter is a rewriting of Chapter 21, in *The Pearl Beyond Price* (Almaas, 1988), to suit our present study. The discussion in the

526   above book focuses on the development of the sense of self in the self-representation, where this sense includes both the sense of being a differentiated and unique existence, and the feeling of identity. The present discussion focuses more on the feeling of identity, but discusses the development of the sense of self, in general, as the larger development. We referred to the essential aspect as the Essential Self in the above book and in other previous publications, but call it Essential Identity in the present book.

64. In ego development, which is the process by which the conventional self develops, the differentiation of the self amounts to, or develops into, separation based on self-boundaries. The experience of the Essential Identity as a differentiated and unique existence does not imply separateness or partitioning boundaries. Differentiation here only means difference and uniqueness. In other words, differentiation is not separateness. It is not easy to imagine how one can experience oneself as differentiated and unique without being separated from others by partitioning boundaries, but this realization is possible within essential experience. It is similar to experiencing oneself as a presence differentiated but not separated from a universal presence, differentiated by qualities unique to it, but not separate because there are other elements that are common. It is like being a unique part of a design, different from the other parts, but not separate from them. We will see how this is possible as we go further in our study.

65. What we are calling the Essential Identity is not the same as the self assumed to exist in the early months of life by some object relations theorists, such as Fairbairn. Fairbairn's self is an entity that is functional and psychical in nature, so it corresponds to our concept of the self or soul, while the Essential Identity is, rather, a presence of Being, in the form of identity. It is neither psychical, in the usual sense of the word, nor functional.

66. This can be ascertained directly by individuals with essential perception. Essential perception makes it possible to directly perceive the inner state of the child and see what aspect of Essence is present in his consciousness.

67. These experiential qualities of the Essential Identity may help explain how one can experience oneself as differentiated and unique

but not separate. One experiences oneself as a concentration of pres-   527
ence and intensity of awareness, but still part of a sea of aware presence.

This also shows that this self is not the self negated in Buddhist metaphysics. The self negated is the sense of being an independently existing
and enduring self. The Essential Identity, although it is self-existing and
ontologically real, does not exist in isolation from the rest of the realm of
Being. In fact, it is an expression of Being, a form that Being assumes as
part of the richness of its manifestation, expressing and manifesting some
of its intrinsic and fundamental qualities and functions. Its properties of
self-existence and ontological reality, instead of setting it up as an independently and absolutely existing entity, merely reflect the properties that
it possesses in lieu of its inherent inseparability from Being-as-such.

68. Truth is one of the aspects of Essence, which expresses its property of essential Truth as the very existence of Truth, rather than as truth
related to some object or idea. This aspect reveals that Truth is ultimately a presence, a self-existing quality of Being, and not only a quality which qualifies something else. Truth is then experienced as a dense
and substantial presence, solid and real. It is a presence that has luster,
warmth, intimacy, and realness. It is a solidity that is not corrupted by
lies and falsehood, but can expose all lies and falsehood. Although it is
dense and solid like gold, Truth possesses heart qualities like warmth
and intimacy. There is a sense of purity to it, a sense of incorruptabil-
ity, a sense of being the real thing. It functions, in part, to give the self
the capacity to discern truth and separate it from falsehood, a capacity
needed not only for spiritual development but for survival. The way it
provides the self with this capacity is the way pure solid gold provides
the jeweler with a way of discriminating it from its imitations and alloys.
This capacity is needed because lies and falsehood usually function to
take the place of truth, presenting themselves as truth.

69. This is a clear example of how the ego-self disconnects the self
from Essence. Any falsehood in our experience of ourselves will disconnect us from the aspect of Truth. And since this is the aspect of
Essence which specifically expresses the fact that Essence is the ultimate
and prototypical truth, any falsehood will disconnect the self from
Essence in general. So falsehood disconnects the self from Essence, and
is also a result of its disconnection from it.

528   This is not exactly a narcissistic issue, but it will disconnect the self from Essence. Therefore, by dealing with narcissism specifically, we see how it disconnects the self from Essence by disconnecting it from a specific aspect, the Essential Identity, which expresses, just as Truth does, something fundamental about Essence. Just as the aspect of Truth expresses and manifests Essence as the ultimate truth of the self, so the aspect of the Essential Identity manifests and expresses Essence as its ultimate identity.

We can do this kind of exploration with the various manifestations of Essence, like Love and Compassion and so on, thus realizing Essence by the clarification and dissolution of the various structures and characteristics of the conventional self. We do this, for example, in *The Pearl Beyond Price* (Almaas, 1988) and *The Void* (Almaas, 1986), related to the aspects of the Personal Essence and Inner Space, respectively.

70. This is similar to the situation in the dimension of conventional experience when one identifies with a certain impression, like the body. She (the self) experiences herself as the body. This identification is not as complete or total as in the essential dimension because although she experiences herself as the body, the identity with it is not complete and not directly experienced. There is still a subject-object relationship to the body, which is an intrinsic and unavoidable expression of the mode of experience in the conventional dimension of the self.

71. The distinction between the two kinds of nondual experience can help us to understand some of the subtle differences between various traditional spiritual teachings. A good example is the difference in the formulation of the ultimate truth between Buddhism and Hinduism, where this ultimate truth is conceptualized as absolute nature in Buddhism, and absolute self in Hinduism. The ultimate truth is understood to be the same, which is emptiness or awareness (which is emptiness coemergent with presence), although the subtle difference in definition appears in both of these traditions. The formulations of the ultimate truth of the final nature or self reflect the differing emphasis in the two traditions: The Buddhist formulation reflects the second way of experiencing the ultimate truth, while the Hindu formulation reflects the third way of experiencing it. So the Buddhist will express his view as "There is only awareness," while the Hindu will express his view as "I am awareness."

This is made abundantly clear when we compare the flavor of the   529
views in the next two passages, the first from the teachings of the
Buddhist Kalachakra tantra and the second by the Indian Vedantist
Nisargadatta Maharaj:

> The innate mind of sentient beings is luminous clarity;
> From the beginning it is detached
> From the absolute attributes of arising, ceasing, and settling.
> Since beginningless time it has been the primordial supreme
>   Buddha,
> Because it has been unmodulated by cause and condition.
> (Takpo Tashi Namgyal, 1986, p. 181)

> As Absolute, I am timeless, infinite, and I am awareness, with-
> out being aware of awareness. As infinity I express myself as space,
> as timeless I express myself as time. (Dunn, ed., 1985, p. 72)

Of course, the difference is a matter of emphasis, and the two kinds
of experiences exist in both traditions. However, this difference, which
reflects two of the functions of the Essential Identity, does lead to wide
differences in metaphysics and mostly in methodology. The main metaphysical difference is that while in Hinduism the ultimate truth is formulated as the true self, in Buddhism it is formulated in the opposite
direction, as no self.

The two kinds of experiences may be seen in the theistic traditions,
in terms of the experience of God. We see this, for example, in the Sufi
teaching, where it is formulated that one may experience God in two
ways; the first is expressed as "Only God exists," and the second as "I
am God." An example of this is the system of Ibn Arabi, where he views
the path as consisting of stations, and considers the "I am God" as a
higher station:

> The traveller in this station finds on his road no one else but
> himself and thinks of everything as tied to himself. . . . He was
> before this the Son of Time and he used to say: 'There is no
> other existence but God.' When he has found this station he
> will say: 'There is only "I,"' and he is often referred to as the
> Father of Time (abu-l waqt). (Ibn 'Arabi, pp. 6–7)

Both of these realizations correspond to the experience of full self-
realization. In this experience, where the primordial presence includes

530   all dimensions of the self, the first way of experiencing truth will be not only that "Only truth exists," but also that "Everything is truth." More accurately, it is the experience of "Only truth, which is everything, exists." This is the coemergence of truth and everything. The second way of experiencing truth in primordial presence is not only that "I am the truth," but also that "I am everything." More accurately, it is the experience of "I am the truth, which is everything." This is the coemergence of truth, identity and everything.

Book Two Notes

─────────────────────────────────────── •

1.   When the focus is on the other forms of narcissism and this is not clear from the context, we will indicate the form we are discussing.

2.   The understanding we are presenting has a much wider range of application than its usage in the Diamond Approach^{SM}, or for that matter, in spiritual development in general. It is an understanding that does not only contain a view of self-realization, but a very comprehensive and fundamental comprehension of narcissism, which is a significant contribution to the growing research into this disturbance of the self.

3.   A further, unselfish interest develops by now, manifesting as the desire to help and serve other beings. We learn increasingly that we are not so separate from other human beings and from life in general, and we begin to see that our own interests and the interests of others are very connected. This impels us to want to free and realize ourselves on more and more profound levels so that we will have the capacities to be of help. This selfless desire grows out of the love and compassion that we experience in greater depths, but ultimately, the more it is impregnated by its essential qualities, the more it is recognized to be a natural functioning of the self. In other words, something akin to what the Buddhists

532   call the "Bodhisattva attitude" develops spontaneously as part of the natural spiritual development of ourselves.

4.   It is interesting that Kernberg conceptualizes self-esteem as having affective components at primitive levels of organization, components that he describes in the same way we will describe affects characteristic of Essence:

> Self-esteem or self-regard represents, therefore, the more differentiated levels of narcissistic investment, while diffuse *feelings of well-being, of pleasure with existence, of affective states expressing euphoria or satisfaction,* represent the more primitive expression of narcissism. [emphasis added] (Kernberg, 1975, pp. 317–718)

We may consider the feelings characterizing essential presence to be primitive, in the sense that they underlie and antecede the ones dependent on the development of psychic structures, but they are definitely not primitive in the sense of being vague or undifferentiated, for they possess the property of being experienced and recognized in a very clear and differentiated way.

5.   Kernberg writes:

> These patients present an unusual degree of self-reference in their interactions with other people, a great need to be loved and admired by others, and a curious apparent contradiction between a very inflated concept of themselves and an inordinate need for tribute from others. Their emotional life is shallow. They experience little empathy for the feelings of others, obtain very little enjoyment from life other than from the tributes they receive from others or from their own grandiose fantasies, and they feel restless and bored when external glitter wears off and no new sources feed their self-regard. (Kernberg, 1975, pp. 227–228)

6.   Kernberg, whose discussion starting with manifestations that we have mentioned but moving to more pathological one, states:

> They envy others, tend to idealize some people from whom they expect narcissistic supplies and to depreciate and treat with contempt those from whom they do not expect anything (often

their former idols). In general, their relationships with other 533
people are clearly exploitative and sometimes parasitic. It is as
if they feel they have the right to control and possess others and
to exploit them without guilt feelings—and, behind a surface
which very often is charming and engaging, one senses cold-
ness and ruthlessness. (Kernberg, 1975, p. 228)

The psychopathological flavor may also be seen in other kinds of
manifestations, mixed with the ones we have enumerated, as Kohut
points out:

(1) in the sexual sphere: perverse fantasies, lack of interest in
sex; (2) in the social sphere: work inhibitions, delinquent activities; (3) in his manifest personality features: lack of humor,
lack of empathy for other people's needs and feelings, lack of a
sense of proportion, tendency toward attacks of uncontrolled
rage, pathological lying; and (4) in the psychosomatic sphere:
hypochondriacal preoccupation with physical and mental
health, vegetative disturbances in various organ systems.
(Kohut, 1971, p. 23)

Some of these may manifest for some individuals, even with a normal development of self as part of dealing with central narcissism, but
they tend to be not so severe or chronic, and not the central manifestation. The more severe they are, the more chronic and central, the more
we may feel that the particular individual suffers not only from the fundamental narcissism characteristic of the normal self, but of some degree
of abnormal development.

7. Kohut defines a third kind of selfobjects, in his last writings,
related not to the two poles of the bipolar self, "but to an intermediate
area of basic talents and skills that are activated by the tension-arc that
establishes itself between ambitions and ideals." (Morrison, 1986, p. 177)

In other words, the bipolar self is defined not only by its poles of
ambitions and ideals, but also by the integration of skills and talents
that are needed for the self to express itself when activated by the
tension-arc.

The third type of selfobjects are the objects who affirm and support
the child in assuming and developing her skills and talents. Kohut calls
these "twinship" or "alter ego" selfobjects, in the sense that they are

534   objects who support the self by being similar to her. The little girl's skills
are supported and affirmed, for example, by her kneading dough along-
side her mother, who is doing the same thing. Kohut's original formulations included the twinship kind of selfobjects into the category of
mirroring selfobjects, but he later decided that it is a specific type that
has its own line of development. (Kohut, 1984, Chapter 10).

8.   Kohut believes the grandiose self is only an image in the child's
mind, and not a true perception of herself; yet she needs it to be mirrored to help her maintain her narcissistic well-being. In his first theory, Kohut maintained that the child needs this grandiose self to preserve
the original perfection of primary narcissism. But in his latter theory,
he merely sees the grandiose self as a natural developmental step and
the need for its mirroring as also a developmental need. As we will see,
we view the grandiose self from a different perspective, one in which it
is not an inaccurate image of the self. Hence, the child's need for its mirroring becomes the need to be seen for her true self. See Chapter 20
about the relation of grandiose self to the Essential Identity, where the
truth underlying the former becomes clear.

9.   Kohut writes:

> It is in the matrix of a particular selfobject environment that, via
> a specific process of psychological structure formation called
> *transmuting internalization,* the *nuclear self* of the child will crys-
> tallize. Without going into the details of this structure-building
> process, we can say (1) that it cannot occur without a previous
> stage in which the child's mirroring and idealizing needs had
> been sufficiently responded to; (2) that it takes place in conse-
> quence of the minor, non-traumatic failures in the responses of
> the mirroring and the idealized selfobjects; and (3) that these fail-
> ures lead to the gradual replacement of the selfobjects and their
> functions by a self and its functions. (Kohut, 1984, p. 181).

10. Kernberg writes in his paper, "Factors in the Treatment of Narcissistic Personalities":

> At this point, there is a fusion of ideal self, ideal object, and
> actual self images as a defense against an intolerable reality in
> the interpersonal realm, with a concomitant devaluation and

destruction of object images as well as of external objects. In
their fantasies, these patients identify themselves with their own
ideal self-images in order to deny normal dependency on external objects and on the internalized representations of the external objects. (Morrison, 1986, pp. 216–217).

535

11. Kernberg's perspective of the nature of this defense is clear in the
following statement from another paper, "Further Contributions to the
Treatment of Narcissistic Personalities," in which he differentiates
between the borderline conditions and the narcissistic personality in
that the latter has an integrated grandiose self which reflects:

> a pathological condensation of some aspects of the real self
> (the 'specialness' of the child reinforced by early experience),
> the ideal self (fantasies and self-images of power, wealth, omni-
> science and beauty which compensated the small child for
> the experience of severe oral frustration, rage and envy) and
> the ideal object (the fantasy of an ever-giving, ever-loving and
> accepting parent, in contrast to the child's experience in
> reality; a replacement of the devalued real parental object).
> (Morrison, 1986, p. 247)

12. Our approach lies between those two. Since ego deficiency is a
borderline issue, we see that Kernberg's formulation makes most sense
with narcissistic individuals who have strong borderline features. The
more borderlines features a person has, the more her grandiosity will
be used for defense. He emphasizes aggression a great deal in terms of
defining narcissism and the grandiose self, and considers splitting as
part of the defensive narcissistic structures because it is specifically a
defense against oral rage. Kernberg's formulation will be useful in our
understanding of the oral form of narcissism, in which oral aggression
and splitting are important.

13. We say a human being is born a soul, instead of with a soul,
because we take our view from the experience of full self-realization in
which the primordial presence includes the body as its embodiment.
However, our view of the development of the self and narcissism does
not need this specific refinement, and may be seen entirely from the
view that an individual is born with a soul.

536   14. The child can be born with different kinds of disturbances and deficiencies such as physical inadequacy and damage or disturbances and deficiencies can be the result of the effects of prenatal life on the growing organism. The questions of whether the newborn soul already has a structure and whether it is an entity remain unanswered. We definitely know that the child is not born with a sense of being a person. But is the newborn child an entity in the sense that there is an awareness in the child of itself as an entity separate from the rest? According to Mahler, the sense of being an entity develops as part of the separation-individuation process, just as the feeling of identity does. The psychic organization, in conjunction with the physical functions, is termed the undifferentiated matrix by Hartmann, and the psychophysical matrix by Jacobson; both terms infer an existence that lacks the differentiation necessary for a sense of entity.

We believe this is most likely the case, which is what Kohut is referring to when he says that there is no self at the beginning of life: "To begin with, it seems safe to assume that, strictly speaking, the neonate is still without a self." (Morrison, 1986, p. 181) In other words, the neonate does not have a sense of being an entity with a sense of identity. We will not use Kohut's terminology here because the self is the soul in our view and not merely the soul's later structuralization. In other words, the self exists in the beginning as the psychic life of the infant. In fact, the psychic life as commonly known is not exactly the psychic life of the infant because, as seen in Chapter 4, she lives in the condition of primary self-realization, in which psychic life as we understand it exists as an expression and manifestation of presence.

15. In fact, we see these latter theories as limited because they take the human being to be very impoverished and denuded. They view the human infant basically as a physical body with some psychic functions and potentialities. They do not include in the human being a reality that is intrinsically rich, full, or a source of psychological nourishment, love, pleasure, and satisfaction. It is our view that they view him as empty of a self-existing goodness and richness because they see him only from within the conventional dimension of the experience of the adult, namely, from within the perspective of the narcissism of everyday life. Looked at from the experience of self-realization, almost all the depth psychological theories of the self are adultomorphic because they

do not include the ontological ground of the self with the intrinsic and 537
self-existing richness of its essential presence. These theories take the
view that whatever capacity for self-nourishment, self-soothing, understanding, value, love, and compassion that an individual develops is
due to the internalization of these qualities and functions from external sources (adults), giving him nothing of his own that is of any psychological value. The most that these theories give him is the potential for
such capacities, but even such potential is understood as the potential
to internalize them from others. Hartmann's concept of ego functions,
or the apparatuses of primary autonomy, comes the closest to our view
of the intrinsic existence of richness in the neonate, but it fails to give
the human being a real ground of goodness, because it views such functions or apparatuses largely as ways for getting the needed richness from
outside. This situation continues to be the case for most depth psychological theories; the only exceptions are the ones that have a spiritual
dimension, like those of Jung. Their conceptualizations prevent them
from seeing that these capacities depend on experiential qualities that
a human being is born with and that the internalization process merely
organizes these already existing qualities into the developing structure
of entity and identity.

This truth is obvious in our common sense experience of children.
It would also be included in psychological formulations of the human
self if theorists were open to the insights present in many of humanity's
spiritual teachings. It is difficult not to agree with Kohut's characteri-
zation of psychoanalysts' attitudes as being generally close-minded:

> Even though the claim of open-mindedness is always made—
> how could it be otherwise?—I believe that on the whole ana-
> lysts do not study opposing viewpoints extensively, do not give
> wholehearted trials to new modes of depth psychological
> thought, and are unwilling even to shift their observational
> position to new vantage points from which to make the clini-
> cal observations that bear on alternative theoretical positions.
> (Kohut, 1984, p. 164)

This is, in our opinion, even more applicable when it comes to understanding the nature of the self, and the well-known areas in which such
understanding already exists. Of course, Kohut's criticism can also be

538   applied to his developing a psychology of the self which he undertook without investigating the knowledge about it which might already be available.

16. This has been corroborated in many areas, including brain research, where it has been found that the brain grows in spurts:

> Brain 'growth spurts' take place in utero, at birth, and at the beginning of each stage of development.... (Pearce, 1992, p. 99)

17. Structure can be built before the conceptual faculty develops, as some depth psychologists have been discovering. This is part of Daniel Stern's thesis where he proposes that a sense of self forms before the development of conceptual knowledge. He writes:

> It is a basic assumption of this book that some senses of the self do exist long prior to self-awareness and language. (Stern, 1985, p. 6)

This corresponds with some of our observations, but it does not mean that Essence can become part of these early structures. There are several reasons for this, some we have already discussed.

One important reason is that these early senses of self contain elements related primarily to functioning and not to innate nature, which is a much subtler thing to structuralize because not only is it not conceptualized, it is not even discriminated in experience. Another reason is the fact that these early senses of self are transformed later by the conceptual operations of the mind. Stern, in fact, mentions these two points in the continuation of the above quotation which enumerates some of these early senses of self:

> These include the senses of agency, of physical cohesion, of continuity in time, of having intentions in mind, and other such experiences we will soon discuss. Self-reflection and language come to work upon these preverbal existential senses of the self and, in so doing, not only reveal their ongoing existence but transform them into new experiences. (Stern, 1985, p. 6)

There is another reason that early structures of the self cannot include Essence, which we will discuss only briefly, for it will take us far afield to the larger context of the self and its properties. This is the fact that a

structure is relatively invariant, as Stern puts it. As a fixed structure   539
along the axis of time, it is not permeable to Essence. Essence, as we
have seen in Chapters 4 and 8, has a dynamic quality that gives the self
an unfolding property. A fixed structure (and the more fixed the structure, the more this is so) will automatically be antithetical to the presence of Essence, for it will impede the spontaneity and flow of its
dynamism.

18. This capacity for perceiving the content of his experience is aided,
and partly developed, by the mirroring of people in his environment.
In other words, the fact that his mother relates to and touches his body,
for example, helps him feel it and perceive it. This help, however, is
rarely available when it comes to the experience of his essential presence. Most parents are not self-realized, so they not only do not experience Essence; most of the time they do not even know of its existence.
As a result, they do not and cannot provide mirroring for the child's
essential presence. We will discuss this shortly, as part of the environmental factors which cause narcissism.

19. This is probably the most important reason every individual loses
his self-realization as he grows up. The nature of the human mind is such
that it does not allow the self to recognize its initial condition, which is
a form of self-realization. The self always develops as the ego-self, a psychic structure whose identity situates its consciousness in the dimension of conventional experience. In other words, the nature of the self
and its development causes it to lose contact with its essence, regardless of the quality of life in the early years.

20. The possibility that the child will experience the Essential Identity
in a somewhat objective manner must be discussed to complete our
exploration into the maturational factors behind the development of
narcissism. This does happen occasionally, just as it happens in some
of the stages of spiritual development. This is because the Essential
Identity is an aspect of Essence, and can be experienced in the three
ways we discussed in Chapter 14. In the first type of experience, the
Essential Identity is experienced in a dualistic manner and hence as an
object separate from the self. However, this is not the experience of self-
realization; it means that a person will not know that what he experiences dualistically is what he is experiencing when he is being himself,

540   when he is simply being. So it will not be possible for him to see it as himself. This fact and the fact that most children rarely experience it supports the validity and significance of our discussion. We must also remember that this discussion pertains to the development of narcissism, which is a specific reflection of the loss of self-realization.

    21. In discussing Mahler's contributions, Greenberg and Mitchell write:

> The child's development results from the interaction between his subphase-specific behaviours and the mother's responses. As the child passes through the various subphases, his needs change, including his need for different modes of relatedness with the mother. (Greenberg and Mitchell, 1983, p. 280)

    22. This situation—of reactivity causing narcissism—is appreciated both in spiritual teachings which develop practices for learning not to be reactive, and also by some object relations theorists. A specific example of the latter is the case of R. D. Winnicott who understood that reacting leads to disconnection from being:

> The alternative to being is reacting, and reacting interrupts being and annihilates. (Winnicott, 1980, p. 47)

    Thus, since the loss of the capacity to be is exactly the fundamental cause of narcissism, it follows that Winnicott understands how reacting causes narcissism. He does not use the term *narcissism,* but he does use the term *false self,* which he conceptualizes as the manner in which the self develops when it is based on reacting. (Winnicott, 1980, pp. 140–152)

    The false self is actually what the narcissistic self is, and it is basically the result of the alienation from Essence.

    23. Kohut and most depth psychologists understand the child's need for adoration, but take the position that this means the child needs a reflection that does not correspond to the truth of what and who he actually is. The implication is that the self of the child needs something not true—a falsehood—for it to grow. We find this to be a gross misunderstanding of the human being and his or her needs. Obviously, this misunderstanding reflects a fundamental limitation in the formulations of depth psychology with regard to the self.

In any case, a child needs an adoring attitude not because he needs 541 an unrealistic view about himself, but because he is actually adorable; in other words, it is not an unrealistic view about him because his essence does actually possess such unusual and adorable qualities. We find something real being interpreted as imaginary and delusional in many of the formulations of depth psychology. It suggests a belief that the human self has a fundamental need for falsehood, in the form of delusions. This contradicts the deepest and most fundamental truth about the human self, which is that its ground and ultimate nature is pure truth.

This misunderstanding has other consequences, as we will discuss elsewhere in this study. Kohut's view about the needs of the self extend to believing that one needs to feel understood regardless of whether or not the understanding reflects the true condition of the self. This would mean that a true and realistic sense of self could develop out of a delusional sense of who one is, a view which contradicts both common sense and logic.

These remarks will become significant for our view of the grandiose self and its genetic origin, which takes the essential truth of the self into consideration. This view is quite different from those offered by Kernberg and Kohut. We believe it to be more balanced in that it explains the unrealism of the grandiose self without having to assume that a delusional view of oneself is a necessary developmental stage. This is significant for a study of narcissism, since correctly understanding the grandiose self is recognized to be important for understanding narcissism not only by us, but by all of the theories in depth psychology.

We will make only a brief mention of our understanding of the grandiose self here, since a full discussion appears later in Chapter 20, which is devoted to the exploration of the grandiose self. Our understanding of the grandiose self requires the recognition that the Essential Identity is a presence of Being, beyond the body and mind. It is basically indestructible, powerful, precious, and beautiful beyond bounds. Its love is limitless and its brilliance is boundless. But these are the qualities of Essence and not the body or mind, and they cannot be transposed and applied to the physical or psychic sphere except in a very limited way. The child is identified with the Essential Identity with all of its qualities, but he does not know what he is being, as we have seen.

542   At some point, for various psychological and developmental reasons, the child starts believing that these unusual qualities characterize his body and mind, and behaves accordingly. This is how the grandiose self begins. This means that the depth psychological understanding that the grandiose self is a delusional formation is partly, but not completely, accurate, especially in relation to narcissism. This understanding discounts the fundamental truth about the child—that there is an element in him that truly has grand characteristics—and in this way also discounts the most important part of the child's potential, his Essential Identity, and his capacity to be truly himself.

24. This point actually illustrates that ego development, even though it is basically a conceptual process, is inextricably linked and dependent upon the unfoldment of essential presence. The reader may find more details about how early childhood ego development, specifically, the development of psychic structures, is intertwined with the arising of pure essential forms, in our previous book, *The Pearl Beyond Price* (Almaas, 1988). In this book, we discuss the development of the self into an individual with a sense of entity and identity in specific detail, including the way in which the various phases of development, such as the symbiotic stage, rapprochement, and so on, are related to the corresponding forms of Essence, the essential aspects.

25. Portions of the following few pages are adapted from Chapter 21 of our book, *The Pearl Beyond Price,* for our present study.

26. What does it mean when we say the Essential Identity has no limitations on the Being level? This is not an easy point to grasp if one does not directly experience the Essential Identity. One way of describing it is that the Essential Identity is an element of the self that shares with Being-as-such the characteristics of being indestructible, eternal, and absolutely positive. Its truth transcends our common sense of time and space, so it is a timeless reality. This timelessness makes it something to which we cannot apply the concepts of destruction or limitation. It is also the self's true ontological source of love, goodness, intelligence, compassion, power, and so on, and hence, one feels the limitlessness of these qualities when one is the Essential Identity.

This limitlessness is usually attributed to God in the various theistic traditions, and to the enlightened person in the Far Eastern religions.

These characteristics are really the attributes of pure Being, and the 543
Essential Identity is the reflection of this pure Being in the human self.
However, we cannot say that the self in general possesses such attributes,
for the self has mental and physical manifestations that definitely do
not possess such attributes. The degree to which an individual truly
possesses such attributes, meaning the degree to which he can actually
feel and express them, depends on his level of self-realization. Even then,
one does not experience this limitlessness on the physical and mental
level, for these dimensions are simply unable to manifest these characteristics completely. Some traditional spiritual teachings—such as
Buddhism's descriptions of the fully realized Buddha and some Hindu
schools—say it is possible for a human being to express such qualities
completely, even in the physical plane. Since we have not experienced
this firsthand, we have no familiarity with it.

27. It is interesting and instructive that the Sufis refer to the spiritual or essential core as the "meaning" (m'ana, in Arabic), differentiating
it from the "form" (sura, in Arabic), which is the external manifestation of experience. They definitely do not refer to conceptual meaning;
they are very clear in their communications that they are referring to
the inner truth of Being, the essence of the manifest, as is amply clear
in the following excerpt from a poem by Rumi:

> Know that the outward form passes away, but the World of
>   Meaning remains forever.
> How long will you make love with the shape of the jug? Leave
>   aside the jug's shape: Go, seek water!
> Having seen the form, you are unaware of the meaning. If
>   you are wise, pick out the pearl from the shell.
> (Chittick, 1983, p. 20)

28. He discusses idealization as being different types. One is the
primitive type, characteristic of borderline pathology, which reflects
the defensive operation of splitting in which the object is idealized as
"all good," powerful, and gratifying, to defend against the "all bad"
image of the object. Another form is the neurotic idealization, which
expresses the individual's ambivalence, and yet another is the more
mature kind, which includes the projection of higher level superego
functions.

544   These different types of idealization can be seen as a continuum, from normal primitive to normal adult functioning. All of them, however, are in striking contrast to the idealization of the narcissistic personality, which reflects the projection onto the analyst of the patient's grandiose self. (Kernberg, 1975, p. 277)

29. We do not have direct evidence that supports the Jungian view that it is always natural for the child to project its spiritual qualities as part of its normal development, as is stated in the following passage:

> This one-sided projection (or transference) is a necessary stage during which the spiritual aspect of the Self unfolds, becoming a psychic structure that performs vital functions. (Schwartz-Salant, 1982, p. 43)

It is possible that such processes do occur, and it is a reasonable assumption, but it is also possible that there are alternative explanations. We do observe this process in the idealizing transference of most students at certain stages of their work on spiritual transformation, but this is not necessarily sufficient to hypothesize the same process in childhood. Part of our reluctance to totally accept the Jungian view is due to our observation that the child does experience the Essential Identity and does not normally project it on the parents. Of course, the question of the origin of idealization in childhood development of the self remains, but the observation that the child does not normally project all spiritual qualities of itself on the parents does indicate that idealization—if it is a projection of a spiritual quality of the child—is not a projection of the Essential Identity. So what is it a projection of?

30. This is a significant juncture. It is the place at which our work takes a spiritual direction and ends up fundamentally separate from Kohut's work and that of any other psychotherapeutic approach. This juncture occurs not only in the work on narcissism, but also in the investigation of any ego manifestation. In understanding a particular manifestation, we always discover that at a certain juncture our work bifurcates from that of psychotherapy and reveals what it truly is, a method for spiritual transformation. A psychotherapist would stay at the same level of discourse at this juncture, while in our work, it becomes the stepping stone to spiritual dimensions.

31. As we will see in due course, these correspond to the two kinds 545 of narcissistic transference: the loss of idealization leading to loss of support, and the loss of mirroring leading to loss of identity.

32. This attitude of total openness which underlies our method of inquiry provides a certainty in our findings about this emptiness. We feel certain that these findings are more accurate, or at least more complete, than those of Kohut and others in depth psychology. This total openness is specifically necessary for exploring narcissism at this juncture because, as we will see shortly, it is the essence of the full understanding of the deficient emptiness under consideration.

33. See *The Pearl Beyond Price* (Almaas, 1988) for a detailed discussion of ego deficiency, which has to do with the absence of the Personal Essence, the essential aspect that supplants the ego experience of being an autonomous and separate individual. This ego deficiency is related to the weakness of the psychic structure of self-entity, while the helplessness related to lack of support is connected to the weakness of the psychic structure of self-identity.

34. Working with the more well-known ego deficiency, that of ego weakness, leads to the discovery of a certain essential manifestation of Being. Since this inadequacy relates to functioning, and hence to all of the ego functions, its transformation leads to a different kind of support, the support for true functioning. This essential manifestation is discussed in detail in *The Pearl Beyond Price*, where we refer to it as the essential conscience, or The Citadel, the defender of Essence. It is the support for the general process of transformation, for living a life that will support and enhance the work of self-realization. It is a manifestation of the will of Being, the source of wisdom regarding external discipline with regard to one's behavior, conduct, lifestyle, and environment. It functions as the conscience of the work of transformation by clarifying how one is not living one's life to support transformation and by offering guidance as to how to get that support.

This support is different from the support we are investigating which is related to being who one truly is. However, it is necessary for the support of identity because it forms the external ground required for true self-realization. It provides the guidance for what can be done so that one may arrive at the stage where nondoing is required. If its teaching

546   is followed, it will eventually expose the emptiness of the normal identity, and more than anything else, it will confront us with the emptiness as the final and primary barrier to self-realization.

    The support we experience when we deal with narcissism is of a different kind. It is a subtler dimension of support, a support for the central part of the work of transformation. It is related not to one's external life, as in the case of The Citadel, but to the immediacy of one's inner experience of oneself. It is the support for nondoing, which we may term "the support for Being." The Citadel resolves the deficiency related to the self-entity while the support of nondoing resolves the deficiency related to the self-identity.

    It is possible to experience self-realization and its essential support in a time-limited way before integrating The Citadel, but it cannot become a permanent realization without this integration. To live a life that does not support the process of spiritual transformation (which is the meaning of not integrating the dimension of The Citadel) indicates that one's actions are dictated by the needs, desires, and biases of the normal identity, which can only support and prolong its delusions, including the delusion of its reality. Simply put, one cannot work on transcending the normal identity of the self when one continues to live its life.

    Although the support for the identity of being is a much subtler dimension, the realization of The Citadel is a much more difficult attainment. It is difficult because it means the loss of most of the comforts that cushion our delusions. It is emotionally difficult because it means living a life of discipline and maturity in which the first and foremost commitment is to the transformation of the consciousness.

    In contrast, the difficulty in realizing the dimension of essential support related to the simplicity of Being is mostly cognitive and epistemological, and hence, more subtle.

    35. As far as we know, Kohut does not offer a new definition of psychic structures, leading us to conclude that he accepts the classical psychoanalytic definition. This means that he accepts that a psychic structure is an integrated organization of past impressions, composed mostly of representations; or, by our definition, it is a segment of the self that is structured by this organization. We conclude that the resolution of the idealizing transference, according to Kohut, will end with the establishment of such psychic structures.

36. This is similar to Kernberg's view of the idealizing transference as a defense against painful, narcissistic vulnerabilities. It is also similar to his view that the idealizing transference is a projection. There is, however, an important difference: he believes the projection is of the grandiose self, while in our view it is a projection of the Diamond Will, the true support of Essence. This is a significant difference that brings our work closer to the Jungian perspective of Schwartz-Salant.

37. This supports our thesis that the self's ultimate nature is truth, and hence, its needs always reflect truth. Grandiosity and idealization are not delusional in the ordinary sense; they are expressions of deep and real knowledge about the true potential of the human being. The distortion, which is technically not a delusion, is to attribute these perfections to the psychophysical apparatus of the self and the external object, respectively, while they are the real and true qualities of the Essential Identity and the Diamond Will.

38. This fine discrimination may not be significant in the treatment of pathological narcissism, but it is quite important in understanding the mirror transference and the need for mirroring in the narcissism of everyday life. It is even more necessary when we are engaged in any work of spiritual self-realization.

39. Empathic mirroring depends, of course, on empathy, and/or empathic perception. It is the communication of understanding obtained through empathy. Kohut's definition of empathy is adequate for our discussion here.

> We define it as 'vicarious introspection' or, more simply, as one person's [attempt to] experience the inner life of another while simultaneously retaining the stance of an objective observer. (Kohut, 1984, p. 175)

40. Generally the mirror transference arises as the idealizing transference is understood and its underlying structures—be they ego structures or the Diamond Will—are integrated. More specifically, with the fundamental narcissism of everyday life, and in particular with central narcissism, the idealizing transference is generally established first, and only as its underlying structures are integrated does the mirror transference become established.

548   There is, however, a great deal of overlap between the two kinds of narcissistic transferences. Frequently, the two kinds alternate, and may, in some cases, occur simultaneously. There is then an idealization of the teacher and a need for his or her mirroring. This is actually the case in almost all instances, but one of the two transferences is usually in the foreground. We also find that each individual develops a self-structure that depends on some form of narcissistic transference to shore up the sense of self; some individuals depend mostly on idealization and others mostly on mirroring, although both types are present.

41. Kohut gives more pathological reasons for the defenses against the establishment of the mirror transference:

> fear of loss of contact with reality and fear of permanent isolation through the experience of unrealistic grandiosity; frightening experiences of shame and self-consciousness through the intrusion of exhibitionistic libido; and hypochondriacal worries about physical or mental illness due to the hypercathexis of disconnected aspects of the body and the mind. (Kohut, 1971, p. 153)

In our experience, these fears are more present in more narcissistically disturbed individuals and reflect the reactivation of an unrealistic sense of self or the lack of integration underlying it.

42. Kohut is, of course, referring to the bipolar self, and in particular to the ambitions pole, when he is considering the narcissistic unity of the self. As discussed in Book One, we consider the bipolar self to be only a part of the self-identity structure and consider the latter to be involved in the mirror transference. Kohut's understanding of the mirror transference still applies to our definition of the narcissistic sector, and so does his elaboration of its disruption. Our view is that his observations are similar to ours, but his conceptual elaborations differ in varying degrees depending on the areas of research.

43. He writes about the patient who is usually more pathologically narcissistic than the population of students we work with:

> He begins to experience the regressively reinstated hypercathexis of isolated body parts and mental functions (elaborated as hypochondria) and turns to other, pathological means (such as

perverse sexual activities) in order to stem the tide of regression. (Kohut, 1971, p. 121)

44. He writes:

The patient's efforts to hold on to his grandiose self, and to avoid acknowledging the analyst as an independent, autonomous person, consistently reveal his defense against the intense envy, against the feared relationship with the hated and sadistically perceived mother image, and his dread of a sense of empty loneliness in a world devoid of personal meaning. (Kernberg, 1975, p. 287)

45. Kohut writes:

The acceptance by the analyst of the phase-appropriateness of the analysand's narcissistic demands counteracts the chronic tendency of the reality ego to wall itself off from the unrealistic narcissistic structures by such mechanisms as repression, isolation, or disavowal. (Kohut, 1971, p. 176)

Now, the analysand has the developmental chance to see and acknowledge unintegrated parts of himself—especially his need to exhibit grandiose conceptions of himself—and have them seen and admired. Contrast with reality within the empathic milieu and analysis of the various defenses that arise against the various self-images and affects, will have the effect of modifying his grandiosity and transforming it into more useful and realistic self-structures.

Being thus, on the one hand, continuously reactivated without being gratified and, on the other, prevented from regressive escape, only one way remains open to the infantile drive, wish, or need: its increasing integration into the mature and reality-adapted sectors and segments of the psyche through the accretion of specific, new psychological structures which master the drive, lead to its controlled use, or transform it into a variety of mature and realistic thought and action patterns. (Kohut, 1971, p. 197)

46. In the work of self-realization that we do with our students, we observe that the aspect of Loving Kindness generally arises for the normal

550   self, much earlier in the process than the aspect of the Essential Identity, and hence, before dealing with the narcissistic sector of the personality. Loving Kindness is a basic quality of Essence that the student must activate and embody to some degree before she will be able to work on her narcissism, and later, the realization of the Essential Identity. For further discussion of the aspect of Loving Kindness (also referred to as Compassion) see *Diamond Heart, Book One,* (AH Almaas, Berkeley: Diamond Books, 1987) and *The Pearl Beyond Price* (Almaas, 1988).

47. A useful way of picturing this process is Masterson's conceptualization of object relations. In terms of working with the disorders of the self, he discusses, two primary object relations units: the withdrawing object relations part-unit (WORU) and the rewarding object relations part-unit (RORU). The first refers to the situation where the individual finds herself in a relationship where the other is disapproving, rejecting or withdrawing, and the second is an object relation where the object is approving and rewarding.

The child finds herself in the position of the WORU, which means there is no love or acceptance for how she is and how she expresses herself, so she resorts to an alliance with the object, through the RORU.

> To compensate for the fact that self-expression is not available for motivation, the patient turns instead to the alliance of rewarding object relations part-unit (RORU) and pathological ego which, while providing him with a defense against the abandonment depression, at the same time provides him with a response to deal with the environment—a form of adaptations. As these patterns become familiar, stereotyped and repetitive, the patient identifies them as his self. But it is a false self. . . . (Masterson, 1985, p. 103)

This formulation applies both to severe disorders of the self, and also to the development of the normal self because the child experiences the Essential Identity in the withdrawing object relations situation. Turning towards the rewarding object relation and developing an identity based on these two object relations becomes the process by which the shell develops. In other words, the individual abandons herself to avoid the abandonment depression.

48. Kernberg writes:

> The subjective experience of emptiness represents a temporary   551
> or permanent loss of the normal relationship of the self with
> object representations, that is, with the world of inner objects
> that fixates intrapsychically the significant experiences with
> others and constitutes a basic ingredient of ego identity. (Kern-
> berg, 1975, pp. 219–220)

Not all depth psychologists share Kernberg's view of the meaning of emptiness, as we see in the following passage from the paper, titled "Depression and Grandiosity as Related Forms of Narcissistic Distur-bances," by Alice Miller:

> What is described as depression, and experienced as emptiness,
> futility, fear of impoverishment and loneliness, is frequently rec-
> ognizable as the tragedy of loss of the self, or alienation from the
> self. (Morrison, 1986, p. 323)

49. The experience of not knowing what to do in one's life that we describe here is not the same as the sense of helplessness that results from the absence of inner support. The latter is the feeling of "I do not know what to do" in relation to being oneself, specifically. It is associated with the deficient emptiness of the disconnection from the Diamond Will.

In our present discussion, the feeling of "I do not know what to do" is related to the lack of orientation in one's life. It is not a sense of help-lessness; rather, it is the absence of clear guidelines for significant involve-ment in one's life. One does not know who he is, so he has no idea what he wants to do or become involved in. So it is a sense of being lost, instead of being helpless.

50. The disconnection from any manifestation of Being, any aspect of Essence, leaves not only a wound, but an emptiness. The disconnec-tion is experienced as the state of the self when the essential aspect is missing. This state of deficiency is always experienced as a deficient emptiness, a hole in the self. This understanding is what we have termed the theory of holes. See *Elixir of Enlightenment* (AH Almaas, York Beach, Maine: Samuel Weiser, Inc., 1984), *The Void* (Almaas, 1986), and *Diamond Heart, Book I* (Almaas, 1987).

Narcissistic emptiness indicates the presence of the specific hole of the Essential Identity. This is the reason that its affect feels like not being

552   oneself, not having a self, not being real, not being centered, not being present.

51. This is the narcissistic form of Masterson's withdrawing object relations part-unit (WORU). (Masterson, 1985; see, also, note 46, above)

52. The sense of duality does not disappear completely until the advent of full self-realization, which is the realization of nondual presence. This requires the resolution of narcissism at deeper and more primitive levels than that of central narcissism, as in the resolution of oral narcissism. (See Chapter 38.)

53. We may become concerned that this means resignation to states of egoic identification, or succumbing to negative manifestations of the self. Deeper contemplation of what we are discussing will show that this is not the case. To experience ourselves without any judgment or opinion does not dispose one towards distorted states, but towards the condition of self-realization itself. Not having an ideal state to strive towards already indicates a transcendence of all unrealized states.

The freedom we are discussing is one elaboration of the subtle teaching in some spiritual traditions that there is no technique or method for arriving at enlightenment, that one merely finds oneself in it, simply leaving oneself alone. All techniques are merely ways to learn how to leave oneself alone, to stop fooling around with one's inner condition. This, of course, implies the cessation of ego activity.

54. The following Sufi passage exemplifies the theistic formulation of this understanding:

> The lover must keep company with the Beloved devoid of all motive; he must wipe out all desires, deliver himself to the Beloved's want, and abandon all ambition, for aspiration only blocks his path. . . . Give up desire therefore, think that whatever you get is what you want, and in this acceptance find ease and joy.

> Renounce desire
>   a hundred times
> or else not once
>   will you embrace your Desire
> (Iraqi, 1982, p. 114)

The path of meditation is exemplified by Buddhism, as in the fol-   553
lowing poem by Saraha, an ancient sage of Tantrism, on the yoga of
nonmeditation, the final yoga of the teaching of Mahamudra:

O, Do not claim to meditate
On that which is empty of any self-nature,
For by conceiving the duality of meditation and meditator
And by clinging to it
You will abandon enlightenment
(Takpo Tashi Namgyal, 1986, p. 394)

Mahamudra, a particular teaching in Tibetan Buddhism, views nonmeditation as the final stage of the practice of meditation. In our work,
the finding of where we are and the effortless relaxation into it is not conceived of as a final stage, but as the central element of the approach, reflecting the full state of realization in which there is no duality between the
self and its realization. So the state of nonmeditation, as discussed in
Mahamudra, is not exactly the condition we find ourselves in at the beginning, but it does inform the attitude we take in the work on ourselves.

55. This dimension is still not the full resolution of the need for mirroring. The full resolution requires the total realization of the boundless mirror-like awareness, which happens only with the full nondual
self-realization. The essential dimension we are discussing in the present chapter does, however, resolve the need for mirroring in central narcissism. It is also a primary step towards the mirror-like awareness,
which is a nondual presence. Oral narcissism and the deeper dimensions
of self-realization, including the boundless dimensions of Being, must
be explored to fully resolve the need for mirroring.

Book Three Notes

1. A detailed account of the characteristics and development of the Personal Essence and its relation to the ego individuality appears in *The Pearl Beyond Price* (Almaas, 1988). In this book, we elaborate on the understanding that the Personal Essence is the true prototype for the sense of personhood, or more precisely, that ego individuality is the result of an incomplete development of the self in the direction of the Personal Essence. The study of the qualities and development of this essential form involves us in a detailed investigation of the process of separation-individuation relating the stages of this process to individuation on the essential dimension. The above book can be viewed as a study in the individuation of the self in self-realization.

2. This is a significant insight, for it indicates that the normal experience of personhood, as it takes form through ego development, is ultimately empty, unreal, and therefore, fake. It is the expression of an ego structure, the self patterned by self-representation and, hence, alienated from the core of the self. Ego individuality is an empty form, empty of Essence. It is an imitation, or a distant reflection, of true individuality, the Personal Essence, which is true existence, a fullness inseparable from the feeling of competence.

3. An interesting insight in relation to this perspective is that ego 555
individuality is always a precocious development because it is a development of individuation before the child is able to experience it on the
essential level. For us, the essential dimension determines the authenticity of experience, much more so than the emotional dimension.
Regardless of how secure the individuation of the self is, if it does not
include the essential dimension, it is still precocious. Hence, it is fundamentally empty and meaningless.

4. This realization actually includes several realizations, and the
completion of several tasks. It implies that the conflicts around separation-individuation, including those related to narcissism, have been
resolved. It also implies the transformation of both central and individuation narcissism.

5. At this stage, the child experiences a strong sexual attraction to,
and a desire to possess, the parent of the opposite sex. Simultaneously,
the child also experiences aggressive and competitive impulses towards
the parent of the same sex, which produces the guilt and fear of retaliation from the latter parent, which is experienced as castration anxiety.

6. In some instances, a sexual abuse survivor manages to stay in
touch with a certain depth of the self which may include some contact
with Essence. However, this can happen only at the expense of a deep
splitting in the structure of the self, in which the individual has a depth
of experience, but must employ, unconsciously, some radical means in
order to remain unaware of the content of early abuse. This defense is
easily threatened by a variety of life situations, or by deep work on oneself, which leaves the survivor vulnerable to unexpected states of dissociation and disorientation.

Early abuse, sexual or physical, needs to be addressed adequately if an
individual is serious about pursuing the process of self-realization. It is
best to do some work with the abuse itself, at least to some degree, before
commencing on the deep process of spiritual realization, but it can be done
concurrently. Frequently, an individual will not discover the abuse until
going very deep in the work on self-realization, causing a great deal of suffering and confusion.

7. We must mention here that transformation of oedipal narcissism is only one of the requirements for the capacity to establish an

556   enduring love life and for the capacity to fall in love. Others include the development of the capacity for personal love, object constancy and orgastic potency, amongst others. As an example of these other necessary conditions, we mention Kernberg's view, which posits two major developmental achievements necessary for falling and remaining in love:

> a first stage, when the early capacity for sensuous stimulation of erogenous zones (particularly oral and skin eroticism) is integrated with the later capacity for establishing a total object relation; and a second stage, when full genital enjoyment incorporates earlier body-surface erotism into the context of a total object relation, including a complementary sexual identification. (Kernberg, 1979, p. 185)

    8.   This passionate, erotic, and loving presence, which is the self of the oedipal phase, makes it possible for us to experience our bodies and emotions deeply and fully. We experience the body then as vibrant and alive, and the emotions as deep and expansive. In other words, the oedipal self includes the emotional and physical dimensions of the self. This means the work on oedipal narcissism requires work on opening the emotions, feelings and sensations. This also indicates that disturbances in the oedipal stage may lead to emotional repression and general alienation from our feelings and the aliveness of our bodies.

This aspect of oedipal narcissism forms the central thesis of Lowen's view on narcissism and its transformation:

> Therapy is a process of extending self-awareness, increasing self-expression, and achieving self-possession, which is the ability to contain and sustain strong feelings. Bodily tensions and rigidity have to be gradually reduced so that the body can tolerate the higher level of excitation associated with strong feelings. (Lowen, 1983, pp. 61–62)

Transformation of oedipal narcissism requires all that Lowen describes above and a great deal more. It requires the realization of sensuous and passionate presence, the essential core without which the deep feelings will only be a manifestation of an empty shell. However, if feelings are authentic, they may reach to presence when they go to a profundity of depth.

9.   It may be clear to the reader by now that the term *oedipal self* is
not satisfactory for describing the self realized through the transformation of oedipal narcissism. This is the self which experiences itself as a presence containing several essential aspects. In the language we use in our
work, it is actually the presence of the soul (the actual self) coemergent
with the essential aspects of Personal Love (Affectionate Love), Ecstatic
Love (Passionate Love), Merging Love (Merging Essence), Strength, Power,
and Will, all experienced as a personal manifestation.

This discussion is taking us, however, to considerations of oral
narcissism.

10.   This is a case of splitting and projective identification, a primitive defense against the oral rage and hatred to safeguard one's all-good
identity and its positive object relations from destruction or contami-
nation. Splitting is a normal defensive operation at such an early developmental stage, and its constituents seem to survive in the normal self,
although hidden in its underlying structures. This is contrary to the
position of object relations theory, which believes these constituents
survive only in pathology.

11.   We differ from Kernberg in our understanding of oral narcissism, in that we see this manifestation of the self as more significant
than the conflictual and primitive object relations it engages in. It is this
empty and hungry self which is the heart of oral narcissism; the object
relations either produced it, or are its reactions to the situations it found
itself in. Narcissism, in our view, has to do with our experience of identity, with our self-recognition.

12.   This is the condition of the self the Buddhists have called the
"hungry ghost," a being with a huge belly but with a tiny mouth. It never
feels full, and is always hungry and empty. Calling it a ghost is actually
quite appropriate because it is a narcissistic structure of the self; in other
words, it is an unreal manifestation of the self.

13.   Schwartz-Salant divides the process of the working-through of
narcissistic disturbance into two stages. The first concerns the transformation of the masculine—which he relates to doing—and the second, that of the feminine aspects of the self—which he relates to being:

> My consideration of the first stage of transformation follows
> much that Kohut describes. There are major points of difference

558   which shall later become clear, but his emphasis on the formation and transformation of the narcissistic transferences is crucial to this stage. It is the stage described by the Narcissus myth
according to Ovid. The second stage concerns the redemption
of the Self, the emphasis being on its feminine aspects. (Schwartz-
Salant, 1982, pp. 22–23)

He does not view these two stages as reflecting two forms of narcissism, but as two stages of transformation of narcissism in general, which
point to two layers in its structure. His second stage, which concerns
the deeper layer of narcissism, seems to be related to the transformation of what we have termed oral narcissism, especially in that he views
the inception of its corresponding layer as taking place in the first few
months of life. He views the early disruption to the wholeness of the self
at this early stage as resulting into the splitting-off of a part of the self
that has the connection to archetypal energies. This way the child loses
his contact with joy, as we see in the following passage:

> The major quality of the split-off Self that appears with the dis-
> solution of the narcissistic and primarily idealized transference
> is joy. It is the "child of God" that defines every newborn child.
> (Schwartz-Salant, 1982, p. 159)

This might be the loss of the essential core of the self, expressed in
Jungian archetypal terminology. The essential core includes, however,
more than Joy; Joy is only one of the essential aspects.

Viewing his perspective from ours, he seems to deal mostly with central narcissism in the first stage and oral narcissism in the second,
although he conceives only the second stage as dealing with the redemption of the spiritual core of the self. So for Schwartz-Salant, the regaining of wholeness is a matter of healing the split in the self: "In our
framework we would speak of the split-off Self reconnecting with the
ego, gaining ego-quality." (Schwartz-Salant, 1982, pp. 155–156)

14.   There is some disagreement between the various Buddhist
schools about the nature of Being, specifically in the conceptualization
of ultimate reality. Ultimate reality is conceived of sometimes as emptiness (sunyata), sometimes as clear light, and sometimes as a presence
that combines the two in a nondual manner.

15. One possible resolution of the debate is to conceive Being as 559 manifesting various dimensions, and that one of these dimensions, the final one, is that of nondual presence.

16. This is in contrast to the approaches of many other teachings, especially those of sudden or direct enlightenment, as in Zen or Dzogchen. Dzogchen calls its approach direct, and relies heavily on "direct introduction," which means that the student has an initial contact with the ultimate reality, the nondual presence, by opening himself to, and merging with, the realized consciousness of his teacher. He is then given some meditational practices to remember or to invoke this initial experience and to increasingly establish it. This is supported by repeated experiences of direct introduction, or what is sometimes referred to as direct transmission.

This usually sounds very attractive to many individuals, who believe this method to be a short and direct route, regardless of the exhortations of the Dzogchen masters that a great deal of preparation is required before one can benefit from this approach. It is our observation that very few individuals benefit from such an approach, and that most individuals do not contact nondual presence when they experience the direct introduction. Most seem to contact some limited experience of presence, and they must do a great deal of work to recontact it on their own. The progression to deeper and more complete experiences of presence seems to be present, in other words, even in a teaching like Dzogchen, that conceptualizes only nondual presence.

Our observations of the effect of such teachings are limited, and limited only to Western students, and this must be taken into consideration regarding the above comments. We appreciate Dzogchen, and other traditions that fall within this category, as providing possibly the best and most complete teaching on the realization of nondual presence. The Dzogchen texts elaborate on the properties and nature of nondual presence in a much greater detail and specificity than we have found anywhere else.

17. When this experience of the cosmic shell—or universal narcissistic emptiness—arises, some individuals conclude that the world is inherently empty and life is meaningless. This experience is also the origin of some beliefs that the world is illusory, does not have a true existence, or is only a dream.

560   These are mistaken interpretations of this experience, which is simply a deep experience of the ego-self. It is a mistake to think of the experience of the emptiness of everything as the same thing the Buddhists are referring to when they say that everything is empty, or as what the Hindus mean when they say that everything is maya, illusion. They are not referring to this experience. The emptiness that is revealed in Buddhist practice is a clear space, without the sense of deficiency that characterizes the emptiness of the cosmic shell.

Having the cosmic shell experience with its sense of deficiency indicates that one is experiencing the mental structure of a self that is still not differentiated from the world. Both the self and the world are experienced in this way as a result of a mental structure, a structure that patterns experience to be the normal self living in the conventional dimension of experience. We recognize now that this experience of universal emptiness is the experience of this structure, so it is empty.

That the world the ego-self experiences is the result of the development of a psychic structure has been formulated by object relations theorist Joseph Sandler as the concept of the representational world:

> Thus, self and object representations, culled from a multitude of impressions, constitute a network of concepts and enduring images, a 'representational world' which provides the basic organizational framework for the child's experience. (Greenberg and Mitchell, 1983, pp. 373–374)

In other words, the experience of the ego-self is underlain by the structure of the representational world, such that when one finally experiences it completely, it is seen as a representation, not the real world. The emptiness is the emptiness of the representation, but we see it as the emptiness of the world because we do not know that we have been experiencing a representation.

18. The loss of oneness, the unity of Being, has been understood in some circles to be equivalent to the concept of the "original sin" that started with the fall of man. The regaining of the unity is understood, then, as the union with God in Christian mysticism and as God-realization in some of the Hindu traditions.

19. The process of transformation of duality at this level of experience is an involved one, and the interested reader will find a short

discussion of it in *The Pearl Beyond Price*, Chapter 35 (Almaas, 1988). 561
The idea is that the student will alternate for some time between the experience of duality, in which he is identified with the ego-self and the experience of unity, or being the pure Being. This begins the process of clarification of the ego-self, in which the student increasingly experiences the self clarified from the mental representations. This finally leads to the experience of being absorbed into the pure presence of Being.

20. The older needs for mirroring—to be seen and admired—which are relevant to the Essential Identity and pure Being tend to reemerge at this point, but with an added sensitivity to being conceptualized, or having to conceptualize. This new wound is quite sensitive because people cannot communicate without conceptualizing.

This does not mean the student needs the absence of conceptualization, but rather that she needs an understanding of her sensitivity and the ability to see herself, or be seen, as presence beyond any conceptualization.

21. This part of the process of self-realization reveals how the presence of the phenomenological, epistemological and representational factors cause narcissistic alienation. This is, in other words, no longer a matter of dealing with psychodynamic issues or with one's history.

22. Zen deals extensively with these paradoxes and uses them as bridges to this experience of Being. It seems to emphasize this particular realization of Being, and hence considers itself beyond the grasp of the conceptual mind.

23. There exists only one empty shell that returns with deeper, more primitive, and fundamental layers of its structure every time that Being presents itself in a subtler manifestation. This is in accord with the formulations of object relations theory, which views each psychic structure as composed of many representations, from various stages of development, integrated as a cohesive whole. Investigating such a structure means it will reveal its constituent representations. When we investigate the self-identity structure, these appear as different levels of the empty shell.

24. The empty shell of oral narcissism is actually a structure patterned by the experience of the stomach, or the alimentary tract. The baby at this stage of development relates to the world in a predominantly oral way, in which it puts everything in its mouth, for nourishment, but also

562 for contact, exploration and information. Students frequently experience the empty shell as composed of a thick, alive, and pulsing membrane or wall around a gnawing emptiness, the way a hungry stomach feels.

25. Observing that the self at this level of structure has lost all distinguishing features that can give it a sense of identity except for the fact that it is an entity, we give this manifestation the label of "entity-identity." Here, the self resorts to the separating boundaries as a last strategy to recognize itself.

26. These reflect the three main characteristics of ego structures in general, indicating they are facets of the same disruption. Withdrawal reflects the schizoid; weakness and inadequacy reflect the borderline; and emptiness and impoverishment reflect the narcissistic characteristics. In other words, it is inherent to the ego-self that it possesses all the three structural characteristics. Individual differences are due to the degree and proportions of these characteristics in the pattern of the self-structure.

27. This is possibly what Freud called the longing for nirvana, which he postulated as underlying the death instinct. In fact, some students misinterpret this deep longing as the desire to die physically, which can provoke a tremendous terror, or a desire for suicide if there still remains some self-hatred that the student has not seen and understood. The desire for physical death at this juncture is not due intrinsically to this longing; rather, it is due to the remaining identification with the physical body. The student longs for the peace of total cessation of the structure of the ego-self, but believes she desires the death of her body because she cannot differentiate between a psychic structure and the actual body.

We agree with Freud that there is a nirvana principle and that there is deep in the self a fundamental wish to cease. But we disagree with him in seeing this as a death instinct. The longing is not for the death of the body; it is for the death of the ego, the structure that separates the self from its nature. And when there is still a great deal of self-hatred present, this longing becomes a masochistic suicidal tendency. In other words, Freud's death instinct is a distortion of the longing for the cessation of psychic structures.

The longing for cessation is a yearning for peace, for a peace that one vaguely intuits, at this juncture, but can not yet fathom. Theravada

Buddhism actually recognizes this longing as a sign of the approach of the "trance of cessation," the entry into nirvana which is the release of enlightenment.

28. This state has been recognized by some of the spiritual traditions, especially those of Sufism and mystical Christianity, and is valued as an absolute necessity for spiritual transcendence. It is referred to as the station of "mystical poverty" and understood as the recognition that the soul is totally poor and lacking in relation to God, who is the source of everything.

It is important to realize that this religious view still remains bound to the oral way of relating to reality, that the soul is empty, and God the all-providing source. The student must see these traces of orality for her experience to take her to full self-realization; otherwise, she will remain bound to an object relation of a poverty-stricken soul relating to an omnipotent and all providing God (selfobject). This may lead to a deep spiritual life, but it will not resolve fundamental narcissism. The important step is recognizing that as long as she is relating to Being within any object relation she is still within the conceptual mind, and so is operating from within mental representation. She needs to transcend the concept of relationship and utterly surrender all separate existence.

29. Some mystics, such as St. John of the Cross, view this state as that of the soul being penetrated by the light of God, which cleanses it of all of its qualities and faculties. The soul experiences God's light as its poverty, not knowing until later that she is actually experiencing her greatest boon. This is the reason that St. John sometimes equates the experience of the dark night of the spirit with that of the light of God. (St. John, *The Spiritual Canticles*)

30. The Sufis have a saying that they take from the Quran, where God says something to the effect that: "You may look for me in the mosque, the church or the temple. You may look for me in the various quarters of the world. But to find me look into the heart of my lover."

31. This view is the counterpart to that of Nagarjuna, the madhyamaka philosopher, who understood the Buddhist notion of emptiness to mean that we cannot say anything positive about it—that emptiness is not only negation, but the negation of negation and affirmation.

564   Our view is not that we cannot say anything about the ultimate truth, but rather that whatever we say, regardless of how accurate it may be, will not exhaust it. It cannot be described, not because no description can be found, but because whatever description we find will fail to give it justice. In fact, mystical poets are always describing it, but all the poetry possible is a paltry limitation of what it is. In other words, the absolute truth is indeterminable because of its inexhaustibility.

This does not contradict the view of prasangika madhyamaka; rather, it complements it. It does not contradict it because the inexhaustibility of the absolute truth is a consequence of its utter simplicity, which is the essence of Nagarjuna's view. Simplicity and inexhaustibility are the two paradoxical poles of this ultimate truth, just like emptiness and fullness.

32. Although emptiness is the ultimate truth, ultimate realization is the establishment of the coemergence of clear light with this emptiness.

33. Nonduality is known and stressed by traditions other than Dzogchen. It is a basic view of Kashmir Shaivism, central in Taoism, and also important in Sufism. The following passage demonstrates the view of nonduality in Sufism expressed in a theistic language:

> And, universally, thou mayest understand that seer and seen, and Creator and created, and knower and known, and perceiver and perceived are one. (Ibn 'Arabi, 1976, p. 22)

Nevertheless, the teachings of Dzogchen, of all of the traditional teachings regarding nondual realization, seem to be the most known in the West at the present time.

34. The following passage from a later book demonstrates more clearly how he views emptiness, absence or negation, as fundamental:

> Within the luminous vitality of such a knowing existence would be transformed into 'appearance as'. 'Was' would be 'as' and 'is' would be 'as'; *essence would be transformed into absence. Negation would be present within all appearance, as the heart of appearance.* [emphasis ours] (Tarthang Tulku, 1987, p. 409)

35. The translated Dzogchen texts and the teachings of its living masters seem to vary in terms of subtlety of understanding nondual presence. This may be interpreted to mean that the teaching includes a view

of different levels of presence. However, we are not sufficiently familiar
with this tradition to know whether it actually holds a view of different
levels of the experience of nondual presence.

36. The process of spiritual development, which is the maturation
of the human being, can be divided into two complementary facets.
One is the self-realization of Being in its various aspects and manifestations, and the other is the integration of this self-realization in the
everyday life of a human person. The latter is a progressive process of
maturation of the self, in which the unfoldment of Being expresses itself
in an individuated personal life with other human beings in a real world.
Self-realization connects the person to his true identity, which is his
Being, and this makes it possible for him to mature in everyday life and
to fulfill his humanness. Human life becomes then the personal expression of one's realization in the context of normal life situations.

So we can say that the process of individuation makes it possible for
us to be in the world, while that of self-realization connects us with the
transcendental source of our Being, which is beyond the world of appearance. The present book is an attempt to understand the process of self-
realization, while *The Pearl Beyond Price* is an attempt to understand
the individuation of Being, which is a process of the personalization of
its various facets and manifestations.

37. The experience Roberts describes, and her understanding of it,
is of particular interest to our work in light of the related experiences
of our students. When experiencing the Essential Identity, some students describe it as a point of light or sometimes as a brilliant star.
Students have also referred to it as the star of Bethlehem, especially
when they experienced it in conjunction with the arising of the Personal
Essence. Bethlehem means the house of flesh, the body where the
Personal Essence is born. The correspondence to Roberts's understanding becomes clear when we understand that the Personal Essence
is the true maturation and individuation of the soul. (See *The Pearl
Beyond Price* [Almaas, 1988].)

38. This is reminiscent of some passages in the Quran, where the
creation is described as the function of a pen (the divine intellect) writing on a tablet (the universal soul). The unity of the two is seen as the
creative logos, what the Sufis call the Mohamadan Spirit.

566   39. The usual name for the point in Sanskrit is *bindu,* which literally means point or center. It is usually seen as the center of the mandala, representing our experiential universe. Buddhism uses this word *bindu* to refer to the center of the mandala, but there is no explicit emphasis on the point of light. This most likely is a result of the fact that Buddhism arose as a corrective response to the Hindu overemphasis on the question of the individual self, the atman. Buddhism emphasizes true nature as the anatman, the no-self. However, some branches of Buddhism, like that of Vajrayana of Tibet, work with the experience of the point of light in their practices. The term for point in Tibetan, the translation of the Sanskrit term *bindu,* is *thigla. Thigla* means both point or drop, and a visualization of a brilliant thigla is frequently an important part of Tibetan tantric practices. The visualization of thigla is not, however, always the visualization of the essential point. The essential point appears only in some practices.

Appendix C Notes

---•

1. The view that spiritual experience "can't be described" was made commonly popular in rather naive spiritual circles, such as those interested in Zen in the 1960s. Zen masters were interested in the direct and immediate experience of self-realization, and not in describing it conceptually. Their particular method is to precipitate the experience by the transcendence of all conceptualization. And since discrimination, for the conventional dimension of the self, is bound to bring up concepts from personal history, their methods did not use nor emphasize, but actively avoided and shunned, the conceptualization of experience. This does not mean that the experience of self-realization is not capable of discrimination, as the study of many of the authoritative spiritual texts of the major spiritual teachings, like those of Tibetan Buddhism, the various Hindu yogas, Sufism, the Kabala, and so on, will testify.

2. By the "nonconceptual" dimension of experience, we mean experience before it is discriminated, recognized and cast into labels. It is known that infants, for instance, do not, at least sometimes, experience things in a differentiated and conceptual manner. Their capacity for differentiation develops slowly, which gives them the ability to discriminate the details of their perceptions, needed before they can employ

568   concepts. This does not mean that perception totally loses its nonconceptual dimension; it merely indicates that our conceptualizing activity happens so fast on the heels of our perceptions that we do not notice, under normal circumstances, the original nonconceptual nature of our experience.

The nonconceptual dimension of all perception or experience remains the fact of pure perception, as the ground for all of our discrimination, recognition and labeling of our experience. We can retrieve, or more accurately, isolate this nonconceptual dimension of experience by suspending our habitual tendency to conceptualize. This occurs in some of the deep spiritual experiences, which make it possible for us to see firsthand that our perception is originally nonconceptual. When we become attuned to this dimension of experience, we may see that conceptualization requires first differentiation and then discrimination. Labeling occurs as a third step and helps in giving the conceptualizations a greater clarity and fixity, and the possibility for use in memory and communication. Concepts become the building blocks for representing the objects of our perception.

It is actually when we experience ourselves nonconceptually that we recognize our quality of presence, which is the mere perception of our factness.

3.   Enlightened consciousness is described as possessing five primordial facets or dimensions, coexisting in it and functioning as the fundamental fabric of all perceptions. Amitabha is one of the five dhyani buddhas, each representing one facet of enlightened consciousness. The five are usually arranged spatially in the shape of a cross with a center.

> This spatial unfoldment corresponds to the spiritual differentiation of the principle of Enlightenment in form of the five transformed constituents of consciousness and their corresponding Dhyani-Buddhas, in whom the consciousness of Enlightenment appears differentiated like rays of light passing through a prism. (Govinda, 1969, p. 62)

The other facets are the wisdom of infinite expanse, the wisdom of mirror-like awareness, the wisdom of equality, and the all-accomplishing wisdom.

4. Ibn Arabi, and Sufi ontology in general, thought of "creation"—   569
the manifest universe of experience—as the universal feminine, and the
source of creation as the masculine.

5. This characteristic of intrinsic discrimination inherent in the
dimension of essential presence forms the prototypical ground for the
self's capacity for discrimination on all levels of experience. It provides
the self with the possibility for understanding on its various levels of
experience. It is actually this inherent characteristic of our true nature
that makes it possible for us to realize this true nature. In other words,
it provides the self-existing and intrinsic discrimination in the innermost dimension of experience that appears to us on the various levels
of experience as the deeper discrimination. This makes it possible for
us to go deeper in our experience and understanding of ourselves. More
accurately, the closer we are to the dimension of primordial presence,
the closer our discriminating capacity is to the wisdom of discrimination, and the deeper, more accurate and objective our experience and
understanding of ourselves is. Again, this precise and clear discrimination that exists in the depths of the self as an intrinsic facet of its primordial essential nature, makes possible ever deeper, more precise
experience and understanding of experience. This deepening in understanding arises through genuine interest in clearer, more precise, and
real discrimination of experience.

This is the basis for the concept of the inner guru or teacher in some
spiritual traditions. The inner teacher is nothing but the guidance of the
primordial presence through its discriminating property, which appears
in many dimensions of experience, but we have understood it more
clearly in the deeper spiritual dimensions because of the latter's nearness to the primordial presence. This is the reason that in the Sufi tradition it is the intellect, the discriminating faculty, that is seen as the
necessary ingredient for the transformation of the self, even though it
is a teaching primarily of love.

> There are two forms, for instance, of aql, intelligence—the
> intelligence of the ordinary man, and that of the religious one.
> The first is fit for this world and its affairs, the latter for the
> next world. This is characterized by guidance, sometimes
> referred to as illumination. (Shah, 1964, p. 270)

570   The intellect considered the inner guide for the spiritual journey is not the intellect in the domain of common experience. This latter is only a reflection of what is called the real or higher intellect, the "nous" of the ancient Greeks, which is the appearance of the primordial discrimination, the wisdom of discrimination, in an essential form, a form of presence that can appear in the midst of the dimension of conventional experience. The essential or real intellect, the "nous" of the ancient Greeks, is actually the wisdom of discrimination, viewed from a limited perspective because of the incompleteness in our understanding of ourselves. At this point of spiritual development, we are able to have experiences of essential presence, but we are still not in the full self-realized state. As the spiritual development progresses towards the dimension of primordial and nondual presence, with the assistance of the inner guidance, it reveals progressively the true nature of this guiding presence until it finally reveals it as the wisdom of discrimination at the point that the development reaches the primordial presence.

REFERENCES

Almaas, A.H., *Diamond Heart Book I*, Berkeley: Diamond Books, 1987.

Almaas, A.H., *Diamond Heart Book II*, Berkeley: Diamond Books, 1989.

Almaas, A.H., *Diamond Heart Book III*, Berkeley: Diamond Books, 1990.

Almaas, A.H., *Elixir of Enlightenment*, York Beach, ME: Samuel Weiser, Inc., 1984.

Almaas, A.H., *Essence—The Diamond Approach to Inner Realization*, York Beach, ME: Samuel Weiser, Inc., 1986.

Almaas, A.H., *The Pearl Beyond Price—Integration of Personality into Being: An Object Relations Approach*, Berkeley: Diamond Books, 1988.

Almaas, A.H., *The Void—Inner Spaciousness and Ego Structure*, Berkeley: Diamond Books, 1986/1992.

Bettleheim, Bruno, *Freud and Man's Soul*, New York: Alfred A. Knopf, 1982.

Blanck, Gertrude and Rubin, *Ego Psychology: Theory and Practice*, New York: Columbia University Press, 1974.

Blanck, Gertrude and Rubin, *Ego Psychology II: Psychoanalytic Developmental Psychology*, New York: Columbia University Press, 1974.

Blum, Harold P., editor, *Psychoanalytic Explorations of Technique*, New York: International Universities Press, 1980.

Blume, E. Sue, *Secret Survivors*, New York: Random House, 1990.

Castaneda, Carlos, *The Fire From Within*, New York: Simon and Schuster, 1984.

572   Chessick, Richard, *Psychology of the Self and the Treatment of Narcissism*, Northwale, NJ: Jason Aronson, 1985.

Chittick, William, *The Sufi Path of Knowledge*, Albany, NY: State University of New York Press, 1989.

Chittick, William, *The Sufi Path of Love*, Albany, NY: State University of New York Press, 1983.

Corbin, Henry, *Creative Imagination in the Sufism of Ibn 'Arabi*, Princeton, NJ: Princeton University Press, 1977.

Dalai Lama, The XIVth, His Holiness Tenzin Gyatsho, *Kindness, Clarity and Insight*, trans. Jeffery Hopkins, Ithaca, NY: Snow Lion Publications, 1984.

Dunn, Jean, *Prior to Consciousness*, Durham, NC: Acorn Press, 1985.

Fairbairn, W. Ronald D., *Psychoanalytical Studies of the Personality*, London, Henley and Boston: Routledge and Kegan Paul, 1984.

Fenichel, Otto, *The Psychoanalytic Theory of Neurosis*, New York: Norton, 1945.

Freud, Sigmund, *The Psychopathology of Everyday Life*, New York: W.W. Norton & Co., 1960.

Govinda, Lama Anagarika, *Foundations of Tibetan Mysticism*, New York: Samuel Weiser, 1969.

Gray, William, *Ladder of Lights*, Toddington, England: Helios Books, 1968.

Greenberg, Jay R. and Stephen A. Mitchell, *Object Relations in Psychoanalytic Theory*, Cambridge: Harvard University Press, 1983.

Guenther, Herbert, *Matrix of Mystery*, Boulder, CO: Shambala, 1984.

Hartmann, Heinz, *Ego Psychology and the Problem of Adaptation*, NY: International University Press, 1939.

Horner, Althea, *Object Relations and the Developing Ego in Therapy*, New York and London: Jason Aronson, 1979.

Ibn 'Arabi, Muhiyddin, *Kernel of the Kernel*, London: Beshara Publications.

Iraqi, Fakruddin, *Divine Flashes*, Ramsey, NJ: Paulist Press, 1982.

Jacobson, Edith, M.D., *The Self and the Object World*, New York: 573
International Universities Press, Inc., 1980.

Jung, Carl, *Psychology and Alchemy, The Collected Works of C.G.Jung 12*, Princeton, NJ: Princeton University Press, 1953–1979.

Kelsang Gyatso, Geshe, *Clear Light of Bliss*, London: Wisdom Publications, 1982.

Kernberg, Otto, *Borderline Conditions and Pathological Narcissism*, New York: Jason Aronson, 1975.

Kernberg, Otto, *Object Relations Theory and Clinical Psychoanalysis*, New York: Jason Aronson, Inc, 1979.

Kernberg, Otto, "Self, Ego, Affects and Drives," Journal of the American Psychoanalytic Association, 30: 374–375, 1982.

Kohut, Heinz, *How Does Analysis Cure*, Chicago: University of Chicago Press, 1984.

Kohut, Heinz, *The Analysis of the Self*, New York: International Universities Press, 1971.

Kohut, Heinz, *The Restoration of the Self*, New York: International Universities Press, 1977.

Kohut, Heinz, *The Search for the Self*, ed. P. Ornstein, New York: New York International University Press, 1978.

Krishnamurti, J., *Krishnamurti to Himself*, London: Krishnamurti Foundation Trust, 1987.

Laing, R.D., *The Voice of Experience*, New York: Pantheon Books, 1982.

Laksman Jee, Swami, *Kashmir Shaivism: The Secret Supreme*, Albany, NY: State University of New York Press: 1988.

Longchenpa, *You Are the Eyes of the World*, Novato, CA: Lotsawa, 1987.

Lowen, A., *Narcissism, Denial of the True Self*, New York: Macmillan, 1983.

Mahler, Margaret, and Louise Kaplan, "Developmental aspects in the assessment of narcissistic and so-called borderline personalities," in *Borderline Personality Disorders*, Peter Hartocollis, editor, New York: International Universities Press, 1977.

574   Mahler, Margaret, *On Human Symbiosis and the Vicissitudes of Individuation*, New York: International University Press, 1968.

Mahler, Margaret, Fred Pine, and Anni Bergman, *The Psychological Birth of the Human Infant*, New York: Basic Books, Inc, 1975.

Manjusrimitra, *Primordial Experience*, Boston: Shambala, 1987.

Masterson, J., *The Narcissistic and Borderline Disorders*, New York: Brunner/Mazel, 1985.

Masterson, J., *The Real Self*, New York: Brunner/Mazel, 1981.

Mitchell, Stephen, *Hope and Dread in Psychoanalysis*, New York: Basic Books, 1993.

Morrison, Andrew, editor, *Essential Papers on Narcissism*, New York: New York University Press, 1986.

Nisargadatta Maharaj, Sri, *I Am That*, Durham, NC: Acorn Press, 1982.

Ouspensky, P.D., *In Search of the Miraculous*, New York: Harcourt Brace Jovanovich, 1949.

Pearce, Joseph Chilton, *Evolution's End*, San Francisco: Harper Collins, 1992.

Plotinus, *The Enneads*, London: Penguin Books, 1991.

Reich, Wilhelm, *Character Analysis*, New York: Simon and Schuster, 1945.

Reynolds, J., translator, *Self-liberation Through Seeing with the Naked Awareness*, Barrytown, NY: Station Hill Press, 1989.

Roberts, Bernadette, *The Path to No-Self*, Boston: Shambhala Publications, Inc., 1985.

Saraswati, Swami Yogeshwaranand, *Science of Soul*, New Delhi: Yoga Niketan Trust, 1987.

Settlage, C.F., "The Psychoanalytic Understanding of Narcissistic and Borderline Personality Disorders: Advances in Developmental Theory," Journal of American Psychoanalytical Association. 1977, 25:805–833.

Shah, Idries, *A Perfumed Scorpion*, London: Octagon Press, 1978.

Shah, Idries, *The Sufis*, New York: Doubleday, 1964.

Shah, S.I.A., *Islamic Sufism*, New York: Samuel Weiser, 1971.

Singh, Jaideva, *The Yoga of Vibration and Divine Pulsation*, Albany, NY: State University of New York Press: 1992.   575

Stern, Daniel, *The Interpersonal World of the Infant*, New York: Basic Books, 1985.

Schwartz-Salant, Nathan, *Narcissism and Character Transformation*, Toronto: Inner City Books, 1982.

Takpo Tashi Namgyal, *Mahamudra, The Quintessence of Mind and Meditation*, Boston: Shambala, 1986.

Tarthang Tulku, *Love of Knowledge*, Oakland, CA: Dharma Press, 1987.

Tarthang Tulku, *Time, Space and Knowledge*, Oakland, CA: Dharma Press, 1977.

Tsultrim Gyamtso Rinpoche, Ven. Khenpo, *Progressive Stages of Meditation on Emptiness*, New Marston, Oxford, England: Long Chen Foundation, 1986.

Tulku Thondup Rinpoche, *Buddha Mind*, Ithaca, NY: Snow Lion Publications, 1989.

Weiss, Fredrick, *Hegel, The Essential Writings*, New York: Harper and Row, 1974.

Wilbur, Ken, *Spectrum of Consciousness*, Wheaton, IL: Quest Books, 1977.

Winnicott, D.W., *The Maturational Processes and the Facilitating Environment*, New York: International Universities Press, 1980.

INDEX

A.H. Almaas's background is in physics, mathematics and psychology. He is a teacher who for the last twenty-two years has guided students and groups worldwide using his unique method of personal realization called the Diamond Approach[SM]. Since founding the Ridhwan School in 1975, Almaas has guided students and trained teachers in this method in California, Colorado and elsewhere, in addition to publishing eight books describing various aspects of the Diamond Approach[SM].

The Diamond Approach is taught by Ridhwan teachers, certified by the Ridhwan Foundation. Ridhwan teachers are also ordained ministers of the Ridhwan Foundation. They are trained by DHAT Institute, the educational arm of the Ridhwan Foundation, through an extensive seven-year program, which is in addition to their work and participation as students of the Diamond Approach. The certification process ensures that each person has a good working understanding of the Diamond Approach and a sufficient capacity to teach it before being ordained and authorized to be a Ridhwan teacher.

The Diamond Approach described in this book is taught in group and private settings in California and Colorado by Ridhwan teachers.

For information, write:

> Ridhwan
> P.O. Box 10114
> Berkeley, California 94709-5114

> Ridhwan School
> P.O. Box 18166
> Boulder, Colorado 80308–8166

Satellite groups operate in other national and international locations. For information about these groups, or to explore starting a group in your area, taught by certified Ridhwan teachers, write:

> Ridhwan
> P.O. Box 10114
> Berkeley, California 94709-5114

Diamond Approach is a registered service mark of the Ridhwan Foundation.